MUSIC IN MY TIME

AND OTHER REMINISCENCES

THE MACMILLAN COMPANY
NEW YORK · BOSTON · CHICAGO · DALLAS
ATLANTA · SAN FRANCISCO

MACMILLAN AND CO., Limited
LONDON · BOMBAY · CALCUTTA · MADRAS
MELBOURNE

THE MACMILLAN COMPANY
OF CANADA, Limited
TORONTO

After-dinner Gathering at Le Flonzaley. Inscribed: "*To our friends Daniel and Mary Mason, in remembrance of the evening of September 13th, 1913 spent at Le Flonzaley. E. J. de Coppet. Pauline de Coppet.*"

BACK ROW: Iwan d'Archambeau, Ugo Ara, Adolfo Betti, Felix Weingartner, Josef Hofmann, Mrs. Rudolph Ganz, Mrs. E. J. de Coppet, Ernest Schelling, Mme. Sembrich, I. J. Paderewski, Sigismund Stojowski, Daniel Gregory Mason, Alfred Pochon, Juliet de Coppet, Mr. Stengel. FRONT ROW: Mrs. Mason, Mrs. Louis de Coppet, Mrs. Weingartner, Rudolph Ganz, Edward J. de Coppet, Mme. Paderewska, Mrs. Hofmann.

DANIEL GREGORY MASON

MUSIC

IN MY TIME

AND OTHER REMINISCENCES

THE MACMILLAN COMPANY · NEW YORK · 1938

PRINTED IN THE UNITED STATES OF AMERICA BY H. WOLFF, NEW YORK

FOR M. L. M.

Do you remember my reading you, in Norfolk one windy autumn morning, hardly an hour after we had come in from the walk and talk that suggested it, a sentence beginning: "I remember a garden orchard high in the Berkshires"—and your laughing at me in your delightfully irresponsible way and saying: "Well, that isn't hard to remember—I remember it myself."

Most of the doings here set forth, though some of them happened longer ago, you will likewise remember; and you may recall having directed on many of them the gentle laughter, one of your divinest gifts, that helped me not to take myself too seriously. . . . My thanks and my love.

D. G. M.

"Commemoration is itself creation. A wise communion with the dead renews our own life, and restores to us their very presence in a form that may be deeper, truer, and more potent than the literal human companionships of the old days ever could have shown to beings who, like ourselves, understand our present human friendships so little, and so ill."

JOSIAH ROYCE
The Hope of the Great Community

"There is an element of vanity in waiting until we think we are all that we admire before we allow ourselves to communicate our admiration. To know that we work less through what we are than through what we worship is a great economy of pride."

WILLIAM ERNEST HOCKING
Human Nature and Its Remaking

" . . . Heart, we have chosen the better part!
Save sacred love and sacred art
Nothing is good for long".

WILLIAM VAUGHN MOODY
Song-Flower and Poppy

O beauty, shine afar!
The world is a bad place,
Full of bawling and squabbling, of pushing and shoving,
And men are like silly hens
Cackling for the grain
And raising a dust.

O beauty, shine afar!
I have loved thee long
And served thee a little.
I have caught thy gleam, and that is enough.

Others too I have known who have loved thee:
Some that lived centuries ago,
Some whose hands I have touched.
All are my brothers, all my dear companions.
They have warmed and lighted the world for me
And made it home.

O beauty, shine afar!
For I see clearly now, as at evening,
When stars first glimmer faintly
And then shine quietly forth;
And I see that one of your rays
Is more real and can traverse farther
Than all the noise and the strife,
Than all the illusions and the chimeras;
And I am content.

O beauty, shine afar!

D. G. M. January, 1919

NOTE

PARTS of Chapters XII and XV are here reprinted from *Musical America*, a part of Chapter V from the *Musical Quarterly*, and a part of Chapter XXI from *Harper's Magazine*, with the kind permission of their Editors. The passages quoted from my *Music as a Humanity* are used with the consent of its publishers, the H. W. Gray Company of New York.

For permission to use various letters, photographs, and other material I extend my cordial thanks to Adolfo Betti, Van Wyck Brooks, Ulysse Buhler, Chalmers Clifton, Dr. James Francis Cooke, André de Coppet, Gaston Dethier, Clara Clemens Gabrilowitsch, Mrs. Henry F. Gilbert, Miss Grace E. Hadow, Hermann Hagedorn, Professor Edward Burlingame Hill, Josef Hofmann, M. le Comte Jean d'Indy, Professor Lionel S. Marks, Henry Lowell Mason, Mrs. Edward MacDowell, Mrs. Frances McFarland, Douglas Moore, Mrs. Ruth Nivison, Louis Noyer, John Powell, Pierre laRose, Howard G. Schmitt, Miss Emily Spackman, Randall Thompson, Ridgely Torrence, and Bruno Walter.

D. G. M.

Little Cedars,
New Canaan, Connecticut,
July, 1938

CONTENTS

ILLUSTRATIONS

MUSIC IN MY TIME

AND OTHER REMINISCENCES

CHAPTER I

A BOYHOOD IN BROOKLINE

I WONDER if our place in suburban Brookline, where I was born early in the morning of November 20, 1873, was really as spacious as it stretches in my memory, in contrast with the crowdedness of modern cities, or if it only seemed so in relation to my own small-boyhood. Our piazza looks wide as I recall it, stretching across the front of the house facing Harvard Street and turning at right angles along the smaller Green Street, which you would have to your left as you looked out our front door. To your right was the Bretts' place. From our door the lawn stretches, in my mind picture, leisurely and long, until you come to the asphalt sidewalk so agreeable to my velocipede, with the big horse-chestnut tree at the left of our front walk. The chestnuts, in their rich seal-brown, shiny and polished, used to fascinate me as they fitted so neatly their gaping green shells; it always seemed as if I could make something wonderful from them, but when I tried to cut them they wilted into shrivelled shards. Across the street was the Thomases' house. Reverend Reuen Thomas was an Englishman, and our "minister" of Harvard Church, at which my father played the organ for Sunday School, and to which he later gave a bell. Mrs. Thomas's habit of serving unsalted butter at her table filled my mother with an astonishment tinged with horror.

One thing that contributed to the sense of space, I imagine, was Patrick's geranium trees, in tubs, set at stately intervals at the edge of the piazza. "Trees" is hardly an exaggeration; by keeping the plants from year to year, wintering them in hotbeds and bringing them forth in spring, watering them with liquid manure of which I loved the rank, rich smell, he would coax them to heights of eight or ten feet, and people driving by into Boston would stop to admire them and ask us how we got them so big. Patrick McNamara had a high arched nose, a reddish chin beard and a rich brogue. He did not mind my tagging after him, seemed rather to like it, and I simply loved to follow him among all the things he was making grow. James, the coachman, was nice to me too—indeed they all spoiled me, as I was ten years younger than the next of my three older brothers—but James was not quite so leisurely, dream-walking and patriarchal as Patrick.

We children, my playmates and I—for of course my brothers were too old for such childishness—were led by the peculiarity of the piazza to the invention of our most exciting game, "Piazza Chance". There was no entrance to the piazza on the Green Street side, only railing; and we early discovered that though we could climb the railing and run off towards Green Street, my Saint Bernard dog Ponca, so much bigger than we, could never learn the trick of the railing, but had to run all the way back to the single Harvard Street entrance before he could chase us. What a start it gave us! how we would scream as we ran! and when at last he caught us how delightfully he would knock us down!

From the Green Street side came in the carriage entrance, cutting right across to the barn, behind the house and almost on the edge of the Bretts' grounds. To the left of the barn was the billiard room, and still to the left of that, outside, was a big dog-kennel in which Mabel Brett (nicknamed "Pussy") and I used to play house. It was musty, damp, and dark, but it was fun to arrange things in it. The billiard room, on the contrary, had a clean, dry smell, and the rows of cues against the wall looked neat. The great game there was to make railroads by putting two cues together and rolling the balls along them. Their blunt ends could be met by the blunt ends of two other cues, and *vice versa* with the pointed ends; and in this way with proper supports you could run your railroad clear across the billiard room, though of course the balls would sometimes fall off in spite of your best efforts. And the grown-ups, too, would want to play billiards inopportunely.

On the opposite side of the barn from the billiard room, to your right as you faced it, and therefore on the edge of the enchanted terrain of vegetable garden, orchard, hotbeds, summer-house and lily-pond that stretched back for several acres, was the entrance to the dark, cool, ammoniacal barn cellar. You descended to it by a gentle incline, with whitewashed walls on which someone had scribbled in black paint the record of a snow-storm remarkably late in spring—April 28, I believe, in some year such as 1883. You stole down the ramp on a hot summer day, and the baking heat receded behind you, giving place to semi-darkness, ammonia-scented coolness, and a stillness broken only by the occasional stamp of a horse overhead.

This beloved barn cellar was approached by a path that bordered the tennis court. Curiously I do not remember the tennis court in summer at all, but only in winter when a miniature lake would form in it and freeze over, with snowy inclines at the edges, over which we would proceed on sleds urged along by picks held in both hands. But the pear trees that bordered the court at right angles to the path come back to me rather in late summer and fall, when the little seckles made hardly more than a tart mouthful each, and the "Beurre-bosques" (if that is the way to spell them) would lie on the ground in embarrassing profusion, their spicy flavor even more spicy, we fancied, along the cracks that covered them as railroads do a map. Still further back were vegetable garden, grape arbor, Patrick's hotbeds, and fruit trees standing around the open space of the lily-pond—acidly juicy early Astrakhan apples, and some veteran cherry trees ravishable only with ladders.

The lily-pond was nothing much—a depression in the ground ten or fifteen feet across, lined with concrete, supplied by Patrick with water-lilies and by us boys with tadpoles, turtles, and other aquatic miscellanea. The pond hardly did more than mark the

centre of the upland field in which our place terminated, until my
brother Alan decided to build a rustic summer-house beside it. That
was an excitement; and we smaller boys, my playmates and I, used
to help not only by the interest expressed in endless questions, but
by supplying the workmen with bottles of sarsaparilla, rootbeer,
and lemon soda from Coolidge's store, at Coolidge's Corner, a
stone's throw from our house, where Harvard Street crossed Beacon
Street and you turned left to go into Boston. Back of summer-house
and pond was a high wooden fence, the extreme limit of our grounds,
over which we boys would swarm when minded to go an excursion
to Babcock's Woods and Babcock's Pond. These were in really unspoiled country in those days, though so few miles from Boston;
my brother Harry once shot a sparrow hawk in Babcock's Woods,
and we used to catch horn-pout and perch in the pond as well as
collecting marsh-gas from it while in our chemical phase. The
walk back would sometimes seem long, and it was a regular rite,
after we had climbed the fence and reached the grape arbor, to
proclaim, "I think we deserve a grape," and to proceed to engulf
Concords and a kind of Tokays that vanished with my childhood.

Years after we had moved away from Brookline—let me inter-
rupt myself to tell—years after my father and mother had died,
my brothers had scattered, and I had gone to live in New York,
I returned once to take a Rip Van Winkle glimpse of my birthplace. I could hardly find it. The house had been bodily turned on
its axis, to face Green Street instead of Harvard. New houses bordered and crowded it. Tennis court, vegetable garden, and orchards
alike had become mere house lots. Even Babcock's Woods, forlorn
hope, had been cut down, Babcock's Hill had been bodily shovelled
into Babcock's Pond, and cheap apartment houses sprinkled the
dusty plain that was all Babcock's ghost could find to walk in. Yet
there, paradoxically enough, were still the lily-pond and the summer-house, left as if by accident in one of the eddies of change,
absurdly diminutive and distressingly prosaic. I almost preferred
having things vanish completely, rather than remain like corpses
without souls, outliving their youthful spaciousness and romance.

As memory strays beyond our own grounds, for instance down

Harvard Street, I find the same sense of spaciousness accompanying me. Coolidge's Corner, to be sure, with its grocery store redolent of kitchen soap, was only a stone's throw from us; but as you passed it, crossed Beacon Street, even then something of a thoroughfare, and continued on Harvard Street past Harvard Church to "the village", you had a sense of exploration sometimes exciting, sometimes terrifying. I would start after a day's play to walk home with "Willie" Nash—Auburn Street could not have been more than half a mile—and becoming panic-stricken half way, persuade him to walk home with me. The process could be extended *ad libitum.* . . . As for "the village" itself, it seemed to me truly remote, and I only sought it when I went in the company of elders to dancing school. There was a horse omnibus, or, as we called it, "coach", that went up Harvard Street from the "village" to Coolidge's Corner, thence into Boston by Beacon Street (all of three miles) and thence once more to "the village". I was put into it by a playmate's mother late one afternoon, to go home. When it reached Coolidge's Corner I was too shy to ask to be let out, and was taken all the way into Boston, finally reaching home, I forget by what intercession, in tears. What an adventure!

When I was a few years older I would sometimes walk up Corey Hill to "Johnnie" Adams's house, almost at the top of the hill, and we would play a nameless but exciting game, of our own invention, in the square stretch of asphalt, shelving down to a drain in the middle, intended for washing carriages. Each of us would take an empty barrel as a "horse", and a broom to propel it, and strive to separate our adversary from his horse. These barrel horses were singularly balky beasts. You would give your barrel an immense push with your broom, and it would do nothing but revolve on its axis. If you tried to control your ardor you would find that a milder propulsion would merely deflect it in a totally unexpected direction, and put you for the moment out of the running. But the more unmanageable our barrels proved the better were we pleased; and we would finally sit down on them suddenly, weak in the knees, perspiring, breathless, but happy.

The only more organized sports I can remember were at "Willie"

Nash's, where the B.J.A.A. (Brookline Junior Athletic Association) held broad jumps, high jumps, and hundred-yard dashes. Very soon, however, probably under the influence of Willie's legalistic mind and fondness for public speaking, which we all felt confident would eventually land him in the mayorship of Brookline—if not in the presidency of the United States—the B.J.A.A. metamorphosed itself into the B.J.D.C., a debating club that held its deliberations in somewhat crowded quarters in the loft of the Nash barn. The room was a small one, under the sloping eaves; entrance to it was by an almost vertical step-ladder; and my Saint Bernard dog Ponca, larger and more enthusiastic than any of us, was an embarrassment from the start. His interruptions of our eloquence finally became unbearable, and a vote was taken to exclude him, in which mine was the only dissenting voice. My resignation followed, an impressive document, culminating in the phrase "on account of cruelty to me and my dog".

Formal documents of this sort were very much in Willie Nash's line; I blush when I recall the "written apology" that he once demanded of me, and my reason for finally according it. He was the prime favorite of our teacher, Miss Bean, frequently honored with her confidence. One muddy spring morning, as he was carrying some of her precious papers, jealousy maddened me and I (very much out of character, for I was always physically timid) took to fisticuffs and managed, much to my surprise, to knock the papers out of his hand and into the mud. Entirely justified, surely, was his demand for the written apology; inexcusable was my refusal of it. But still more inexcusable were the circumstances under which I eventually vouchsafed it. Months passed. Spring mud gave place to early summer warmth. One afternoon, passing the corner of Auburn Street, I saw Willie and his friends on a ladder in his cherry tree, fairly gorging themselves on the big juicy cherries. I looked about me. A curving grey stone wall on the corner of Auburn and Harvard streets was breast-high, just convenient for writing. I had in my pocket a pencil and a scrap of paper. Almost before I knew it, the long-belated apology was written, presented, and accepted. Little Jesuit that I was, I got the cherries.

While I am making confessions, let me add that a friend tells me (what I had wholly forgotten) that I used to rent my two tricycles, the old one for two cents an hour, the new one for five. It was from the Gregory family, I suppose, that I got my Scotch blood.

II

In the little "sitting room" to the right of our front door was an arm chair where my father would receive me on his lap of a Sunday morning, to cut my finger nails. He performed this rite with a small, bright, very sharp pen-knife, as neat and exact as himself. He would press my finger hard so as to make a clean edge. His own finger nails were super-clean, and close-textured, flat on top, and like all his person scrupulously cared for. He was fond of cologne-water, Bay rum, and other toilet whimsies, and when I climbed into his lap those Sunday mornings cigar smoke would be only an over-tone of sweeter scents. Week-days he paid little attention to me. James would drive him into his office at the Mason and Hamlin Company, and out again at night. Sometimes I would go along, and if it was spring James would stop the two horses at a dip in Beacon Street where willows grew, get out of the "carry-all" and cut me a whistle.

With my father I was always a little timid. Despite a fund of essential kindness his temperament was nervous, even irritable. Yet I admired him too, for his personal distinction, for his way of look-ing over the tops of his eye-glasses, for something chivalrous in his love of truth which I only half understood, and for his piano play-ing. His playing, to be sure, had fallen into certain bad habits in the days I heard him; like most pianists of his generation he leaned some-what to empty brilliance and dashing virtuosity, and he liked to put the pedal down when he began and hardly lift it until he stopped. Yet he had true musicality too; in his touch was something of that clinging, singing, caressing quality that made my Uncle William's —his brother's—the most beautiful touch I have ever heard; and their father, Lowell Mason, used to say that his talent was almost as marked as William's had it only been developed. The piece he played to my greatest delight was Beethoven's *Pathetique Sonata*, especially the slow movement.

Even before my father and mother were born, it seems, their families had been brought together, through music, in the following curious way. When my grandfather, Lowell Mason, commenced as choir-master of the Bowdoin Street Church in Boston the work for church and school music destined to contribute so much to American musical culture, he invited to live in his house, in order that he might have her rich soprano for his choir, Miss Anne Folsom of Exeter, for whom he later named his tune *Folsom*. In this way Anne Folsom met Asher Palmer, already a member of the choir, married him in 1833, and bore him first a son whom they named Lowell Mason Palmer, and in 1836 a daughter, Helen Augusta Palmer. In some unpublished reminiscences, set down many years later for us her sons, this Helen Palmer, then Helen Palmer Mason, writes: "At the time my mother came to Boston in 1831 to accept Dr. Mason's hospitality and to sing in his choir, Dr. and Mrs. Mason had a little fair-haired boy of eight months old, and that little boy was Henry Mason, my husband in later years. When my dear mother's first child was born, Mrs. Dr. Mason gave to my mother *her cradle*—she having got through with it, my husband being her last child, and the cradle having served for three sons older. So my mother's children all went through that cradle, and when my first child was born my mother gave the cradle to me. So my husband and I, and our children, were all rocked in the same cradle, and when my eldest son was married and had children I gave that cradle to him."

Under the circumstances it was natural that when Helen Palmer visited her Exeter cousins, and girl-like they discussed their "beaux", she should name as hers Henry Mason. Yet she really knew very little of him. When he was fourteen or fifteen she saw him once at a choir rehearsal, but before he was twenty his father sent him on a trip to Germany to share the musical experiences of his next older brother William. Lowell Mason, by that time widely known for his pioneer work in music, allowed some of the Boston and New York newspapers to print the crude but enthusiastic letters sent him

Dr. Lowell Mason (1792–1872) and Mrs. Mason

by his two sons; and no doubt such experiences as theirs were then unusual for American boys. William, who stayed several years, studying with Moscheles, with Alexander Dreyschock, and eventually with Liszt, has rendered a fairly full account in his *Memories of a Musical Life*. Henry's comments, culled from yellowing newspaper clippings, paint to the life the innocent, honest, musically sensitive but uncultivated youth he then was.

"Prague, February 4, 1851. This morning a new mass was performed, composed by Herr Kroup, a resident of Prague. The music pleased me; it was quite Mozartish I thought. The choir is a very good one. . . . They do not play with one another and behave silly, as we often see our young ladies do in our American choirs. Oh! how insipid many of our choirs, and especially our church quartets, appear when compared with the well-trained choirs here.

"Dresden, March 12. Dreyschock showed me an old piano, eighty years old, on which Beethoven had formerly played. I played the scale, and felt almost a musical inspiration coming over me, as I pressed with my own fingers the keys that have yielded to the touch of the great Maestro. . . . I called at a small two-story house in a poor part of the city, in which lives the great Johann Schneider! Yes! I was astonished indeed, to find so great a man living in so small a house. . . . He is still regarded as the greatest organist in Germany.

"Berlin, April. We visited the new palace which was built by Frederick the Great at the close of the seven years war, in order to show his enemies that he still had some money left. . . . The celebrated *Passion Music* of Bach was given by the far-famed Sing-Academie. The performance was admirable. But I did not much like the music. I doubt not you will say that it is because of my ignorance or want of taste; but still the fact is that with the exception of four or five most splendid Fugues, and the Chorales which are scattered along through the work, I thought it dull, dry, and uninteresting. . . . I was truly glad when the performance was over, and I could say in truth, I have heard Bach's *Passion Music*. . . .

"It was a treat to hear Mendelssohn's *A minor* so perfectly performed. Before the orchestra had played the first measure through, association carried me back to the great Chorus of the Musical Convention in August last, and I could almost hear a thousand voices singing that splendid tune *Menville*, from *Cantica Laudis* [1], which is taken, you will remember, from the first part of this glorious *Sinfonie*. Is not this Mendelssohn's greatest work?"

After his return home my father founded, in 1854, with Emmons Hamlin, the Mason and Hamlin Company, which prospered for many years in the manufacture of reed organs, at that time widely used over all America. Then in June, 1857, Dr. Lowell Mason brought his son Henry to pass a Sunday with his old friends the Palmers in Cambridge where he was holding a "praise meeting" and lecturing, as he did all over the country, on congregational singing. "They spent the Sunday with us," writes my mother, "and on Monday I went with them to North Reading to spend the day in attending a musical convention which Dr. Mason was holding there. We were there together, Henry and I, Saturday, Sunday and Monday, and by the time we got home I was pretty deeply in love."

As for Henry's sentiments, we can read them even now, with a little imagination, between the quaintly formal lines of his letter to Helen's parents, with its underlinings that give it such a flavor as of Richardson's novels. Here are some sentences from it.

"Boston, July 2nd, 1857. My dear Mr. and Mrs. Palmer, My acquaintance with your family has been of so recent a date, that what I am about to declare *may* appear to you to be premature. Yet I feel that I cannot trust myself to visit longer at your house without informing you of my *most earnest desire* and obtaining your consent thereto.

"I deeply and truly *love* your daughter, Miss Helen. Mrs. Palmer must already have noticed, I think, that I was greatly interested in her from the Saturday evening (it seems scarcely possible it was less than *one* short week ago) when first we met. . . .

"You will please to bear in mind that my acquaintance with Miss Palmer was formed under peculiar circumstances. Our families have long been intimately acquainted. I was with Miss Palmer almost

[1] One of Lowell Mason's collections of tunes.

Helen Palmer Mason (Mrs. Henry Mason)

From a Daguerreotype taken at about
the time of her marriage

the whole of Saturday evening, the following Sabbath, and Monday, and in that time, *under the circumstances*, became better acquainted with her than I should probably have become in six months or more of ordinary callings and casual meetings.

"I have already spoken to my Father about it, and he has bade me Godspeed, and assured me of both his and my Mother's most cordial approbation. I have then only *your* consent to obtain, before telling *her* of my affection.

"If you should approve (which may God grant) I should prefer to be the first one to tell her of my love, and to offer her my hand and heart. Should you disapprove (Oh! heaven forbid!) it is unnecessary for her ever to know aught of this. *Earnestly soliciting* an answer at your earliest convenience, I am

"Most Respectfully Your Friend
"HENRY MASON."

One or two more excerpts from my mother's memories complete the story. "I remember so well," she writes, "the day he first took me for a buggy drive, June 29th, 1857. I realized perfectly that I ought not to go unless I really meant to encourage his suit. . . . While he waited at the door and I went for my hat and wrap I dropped on my knees in my own little attic room and earnestly prayed for some light to guide me on my way. . . . The date of my engagement was July 15, 1857. It was Commencement Day at Harvard College. We walked on Quincy Street and about the college Yard, and finally sat down on the steps of the University Library (Gore Hall). There we plighted our troth. . . . Every day after business hours he would come out, take tea, and pass the evening. He brought a good deal of music which he played, and he and I played duets sometimes. The opera of *Trovatore* had shortly before come out, and he brought the score and played and sang it constantly to our delight. He was the musical correspondent for one of the New York papers, so he had tickets free for all the operas, concerts, etc. . . . In December of 1857, Christmas Eve, we were married."

III

The first two of my brothers, "Ned" (Edward Palmer) and
Alan, were born in Cambridge, but the third, "Harry" (Henry
Lowell), in Boston, where my father bought a house and greatly
enjoyed his weekly evenings of chamber music with Gärtner,
Hause, Jungnickel, Wolf Fries, August Fries, and other Boston
musicians. In the parties held more or less regularly for the playing
of quartets and quintets—parties less usual in those days than now
—my father took the piano parts. After the move to Brookline the
billiard room, long before it knew my cue railroads, was the scene
of many an orchestral performance by local talent. My brother
Harry was one of the two or three second violins, there were six
or eight firsts, Handasyd Cabot played cello, my brother Ned
double-bass, James Stearns trombone, and the whole was led by
Harry's violin teacher Albert van Raalte, a thin, near-sighted young
Jewish musician whom even I can remember. Their ambitions rose
to Beethoven's *First Symphony*.

The room to your left as you entered our front door, the "parlor"
as we called it, was more than twice as large as the "sitting room",
ran indeed as far back as both sitting room and dining room on the
other side, contained piano, Mason and Hamlin organ, and music-
box, and had a large bay-window looking toward the Bretts'. It
had a thick carpet into which my feet sank luxuriously, a carpet
with large figures boldly outlined against a blue-white ground. For
that carpet I have a tender place in my heart, since it was upon it
that I lay down and sobbed when I could not play all those horrid
double sharps in Schumann's *Mai, lieber Mai*—while I was planning where to play one of them I forgot about the others. *May, dear
May*—which I loved musically as much as I detested it technically
—must have been given me, I fancy, by Clayton Johns, my first
real man teacher, who lived in Boston and to whom I was pro-
moted from "Nellie" Coolidge, Brookline-bred, of the same family
indeed as the Store and the Corner. "Mr. Johns" had a lovely curly
moustache and eyes half-quizzical, half-merry, as he explained the
mysteries in friendly confidence. Another Schumann piece he gave

me, *Erster Verlust (First Loss)*, I played with too little expression
to please him, and he suggested I think of some dear friend who
had died. The trouble with that was, as I said at once, that none of
my friends *had* died. This seemed to bring us to a standstill, until
I bethought myself that my little dog, Rhea Sylvia, a tiny Skye
terrier, "Rhea" for short, had died, and I might think of her! Mr.
Johns approved the idea, but whether with satisfactory results to
the performance I do not know.

It was at about this period, too, that I made my first attempts at
composition, urged on very likely by emulation of my brother Ned,
who, graduating at Harvard in 1881, when I was seven years old,
not only led the Glee Club but composed some of the songs for
the Hasty Pudding Club theatricals. One of his songs I remember
clearly, for the grace of its tune and a sort of leisurely luxuriance
in its harmony, but also for an eccentricity of form by which each
stanza modulated further away from the original starting point, and
the whole never really ended! My own sense of form in those days
was equally erratic, to say the least. My first little piece, played off
at the piano when I was seven and kindly noted down for me by
this same brother, stays to be sure almost pusillanimously in G
major; but the two pieces I still have in my own boyish handwriting, dated August, 1882, never get back to their native G major at
all, one coming to an unequivocal end in E minor, over which, to
make assurance doubly sure, I have printed FINE in large capitals,
the other simply losing itself in modulations that I evidently found
as unmanageable as Schumann's double sharps. (I seem to have had
considerable difficulty in even notating these pieces. One of them
bears the direction "Octave lower" against both right and left
hand parts!)

Another manuscript, of considerably later date, and entitled
Souvenir, reminds me of family discussions we used to have about
it, that seem interminable in their futility as I look back on them.
Its meticulously regular four-measure phrases march in precise
formation until the last one—which is suddenly five measures. It is
simply that the next to the last chord has been lengthened to a
whole measure in order to give a certain amplitude to the cadence,

but it brings back vividly to mind the limitations of our musical world when I think of all the breath we wasted on whether that fifth measure was "permissible". The truth is, our whole view of music was based on the style of the classic and romantic symphonists, beginning with Haydn and Mozart and ending with Mendelssohn and Schumann. Even Bach was rather on the edge of the music we recognized, and the rhythmic freedom or unmetricality of, say, Gregorian chant was decidedly beyond our horizon. My father's doubts about the *Passion Music* were quite natural in one whose favorite composer was probably Mozart. It is not surprising that a five-measure phrase struck us as needing justification, but it is interesting to note how limited was our conception of musical style, passionately attached to music as we all were.

My second and third brothers definitely shared the family interest. Alan, graduating from Harvard in 1886, led the Glee Club, and founded the Band, not in existence before his time. He played the cornet. My brother Harry, graduating in 1888 (and thus celebrating this year his fiftieth anniversary with his class-mates), played the violin as a boy, the piano later, and after joining the Mason and Hamlin Company, of which he eventually became president, was the congenial companion of many musicians. It was through my brothers that I came later to study piano with Ethelbert Nevin, and that I met MacDowell, Loeffler, Chadwick, Foote, and other Boston musicians, as well as Henry Holden Huss of New York, to whose comradely interest my early musical efforts were deeply indebted. . . . When a brother is also a friend—the conjunction is rarer than we like to believe—he is apt to be a particularly good one. I was fortunate in being united to my brother Harry not merely by early associations with their incomparable magic but by the stouter if soberer bonds of common ideals and many common tastes. With his impulsive affection and generous practical help he has been in my life, both in the excitements of youth and the realizations of age, a sort of overtone, so to speak, given by nature: not by any means always consonant, but even in dissonance enriching the timbre.

As I consider the old problem of heredity and environment, then, in the light of my own experience, I feel sure that friendly environment in the form of grandfather, father, uncles, brothers and companions did for my music what no heredity could have done alone. It is true that the musical interest of the Mason family goes back many generations, and that even my great-great-grandfather Barachias Mason (1723–1783) "taught music" twenty years in his native Medfield; it is true that in my own generation and the two preceding ones most of the male Masons (who so greatly outnumbered the females that my mother mentions in her memoirs that "in six generations there were twenty-four boys to only four girls") were interested in music in one way or another; it is true that one man in each of those three generations became a professional musician. Yet for all that, the daily companionship with music that arose naturally from this widely diffused interest, the habit of taking it as "part of the day's work", was for me, I feel, the decisive element. It was because I heard music daily from piano, organ, glee club, or music-box—it was because my family entertained musicians and discussed their problems—it was even because I cried on the floor over double sharps instead of broken shins—it was for all these environmental reasons that music became for me so early the most vivid thing in the world. How vivid it was to me, with what almost pathological intensity I took it, I may finally suggest by quoting an absurd and yet perhaps slightly pathetic letter I wrote my brother Ned in 1886 when I was twelve, and when our idyllic Brookline existence was just about to end, and we were to move into Boston.

"Dear Ned,—I write to you to let out some of my pent-up feelings, I go for something higher than this world,—for music,—the highest of all arts, more than an art,—a sublime purpose. Music is not for this world, and yet it is in this world—I do not see why. I have been reading the biography of that greatest of musicians *Beethoven*. The very name is almost sublime. My nerves were strained to their utmost—I was perfectly "carried away" with Beethoven and all his actions. Mamma said something, I forget what, but my nerves were all gone. I couldn't bear to have anything common spoken of just then, and so I answered crossly. Mamma reproached me and—that was the last straw—I threw myself on the bed and sobbed and sobbed and sobbed!

"But excuse me for bothering you with my troubles. I wanted to tell them to somebody, now I have done it. This was the most earnest letter I ever wrote, I guess.

"Affectionately, GREGORY."

There my boyhood, so naïve and yet so serious, came to an end. When we left Brookline, with its delicious freedom, its careless playmates, its fresh sights and sounds and smells and tastes, for the Boston world of school, library, concert, and theatre, I left my childhood once for all behind, and ventured timidly into youth.

CHAPTER II

AT HARVARD IN THE NINETIES

IN THE fall of 1891 Pierre la Rose and I settled into 14 Matthews, where we continued as room-mates for the whole of our course at Harvard, until our graduation in June, 1895. Number 14 was on the third or fourth floor at the back of Matthews, and as you sat in our window-seat you had to your left Harvard Square, to your right the beautiful rose-brick oblong of Massachusetts Hall, with its ancient thick walls and incongruous modern fire-escapes, which at certain hours would be black with students retiring from Charles Eliot Norton's course in fine arts on the upper floor. La Rose, whom I had met the year before at Exeter Academy, had pretensions to taste in furnishing, and we had orange sash-curtains, and over the upright piano a bust of Richelieu (why Richelieu I cannot remember) set off against an India shawl. There was a crucifix, too, more, I always felt, for artistic than religious reasons, though la Rose, who had an ecclesiastical turn of mind, insisted upon it. He used to madden me by talking about *"The* Church"—with none of the adjectives I was used to adding—and about doctrinal subtleties incomprehensible to me, with his friend Gaillard Lapsley and other upper-classmen. Lapsley intimidated me with his strenuous learning. The court fool of our group, the irreverent and ribald jester, was John Mack; and his translation of Newman's title *Apologia pro*

17

Vita Sua as *Apology for Living in a Sewer* solaced my wounded sense of being nothing but a sectarian and outsider.

On the whole I was fortunate in my room-mate. As a youngest son, ten years younger than my next older brother, I had been somewhat spoiled in boyhood, so that my early tastes were hardly more than boyish enthusiasms and headstrong prejudices. I idolized Dickens, for instance, but despised Thackeray; along with Moszkowski, Grieg, and Nevin, whom I admired for their prettiness, I placed Beethoven, but could not abide Mozart; Bach I admitted to my pantheon, while excluding Handel. All this captiousness received its first check when at Exeter, where most of the healthy young animals despised me as a "mother's boy" and were in turn despised by me as barbarians, la Rose sought me out for my love of books and music, and commenced my training. Of all my classmates he had the surest nose for the best, whether in letters, music, the graphic arts, or the more general arts of life; and if it was a nose that would also tilt to a supercilious angle at what he thought less than best, it was good for my independence to have to make the correction needed. He was quite capable of enthusiasm, too. His style in college essays and stories was fairly Jamesian. He could draw exquisite book-plates. As for his piano playing, I can see him yet at our upright, stocky but erect in shirt-sleeves and red hair, facing the bust of Richelieu, getting over the keys with surprising facility, drooping his inseparable cigarette from a corner of his mouth, and never dropping it in the most complex mazes of Grieg or Chopin, nor when he stopped to exclaim over their beauties, nor even when he coughed—for he had in perfection the necessary art of coughing without losing his cigarette.

As you entered our room through its double door, with vestibule between, you had the piano and Richelieu at your right, and the coal grate at your left, with well stocked book-case above it. There was a side-table for tea, of which we made an important function, and to which our Boston friends would sometimes come out. Then la Rose would officiate at the tea-table and guide the conversation. My part was the humbler one of replenishing the hot water, and alas, even this I did once in a far from seemly manner, and instead of

discreetly taking the kettle to the bedroom, brought forth to shock
all eyes the huge crockery water-pitcher that should have stayed in
a decent privacy. If I am laughing a little at our youthful affectations it is probably as a compensation for the sense of inferiority.
I had been a rather solitary child, had stayed only one year at preparatory school, where I had felt completely isolated, and remained
among our freshman group of sophisticates or would-be sophisticates singularly and incurably innocent. The contrast is symbolized
for me by a discussion of Hardy's *Tess of the d'Urbervilles* in which
my friends were outdoing each other in epigrams (we always made
"epigrams" about everything). I thought them unsympathetic to
Tess and too tolerant of her lover—was his name Clare?—who was
so unimaginative about faults in her in which he had himself freely
indulged. At last, after standing it as long as I could, I burst out:
"But, for Heaven's sake, fellows, she *apologized!*" I never heard the
last of that.

II

One day la Rose brought to our room a classmate I found it difficult at first to place. To begin with, he was a little older than most
of our set, or perhaps only appeared so because of the preposterous
heavy, almost military-looking moustache he had not yet shaved off,
which went most incongruously with his wavy sandy hair and his
blue eyes at once friendly and mischievous. Then he was not a Bos-
tonian, not even a New Englander, but that doubtful quantity a
"middle Westerner"—he hailed from St. Paul. Finally, while he
could make epigrams with the best of us, and kept us in gales of
laughter with his odd conceits, his wit was quite devoid of self-complacency, on the contrary he seemed to be poking fun at himself as
much as at what he happened to be talking about. His gay irresponsibility infected even the most self-conscious of us, and although his
name appeared in the catalogue as Flandrau, Charles Macomb, we
quickly shortened it to Charlie Flandrau, and frequently lightened
it to the nickname "Charlie Bolo". Readers of his delicious *Viva
Mexico* can perhaps form a faint idea of how irresistible he could be
in daily life. Strolling into his room one day I noticed a porcelain

miniature lying on his table. "Is this Dante, Charlie?" I asked. "No," said he, "that's Alice in Wonderland—Oh, *that*—that's George Eliot." Once we were rash enough to try to "grind" with him on a history examination. The name Odo seemed to fascinate him, and he suggested as a title for a novel: *Odo, a Detail of the Day*. When towards dawn we were all reaching the breaking point he retired to the bedroom and reappeared with a powder puff in his button-hole as a chrysanthemum.

In our meetings of later years, unfortunately few, I have always savored in Charlie the same irresponsible humor. His report to our class secretary, twenty-five years after graduation, begins: "Since leaving Harvard I have done all sorts of things, none of which has been of the slightest importance to anyone but me," and ends: "This brings up to date the record of a life that, as far as I know, has always been quite aimless and exceedingly contented." In a later report, written from his retreat in Majorca, he remarks that he seems to have joined "that sturdy band of patriots who would do almost everything for their country, except live in it", but adds: "In regard to your suggestion that I may have retired, there has never been anything to retire from." This last statement was of course not literally true—no more so than any of Charlie's statements ever were. In 1924, for instance, he was writing regularly for the *St. Paul News;* and this led to a delightful renewal of our college friendship when my first symphony was played in St. Paul and he discussed it in an article of which I will quote the opening, since it takes us back again to college days.

"At a memorably agreeable period of my existence," he says, "when in the college rooms of Daniel Gregory Mason some of us frequently sat up most of the night listening to Mason and his roommate play Grieg and Brahms, Chopin, Bizet, Tschaikowsky, occasionally his own youthful works, and a dozen others, until a light repast of hot dogs, scrambled eggs and beer was indicated, one used to return home in the steel blue Massachusetts dawn wondering whether Mason would become a pianist, a composer, a philosopher, or a writer, for at that time he was a good deal of all four. Well, he still is, although, as one can't very well dedicate oneself with equal fervor to four activities, philosophy, and the piano in at least its virtuostic (there should be such a word although it seems that there really isn't) sense have made way for the composing of music and the writing of . . . books and essays about it."

III

La Rose and I used occasionally to take stray meals at a dingy restaurant, Allnutt's by name, up a dark flight of wooden stairs, near the corner of Harvard Square. Its nondescript clientele, mostly poor students with a furtive and hungry air, was as depressing as its habitat; but its liver and bacon, to youth and in spring, could be almost exciting. One evening in the spring of our junior year la Rose recognized there an old school friend, a man of middle stature, full-blooded complexion, and studious air, whose deep liquid blue eyes seemed to look through appearances into essences. His manner was reserved but friendly. We fell into talk, or at least la Rose and I did, while his friend smoked a pipe ponderingly, pressing it with thoughtful fore-finger, and from time to time dropped brief comments, often hardly more than resonant ejaculations, somehow more liberating, more refreshing than volumes of the carefully manicured epigrams current in our set. Unusual, too, seemed to me his dress: both florid and careless, as if a barbaric taste for magnificence in waistcoats and neckties found itself unsupported by an attention that was set on things more worth while. Most of our friends were trim with a New England trimness; this man breathed the freshness, almost uncouth, of the West. Yet his unconventionality, far from seeming eccentric, was delightfully friendly and intimate; and even in that cheerless place and casual meeting, to talk with him, to bathe one's spirit, after struggles for cleverness, in his rich silences, was like coming home to truth and beauty. Before leaving him that evening we spent an hour in his room, and I, taking away some of his poems for possible musical setting, felt that I had made a new friend, though little knowing how unique a one. His name was William Vaughn Moody; he had graduated in '93, but was staying on for further study and to teach.

During the whole of my senior year, 1894–95, he was assisting his friend Lewis E. Gates in English 22, and acting as proctor in Gray's Hall, just across the corner of the Yard from Matthews. It was easy to arrange those long walks and talks in which congenial youths discover each other—and themselves. In winter there was hot rum toddy over my open coal fire, or walks in bleak sunsets across Harvard Bridge to Boston, to dine at Marliave's, where as Gates said "one played at being abroad", or to hear the Boston Symphony concert and discuss it afterwards over beer and welsh rarebits at the Old Elm. There were in those days some new symphonies worth hearing. There was that feverishly exciting but terrifying *Pathetique*, in which Tschaikowsky had put into music all the sense of metaphysical mystery and dread, of horror even, that we found so haunted us in our more serious moods, and that seemed to be always lying in wait for us when we were tempted for the moment to fancy life comprehensible. There was the fascinating *New World* of Dvořák, with its opening theme that Charlie Flandrau thought resembled *Where Did You Get That Hat?* and its finale that seemed to Will Moody "a sort of celestial cake-walk". Preserved in my journal I find a program of the concert of February 14, 1895 on the back of which are jotted in pencil, as well as I could get them, the main themes of the symphony, which I then heard for the third time, with, as I record, "shivers of delight". As spring came on there were mint juleps in Boston, or boating at Riverside, or long afternoon trudges; and in the evenings there were magical walks up Brattle Street, fragrant with lilacs, or to Fresh Pond, ghostly in mist and moonlight. And always there was the fascination of Moody's imagination-releasing figures of speech, his fertile silences, his irresponsible humor, comical slang and shouting gusto of laughter, his deep contagious sense of the infinite mystery and richness of life.

The longest and best walk of all came neither in winter nor in spring, but in the summer holiday following my graduation. Why should we not try a walking tour in Belgium and France? Europe, to be sure, was not new to him, but to him nothing could ever be stale. To me it would be one long magic. As early as January we began the luxury of considering it; I find in my journal his remark:

"Stevenson's donkey made his book better, but he probably didn't have half so good a time:—which is only another instance of the discrepancy between art and life." By spring we had got down to practical details such as rubbing two samples of flannel shirtings on the path in the Boston Public Garden to see if they would show dirt. One was a dingy blue-grey, the other a full dark blue, and their capacity to absorb dirt without revealing it surpassed our hopes. On July 3 we actually sailed.

After all these years I find that two traits of my incomparable companion stand out for me as the ground bass to all the varied music of that legendary holiday—traits that a few excerpts from the journal I kept may at least dimly suggest. The first was his immense gusto in the picturesqueness of the commonest daily life. In the introduction to his *Letters* I have told how "Pritchard", the name of a young working-man we met in Cambridgeport, became for him a symbol of the divinity in the average men; if there was one subject on which we could never agree it was Walt Whitman, whom he idolized for his humane inclusiveness, without seeming to notice the lack of discrimination and distinction that always troubled me; and it was because his own love went out so instinctively to all life, not to selected life, that my nickname for him, "Lover of Life", seemed to me so inevitable. If he had in him any snobbism at all, it was the inverted snobbism of the radical. Josephine Peabody hit off the attitude as it showed itself in his religious freedom of thought when she said that he was "tolerant of everybody except Episcopalians".

The second trait I have in mind was closely related to the first; perhaps it was only the manifestation to his closer friends of the same love that the other spread more widely over the world; I myself experienced it in his affectionate, elder-brotherly protectiveness toward my weaker health and slighter strength. To his robustness my limitations must often have seemed unreasonable, absurd, almost perverse; yet keen as was the love of adventure in him they so annoyingly curbed, his affection was vivid enough to make him endure and even make light of them. His humor helped, too. When it came to choosing restaurants, where he looked chiefly for vivid human contacts, he was amused at my anxiety that the food should be "nourishing"—the word became a sort of standing joke between us.[1] . . . Indeed, his friendliness expressed itself in all gradations from a casual pat on the shoulder to the imaginative reconstruction of a comrade's cosmos, in order to bring solace.[2] . . .

[Journal] "S. S. Rhynland, July 3, [1895]. A cheap, unattractive, and innutritious [*sic*] breakfast, which I ate with difficulty, and Will hardly at all. We arrived tired and faint at the dock. . . . The Rhynland seemed to our jaded vision a rat-trap, shabby, malodorous, and ridiculously minute. Greasy seamen were swabbing greasy cubby-holes with greasy mops. . . . There was an unbelievable compound smell of paint and onions. . . . My spirits fell to zero. Will laughed immoderately, while I could scarcely hold in from crying.

"July 6, Saturday. Tonight, about sundown, the steerage passengers all collected on their deck. They grouped themselves about, many of them eating the supper they had brought from below out into the fresh air in tin dinner-cans and rough crockery dishes. . . . Two happy men thrummed and piped popular songs on a zither and a penny flute. They did it for the pure joy of it, melody alone, scorning harmony, and sometimes even rhythm. When they got to *Home, Sweet Home* the company joined in with a monotonous sing-song croak, the friction of many throats, but as heartfelt as warbling. . . .

"The stern deck has just been flooded with a horde of first-cabin passengers, who stood stolidly between us and the sunset, staring at the ineffable colors blankly and talking commonplaces with an empty giggle. The most unbearable of them all is a smooth-faced little cad whom I heard playing Schumann novelettes the other day with a stiff wrist, and who is now arrogantly puffing an Egyptian cigarette at my elbow.

"Monday. I have been whiling away an hour by getting the Philistine medical student to express his opinions. The music he likes is Nevin's *Water Scenes*, Chopin's *Waltzes*, and 'a piece called Eng-

---

[1] See, for example, *Some Letters of William Vaughn Moody*, page 107.
[2] *Some Letters*, XXVII, page 80, etc.

lish Suites by Bach'. He said in regard to the Nevin, 'When a man's feeling down in the mouth, *Ophelia's* the thing.' He told us of one of the stewards who recited to him some lines of Shelley, and opined that 'he was a fool'. Will entirely failed to react on this occasion, and was simply bored by the man's vulgarity and Philistinism, which I confess soon sickened myself.

"Friday. Last night after supper the men in the steerage improvised a dancing bout, much to the edification of themselves and everybody else. Music of a primitive but genuinely organic character proceeded from a violin, a piccolo, and a harmonica. The pieces were funny little jigs. Eight of the roughest-looking but jolliest of the men joined hands and hearts in a square dance, a strange mixture of grace and uncouth antics. A little girl we have nicknamed 'Trilby' was much amused by the masculine cumbrousness of the dancers. . . . One felt that before one's very eyes were bubbling up from the people's hearts the primary and eternal fountains of art.

"July 15, Antwerp. Yesterday afternoon, amid a jargon of foreign tongues, a rain of trunks, and a particolored throng of people, we set foot on Europe. . . .

"July 18, Ghent. Boy's voice. Light on canals and houses.

"July 19, Ypres. Wonderful melting mood on a haystack in late twilight. Beautiful colors. Passed the French border at Comines. The names of the stations are poetic, *Sainte Marguerite*, *Vertgalant*, *La Madeleine*. Will gave the waitress at the way-station at Comines an English lesson, translating raspberry jam for her to try to pronounce—"R-r-r-redgoo!"

"July 20, Amiens. Will called the rose window in the cathedral 'God's Spider-web'.

"July 21, Beauvais. *Concours des Pompiers.* Wild jollifications. Dancing in the square. The billowy sweep and onrush of the galop.

"July 22, Rouen. Walk to Bonsecour. Afternoon of dreaming in the sunshine. Will's first sketch.

"Began our walking, July 26. Train to Brionne, thence walked to l'Hotellerie, about 17 miles. Rain, peasant woman in hut, horrible supper, rainbow. . . .

"July 31, Saint Lo. Menagerie. Cathedral 'index fingers'.

"August 1. Walked to Tessy-sur-Vire. This day was most mythic, fairy-like, indescribable. The little stream called the Vire led us all the way, an inexpressibly quiet, slow rivulet, wherein we could see the whole of the opposite bank reflected, but merged and softened by what Will called its 'blur and drizzle'.

"Gray landscape at twilight, with the soldiers of the 146th regiment on drill. At three in the morning they marched past, raising the echoes of the universe, with inspiring military music on the 'full brass'.[1]

"August 26. Boat from Rouen to Caudebec. Thence to Yvetot on foot. Met on the open road an old man dressed very meagrely, with carpet slippers open at the toes, ragged shirt and bare head, who lifted his hands eloquently and chanted to the empty landscape, 'Pourquoi, pourquoi?' " [2]

"September 7. Sailed for home."

What these brief notes are but dimly able to suggest is the bewildering mixture of poetry and comicality in our adventures, of which Will's relish was insatiable. Take as an instance the epic day of Old Pourquoi. We were late for the Seine boat at Rouen, and it had to be delayed for us by special official dispensation, always impressive in France; we jumped aboard to the accompaniment of staccato Dépêchez-vous's from the attendants. Excitement was succeeded at Caudebec by boredom; not even the inch-high tidal wave that was shown us in the Seine as we sat at lunch on the verandah of the hotel could induce us to pursue our original plan of spending one day at each river-station; and we decided on the spot to walk the ten miles to the railroad at Yvetot (immortalized in Beranger's ballad) and take train there to Havre. Then came the long hot walk of the interminable August afternoon, with, towards sun-down, the great event of the day in the meeting with Old Pourquoi. Finally,

---

[1] This was the origin of Moody's lines in Act IV of *The Masque of Judgment:*
> But always ere the dayspring took the sky,
> Somewhere the silver trumpets were acry,—
> Sweet, high, oh, high and sweet!
> What voice could summon so but the soul's Paraclete?
> Whom should such voices call but me, to dare and die?

[2] See Moody's poem, *Old Pourquoi.*

arriving hot, dirty, and tired at Yvetot station, we found a train actually waiting, a *rapide* of first-class cars only, which like the boat of the morning had to be specially detained for us. Dashing down a gold coin at the ticket window, hastily pocketing the change handed us without counting it, we were ushered, all steaming as we were, into a decorous, richly furnished first-class compartment where a staid business man, in black, regarded with disfavor our dusty shoes, our knapsacks, our dirt-proof dark blue flannel shirts, now put to their supreme test.

A brief respite came in leaning back luxuriously against the immaculate cushions after our long walk. But alas, one final incongruity awaited us. As we alighted at Havre we were arrested—no less—for having accepted too much change from the Yvetot ticket-mistress. Will suddenly saw Yvetot through less romantic eyes than Beranger's. Long and fiercely he argued with the *gendarme*, but how the battle was going, as I could not hear French as fast as he could talk it when angry, I could only guess from his gesticulation —even in that moment of stress not quite Gallic. At last, on payment of balance due, we were allowed to proceed to our hotel. He told me he had never learned more French in half an hour.

My own efforts at French were mostly confined to answering the chambermaid who asked us each morning if we were to stay for the night. (I had to do this, because he was always downstairs at the moment paying the bill.) I ended by acquiring a certain facility— almost an air, I fondly hoped—with the phrase *"Nous partons aujourd'hui"*. This went very well as long as I got the expected *"Oui, monsieur"* in answer. Anything unexpected usually plunged me into confusion. Vivid even now is the qualm of horror, the sense of being lost in a mad hurly-burly, I felt on our arrival in Beauvais in the midst of the firemen's ball I have described in my essay on Berlioz in *The Romantic Composers*. This was after we had been joined by Lewis E. Gates, as eager as Moody for adventure and the picturesque.

"We arrived in Beauvais", I wrote my mother, "tired and hungry after two hours in the train, only to find the whole town absolutely given over to a *Concours des pompiers* which was on for the day.

The streets were full of processions, bugle-calls sounded strepitantly
from every corner, crowds of firemen filled every restaurant and
café, singing songs and making speeches to each other, and everybody seemed slightly fevered by alcoholic as well as social stimula-

tion. We could get no rooms at the hotel we had had our baggage
sent to, and found that there was only one other hotel, and no trains
to take us out of the hubbub. Also it was raining.

"We went to the other hotel and struggled through a wriggling, particolored mass of inebriate but enthusiastic *pompiers* to the *bureau*, where we found that we could get one room for two persons, and another single room. The rooms were full of boots, swords, and luggage of transient *pompiers*, who, we were assured, would leave by evening. The smell was indescribable, and the beds looked sinister.

"Then came dissension to add to our discomfort. Will and Gates wanted to stay and accept even such rooms in order to have the experience of the fête-day. I was tired and very nervous, and wanted at any cost to leave the confounded noisy hole, even if we had to sleep outdoors. Meanwhile we must decide quickly, and have our luggage sent over. The majority carried the day, and a procession of five left to discover the luggage, two stalwart porters preceding and three bedraggled tourists bringing up the rear.

"When we got back we went immediately to our rooms. Mr. Gates afterwards told us that everything in his room broke as soon as he touched it. We had even worse luck: before we had time to wash we discovered a lady's cape on the wall and almost at the same moment a man came to tell us the room was engaged and we must take another. The other, which we immediately sought, contained two large tables set out for a grand dinner of the eternal *pompiers*. Our man tried to stow away our luggage, but thereupon the maid who was to wait on table descended about his ears in a string of the most virulent and untamed vituperation, gesticulating madly and tossing her indignant arms in the air. After a few moments' feeble resistance our man takes up the baggage again, and we follow him dumbly to the first door with a key in it he sees. This he unlocks and opens unceremoniously, waking up an elderly gentleman who has been asleep inside, and notifying him that our luggage must be left in his room till the dinner in ours is over. Without waiting for his acquiescence we rush downstairs again and out into the streets, where the same hullabaloo is being enacted as before.

"Finally we did get some dinner, and after it sallied forth into the middle of the festivities. All the streets were illuminated with lanterns, candles, and colored fire. Booths were set up all round the public square, for candy, tobacco, shooting at targets, and gambling by roulette. Innumerable hordes of *pompiers* and miscellaneous citizens strolled about in squads. Early in the evening the weather cleared, and the stars came out. The scene was fascinating; it reached its acme when the band began playing and the people all dancing, on the public square. They were middle class *bourgeois* for the most part, very respectable and decent, but having the best time in the world. Their politeness was, as always, astonishing. For instance, a boy rushing by with some friends in a mad chase hit Will's foot. Immediately he stopped in his headlong pursuit, left his companions to go on, and came all the way back to beg Will's pardon. . . . Festivities lasted until the small hours. Will and I however slept very well, though Mr. Gates had a three hours' encounter and war to the death with the small nocturnal terrors of European beds."

To this never-to-be-forgotten *Fête des pompiers* Will later consecrated a pencil sketch filling a page of my journal. At the top of the page a mouth with a highly French moustache blows from a bugle the words "*Grande Fête des Pompiers*", and just below appears in colossal letters the motto "*Honneur aux Victimes du Devoir*" (which the victims of duty, most of them at the moment also victims of alcohol, had placed proudly over the main street of Beauvais). In the middle of the page is an R. F. in a wreath flanked by a bottle of "*Vin Beauvaisien*" on one side and two umbrellas dancing on the other. Below is a memory of the roulette table: "*Voici l'arrivée. Numero huit va mieux. Huit a gagné!*", and at the bottom of the page our three bags, Gates's enormous, Will's and mine tiny, and our three profiles, Will's and Gates's with pipe and cigarette and beards meant to be beards, mine with a mottled effect from infrequent shaving.

The test which proved too much not only for my fragile French, but for my powers of adapting at short notice the *mores* of my native Boston, came cruelly early in the trip, in a music hall at Brussels, when some of the chorus girls swooped suddenly down upon our table and demanded that we buy them wine. According to Will I at first turned pale, then by a visible effort pulled myself together,

Chicago's smoke cloud, and in that infernal seat of contemplation have often mused upon your goings and comings in the Latin Quarter. J'ai pause. Nous partons aujourd'hui By pronouncing these mysterious formulae I have many times evoked you in confrontation with that so elusive world of will and idea which we once endeavored to comprehend together and found and shall find entirely incomprehensible. I hear from Papa Bartlett that you are back

drew myself up, and with a noble disregard of auxiliary verbs announced: "*J'ai pauvre!*" As may be imagined, my companions never stopped rubbing that in.

As I contemplate the sympathies that drew Will and me together, I find that deeper than our sense of the poetically comical, deeper than our love of letters and of music, possibly as deep even as our sense of beauty and of course needing solace far more than that, was our common feeling of the metaphysical mystery of life. I have told in the *Letters* how once in my Matthews room, of a winter evening over our toddy, "leaning out from swirls of smoke and emphasizing his points with outstretched pipe, he drew a picture of man in the universe as a frog in a well, condemned always to darkness, destined never to know what was in the world above." I recall a dinner at Marliave's, not long after our return from Europe, when, in the grip of a black mood, I asked him how one was to endure the skull-and-cross-bones aspect of existence, and he answered "By dwelling on the birth-and-bridal aspect". I compare these memories with his statement, several years later, in his letter of August 30, 1901: [1] "*J'ai pauvre. Nous partons aujourd'hui. . . .* By pronouncing these mysterious formulae I have many times evoked you in confrontation with that so elusive world of will and idea which we once endeavored to comprehend together and found and shall find entirely incomprehensible." And I feel that there is something sacred in these first stumbling efforts of youth to find its way through the labyrinth of this world, and that in all the years of interesting life that separate me now from senior year I have found nothing else quite so formative as those magical walks with Will Moody up lilac-scented Brattle Street, and those summer wanderings with him along the placid Vire, and through the Normandy fields and villages.

[1] *Some Letters*, p. 139.

CHAPTER III

FRIENDS AND TEACHERS

DURING our junior year we would rather frequently be startled by the sudden irruption through our double doors, with a slam for each, and a torrent of greeting, apology, explanation, and casual comment which foamed over itself like a river in flood, of "Neddie" Hill, now more staidly to be referred to as the distinguished composer Professor Edward Burlingame Hill of the Department of Music at Harvard. He was at that time a senior, graduating, a year ahead of us, in 1894. Impossible to imagine a greater contrast to the pondering and poetic Moody than Hill with his facile impulsive talk, his witty snapshots at whatever came up, his constant interruptions of himself, his apparent inability to finish a sentence or keep a seat. (Arthur Whiting said of his piano-playing that he was "too much interested in the next note".) I always felt, as I know he did too, that the endurance of our friendship for a day was a triumph for our mutual affection and toleration, so opposed were we in temperament; yet it has endured already over forty years. He was as social in habit as I was solitary; athletics and all forms of sport, so boring to me, filled him with enthusiasm; touching were his repeated protestations that he would read Schopenhauer and try to understand my excitement over philosophy—only second in those days to what laRose called my "war whoop about art"; in short, in all

33

things he was as impulsive as I was cautious. Yet his New England blood and even the long association of his family with Harvard (he was of the third generation to be actively connected with it) were not for nothing in his curiously compounded personality. Under all his meteoric brilliance there were a steadfast affection, an undemonstrative manliness, truly puritan in the best sense, for the comfort of his friends.

From the first we were thrown together by the writing of the music for the Hasty Pudding Club annual theatricals. Jack Oliver, a classmate of Hill's, had written a libretto called *Granada*, for which Hill and I between us provided most of the score. Unfortunately it was the custom for the music to be only composed by the students —and scored for orchestra by professional hacks; so that this part of the training went to the hacks, and not to us. Even so, the experience was invaluable. You had to produce so much copy, under conditions almost professional in their routine; there were no arbitrary prohibitions to be submitted to, of which you could not understand the reasons, as there were in the music courses given by Professor Paine; on the other hand, if what you wrote did not sound well, or hold the interest, you had to "face the music", or rather, recognize with salutary self-criticism that there wasn't any music.

In my senior year I no longer had Hill's help, but wrote the entire score of *Proserpina*, text by Winthrop Ames, destined in later years to do so much valuable pioneer work for the New York stage. In these early days he was an agreeably sophisticated youth, long and thin, with a slightly drooping nose and an air of worldliness that impressed me immensely. In addition to writing the libretto he took the part of Exemplicus, introducing himself with the song, "I'm a Professional Hypocrite", and thoroughly looking the part with his clergyman's collar, silk hat with crape band, hands encased in black kid gloves—fingers held tip to tip—light flesh tights and gaiters, eyeglasses low on nose over which he peered with an unctuous leer. In a side act he made a most sinister Svengali to "Ned" Merrill's buxom Trilby. "Pat" Brice was Pluto—

> I'm Pluto or the devil, both my titles mean the same,
> Tho' I prefer the former as the more euphonious name.

Ivers Adams made a pretty soubrette Proserpina, Charlie Flandrau a most exemplary, almost ultra-respectable Ceres, and "Jimmie" Purdon a Cupid that never was, on sea or land. Made up with side whiskers, wrinkles, and a bald head, he wore a baby's muslins, pantalettes, and pumps, and carried a hoop and doll.

Because my mother, Venus, is immortal,

he explained melodiously,

> She's made me dress like this for fifty years,
> For people are so awfully suspicious
> If I revealed my age she says she fears
> They'd look askance at her unchanging beauty,
> And then, in whispers ask: "How can it be
> That Mrs. Venus, who is barely twenty,
> Should have an only son of fifty-three?"

And the conclusion, expressed in a philosophic refrain, was

> So I'm compelled to be a chronic infant;
> Compared to mine the hardest lot is mild;
> For I'm a man of fifty-three,
> Condemned by fatal chance to be
> A young professional beauty's infant child!

No doubt Ames's text owed much to Gilbert, as my music did to Sullivan, for in spite of our proud sophistications we were really not far beyond "chronic infancy" ourselves; but at any rate it bubbled with youthful irresponsibility and a merry humor.

Besides playing the piano, or, in the college idiom of that day, "hitting the box", for rehearsals, Hill and I would sometimes venture further afield, into Boston drawing-rooms or studios, to regale our friends with music, two-hand or four—serious or frivolous. One of our favorite battle-horses was *Between Two Bands*, a graphic representation of one march (E. B. H. in the treble) beginning very near and loud, and gradually disappearing into space and *pianissimo*, while a different march (D. G. M. in the bass) would begin very far and soft, and equally gradually approach into deafening *fortissimo*. There was a crucial moment when both bands were about equidistant, supremely relished by us if not always by our audience. The best of all our music-making, I think, was the leisure hours spent browsing over the scores with which the college library was plentifully supplied. The Brahms chamber music scores were bound in black; and a black binding has ever since seemed to me, by association, particularly cheerful. We would often bring back to our rooms four-hand arrangements to try over, I pleading for an easy pace and time to ponder, while Hill would equally instinctively cry out, it seemed to me almost before we began: "A little faster!"

Our musical tastes, of course, reflected the general polarity of our temperaments, he leaning far more than I to the brilliant, the color-ful, and the picturesque, and in those college days falling much un-der the spell of MacDowell, as he later took the French impression-ists and the Russian primitives more seriously than I could. In the summer after he left college I sent him parts of my first piano so-nata, an ambitious if inchoate work (never completed), to which he characteristically responded with this "confession":

"I told you that I should commit all manner of loathsome musical sins this summer, you remember? Well, I hereby appoint you my father confessor. I've gone and done one silly sin. I got hold of a little tune which seemed to me to be rather 'nigger' and I have worked it into a little *Scherzino*. I can imagine your groans and other exhibi-tions of disgust when you receive it, but just the same I must con-fess it. Strangely enough this little piece has for me a programmistic flavor about it. I can see the niggers, men and women, dancing un-der the sway of the fascination of rhythm until the sweat fairly rolls off them, and the little singsong tune goes on and on with monotonous persistency. There! I feel better now."

And under the signature is the notation: "To my Father Confes-sor, D. G. M. You needn't return it [The Sin]. These are the best things for it." [A sketch of a match and a can of kerosene.]

Yet it was in that very summer of his being first thrown on his own artistic resources, without the protection of college, that, as so often happens, he began to outgrow his boyish attitudes and to take his art with a new seriousness. I shall let his own words, written at the time, complete the picture.

Greetings from
a friend of long standing
Edward Burlingame Hill
Cambridge, Mass. Nov 25th 1927.

Edward Burlingame Hill, 1927

"August, 1894. Cornish is quite extraordinary. There are many very artistic and beautiful houses there, and the people are decidedly polite and interesting. What I most enjoyed was meeting Whiting. His acquaintance somehow has practically unloosed the last link in the fetter-chain of Picturesqueness. I have, as you may imagine by this last sentence, been undergoing a radical musical reformation. I feel like some strange, abnormal fish who can neither swim in water, nor live in earthly atmosphere. To plunge boldly into classicism seems a deliberate abandoning of originality, while picturesque is at present distasteful! In consequence I have written nothing, as everything I tried to start seemed equally blasphemous.

"October, 1894: I was very glad to hear your opinion of my sonata-theme. It never occurred to me that it was freakish. To me it seemed almost too uninteresting to develop, and rather unsusceptible to treatment, but I shall try to push it on as bravely as I can. . . . It took a good deal of push to get started again. . . . I started bravely to work and evolved some absolutely putrescent music. The next day my efforts were better rewarded with the sonata-theme and a page or so of a suite for violin and piano. I take alternate whacks at them with a touching lack of favoritism, and I make bold to say that one of them will be finished some day. It will undoubtedly be a spontaneous and imaginative composition."

And from two later letters, written when he was working with Whiting in New York:

"A. W. said when I was playing the last of Brahms's Handel-theme variations with bravura but lack of accuracy, 'You could exchange that speed for more solidity and get the best of the bargain.' Unkind, wasn't he?

"I believe I shall realize the seriousness and one-chancedness of life some day. I am making visible improvement therein. But it seems at times as if the starch had left my upper lip for good and all. . . . However, give me more realizing powers, and perhaps my naïve insight such as it is may go down. Damned if I can tell it in English, but I see something in life that is worth telling, blowed if it isn't. If God grants me the time and the mood I may get a little of it on paper this summer.

"Whiting is as Whitingesque as ever, you know what that is: *legato* octaves and phrasing, and his quiet, virile philosophy delivered from teeth that hold a pipe."

II

Much as Hill was to be envied the companionship of a man like Arthur Whiting, I had in Cambridge my own older friends close at hand. Indeed, as I look back on the working in my case of the elective system for which Harvard was then so noted—to some minds so notorious—what impresses me most is not the wide range of subjects at my disposal, not even the freedom to choose them for myself and, quite outside of them, to browse for hours in a kind of play as enriching as work, but the magnificent constellation of great personalities through which my studies were made to live in my mind. Aside from the lifelong stimulus of having known men like Norton and Santayana, James and Royce, more casual contacts with lesser men were not to be despised. Though I recall no word he said, I like to remember the virile and chivalrous figure of Shaler on his platform, with his red, rugged face and his thrown-back shock of gray-white hair. I am glad I was of those for whom the mild-mannered old chemistry professor (was he Josiah Cooke?) performed his time-honored joke of holding in his palsy-stricken, shaking hands two chemicals, and as the hands approached each other in ever wider swoops observing: "Gentlemen, if these two substances should touch, there would be a terrible explosion and we should all be blown to atoms." I am even not sorry to have discovered for myself how petty and pedantic could be a teacher in Shaler's own subject of geology. Mr. X. was a martinet we all disliked. One day he opened a cabinet and picked out a specimen to show us, saying in his dry, rasping voice before he even looked at it: "Gentlemen, this is Tufa." Then he found he held a couple of cheap cigars some humorous student had placed there, of the kind we called "Two for five".

Of course it was a danger for any youngster to have such freedom of choice, whether in men or in subjects, and I made my share of mistakes. For example, never having the slightest gift for history, I yet selected in a moment of laziness biblical history—Semitic 12, the course was called—as an easy way of accumulating points, since it was widely hailed as a "snap course". For me it was no snap. The single fact in it I have remembered is Tiglath Pilezar—because of his pleasing name; who he was, or what he did, I do not know. History 1, a large and popular course given by Professor Edward Channing, I also got into by mistake. In that we had conferences with an assistant of Professor Channing's who would present us with a map of Europe and ask us to point out cities on the spur of the moment. He asked me for Vienna, and I gave him Iceland. Any admixture of history was fatal to me, even in English composition, which I usually liked, and got A's in. I wrote, I fear under Gates or Barrett Wendell, both meticulously scholarly minds, a story of the Civil War in which I introduced—George Washington.

My most serious error of omission was giving up German after one fiasco. As a result, to this day I read it painfully and slowly, and always with a trying sense at the end of each page that I am not very sure after all whether it really means that. Since much that I especially want to read has always been in German, this has never ceased to be an annoying obstacle. For giving up the music courses half way through college I take less blame to myself. Professor Paine struck me from the start as arbitrary, as lacking in that first and last gift of the teacher, the ability to see things from the angle of the student. Typical, to give an example, was his blue-pencilling of a dissonance with which I had begun a song. He said it was "unprepared"—as undoubtedly it was; but to me it seemed seizing and exciting, and his prohibiting it merely cold-blanketed my enthusiasm without showing me the way to a wiser one. If Paine could only have taken a hint from the courses in English composition, especially Gates's and Wendell's! There you were shown not only what your faults were, but in what direction lay the cures for them.

The English courses, literature as well as composition, had the advantage no doubt of merely developing a taste already spontaneously present in me, as would have had also those in music, had they only been a little more imaginative. A more difficult achievement, for which I feel an even deeper gratitude, was Charles Eliot Norton's in extending my sensitiveness to beauty from music and literature to the plastic arts of painting, sculpture, and architecture, and indeed in a sense to the whole of life. The inspiring quality of Norton's Fine Arts 3 and 4 lay in their attitude rather than their subject matter—in his power to make you feel by the contagion of example that beauty was the supreme value in life. One had to be a hardened Philistine indeed to resist the charm of his stoop-shouldered, husky-voiced, but supremely urbane and gentle presence; and a high purity and resolution, as of saints and martyrs, that flashed through his gentleness at times must have awed even the slothful low-brow. Of course, the very ardor and superiority to compromise with which he held his unconventional gospel of beauty could not but arouse opposition in the average man. Many of his class, as I have said, would swarm down the fire-escape once their names were checked; or if they stayed it would be to detach the large, round, brimstone heads from the matches then in use, place them under heel, and make diverting detonations. Even the choicer spirits found something almost too rare to be human in Norton's suave insistence on culture, and sometimes rebelled. One of their retaliations was a mythical exchange of telegrams between Ruskin and Norton, like this:

Ruskin to Norton: "You are the only gentleman in America."

Norton to Ruskin: "You forget Moore." [A colleague of his in the Fine Arts Department.]

Ruskin to Norton: "Let in Moore."

Between the lines of my journal I can read the same irritation: my priggish superiority to the fire-escape-scalers and the match-exploders is at times oddly interrupted by a more human note:

"November 24, 1894. A handful of men to hear Professor Norton on Monasteries, the rest being gone childishly to Springfield [for a football game.] This would do for an epitome of college life.

"December 15. A sparrow got in while Professor Norton was lecturing on that everlasting monastery of Cluny, and hopped about gracefully on the platform, calling forth a titter from the class and a benign side-glance from the lecturer."

To these untutored comments I will add two more, one from about the start of the course, the other from near its end:

"October 2, 1894. Norton insisted on the immense importance to humanity of the sense of social responsibility, and the stimulus given to this sense by a study of the expression attained through the fine arts. Through a sense of responsibility to our fellows, a sense of chivalrous manhood . . . we shall seek for that widened sympathy and cultivation of mind which is the real gift of education, infinitely more important than the collection of facts.

"May 23, 1895. Professor Norton, in explaining the renaissance as largely a reaction from ecclesiastical asceticism, said that an expression of its higher spirit would be 'The World, The Flesh, and God'."

As I owed to Norton much widening in the scope of my sense of beauty, so I owed the chief deepening of its intellectual bases to Santayana. It was in my junior or senior year that I took his Philosophy 8, Aesthetics, given as we all sat about a long table in a room in Sever Hall, and consisting first of a criticism of existing systems, and then of a presentation of his own, as it was crystallized a year or so later in his book *The Sense of Beauty*. I usually sat at his left and next or very near him, savoring the clear intelligence of his gleaming dark eyes, the rich repose and ease of his manner, the accuracy and vividness of his analyses, but at the same time involuntarily on guard against what seemed to me the coldness, not to say cruelty, of his wit, against something almost feline in his purring complacency. How much was this curiously double impression instinctive, how far based on reason?—it is hard to say. I had it from the first, long before he read to a group of us students a poem in which he lampooned Moody as "null" (to rhyme with "dull") although he had also told me that he considered him one of our best poets. Such things shook my confidence in his candor; but after all, perhaps the trouble was simply that my Anglo-Saxon nature could not follow the doublings and turnings of his very Latin one.

His mind I always admired. In those days the decadence we know as ultra-modernism was only beginning; yet one already felt the potential value of a philosophy of art that, like his, could give reasons for the eternal health of the classic ideal, and thus expose impartially the menace of eccentric deviations from it. In a review of his *Sense of Beauty* written for the *Harvard Monthly* as early as November, 1896, I said: "Never a whimsical desire for self-expression, such as actuates most of the sentimental artists of a degenerate day, but always a pure zeal to say that which must and would be said, has been the creative germ of all great works of beauty. The influence of this book will arise from its demonstrating, by psychological analysis, the necessity of propagating this larger point of view." About a year later I discussed with Santayana the possibility of applying the principles of his book to the psychology of music; but it was not until 1902 that in my own first book, *From Grieg to Brahms*, I succeeded in making a modest beginning at an application which I have tried ever since to carry further.

III

The two most magnetic personalities of all those I met among the teachers I found in Santayana's colleagues in the Department of Philosophy: William James and Josiah Royce. Despite their close association and warm friendship, they made a striking contrast. Greatly as I admired James, I always felt that his handsome person, easy geniality, and brilliant talk, threw unfairly into shadow Royce's more difficult and solitary, but to my mind deeper and more poetic nature. James's fascination sufficed to transform even the bareness of a class-room. As he arrived flushed with walking on a winter day, without overcoat but with rather rakish cravat and sportive waistcoat, and moved restlessly about the platform chatting with us rather than lecturing us, his frank manliness and friendliness were irresistible. He could make psychology seem as natural as small talk. He almost gossiped about it. One of his sentences comes back *verbatim*—full of the long words he used so unconsciously. He stood gracefully poised at the edge of the platform, and as casually as if he had been discussing the weather, remarked: "There is no primal teleological reagibility in a protoplasm."

Born as he was into the intellectually and socially most elite circles of Boston, his modesty was so alimented by his alert understanding that no one could have been less a snob. I had personal proof of this when, a year or two after graduation, layman in philosophy as I was, I ventured to publish a review of his *The Will to Believe*. Here is his note of acknowledgement:

"95 Irving St., Oct. 13, '97

"Dear Mr. Mason

"I have had it on my mind daily to write to you a note of thanks for the generous notice you have written in the *Monthly* of my Essays—but life's fitful fever has crowded it out until now. The complimentary adjectives are little deserved, but you have entered more closely into the central spirit and meaning of my poor performances than any other reviewer except one, and I thank you accordingly. Such are an author's rewards.

"Truly yours,
"WM. JAMES."

James himself disclaims, in his *Principles of Psychology*, any particular sensitiveness to music, yet his native shrewdness did not forsake him even in so remote a field. He was once inveigled into participating in one of those inept experiments in which the mass methods of politics are applied to the judgment of art. The company were to listen to certain well-known pieces, to write down their individual impressions, and to compare them in order to see if any significant correspondences emerged. One of the pieces was the *F major Ballade* of Chopin, the one with the rather jerky rhythm. James wrote that this suggested to him a man going through life genially, placidly, amiably—"with one leg slightly longer than the other".

Perhaps one reason Royce seemed to me the deeper nature was that his musical understanding was so much more profound. He once told me that he had wished to be a composer himself; one of his so tenderly loved sons has become one; and music always played an important part in his emotional life. But it seemed to me too that he had an intuition of the place of sorrow and tragedy in our lives, which James, for all his delightful chivalry, somehow missed, and

mentary adjectives are
little deserved, but you
have entered more closely
into the central spirit &
meaning of my poor paper.
Manees than any other re-
viewer except one, and I
thank you accordingly
Such are an author's
rewards.

Truly yours
Wm James

which made his philosophy plumb the depths. This intuition, I think, only revealed itself fully to me as I grew to know him well. To his class he was far from a hero. In person he was homely, if not ugly (until you loved him), with his light blue eyes, red hair, and Socratic discord of immense brow over snubby nose. His voice was raucous, and in place of James's easy elegance with words he had a sort of rough practical way of clipping and chopping them. He would challenge us with a "Whutcher mean by reality?" He seldom wore an overcoat to class, and without thinking much about it I spontaneously attributed this to poverty. Arthur Whiting with his usual realism once took me up on the point, and when I admitted

"Whutcher mean by Reality?"

Sketch by P.LaR.

that Royce doubtless possessed an overcoat, retorted with: "Oh, you only mean he was too poor to *wear* it." The incident is trivial, and my explanation was erroneous; but I think most of the class would have shared my instinctive sense that James without an overcoat was sportive and athletic, Royce somehow spartan. In everything, great as well as small, he seemed more impeded than his more worldly and charming colleague, and for that very reason more perceptive and pitiful, more familiar with hardship, effort, and puritan loyalty and aspiration. He was the most loving, devoted friend imaginable; there was no trouble he would not take in order to bring help to a suffering soul; and this was because he had a great heart, and because he knew much of suffering himself.

Endearing was his sly, almost demure sense of humor; and this at least could be relished by casual students as well as by closer friends. He would quote in class the poor old woman who said:

> If I be I
> As I think I be,
> I have a little dog at home,
> And he'll know me.

and then add, with the grin of a naughty school-boy and in his odd, rasping tones: "The poor woman is striving, you remember, to recover the transcendental unity of her apperception, of which a sad and recent accident has deprived her." One of my latest memories of Royce was taking a walk with him when he was working on his theory of numbers and their analogies with ethics. He took the opportunity to deliver a little lecture on what was so dominating his mind. He pointed out that in the series of numbers you keep repeating the same act—adding unity—and getting constantly novel results—new prime numbers. You do precisely the same thing, he insisted, in the moral world. You repeat the same acts, you get novel results. Then he paused and broke into that impish grin of his. "For example," he added, "another bottle."

Any place where so large a number of such great individual teachers were gathered together as there were at Harvard in the nineties could not but have proved stimulating. But Harvard was more than stimulating, it was mellowing, ripening. This was because we students had not only the provocation of these contacts with truly great men, of a surprising diversity of interests, characters, and personalities, but, what is even more precious, liberty in the choosing of these influences, time to digest and assimilate them, leisure to grow from our centres as well as absorb at our points of contact. We were not regimented, standardized, herded and labelled. We were not intimidated into imitativeness, browbeaten into conformity, or nagged into efficiency. Our healthy nutrition was as little in danger from forced feeding as from starvation; for while there was set before us the feast of the whole of human civilization, what we should take was determined only by our own tastes and powers of digestion. No doubt we became less specialized than we might have become under less generous systems. Hill and I have often compared notes on how much more rapidly we might have progressed in our

purely technical, musical skill had we gone to a good conservatory
instead of to Harvard. But technical skill is not all there is in art, nor
is even intellectual power of a purely impersonal kind. Musicians
are especially apt to be narrow, unimaginative, devoid of mental
nuances. Ripeness, fullness, richness of nature come only from many
interests, freely followed, and allowed to cross-fertilize.

And so, when I look back at Harvard as it stands on the dim horizon of my youth, what I see suffused with the ruddiest light of
memory is not the class-rooms, nor even the professors, splendid
men as they were. I see the endless provocation and golden leisure of
the libraries, laboratories, and clubs; I see afternoons on the Charles
River and evenings in Boston; I taste the mint juleps and the rum
toddies; I peer through the moon-bright mists about Fresh Pond;
and I smell the Brattle Street lilacs. Thank God for "Harvard indifference".

CHAPTER IV

WILLIAM MASON AND HIS CIRCLE

THE cold immersion in an indifferent, heedless, and sternly practical world that comes suddenly upon graduation from the protected atmosphere and the selected interests of college is one of the hardest of the experiences, I am inclined to think, that come to a young man —especially an American young man—anxious to devote himself to any form of art. Fortunately for me, I had certain inestimable advantages that helped me over the start of this trying transition, even if they could not, in the sequel, protect me from many years of doubt, bewilderment, and struggle. Even while in college I had had occasion to realize how powerful a springboard for my untried feet was likely to prove the interest and influence in music of my family. Few college boys are fortunate enough to have, as far from home as Belgium, as reassuring a little adventure as I had in the summer of my senior year with my friends Moody and Gates. Here is the account of it I then sent home.

"Rouen, July 22, 1895

"At Ghent we had decidedly the finest time yet, one incident out of ten of which I will relate. As we struggled along a maze of streets to find our way to the Old Nunnery, Will saw a good-looking old chap and inquired the way of him. He talked volubly for a long time, gesticulating and bowing, and finally sent us forth on our quest only to join us again after a block and insist on guiding us in person. He took us first to an old abbey which we only got into through his intercession, and then to several other places of interest, finally taking us to his own house. And now comes the most remarkable part. His house was full of the most marvelous collection of old musical instruments I ever saw, room after room, clavichords, spinets, organs, violins, violas, violi di gambe, violi d'amour, lutes, dulcimers, harpsichords, serpents, oboes, flutes, clarinets, bassoons, horns, saxe-horns, aeolian harps, everything under the sun that ever produced a musical tone. He has been collecting them for over thirty-five years and his collection is now larger than that of the South Kensington Museum.

"After we had seen his collection we went to his study, full of rare books on manufacture of musical instruments, theory of music, history, and indeed everything that could even remotely bear on his hobby. Here he actually brought out of the cellar and insisted on our drinking with him two quart bottles of twenty-five-year-old Burgundy! We then all exchanged cards, and I found that he was M. César Snoeck. I wrote on my card the name of Mason and Hamlin, and he immediately ejaculated when he saw it, and ran to his card catalogue, from which he produced a large card headed in blue pencil 'Mason and Hamlin, Organs and Harmoniums, Cambridgeport, America.' He had, written down, the date of the firm's foundation and several other notes, also a copy of one of the old catalogues, and in another cabinet a notice of Grandfather Mason's death.

"We then became quite enthusiastic, though the question of language interfered somewhat. When we shook hands goodbye with him I called all my wits together and said with enthusiasm, '*Monsieur, je vous remercie mille fois.*' He patted my arm and said with a funny jerky accent, 'When you come here to Ghent again, come and see me.' "

II

The friendly environment of my family, potent as far away as
Ghent and proportionately more so nearer home, could even domes-
ticate for me a little the maelstrom of New York when in the fall of
'95 I decided to plunge into it from my quiet Boston eddy. For one
thing, right across Washington Square from the room I took in the
Benedick was living, with his daughter Mina and her husband Howard van Sinderen, my uncle, Dr. William Mason, as influential in
the musical world as my grandfather, Lowell Mason, had been in
the previous generation. From the first these three made me welcome, my cousin was as kind to my homesickness as any sister could
have been, and I was able to meet on informal terms the stream of
musicians, American and European, who frequented my uncle's
apartment, and later his house in West Sixteenth Street.

His own piano playing was in itself an unforgettable musical experience. His rich and at the same time discriminating sensuous feeling voiced itself in the most exquisite piano touch I have ever heard.
His way of bringing out the tone by pressing rather than striking
the keys made the whole tissue of his melodies literally "sing". All
the ornamental work was done with a delicious evenness and light-
ness that perfectly subordinated it to the more sonorous voices (in
such things for instance as the Chopin études, preludes, and noc-
turnes). Never have I heard him bring a harsh or hard tone from a
piano. Of course the style of the piano music of his prime was more
ornamental than we like today, and his playing naturally had much
of the "string of pearls" quality—but was ever string so smooth,
were ever pearls more lustrous and opalescent! Such a piece as his
own *Silverspring*, now outmoded but once popular, came from his
hands as delicate as gossamer. To hear its fluid tones stealing upstairs on a summer morning was to feel a new gusto for living.

Nor was the beauty of his playing merely the sensuous beauty of
the touch; he was too good a musician to neglect the higher beauty
of proportionate light and shade. To hear him play his little *One-
finger Study* was an illumination of piano art. The one finger with
which it was played was far subtler than the "melodious fore-finger"

so delightfully championed in Stevenson's letters. It had to create and carry, by its varying touches, three separate tonal lines, on three distinct planes: the singing melody in the foreground, the hardly less singing bass slightly behind it, and in the background the more neutral accompanying tones. How exquisitely he guarded the clarity of each of the three lines, yet merged them all in harmony together! I can see him yet, as he would sit at his Steinway grand with his rather rounded shoulders and his air of complete relaxation, his head bent to listen and his usually prominent eyes veiled in concentration, producing with his short unerring finger the deliciously adjusted sonorities.[1]

My uncle had to the full the Mason timidity and naïveté. Having been furthermore always somewhat "spoiled" by his women-folk —first his mother, then his wife, and when I knew him his daughter —he always had a little the petulance and gusty sweetness of the gifted but temperamental child. Also he had little humor, at any rate he had never formed the habit of turning such humor as he had upon himself, and would make without a tremor such remarks as: "I shall never bear a grudge against any man—it might be a bad thing for me in the end." Cordially and genuinely interested as he was in younger musicians, they were obliged to adjust themselves to him, and were wise not to expect much adjusting from his end. He never appreciated, for instance, Arthur Whiting's finely intellectual musicianship, simply because he could not endure the hardness of his touch (and perhaps, too, the biting breath of his sarcasm). It used to be a joke of my friend Hill's that whenever, coming to New York, he would try to show his recent compositions to "Uncle William", as it amused him to call him for my ear only, Uncle William would suddenly discover that he was "tired". Possibly his timidity inclined him to undervalue those near him, his own relatives or his

[1] It was on his seventieth birthday, four years later than the time I now write of, that Messrs. Steinway and Sons presented to him the grand piano which is now one of my most valued possessions, and which bears the following plate: "This piano, presented to WILLIAM MASON, Mus. Doc., by Steinway and Sons, January 24, 1899, in celebration of his seventieth birthday anniversary, became the property of his daughter, Mina Mason, and was given by her husband, Howard van Sinderen, in her behalf and in memory of her father, to her cousin, Daniel Gregory Mason, Professor of Music in Columbia University.

own countrymen—though in the case of MacDowell he manfully
transcended such snobbishness.

When I dedicated to him my first book, *From Grieg to Brahms*,
he was rather surprised, and only gradually assimilated the idea that
a nephew, by nature a liability, might by a freak of nature become
an asset. He tells in his *Memories of a Musical Life* how reluctantly
he showed his teacher, Moritz Hauptmann, some of his father's
hymn tunes, at his father's special request, how long he hesitated
thus to exhibit home products, and how finally, after Hauptmann
had praised their strength, he could not, as he says, "understand how
such a big contrapuntist could express himself in such strong terms
of approval." "But," he adds with disarming naïveté, "I knew him to
be genuine, and so I straightened myself up and really began to be
proud of my father." And with an honesty as much a part of him
as his timidity he remarks that he "recognized his own ignorance in
imagining that a thing in order to be great must necessarily be in-
tricate and complicated." The most amusing example we have of
his cautious preference for values guaranteed by unmistakable labels
occurs in his account of how he declined an invitation of Wagner's
to a walking tour, in 1852. "Of course," he explains, "Wagner was
not then what he afterwards became in the eyes of the world. I now
know what I missed."

III

Our amusement at these harmless simplicities tends to transform
itself into admiration when we note how his taste, despite the primarily sensuous quality of his innate musicality, broadened throughout his life, and by what a cordial interest in the doings of his juniors
his later years were cheered. Even in youth he mingled to some extent the music of Schumann and Brahms with the Chopin and Liszt
to which he more spontaneously turned. He was the first to bring
to this country many of the piano pieces of Schumann, and he sent
the score of the Schumann *First Symphony* to America almost before it was accepted in Europe. He gave in New York, as early as
1855, with Theodore Thomas and Carl Bergmann, the first per-

William Mason
From a photograph by Hascom

formance of the *B major Trio* of Brahms, not only in America but anywhere in the world. In his old age he learned to savor such novelties as Strauss's *Feuersnoth* and Elgar's *Gerontius*. One summer at the Isles of Shoals he played MacDowell's *Sonata Tragica* every day, until his audience learned to like it. (One recalls the answer of his friend Theodore Thomas to a member of his orchestra who complained that the audience did not like Wagner. "Then," said Thomas, "we must play him until they do.") Later MacDowell dedicated to Mason another of his sonatas, and wrote him of it from Boston, November 12, 1895: "I feared you might not like our sonata therefore you may judge how delighted to receive your letter I was. . . . I am thankful I do not have to criticize my things. Parts of the sonata I am fond of and parts of it I have felt deeply, though I am afraid they—the feelings—are not fully expressed. That you however can take the will for the deed in what may not appeal to you in it, and like the rest for its own sake makes me feel the work has found something more than an indulgent god-father. I am proud of having a good sturdy American name at the head of my music let alone the pleasure of offering it to you. The pride is all on my side." Several years later (December 19, 1899) MacDowell wrote my uncle a short note, on university paper (it was after he had come to New York and to Columbia) and by a quaint accident in red ink, worth printing for its intrinsic charm as well as for the unusual glimpse it gives us of the whimsicality ordinarily masked by his shyness.

"My dear friend:

" 'Wine, wife and song,' etc. always seemed to me incomplete until your birthday remembrance came, in which the wine was synonymous with friend, thus making the old *Spruch* cover the whole ground. That I love the friend needs no explanation, any more than good wine needs a bush—so let me say again that your remembrance of my birthday was very lovely—and that the wine shall be drunk *con amore*. Yours affectionately,

"EDWARD MACDOWELL

"Pardon the red ink—a mistake in the bottle—This sounds pretty

far gone I know, and suggests 'Hic jacet' as a proper inscription on
my tombstone. If anything happens to me it will be your fault."

"If anything happens to me": the words so lightly spoken are sad
enough to us who know the poet's tragic fate, even then swiftly approaching. One more letter, written only a year or two before the
final catastrophe, congratulates my uncle on the *Memories of a Musical Life,* then appearing in a magazine.

> "Hillcrest, Peterborough, New Hampshire
> "August 30, 1900
"My dear friend:
"Only a word of delight at your *Century* articles (and from every
side I hear the same) which I trust you will publish in book form.
The fascination of high ideals and hard work breathes from them
and they will help and encourage even those who have never been
inspired with the ardent and fearless enthusiasm Liszt surrounded
himself with. Don't go too fast—everything is precious to us, and
let me whisper to you, it just makes me swell with pride as an American. This is not very clear, but you will understand.
"We shall be back in New York in four weeks (alas!) and my
very first excursion down town will be to you."

MacDowell's mention of Liszt reminds me, by the law of con-
traries, of my uncle's steadily growing appreciation, even to his last
years, of Brahms. In middle life, of course, he had been too much
of a Lisztian to accept Brahms quite whole-heartedly. All the more
remarkable as an evidence of his hospitality of mind was the deep
love he grew to feel, toward the end, for the most recondite of the
intermezzi and capriccios. I remember particularly how raptly he
would commune with one of the most difficult to understand, one
of the least played, but one of the profoundest of them all—the E
flat minor *Intermezzo.* For a taste commencing with the graceful
salon pieces typified by his own *Silverspring,* such a terminus indi-
cates a singular degree of true musicality.

IV

Another great artist besides MacDowell championed by William
Mason before he was widely appreciated (strange as it seems to us
now that there ever could have been such a time) was Paderewski.
An enthusiastic letter sent by Mason to the *Evening Post* of New
York, and later expanded into a *Century* article, did much, while
his fate in America still hung in the balance, to weight the scales in
his favor. This service the noble and generous pianist never forgot.

It was early in November that I myself was introduced by my
uncle to Paderewski, at the end of one of his New York recitals.
Then, a week or two later, in an excitement that comes back to
memory freshly after forty years, I confided one evening to my
journal:

"I hardly know how to write what I have to tell now; I scarcely
know whether it is true or a beautiful dream. I have been dining . . .
across the square, and the only other guest was Paderewski.

"He is impossible to describe—a tall, fair, gracious man, with
fine flaxen hair, small blue eyes rather far apart, a well-shaped nose
and a sensitive mouth. He has a slight difficulty in pronouncing the
S, a sort of Sh-sh sound. He speaks naturally and with a good deal
of enthusiasm, laughing heartily and with unction. He is absolutely
simple and unassuming, talking as if so used to his fame that it didn't
occur to him very often. He happened to mention not caring to
walk much because 'he had the misfortune to be somewhat known,
and the street-boys would call to him to go get his hair cut'—all
with great heartiness and enjoyment of the fun.

"He spoke of Brahms as a great master, and said the Paganini
Variations were great *piano* music, but that most of Brahms's piano
music was 'bad', meaning not idiomatic. He was much amused at
hearing that a man in Philadelphia wrote to ask Uncle William if it
was true that Paderewski was habitually drunk all the time. He said
parenthetically that he could not remember ever having been drunk.
He was very affectionate to Uncle William, shaking him by both
hands at every occasion. He was refined but simple in his manners,
ate rapidly and in large mouthfuls but never unpleasantly, and was

remarkably cultivated and intelligent in his conversation, making al-
lusions to painting and literature which showed him to be an appre-
ciator.

"Then finally he asked me to play him my *Sonata*, and I thumped

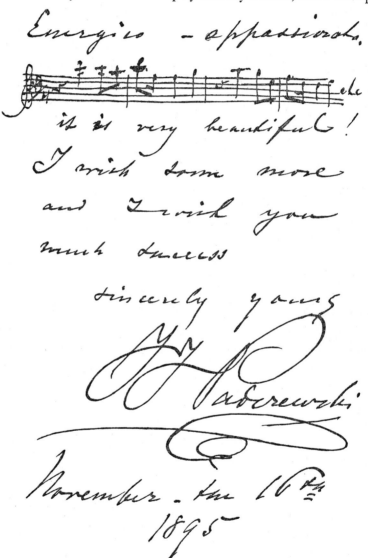

out the first movement in such a tremor of nervousness that I
couldn't see the keyboard and began an octave too high. I calmed

down though, sized up the softness of the action, remembered about repose, and got along fairly, and he interjected encouraging little grunts. When I was through he seemed genuinely pleased, said it was a really interesting composition, commented on the beauty of the second theme, and on the adverse side thought it too brilliant (said it was more in the mood of a concerto than of a sonata) and thought the development rather too long for the general scheme of the whole. He liked it very much, I know. He said it showed 'serious talent', and said: 'You are a composer; you must go on writing.'

"Finally upon my asking him for an autograph, he had the exquisite grace and courtesy to write the first theme from memory, and in the right key, saying underneath: 'It is very beautiful! I wish some more and I wish you much success. Sincerely yours, I. J. Paderewski.' "

V

The young musicians in New York either permanently or temporarily, especially of course the pianists, naturally responded to my uncle's interest in them by gathering for many musical evenings at his West Sixteenth Street house. MacDowell came often, delighted us with the fleetness of his fingers in such pieces as his *March Wind* and with his keen sense of the dramatic in sonorities, and was as good to look at as to hear, with his handsome head held a little sideways as he sat absorbed at the piano. Howard Brockway came, already a fluent young pianist and composer that society and the publishers were taking up, the hare of whom we tortoises were sometimes a bit jealous. (This was however long before his true contribution to American music in his work with the Kentucky folksongs). Occasionally Arthur Whiting appeared, but never seemed to get on too well with my uncle: aside from their Liszt-versus-Brahms opposition in partisanship, they temperamentally rubbed each other the wrong way. Ernst von Dohnanyi came and conquered—a mere boy, enthusiastic, charming, already a brilliant pianist, though no one could then foresee that he would become one of the greatest composers of our time.

One evening a young Russian appeared—none of us seemed to

know whether the second or the third syllable of his name, Gabrilowitsch, should bear the accent. (Later he had to resort to an accent over the O to show how it should be pronounced.) As he wrote the name in the guest-book that first evening someone suggested that it was very long. Quick as a flash came his response: "It's too late to change it now. It's advertised." A phrase fondly supposed to be Russian had been prepared in compliment to him by van Sinderen, my uncle's son-in-law. He received it in silence, with that disconcerting cheerful objectivity of his; and when van Sinderen finally stammered, "That's Russian, isn't it?" he replied drily: "It would be if it were pronounced quite differently."

These examples of his realism remind me of another occasion, years later, when my wife and I happened to overhear a conversation between him and Isadora Duncan, in the artists' room after one of his concerts. In his kindly way he told her he would soon be seeing her brother, as he was to play a recital in his city. "Give him my love," fluted Isadora dreamily, and then, indicating with a sweep of her arm the circle of girls, pupils of hers, that surrounded her like a cloud of incense—"Give him *all* their loves." There was a hush as we all tried to live up to the grandeur of that sentiment, a hush punctured by the realistic Gabrilowitsch's question: "Does he know them?" . . . Ossip's directness of mind never had need of the circumlocutions and petty insincerities by which most of us protect our own and other people's vanity. Always he thought for himself, announcing the results with disarming simplicity and good humor.

Our closer association began when, in playing my first large composition, an *Elegy* for piano in memory of my friend Philip Henry Savage the poet, he unhesitatingly devoted his incomparable art to the performance of a long and difficult work by an unknown young composer of a nation considered unmusical. No one with a less robust confidence in his own judgment or a less healthy freedom from superstitious reverence for his own fame would have undertaken anything so thankless. And he had no illusions about it, either. "I'm going to play your *Elegy* in Europe next winter," he wrote me in the spring of 1897, "and I'll send you all the bad things the newspapers say about it."

To Mr. + Mrs. Daniel G. Mason in memory of pleasant hours spent in their company and in hopes for many returns of them

Ossip Gabrilowitsch in 1907

Sure enough, a letter came from Wiesbaden the following May: "I have played your *Elegy* at my last Berlin recital, and *it was a success*. What I mean by success you probably know—it is the sort of thing that you and I appreciate most: the public did not get wild over the work, they did not stand on their chairs or recall me a dozen times. But I could see many of them (in fact the most intelligent ones) deeply moved by your composition. In short it was not what one would call a 'popular success,' but it was a great *artistic* success, the sort of success I would like for my own composition if it were to be played." And a month later came from London the characteristic word: "I played the *Elegy* at my London recital. The success quite equalled, maybe surpassed, that of the Berlin performance. You will see by the clippings I am sending you how even the press got warmed up by your work. . . . This means a good deal considering what an amount of MacDowell those Englishmen had to swallow within the last few years. In a word you succeeded in touching even the hardened heart of the English journalist! (Which reminds me of the saying of some witty man: 'The mere fact that a thing has been praised in the papers does not absolutely prove that it is bad.')"

Ossip, it will be seen, was that rarity, a man who thinks for himself. His taste, always naturally conservative, was spontaneous and untrammelled. In the same letter, after praising the *Elegy* with all his youthful generosity of enthusiasm, he adds: "I will be just as frank in saying that some of the professional musicians found a strong influence of Schumann and Brahms in it. . . . While I admit a certain resemblance in feeling with that of Brahms's music, that resemblance to me is one of the charms of your work. Thank Heaven you do not remind me of Debussy nor of Richard Strauss!" This half-whimsical exclamation is of couse not to be taken too seriously. If temperamentally Debussy's languor and Strauss's restless brilliance were not entirely congenial to him, Ossip was too hospitable-minded not to admire even such perverse geniuses. But it is characteristic that while he marvelled at the technical skill and immense dramatic effectiveness of *Salome, Heldenleben, Zarathustra,* and other Strauss works, if you had asked him which he con-

sidered the most inspired he would have been likely to select *Don
Juan*. And once when I confessed to him that his admiration for the
Liszt-Strauss-Mahler group puzzled me, he replied: "I would willingly sacrifice the entire work of Strauss rather than a single symphony or a quintet of Brahms. One admires Strauss rather than
loves him. But without Brahms one wouldn't like to live in this
world." [1] His freedom from servility to prevailing fashions comes
out again in a letter he sent me from Munich after he had begun
his orchestral conducting there: "The things I enjoyed most were
Tschaikowsky's *Francesca*, the Brahms *Double Concerto*, Elgar's
Variations and Liszt's *Faust Symphony*. You are probably horrified
at my enthusiasm for this work, but I assure you it is fine. Just
study it carefully and then say if I am not right. The *Pelléas and
Mélisande* Suite by Fauré is also a delicious piece of music. Do you
know it? It is short (lasts only fifteen minutes) but contains a
hundred times more music than all the interminable three acts of
Debussy's sleepy opera. . . ." In this case I happened to agree with
him. But even when I rebelled against his conclusions I had to admire the independence with which he reached them, as when, some
years later, trying to persuade me that three movements were
enough for a symphony, he wrote: "Long live Franck! He understood that—and that, by the way, is one of the few good things I
have to say about his symphony."

This independence of his is symbolized for me by a remark in
which I once heard him summarize his attitude toward the press. In
the course of an after-dinner chat between Arthur Whiting, Percy
Grainger, Ossip, and me, Grainger made, eloquently enough, the
usual plea that press interviews and articles "place the artist's personality before the public". Whiting, Ossip, and I were skeptical.
At last Grainger, stung by Ossip's laughing detachment, challenged him: "But you yourself advertise in *Musical Chit-chat* [nam-
ing a well-known trade paper], don't you?" "Ah," replied Ossip,
"I must tell you a story." And he told of two college classmates,
of whom one had risen in the world, and the other descended,

[1] See *A Conversation on Music with Ossip Gabrilowitsch*, recorded by Daniel
Gregory Mason. *The Century*, May, 1909.

until they chanced to meet in a restaurant where A. was dining and B. was waiting on table. After greetings were over A. effusively invited B. to join him in his meal. "Oh no," replied B., "I wait here, but I don't eat here." "That's the way I feel," concluded Ossip, "about *Musical Chit-chat*. I advertise in it, but I don't read it."

He was armored in advance, then, against the whole tribe of journalists, even those of Boston, with the notorious Philip Hale at their head, and so had the audacity to bring my *Elegy*, early in 1909, to the native city of its composer. Hale ran true to form. "It is said that this *Elegy*," he wrote in the *Boston Herald*, "is in memory of a friend. Grief is sometimes assuaged by the bereft one's indulgence in the variation form. . . . A composer thus paying musical tribute has one eye on the coffin and one on the public—that is, unless he have only one eye. . . ." Ossip had in his own eyes a curious inequality. He once told me, with his usual zest in a joke even on himself, that he had remarked on it to a friend: "You know, one of my eyes is slightly larger than the other," and the friend had replied: "Why, I thought one was slightly *smaller* than the other." This inequality gave to his smile sometimes a sort of quizzical half-squint that I can picture playing over his face as he read Hale's ribaldries. But he never let me know he had so much as noticed them until years later when there was question of playing my *Piano Quartet* in Boston. Instead he telegraphed me: "*Elegy* had fine success. Everyone likes it. Am very happy." And he put the piece on his programs in New York, Cleveland, Chicago, and San Francisco, and a few years later in Paris.

In June, 1909, when my wife and I had just settled for the first of many summers in one of the old farm houses on the outskirts of Pittsfield belonging to our friend Gertrude Watson, we almost persuaded Ossip to settle there too. He was then a foot-loose irresponsible young bachelor who could go where he pleased—not yet "settled down", though already in love with Clara Clemens, daughter of Mark Twain, and thus naturally gravitating to Redding rather than Pittsfield. His letters of that time reveal to the full his high spirits and the insatiable love of banter that never left him. (One often marvelled at how, all through his life, in the artists' room after his most inspired concerts, where he had opened to us the furthest heavens of music, he never could be serious a moment. Repartee was then at a premium, and no joke too threadbare to afford pretext for the relaxing laughter his over-strung nerves demanded. . . . But in these days the gaiety was just sheer youthful exuberance.)

"I am awfully sorry for you," he wrote me in teasing pity in early June, from Redding, "as I know just how you must feel in the present fix, unable to begin any work. This is the way things go when two women undertake to manage them. (For God's sake do not show this letter to Mrs. Mason—she would never look at me again, although of course I do not mean her. She is an exception.) I am glad I did not succumb to the charms of Miss Watson and of Miss Learned and of their five-hundred dollar white house, or else I should probably now also be writing scores on the edge of a dining table and having carpenters and painters for daily company. I do not see how you manage to keep your good humor."

A month later came a dictated letter from a New York hospital, announcing his serious mastoid operation, and dated July 9, the very day a notice had appeared in the newspapers that he was "dangerously ill" and that "recovery was not at all certain." "Don't be alarmed," it ends, "take things cheerfully as I do"; and a tremulous "Ossip" is traced in pencil as signature. (He later told us, with roars of laughter, that a man visiting him in the hospital had exclaimed: "If you had only died, you would have had a *magnificent* funeral!") By the end of July, however, he reported himself out of hospital, feeling "almost like a human being" and "eating four big meals a day". This sounded reassuring, as his appetite was normally as insatiable for good things to eat as for good things to laugh at. It was by no accident that the story "I wait here, but I don't eat here" so registered itself on his memory. Ridgely Torrence once told us that after they had both dined at our apartment they set off together and walked arm in arm down Broadway. Although we had done our humble best to provide a worthy dinner, at the first lunch wagon Ossip proposed reënforcements.

By the end of August, back in Redding, he wrote in answer to my description of my son Billy's device for irrigating watermelons by means of strings leading water from a milk bottle: "You are certainly criminally modest when you compare your composing to Billy's watermelon growing. I suppose more composers than we realize have been raising their works 'on the bottle' and have accomplished great things just the same. I hope the *Quartet* is progressing finely, and when I come to Pittsfield I expect to have watermelon for dinner and at least two movements of the *Quartet* after dinner."

Then, at the end of September, addressed to both my wife and me, came proclamation of the fulfilment of hopes that had been in his mind for years. "I have a great piece of news to tell you," he writes. "Miss Clemens and I are to be married on Wednesday next, October 6th." But he warns us, with canny attention to detail even in his great moment, not to let the newspapers get hold of it. . . .

Almost a year later came a note that proved to be signed with an unfamiliar name. Dated Stormfield, August 18th, 1910, it read:

"My dear Friends:

"I have the pleasure of informing you that I was born in Redding, Connecticut, this morning at 8.15. Mother and I are well.

"Very truly yours,
"Nina Gabrilowitsch"

As no one who knew the author of this, even if still unacquainted with the signer, could possibly leave it unanswered, I sent the brand-new Gabrilowitsch a few lines.

"My dear Nina: I hope you will set your father at work writing a cradle-song for you at once. It is not well for him to be idle. . . . I want to whisper in your ear that he is inclined to sleep too much. Please see that he is waked up every hour or so to keep him from getting gluttonous. . . . I notice you don't mention him at all in your letter—you say 'Mother and I are well.' This is right. It is just as well to snub him a little. Let him down easy, and get him tame and nice. . . ."

Of all the musicians I met at my uncle's, Ossip seemed to me the most unpretentious, genuine, and greatly simple. None of the others quite combined as he did a deep seriousness and love of beauty with a truly American sense of fun. And of them all he has been, through the years, the longest and the staunchest friend.

CHAPTER V

ARTHUR WHITING

My MEMORY of Arthur Whiting goes back to the autumn after my graduation from Harvard, when as his pupil in New York I first felt the full impact of his manly and stoical character. Gradually I had been coming to appreciate the idealism beneath the cross-grained surface of his artistic attitude, often at first sight so ruthless toward human frailty, yet in the long run vitally human, sanatively preservative of all genuine values. "I find nothing cold about Whiting," I find myself writing my mother in November 1895. "What you are probably thinking of is either his severity as a critic, which comes from high ideals, conscientiousness, and a somewhat over-developed sense of humor; or his lack of the poetic or mystical element in emotion. *Emotion* itself he certainly does not lack, and I am not even sure about the mysticism, for just look at his enthusiasm for Brahms, the king of mystics in music. . . . But his conception of his art is one of great nobility and unselfishness of zeal: he is in music for the sake of music, not for the sake of A. Whiting, and he expects everyone else to subordinate the interests of Smith, Brown and Robinson to those of beautiful and pure art. Coupled with this is his *triple-sec* humor, which will demolish all weaknesses and leave no outworks in the space of half a minute. He has the classic spirit, and will not brook anything slipshod or mawkish or inept. Therefore I have a certain dread of him. But at the same moment that little D.G. is quivering under his scalpel, big D.G. is glowing with approval."

This scalpel of his was unerring in its searching out of all pretentiousness, all taking oneself too seriously, all shams and false values. His friends had frequently to submit to its painful but salutary operations. In the very early days, when I incautiously played him a song I had composed, boy-like, on a foreign text (*Wie jauchzt meine Seele*) he remarked that it was "as German as *Kraut*". His comment when, years later, Josef Hofmann played in his Carnegie Hall recital of American piano music a piece of mine called *Chimney Swallows*, was: "You might call it *Chimney Sweeps*. It's a little heavy for swallows—about right for sweeps." After the Flonzaley Quartet gave the first private hearing of my *Quartet on Negro Themes* at the house of Edward J. DeCoppet in New York (December 30, 1919), he turned to my brother Harry and asked with the mock-innocent air of one craving information: "Is there any Negro blood in your family?" . . . This naughty-boy kind of mischievousness, by the way, was often an element in his humor. He told me that, when his pupils would admire a picture of Brahms's birthplace he had in his studio, he would tell them it was taken the day Brahms was born. Chuckling, he said they would at first look intensely interested, and then (putting his hand up to his chin in mimicry of pondering) begin to wonder!

The title of the piano piece of another friend of those early days, *le Crepuscule*, sounded, Arthur said, "like the name of a bad cigar". That friend was a stickler for formal correctness in notation, not always practically very important. He ended another of his pieces with a string of notes going all the way up the piano and landing on nearly the top one, the tone of which died out, of course, almost at once. Nevertheless, in order to make a correct "eight-measure phrase", he carefully wrote out this poor little final tone in four imposing-looking whole-notes ("goose-eggs", we used to call them) tied to one another. Arthur, pointing to the fourth and last, said "X., I should put a *hold* over that." Alas, poor X.'s exuberance of temperament made him a preordained butt for the other's deflating

ironies. Once, in a train returning from a suburban school where
the whole party had been teaching and when, after lunch, all were
drowsy, X. took the opportunity to boast loudly of his powers of
sleeping at will, of how he "could go to sleep at any moment, night
or day". A. W., quietly: "Well, X., why not give us a demonstration now?" Of the two species of the genus Bore, however, the
effervescent and the stagnant, Arthur undoubtedly found the second
even more trying than the first. Of a particularly heavy specimen
of it he complained: "Guying S. is like shooting a cow—no sport."

Another victim was that delightful amateur of music, Winthrop
Rogers, later connected with the house of G. Schirmer, and always
a good violinist and an imaginative composer. He had written a
song about a robin, and had not resisted the opportunity to suggest
the song of the bird in the accompaniment. This was a habit of
composers that Arthur loathed. I have heard him scornfully describe
a song about a thrush as a sort of "thrush competition—the thrush
was put in in all the interstices". Once at the Century Club he
went with unctuous detail into the habits of different nations in
the matter of such banal illustration. "You give a Frenchman the
word *cloche* anywhere in a song," he said, "and he simply can't
resist it. Yet Sir Walter Parrott had a text with the words 'sound
the hautboy, sound the shawm', and he set it rigorously without
any reeds at all. Someone asked him why he didn't use some reeds,
and he said: 'Oh, I had no shawm.' Then," he continued, "there
is the American. My friend Chadwick, setting a text which says
'*Not* with trumpets and with drums' has to begin at once with a
trumpet call!" With such convictions, Arthur was naturally lying
in wait for poor Winthrop Rogers's robin, which furthermore
proved rather beyond the composer's powers as a pianist. "That
robin," he observed with a mild judicial air, "needs oiling."

One evening Rogers was telling us admiringly of a violinist who
had so clean a technic that he could go right up to the high F in
the *Kreutzer Sonata* without flinching. "Even a player like Kneisel,"
he said, "is apt to shy at that note." "Yes," agreed Arthur, "to
cough just there." On another occasion at the Rogers', when Mrs.
Rogers was about to go to the piano to sing some songs of Robert

Franz, Arthur murmured in an aside to me: "Now that you've
written an article on Franz's songs, wouldn't you like to hear
them?" And that reminds me inevitably of one of the cruellest
but also most comical things I ever heard him say. A violinist of
the Boston Symphony Orchestra, a genial companion but an indifferent player, was leaving the orchestra after a tenure of decades.
Why was he leaving?—we all wondered. At last we asked Arthur's
opinion. "I suppose," he drawled, "somebody must have *heard* him."

It is only fair to add that he seldom missed a good opportunity to
turn his humor on himself, thereby meeting the severest of all tests.
When someone asked him who was at his first recital, he answered:
"No one who wasn't entitled to kiss me." Working on his *Pedal
Studies* he became so keen over the possibilities of literary expression
of musical truths that he told his wife he thought he might send
away the two pianos in his East Fortieth Street studio, and devote
himself to writing. Later, at his request, Moody and I criticized his
preface in detail. He who always gave criticism so pungently was a
little rueful at having to take quite so much. "I rather think, Grace,"
he said, "I shall keep one piano."

For one so sensitive as he was under his "tough-minded" surface
(to use the Jamesian term) he took banter surprisingly well. An
example was his amiable, even highly amused, reception of a caricature of his style I once perpetrated. I had spent the year 1902–03
at Princeton, at the University, on the initiative and at the expense
of that ardent Princeton man, Rudolph E. Schirmer, trying to
arouse interest in music among the undergraduates. This had been
some years before Whiting's own highly successful efforts in the
same direction in his *Chamber Music Expositions* at Princeton,
Yale, and Harvard, and I had made but hard going of it. So he
would frequently urge me to repeat my story of my Princeton adventures, which he never failed to punctuate with shouts of laughter. The climax concerned an undergraduate who came to me for
information about an evening of Schumann music I was giving, in
order to report it for the college paper. Fresh from Harvard, I
called this paper, I remember, the *Crimson* instead of the *Prince-
tonian*—quite innocently and inadvertently, but no doubt with an

effect of maddening snobbery. The boy, of course, got the facts hopelessly mixed, describing a program of the music of Rudolph Schirmer. "No," I said, "the music is to be by Schumann. Mr. Schirmer is paying for it." "Oh yes," he agreed. Then, with an inspiration of self-defense: "I knew Schumann was dead." It ended with my taking pity, and writing the paragraph for him. Overcome by this unexpected aid, he turned to me impulsively as he was leaving, and asked: "Professor, do you give lessons on the banjo?"

All this was recent history on that gay spring evening in 1904 when Winthrop and Mary Rogers gave a farewell dinner to Grace and Arthur Whiting on their departure for a summer in Europe. He was in his best form in an after-dinner speech in which he referred to me as "recently of Princeton, N. G." (slang in those days for "No Good") and "author of *From Hell to Washington Square*" —my first book had been called *From Grieg to Brahms*. He took with angelic good nature some *Variations on Home, Sweet Home, in the Style of A. W.* which I had founded on specific pieces of his (one, I blush to confess, on his beautiful song, *When I am dead, my dearest*, to the text of Christina Rossetti). "Hereafter," he said, "we will collaborate. First you write the caricature and then I'll write the composition."

From the other side, as the summer wore on, he wrote back:

"Tintagel, Cornwall
"August 6

"I was so gratified at what you all did at the Rogers' in the way of a send-off that my impulse was to write a daily letter to every one of you—for one reason or another, or none, the inclination has been denied. In fact, I have almost forgotten how to write, and take it out in thinking lovingly of my friends who are able to set up such a brilliant evening.

"But let it be said at once that all your good wishes for me have been fulfilled; that the English have stopped work to give me a good time and that, by special arrangement with the weather prophet my umbrella has been under my arm ever since I landed.

"Busses have been run up and down Piccadilly for my benefit;

people have ridden, driven and sat in the Park for my amusement; messenger boys have worn their ridiculous little caps at an acuter angle than usual (they know it never fails to fascinate me), theatres have kept open at an enormous expense whether I felt like going or not (they let *me* have a stall for half a guinea a night); people think America is really the only country and they begin every other sentence with 'I guess'—just because they know I like it so. So you see it is a good thing to dine with friends at the Rogers' before visiting England.

"It was great fun in Oxford—Hadow is as good an host as he is a guest. I had my own suite of apartments in a thirteenth century building (with electric light) and did everything an undergrad. is expected to do. . . .

"Met an interesting musician in London, an Oxford man, named Tovey,[1] some of whose compositions I hope to be able to show you. He is of the grand serious, what some call Brahms and water; but while his music does not smack of the soil, it is good stuff. I looked everywhere for the composer with the English face, but didn't find him. Hadow tried to make me think that Parry is he, but he didn't succeed. . . .

"Tintagel Castle is great and the whole country is swarming with King Arthur. But the new stone cottages and English lady boarder (the summer-girl of the country) are better to hear about than to see. Promise me, dear boy, to take my word for it. . . . Grace and Miss Benedict are wonderful sight-seers—they can see sights like anything and make me feel like a mole."

II

Arthur's ironies, of course, were in large measure protective devices for his own sensitiveness and shy idealism—then most of all when they were turned against himself. His deepest interest, we must always bear in mind, even when in later years he largely gave it up, was composition. On the occasion of a threatened fire in their

[1] This is of course Sir Donald Francis Tovey, now famous especially for his brilliant critical writings on music.

Arthur Whiting

From a snap-shot made in Austria in the summer of 1932

apartment once, Grace told us that while she was scurrying about
ferreting out papers and valuables, he suddenly appeared with a pile
of manuscripts under his arm. It was one of those little incidents
that showed what was truly, in the Stevensonian sense, his "lantern". Even when, in over-critical mood, he felt his own lantern to
be too dim to be worth trimming, the thought made him, not indifferent, but bitter, with a morbid and pathetic bitterness, toward
other people's lamps, or even candles. One of the most unfailing
targets of his scorn was what he thought the disproportion between
the many helps we were ready to give youths of talent—fellowships
of the American Academy in Rome, Guggenheim Fellowships,
Pulitzer Prizes—and the few youths capable of profiting by them.
"All this effort," he once exploded, "to find students to keep prizes
from going begging. We're like the people in Jamaica Plain in the
old days. They all had pear trees in their back yards. You would
meet a neighbor and say: 'Do you know of anybody who needs
some pears?' and he would answer: 'Well, yes, I do, but you needn't
think I'm going to tell *you*.'"

Like his idol Brahms he masked a too tender and idealistic heart
under sardonic gruffness or ironic innuendo. How devastating were
the revenges his deep sentiment took in his scorn for sentimentality!
One evening at the Gabrilowitsches', after the hour for leaving had
come and everyone felt sleepy, some sentimentalist began requesting our signatures to a petition that Galsworthy's *Justice* should
not be allowed performed at Sing Sing, on the ground that it would
be "cruel to the prisoners". In the universal lethargy that met this
suggestion, Arthur was the only person who retained vestiges of
presence of mind. He signed, indeed; but as someone suggested that
Grace sign too, he remarked: "Yes, we'll be sent up together," adding: "We'll get a cell with a double bed." This relieved the sombre
mood, and made us all laugh. As Grace was signing he warned her:
"Look out, Grace. Write indistinctly."

Refreshing was the ridicule he always had ready for all forms of
herd-compulsion, such for instance as routine "patriotism". "The
official and ceremonial hymn of a country," he writes in his essay
The American Composer, "is usually perfunctory and Philistine. It

is pious custom more than spontaneous feeling which brings us to
our feet when we sing that commonplace tune which we borrowed
from England which she borrowed from Germany, the words of
which we vaguely remember to begin—'God bless our 'tis of thee.' "
He would have savored Clarence Day's "Aged Hottentot, of Hot-
tentotenville", in *Sic Semper Dissenters*, who "always stood when
any song was sung."

For some reason he was not present at the first Pittsfield Festival,
held in September of 1918, when war sentiment ran high. At my account of its beginning with the *Star Spangled Banner*, played by a
group of musicians all standing, he asked at once: "What, did the
cellist stand up too?" and commented: "A cellist standing up must
look like a horse sitting down." As always with him, this ridicule
of the spurious was the obverse of his deep love of the genuine. No
one loved more than he the true America underneath all the bally-
hoo. In that same article, he has only praise for one song—"our beloved *Dixie*—which throbs exactly with the national pulse, and is
of such sterling worth that it has survived fifty years of hard usage
and is today as thrilling and impelling as when it led the tired march-
ers to the Potomac." "We are proud," he continues, "that we have
men who have produced music with a flavor of its own. That peculiar energy of *Dixie* is native to them—an energy which is not
out of place in large and dignified form. One hears from them a turn
of phrase, a lilt and catch, which can be stamped 'Made in America'
without reservation."

Patience with whatever was routine or humdrum was not his
strong point. Of one of the most admired New York patrons of
music he remarked: "Of course he's the salt of the earth—but so
tame, so disappointing, a salt that has lost its savor. He's like a
prickly pear salad; the name sounds exciting, but it tastes flat."
Some platitude-mongers at the Century were extolling a certain
choral conductor, one for his energy, calling him a "live wire", a
second rather for his patience. At that point Arthur, who had been
listening with a quizzical smile, interpolated drily: "A patient live
wire." At a box party in Carnegie Hall he criticized so severely a
popular pianist that a tender-hearted person, coming to the rescue,

said that at least the soloist subordinated himself well to the orchestra—did not dominate too much. But A.W., seeming dubious whether that were really a virtue, quoted the Irish captain addressing his men: "What we want from you is Silence—and damned little of that!" A careless conductor, unsure of his *tempi*, he compared to "a reckless chauffeur going over the thank-you-ma'ams at the same speed as the smooth places—you couldn't stop him". Of another, who through nervousness took all the *tempi* too fast, he said: "It was really funny to hear him gallop over all the inequalities of the road. Those *mountains* of Brahms—instead of toiling laboriously up to them he dashed across them without noticing them—as if he'd been in an aeroplane." And the first movement of Beethoven's *Pastoral Symphony*, the one that bears the heading: "Happy Feelings on Arriving in the Country", he scornfully characterized, when played by this man, as "Happy Feelings on Arriving in Central Park".

Of course, loving music above all as he did for its expression, his supreme detestation was reserved for empty virtuosity and cheap sentimentalism. Once when David Bispham, in a Carnegie Hall recital, had fairly wallowed in mawkish sentiment, Whiting remarked on the way out: "If he could only have sung with a little less 'expression', there wouldn't have been a dry eye in the house." He wished that a certain popular pianist would try putting his show pieces in the middle of the program and something really fine at the end—"so that the audience shall go out impressed rather than astonished and combing down their hair". Kreisler, a born virtuoso, once took the place of Kneisel, a born ensemble player, in a concert of the Kneisel Quartet, with disastrous results. "The other three gentlemen," said Arthur, "held the life-net for him while he did gymnastic feats. Sometimes they caught him, sometimes not." Similarly he described a certain famous European quartet as a "one-man quartet—like a rich uncle surrounded by his poor relations". No wonder this sort of thing repelled one who once said that there were in music four values, set in decreasing ratio: "first, what the composer imagines; second, what he writes; third, what one plays to oneself; fourth, what one plays for an audience."

Justly or not, he considered Richard Strauss an extreme example of the commercial procurator in music. On this subject, as Stevenson says in describing Thoreau's similar hatred of commercialism, "gall squirted from him at a touch". "Strauss," he said to me, "is the supreme type of the shopkeeper. He makes it his business to supply the demand. In *Tod und Verklärung* he gives people the description of the death agony that pleases their nerves, and then, as they like to think of the beyond, adds on the Transfiguration. *Ariadne* is for people like me; *Salome* and *Elektra* are for the beer-drinkers and the blood-suckers . . . A shopkeeper of genius!" I compared Strauss to Reger. "Oh no," he retorted, "Reger is sincere, he writes the stuff because he wants to. It is a sort of natural secretion; he has to get rid of it. I don't believe he cares what happens to it after he has once got it out of his system." Strauss he thought a man of brilliant endowment who had got on a wrong track and would end by "giving program music a black eye". "I was overwhelmed," he said, "on first hearing *Don Juan*, but on a second hearing these things are like exploded fireworks—there's nothing to do but step on the pieces and stop the smell." "The successful man," he added meditatively, "is the one to pity because he has to exceed his own standard in every new work. The black horse is the happy man—he has the whole ladder before him—think of it, the whole ladder!" And on another occasion this ruthless critic of shallow Americanism declared that it was better to live in a country where there had never been any more aesthetic life than there was here at present, where it was growing up out of frank commercialism, than in a country like Germany where aesthetic culture had given way before the influx of commercialism.

III

It is a pity that the articles in which he voiced with his customary incisiveness some of his opinions are not more easily accessible.[1]

---

[1] Students will find *The Mechanical Player* in the *Yale Review* for July, 1919; *The American Composer* in the *Outlook* for February 17, 1915; *The Music Layman* in the *Outlook* for October 31, 1908; and *The Lesson of the Clavichord* in the *New Music Review* (reprinted in pamphlet form in 1909).

He thought everything out for himself. Almost morbidly sensitive as he was about his own lack of college background (for
social, one suspected, almost as much as for intellectual reasons),
he used to say almost defiantly that the man with native capacity
for genuine culture had no need to go to college—he would nose
out the good things for himself. He certainly proved his point by
his example—I have known no one more truly and finely cultivated.

Two of his essays particularly, far too characteristic and stimulating to be left buried in old magazines, may be briefly quoted
here: *The Mechanical Player*, which contains some of the wisest as
well as wittiest things ever said about the absurdity of trying to
mechanize art; and *The Lesson of the Clavichord*, an impassioned
plea for the subtle and the suggestive as opposed to the brutal sensationalism prevalent in contemporary music. *The Mechanical
Player* opens with a description of the futile efforts of "Son"—the
scion of any average American family—to learn to play the piano.
The reasons for the failure are set forth as "(a) uncontrollable antipathy to the personality of Miss Boggs, his first, and last, music-
teacher; (b) dislocated forefinger from foul tip; (c) fatal facility
in playing by ear; (d) congenital inability to play anything in
sharps". But all is changed as "the mechanical art meets him not
half way but all the way."

"Provided that our young musical chauffeur has the use of his
feet and has passed the right and left test he is ready for a spin
directly the machine is assembled. Mounted on a high, commanding
bench and being relieved of all digital detail, ever his stumbling-
block, he is at last free; freer even than on the avenue where he
often chafes under traffic regulation, for here there are no laws and
no penalties. It is true that the composer may, after his kind, erect
signs bearing Italian equivalents for 'Speed limit, 8 miles', 'School-
house ahead', and the like, or set up a wail when he sees his pet conceptions fluttering under the mud-guard of the flying player; but
all such preferences and warnings seem small and captious, for son
has found himself, his natural gifts are now realized. His mother
was right."

Meanwhile, however, "Father", with his "furtive love for Beethoven", has discovered that "some ways of playing this wonderful music please him more than others":

"While his eldest daughter's pianoforte gifts and accomplishments are very limited, they serve, although her faltering fingers are not to be depended on for climaxes or sonorities. When the performance breaks down altogether he must make good her shortcomings by humming or whistling. But sister has a sweet touch, and he shares, sympathetically, her struggle to round out a phrase; for, although he does not know it, their combined effort is a part of the emotional experience. He will learn, later, that the dramatic effect of a musical situation depends largely on the gamble in human fallibility, in the excitement of uncertainty as to whether the thing really can be pulled off."

Thus is the stage set for the catastrophe, described in the following inimitably Whitingesque paragraph:

"How different it is the first evening they all stand before the just-arrived mechanical player, which, being entirely self-possessed, has even more platform imperturbability than the applauded virtuoso, even a larger number of decorations on its chest from the hands of grateful sovereigns, as well set up and as shiny, exhaling a delicate odor of the varnish of its native warerooms. After a few introductory sounds which have nothing to do with the music and without relaxing the lines of its inscrutable face, the insensate artist proceeds to show its power. Its security puts all handplaying to shame; it never hesitates, it surmounts the highest difficulties without changing a clutch. Always masterful and headlong, it can, if required, utter notes faster than the human ear can follow. Bouquets of adjectives, thrown by the excited audience towards the unperspiring, unexhausted performer, fall unnoticed at its feet. Since that memorable first appearance, poor sister has hardly touched the keys."

Is the reader prepared for the *dénouement?* To any truly musical person it is inevitable.

"Father discovers, after many trials, that the brazen readiness of the mechanical genius does not attract him; that while all the notes that sister missed are sounded with authority, yet when he anxiously

pushes the button marked 'expression' something is lacking which before gave him satisfaction. Those hard, brilliant scales and tempestuous trills do not, after all, make music; they make only a glittering, repelling noise. He longs to hear again the bashful, hesitating sounds which once charmed him, that human touch which said something to him although imperfectly. In short, he recognizes through this experience the demonstration of that eternal truth of which, as a boy in the early stages of penmanship, he had made some fifty laborious copies, to wit, 'the letter killeth but the spirit giveth life'."

And the moral follows the fable:

"That which is truth to the few will, later, be truth to the crowd, which for guidance should remember the maxim, 'art and mechanics are enemies'. In this slowly comprehending crowd we shall, no doubt, see father; and, as he returns for comfort to sister's human ways . . . , we shall know that his education in the higher branches is coming on."

The Lesson of the Clavichord, different from that of mechanization, is no less winningly set forth. What is more, the two lessons really belong together. The second is that of the strength of suggesting, the weakness of overstating; and the folly it analyses and ridicules, closely related in a thousand subtle ways to our idolatry of mechanism, is that other pet modern folly of sensationalism. A brief excerpt will suffice to show the argument, and may tempt the reader to investigate further for himself.

"It is true the pianoforte can be heard almost a mile with a favorable wind, but it is, congenitally, a chamber music instrument which cannot be properly used in a hall of more than 1,500 seats. . . . The evolution of the overwhelming school has brought into use methods and movements hitherto associated only with the manly art of self-defense. The manly art of pianoforte playing has developed a corresponding type of instrument. Everything in its construction is as stout as may be, and some of our best pianofortes can make a good fight. But when these heroes are introduced to domestic circles they seem to be without the gentle graces which are properly demanded of chamber music.

"Chopin and Liszt stood at opposite poles—Chopin withered in the presence of the public—Liszt was the creation of the public. . . . Chopin's art was one of suggestion. He said 'I only sketch; I let my hearers fill it out'. No collaboration of this kind was demanded from Liszt's audience. He furnished everything and expected from the public only cries of excitement or the silence of awe."

IV

Whiting's best beloved composers, I suppose, were Bach and Brahms. Once when he was transcribing one of the toccatas of Bach he exclaimed that in its *adagio*, a gorgeous recitative without much melodic continuity, its composer was like a fine big cock on a rail fence who throws out his chest and crows. His taste was broad enough, however, to include a good deal of impressionism also, especially Debussy, Ravel, and his friend Loeffler—though he was by no means unaware of its decadent qualities. Someone once called Loeffler's pieces "a mass of decay". "Yes," agreed Arthur, "but such swell decay!"

One of the most memorable evenings at his studio in East Fortieth Street was that of December 10, 1905, during the first visit of Vincent d'Indy to America, when Loeffler's *Rhapsodies* were played by Whiting, piano, Georges Longy of the Boston Symphony Orchestra, oboe, and the composer, viola, and the French poems on which they were based were read aloud with exquisite expressiveness and distinction by d'Indy. Later Francis Rogers sang Loeffler's four songs with viola obbligato. Present were the Kneisel Quartet, the Flonzaley Quartet with Mr. deCoppet, Walter and Frank Damrosch, Richard Aldrich, Lawrence Gilman and W. J. Henderson, Gustave and Rudolph Schirmer, and a few others. Arthur Whiting played the piano parts magnificently, and was the animating spirit of the whole occasion.

In the most important of all musical activities, composition, Whiting almost made up in quality for lack of quantity. When I once urged him to compose more, he replied that he had been asso-

ciating with the masters too much to tolerate his own stuff any
longer, and wondered how some of his friends, at their age, could
tolerate theirs. He saw their defects, and his own, too clearly to
maintain a tolerant or hopeful attitude. I recall his account of an
opera of one of them: how as you listened you gradually grew
languid, then bored, then sleepy; how at a certain point in the
action a live bear was led on to the stage; how you eagerly sat up
and pricked up your ears; how after about one minute the bear was
led off again, and you were, according to Arthur, "left alone with
the opera". Such a satiric attitude was not conducive to composing,
and I always felt that his demand for perfection ended by em-
bittering him with his own as well as with others' inevitable human
imperfections. When his friend Hadow, grouping him in the little
book called *Music* with the three contemporaries who had happened to be born in the same year as he—MacDowell, Loeffler, and
Parker—came to the conclusion that "Whiting, who has written
far too little, possesses perhaps more than any of them the feeling
for a true American Art", Arthur seized on the first part of the
judgment—that he had written "far too little"—and often said, in
his later years, maybe half whimsically but certainly also half seriously, that he would like it as an epitaph: "Here lies one who wrote
too little."

"It was with a pride and satisfaction eminently characteristic of
Arthur," comments one of his most devoted friends, "that he said
this. . . . If there is one thing of which I am quite sure it is his
contentment with his musical ideals. This does not mean that he
would not have liked to be a Bach or Brahms, but that more than
anything else he wished to keep the integrity of his musical standard. Not so long ago I said to him, 'My only regret is that you
haven't composed more'; and he: 'Oh, no! Never regret that. As it
is, I have lived always in the best of company, and think what that
means—always to have had the Best! Had I given more time to my
own compositions this could not have been so.' Nothing could have
been more characteristic of the mixture of pride and humility that
was Arthur."

All his friends will say Amen to that. And yet, when I remember his playing, at a concert of the National Institute as early as 1914, of his *Fantasy* for Piano and Orchestra, and recall what genuinely American music it was, how vivid in rhythm, how reticent yet vibrant in sentiment, how individual in style and concise in form, I for one cannot but wish there had been less inhibition of the creative side of his nature by the critical. We, his pupils and friends, could say of his *Fantasy*, in the very words he had himself used of *Dixie*: "One hears a turn of phrase, a lilt and catch, which can be stamped 'Made in America' without hesitation."

So one cannot but wish he had been willing to tolerate his imperfections a little more. But what he did do, whatever its limitations and shortcomings, is unique in its distinction and in a certain half-shy, withdrawn, reserved tenderness. Deep feeling, hidden but also ennobled by his virile stoicism, finds voice in his *Three Songs for Soprano* and in the *Rubaiyat* settings for baritone, especially in the lovely *But oh, that spring should vanish with the rose*. No deeper, purer note has been struck in American music.

In all his musical activities—composition, piano playing, his expository recitals in the universities, his astringent and exciting essays, his casual letters and uniquely individual witticisms, his influence was tonic, prophylactic, preservative of the true spirit of art in a sentimental age. "Who," he asks in one of his papers, "are the friends of an artist? There can be but one answer, which is: those who love art more than they love the artist." He was himself, in peculiar degree, such a friend, who inspired, and one hopes may still long inspire, not only those of us fortunate enough to have known him personally, but all who can divine his splendid integrity.

CHAPTER VI

E. A. ROBINSON AND T. H. BARTLETT

IN SPITE of the stimulus of my study with Whiting, the inspiring contacts at my uncle's, even the praise of Paderewski—"that auroral head", as Will Moody put it in his gorgeous way, "uttering gold vaticination"—all my hopes of establishing myself in New York, and as a musician, soon proved vain and had to be abandoned. In the first place, ever since my father's death in 1890 our family fortunes had been on the wane. The organ and piano business that had brought us prosperity all through the happy Brookline period of my father's prime and my own childhood, was now running down hill with dizzying momentum, to crash a few years later in bankruptcy. Almost worse still, my health, never strong, as Moody's solicitude had so tenderly discovered during our walking trip, now gave out completely. To the general neurasthenic weakness—what Royce used to call the "nervous burden"— was now added a specific ailment of the right arm, a combination of severe "pianist's cramp" with a milder "writer's cramp", that obliged me to reduce piano playing to zero, and writing to pretty near it, for several years. There was nothing to do but admit myself beaten for the moment, confess the New York episode a fiasco, crawl back to Cambridge, where in the Harvard English courses of my friends la Rose, Gates, and Wendell there were some pennies to be picked up, and thank my stars that Thoreau and Emerson (in those days especially Thoreau) were almost as exciting to me as Schumann and Brahms.

During that difficult time, that long dark tunnel of my life, as it still figures itself to my imagination, I struggled, as never before nor since, with "that impotent sense of his own value, as of a ship aground", to quote Stevenson and mix metaphors, "which is one of the agonies of youth". Fortunately even the tunnel had its happy moments, airier, sunlit spaces of books and friends. The books were Emerson, Thoreau, Stevenson, Royce, and a few others. The friends were a group of young fellow-idealists like Moody, Josephine Preston Peabody, Philip Henry Savage, and Edwin Arlington Robinson, and a few kind elders like Truman H. Bartlett, sculptor and friendly host of young artists, and Josiah Royce, imaginative enough to understand such a predicament as mine. I took the room Number 14, Divinity Hall (Emerson's room at a time of similar discouragement in his life, I discovered—and lost no time indicating in a framed notice fastened inside the door), and tried to console myself for the loss of music as best I could with English teaching, reading, and a little writing.

Although E. A. Robinson and I had been, as it chanced, members of the same Class of 1895 at Harvard, as undergraduates we had never met; indeed he had left college at the end of our sophomore year. We first met in the spring of 1899, when he was slaving in a magazine office in Cambridge and I was drawing small checks for assisting in the English courses of Barrett Wendell. Robinson's real work during that whole period was on his long poem about Captain Craig, a hero whom we used to call familiarly "the Pauper", and for whom we had a real fellow-feeling. "In the evening," I wrote in my journal on March 20, "a good walk with Robinson. He has at last got down to work. He has done, tentatively, 200 lines of his 'Pauper' poem, which he says 'seems to be going to be a sort of humorous poem, with something else underneath'. He works at it only between 11 and 1 at night, 'and then can't sleep'. He spoke with more vigorous approval than almost any I have heard him use, of Thoreau's *Poems*, which I lent him.

Edwin Arlington Robinson
From a photograph taken about 1900

Aside from them he is at present entirely unacquainted with Thoreau." A month or two later I added: "Edwin Arlington Robinson spent the afternoon with me, and a curious chap he is: you have to wait hours for him to say anything; but he is interesting enough nevertheless."

It was on this May afternoon, I believe, that he inscribed his microscopic but meticulous signature in my copy of his *The Children of the Night*. This had appeared the year before, and I had obtained a copy of it in exchange for one, earned by a review in the *Harvard Monthly*, of T. W. Higginson's *Cheerful Yesterdays* (a title extended by my irreverent friend Hill to *Cheerful Yesterdays and Bum Tomorrows*). On the fly-leaf of my copy of Robinson's book is also a photograph of him taken by our common friend William E. Butler, to whose generous help he owed so much; but this portrait, pasted in later, is probably the one to which he refers in his letter of August 24, 1899: [1] "I enclose a photograph which may interest you as a harmless freak. I have a look that might lead one to think that I had just been eating the lining out of my own coffin, but that is the fault of an uncomfortable feel somewhere in my spinal column. I was not properly adjusted for the interminable two minutes. The book and the fore-paws have been removed."

Robinson in these early days was tall and in a sensitive way handsome, with dark, fine hair, flowing moustache, and fresh healthy color. Beautiful were his large and peculiarly limpid dark eyes. They gleamed and glowed behind his spectacles, alternately quiet with poetic penetration and dancing with humorous irony. It was this element of irony, I suppose, that made his personality strike me at first, especially by contrast with the romantic warmth of Will Moody and the delicate idealism of Phil Savage, as dry, almost prosaic.

As a companion he was almost as reticent as Moody, of whom it was currently said at Harvard that "it took him a pipeful to make

[1] For the complete series of Letters from Edwin Arlington Robinson to Daniel Gregory Mason, see the *Yale Review*, Summer 1936, and the *Virginia Quarterly Review*, Winter 1937 and Spring 1937. The original manuscript letters are now in the possession of the collector of Robinsoniana, Mr. Howard G. Schmitt, of Buffalo, who has kindly supplied the facsimile at page 131.

a remark." But Moody's silences were rich, pregnant, profound, whereas Robinson's seemed more difficult and self-conscious, as if the play of his mind were struggling against New England inhibitions. He had even then the mannerism that never left him of snarling up his forehead when puzzled or self-conscious, putting up a rather helpless hand to try to smooth it out. One recognizes this almost morbid self-consciousness in many passages of the early letters. "No amount of declaiming or swearing on your part," he protests in one, "will ever make me believe that you enjoyed the last part of Monday evening. I had one of my intolerable fits come over me and made an ass of myself. I do it as many as twenty-five or thirty times a month. If you forget it, all right; but don't feel obliged to smooth it over." Again: "I went to see Miss Peabody last evening and both she and her sister showed great patience and originality. As these are qualities of the first importance to people with artistic aspirations, I always have altruistic thrills when I feel that I may have been the means of developing them." And summing it all up he says in another letter: "If Miss Peabody tells you that I am an untaught beast, you will tell her that I am by nature as kind-hearted as a caterpillar, though I have a quaint way of smashing people's heads when I wish merely to call their attention to things of interest."

Though less humorous observers than himself may cavil at the caterpillar simile, he is within the truth when he says that kind-heartedness was native to him. Beneath all that queer, difficult, sensitive-plant surface of his, of which he was himself far more painfully aware than anyone else, there was a fund of kindliness, of understanding sympathy, that his friends never doubted. This it was that created the atmosphere of tenderness in such early poems as *Isaac and Archibald* and *Aunt Imogen*, to my taste as fine as anything he ever wrote. And however disproportionate in his mental life his repressions and inhibitions might sometimes seem, they did not make him bitter. His most laconic comments on books or persons, even when most drily flavored by that repressed wit of his, voiced a wisdom both shrewd and magnanimous. "Robinson took a walk with me," I note in my journal in February, 1899, "and then came to my room and ate eclairs. He was more articulate than I have ever seen him before; his conversation bore out more the impression his book gives. Talking about sleeping, he said: 'Eight hours is all a man ought to lie stretched out.'" "Phil [Philip Henry Savage] tells me," I note in another journal entry, "that Nietzsche says: 'Without *superfluous* time the mind cannot perceive.' This is very Thoreau-like." (Next day): "Robinson adds: 'The superfluous time put Nietzsche behind the bars, after all.'"

Penetrating as was his intelligence, there was about him a sort of helplessness in practical affairs that made him arouse pity as well as admiration. This had its physical symbol, for me, in his hands, those hands with the long fingers that seemed made not to grasp objects—saws or hammers, hardly even pens—but rather to rub his forehead when that queer half-scowl of perturbed thought visited it. In my journal I find myself saying: "I am cudgelling my brains tonight to think of just the right niche for Robinson, poor fellow. He has so little prehensile power, so little knack at making people give him what he wants. Tonight he said, speaking of a friend of his: 'He's even more of a misfit than I am.' Yet transcendentally he is richly endowed."

What the rest of us perhaps did not understand was that where he fitted worst of all was into any kind of conventional "job", which always distressed and unsettled him so that he could not do his own work. The danger to Apollo of any service whatever to Admetus was almost an obsession with him. It was doubtless in answer to some counsel of worldly wisdom of mine about a "regular job" that he once wrote me: "There is something in what you say about fellows who sit on their tails, but I have convinced myself that I cannot do much while I have an occupation. While a man is occupied he is absorbing, I confess, but if he happens to be constructed as I am he will not do much in the way of production until he gets a vacation. With others it works just the other way, and I do not say they are not the lucky ones." A letter written after poor Savage's death, developing the idea—to my mind a mistaken one—that his poetry had been injured by his secretaryship in the Boston Public Library, goes on by way of moral: "The octopus of superficial self-respect—he refuses for some reason to take hold of me—is worse than anything that Hugo or Jules Verne ever dreamed of, and I cannot but feel half afraid that Savage lost himself in the black water with which this particular beast is said to bewilder his victims."

On the other hand, when Robinson can elude Admetus altogether he is positively gay. "I have come to the conclusion," he writes me during that same summer of '99, adding a characteristically cautious "almost", "that it will be impossible for me to undertake any kind of useful occupation during the coming year and I have racked my brains to find a way to get the time for myself. Now I think—largely through good luck—that I have done it. I am in ridiculously good spirits just now, sending the Pauper along at a rate that makes him red in the face, eating anything that comes along, drinking nothing unpermitted by the laws of Cambridge, and feeling every morning the joy of a liberated idiot for the thought that I am no longer a necessity in University 5. The beauty of it is that I look on the place with an almost pathetic affection. The pathos, however, is without longing and without qualms. Come to Cambridge and see me go to Provincetown."

And when, in the autumn, he managed to escape gleefully to New York and no salary at all, his high spirits burst out in a joke about asking President Eliot for "a large pension on the ground of Permanent Inability in the College Office". He was now entering, high spirits or no, the hardest period of his whole life: the withdrawn and impecunious poet was quite lost in the noise, confusion, and indifference of New York. His friends were few; he was distressingly poor; he was unknown and in mediocre health. It was only his invincible faith in his poetic mission that kept him going through those sordid, dreary years. He took a small room in Irving Place, in the very house where Moody later suffered so from noise.[1] I too was coming down in the world; my mother had been obliged

---

[1] "There are three hundred and twenty-three hand organs and ninety-seven pianos in our block, and every hour thirty-five thousand drays loaded with sheet iron pass the house. Irving Place, you know, is a quiet old-fashioned neighborhood, so we are justly proud of these slight evidences of animation." William Vaughn Moody, *Some Letters*, etc., page 130.

by the steady decline of the family business, the Mason and Hamlin Company, to sell the Commonwealth Avenue house bought by my father, and take a flat in Newbury Street, the so-called "Small of the Back Bay".

"The competent bedbug," Robinson wrote me in October, "drove me out of my second resting place in Washington Square and I am here in a little box room where everything is new. My wall decorations consist of a red match box and a fifty cent photograph of Beethoven which I bought the other day for the sake of having the presence of a fellow who did things without ears." (Robinson was deaf in one ear, always found himself confused when in a group of people, and felt the affliction with his usual acute self-consciousness.) "I am beginning to feel contented and settled," he adds, "though I confess to an occasional qualm for your den in Newbury Street."

In a letter of nearly a year later he plays a variation on the same evidently unforgettable motive, with an interesting revelation of his frail health in boyhood added as countersubject: "You are doing more moving than I did when I came here last October; and I congratulate you, even in the face of family troubles, that you are not propelled by the familiar and irrepressible Bed Bug. There is nothing in the world just like him, and I get such comfort from the thought that he is not with me in this house that I can wind my longest toes around the rods of my bed and make fun of insomnia. I am fortunate, however, in this respect; it is very seldom that I lie awake for more than two hours after I 'disrobe and tumble in', as my neighbor in Oxford Street expressed it, and that is too slight a matter to worry over. When I was a small boy I used to lie awake pretty much all the time, wondering if the shin-bones of all the rest of the world ached as mine did. I used to grow about an inch in seven minutes when I was a boy, and I suppose that fact accounts for my graceless elongation at the present time. If ever you have a boy who grows in this fashion, knock him kindly but effectively on his head and let the funeral be private. If you let him live, he will never amount to a damn."

In the letters of these first months in New York Robinson some-

times solaces his homesickness with daydreams of that boyhood of
his in the fresh air and quiet of Gardiner, Maine. Once when as a
boy he was eating apples in Gardiner, he told Ridgely Torrence, he
heard a bystander wondering how many apples a boy could eat.
He counted the cores beside him and found thirty. "And," he
proudly added, "I hadn't really begun, either." Here is a letter
worth giving entire.

"26 November, 1899

"Dear Mason. . . . Last week we had the *Fourth Symphony* of
Brahms and it took hold of me like the jaws of something—something that never lets go. I heard it eight years ago in Boston but
kept nothing of it but big vague memory of the second movement.
If I could hear it once a week for the next three months, I would
pay the price of admission, even at the expense of apples. Speaking
of apples, I have a permanent dago around the corner who sells me
three big Northern Spies for five cents—the same as those I used to
eat at home twenty years ago—before I ever questioned the un-
qualified greatness of Mr. Poe's *Raven*—and I have occasional nos-
talgic disturbances after eating them. I have tried sometimes to look
on apples as a thing that we should outgrow—like circus lemonade
—but I have not yet been able to put down the old bucolic appetite
for Spies, Belfleurs (they should be Bell-Flowers), Baldwins, and
Seek-no-Farthers. I never cared such a devil of a lot for Kings and
Greenings, but for the others I was always sore anhungered. As I
analyze my feelings while eating them, I have to confess that my
satisfaction is more than half sentiment. The Virgillian *rusticus es*
in me will not be killed. And on the whole I am not altogether certain that I wish to kill it. I remember one rainy afternoon, the deuce
knows how long ago, when I went down to the orchard with a tin
pail and an umbrella and got Gravensteins. When I got back I
washed off the dried grass and the mud and had a solitary orgy by
the fire. After I had eaten about ten I began to blow scales on the
clarinet. I have not a doubt but that I ate an enormous supper that
night and read *The Raven* with an unaccustomed force, and I may
have added *Lochiel's Warning* and *The Cataract of Lodore*. The

Truman H. Bartlett
From a photograph by the Author

clarinet blowing, however, never amounted to much, and later when I had a machine of my own I never succeeded in getting anywhere with it. I could do *The Flying Trapeze* and *Abide With Me* pretty well, but I could never do the march in *The Prophet*—not because I couldn't finger it, but because I got tangled up in trying to read it. I couldn't get time through my head. . . ."

II

Another friend of those days was "Mr. B." "I am staying," wrote Will Moody to Robert Morss Lovett in August 1900, "with a Mr. Bartlett, ex-sculptor, art critic, and in spite of all a magnificent old goat and man of God." "Immediately on my arrival"—so he wrote me during the same visit—"I was swooped down upon by Mr. Bartlett, and soon transferred bag and baggage to his house, where I am living in undisturbed possession of the upper story. We get our own breakfast and take dinner and supper at the hotel. . . . The old boy is in marvellous form, and stars the passing hours with immortal phrases."[1] Moody's word, "a magnificent old goat" succeeds in suggesting that unique quality of "Old man Bartlett," as we used to call him, or "Père Bartlett"—he was the father of Paul Bartlett the well-known sculptor—or simply, in affectionate diminutive, "Mr. B.", which eludes detailed description. It suggests his skittish independence and unconventionality, his gusto in denunciation of servile respectability, his boyish zest in profanity and in the wildest exaggerations, his passionate prejudices, even somehow his physical aspect: the small bright eyes set wide apart, gleaming with mischief, the two tusks of teeth that did not meet, the pointed grizzling beard over the loose flaps of the open collar, the strong hands with their thumbs powerful to mold the clay, the legs encased in high felt boots against the cold of New Hampshire winters. There was about him always something of the free air, the untrammelled good nature, of his intimate friend Walt Whitman. His voice was another irrecoverable: rasping, raucous, vibrant without sonority, in moments of conviviality or assertion rising to

[1] *Some Letters of William Vaughn Moody*, page 129.

sudden shrillness, full always of chuckles and sly accents that made its harshness delightful—the one inevitable medium for his inspired impudences.

A country boy, he had drifted into stone cutting in the village graveyard, thus attracting the attention of some rich people who sent him to Italy and France to become a sculptor. I remember in early days seeing him at work, in the garret of our house in Boston, on a bust of Jeffries Wyman in clay; but his education had come, I suppose, too late, and he had gradually given up modeling, leaving it to his son Paul. Everything he had, including association with men like Frémiet, Daumier, and other French artists of his student days, and with Walt Whitman and other boldly unconventional fellow-countrymen, he had earned against heavy odds and by an indomitable intellectual curiosity. The natural result was a contempt for facile mediocrities—for what he called "these little tiddy-widdy, two-cent fellers"—which in him was less inhibited by regard for decorum, and more picturesque in expression, than in any other man I have known. He once told me that he had been brought up "like a wild beast", that he had eaten with his knife until he was forty-five, when Mrs. Lombard, to whom he expressed deep gratitude for the lesson, told him at her own table that he "had no manners". In his youth, he said, he had known no better than to wear his hat in the house and to spit on the floor (like Beethoven and other great spirits). Was it any wonder the frequent Philistinism of those who had had the "advantages of education" infuriated him? "When a man like President Eliot," he burst out one day, "advocates one of the damnedest frauds of modern times [St. Gaudens as a great sculptor] what in hell is a plain man to do?" The explosion is interesting for the light it throws, not on St. Gaudens, but on Bartlett. He would ride a prejudice with the same crusading ardor that less daring souls reserve for their convictions. When he was in search of such a "pure hate" as Thoreau thought should "underprop our loves", peddling considerations of reason did not embarrass him; and no one ever followed more whole-heartedly Emerson's advice to write "Whim" on the lintels of the door-post.

Universal education, he said, is "the trotting out of a damn fine thing to a pack of idiots". The State he considered "a necessarily constructed bugaboo for the regulation of fools". The fellow-townsmen of his admired Emerson and Thoreau he once referred to as "those caked and costive Concordians". For New Englanders, indeed, having the misfortune to be one himself, he seemed to reserve a special venom. "I never saw a New Englander yet," he said, "who had his navel-string untied. They're all bound up." And when someone quoted, "God is his own interpreter," he remarked: "That's awfully hard on the average New Englander, who wants to do it all himself." I described to him once the preface in a book of Professor George H. Palmer's I had been reading. His comment was: "Seems as if he'd undertaken a good deal—loaded himself right up, you know. No wonder his head is bald." "Of course," he writes in a letter thanking me for some books, "I shall find loads of good, especially out of Royce, next Thoreau, and then Johnny B. [John Burroughs]. Perhaps he is getting a little moss-covered, with here and there a sprout of vanity that disturbs—for instance, he lets his picture be taken for publication. Walt did so too, but he was a Being, and every phase of his physiognomy revealed." The delicacy of his literary instinct is shown in this scribble on a post-card: "Found F. B. Sanborn's *Life of Thoreau*. Can't read it. Something about it that shocks me. Wonder how it strikes you. Poison ivy running its deathly wind round a rose tree. T. H. B." I showed him Edward Carpenter's *Civilization: Its Cause and Cure*. Mr. B.: "Just like an Englishman—Anglo-saxon all over to have a cure ready for anything. As if it *had* any cure. Let it wobble on! Cure! Reminds me of a horse doctor. [Long pause] Spavin!"

The indescribable fascination of his mind, however, lay only partly in his uninhibited scoffing, liberating as that was, but rather in the queer combination of scoffing with poetic insight, as when someone compared the moss festoons on a tree to jewelry work, and he came back like a flash with "Yes, my boy, the work of the high and mighty jeweler—the Feller that Sneers at Everything". The two sides of his mind, the scoffing and the poetic, were as bafflingly intermingled as the two halves of his vocabularly—the rudely colloquial, slangy, profane, and the fastidiously fine and distin-

guished. One recalls such inspired use of language as his pointing to
the darkening hills of an autumn sunset and saying: "Look at the
gravity of those mountains!" It was that quality that Moody had in
mind (he who shared it so richly) when he wrote me in August,
1901: "If by good luck this finds you at Chocorua, greet for me
the grand old man and his pals the mountains. Cull for me a morning phrase, big as Whiteface and dewy as those morning glories on
the projected and now I trust realized pergola."

The affinity between these two minds, the younger man's so powerfully implemented, the older one's so seriously disadvantaged in
education but by nature so richly endowed, is felt not only in their
instinctive sympathy for each other, but in the spontaneity with
which both struck out their bold inevitable metaphors. "The man's
audacity," cried Bartlett admiringly of Moody's *Masque of Judgment*, "is overpowering. The way he has the Angel of the Pale
Horse scooting around!" "Moody is a treasure," he told me another
day, "and I've got my rake out for more. All this comes of having
a lingering, infantile, incipient love for literature."

Like all really strong natures he felt instinctively that activity is
more important than results, that what we work for is the process
itself, not its products. How inspiringly he could express this insight, with what Moodyesque force and originality of metaphor, a
few examples will show.

"It doesn't make a damn bit of difference whether your opinion
is the true one or not; it's giving your mind a chance and having it
act that counts. Give it room for activity. If you have a damn fine
trotting horse, you don't run him over ploughed ground. You make
a track for him."

Someone was spoken of as having "put his foot in it". Mr. B.:
"No one can step, my boy, without putting his foot in it. That's all
right. But what is wrong is thinking that when our foot is all covered with mud, we can wrap it up in someone's handkerchief."

I quoted Clough's couplet:

It fortifies my soul to know
That though I perish, truth is so.

Mr. B.: "Yes, but what *is* truth? Every man piles up his little heap of stones and sticks a red flag on top of it. Everything is relative. And that's a comfort, too, because, by jingo, it keeps a man from nailing himself up like a woodchuck skin on a barn-door to dry."

We agitated the old question of continuity of intellectual and artistic history versus individualism. He finally permitted me to keep my "little landmarks" as he called them, but said that *his* experience had been with men so great that they didn't fall into such classifications at all. "Well," said I, "that impresses me as it would you if I said that although stones often fall to the ground when thrown up, *I* had seen some that didn't." "Well," says he with his most lovable grin, "there *are* some stones that are so damned handsome they *do* stay up—held up by angel's wings!"

Of Royce's book, *The Conception of Immortality:* "There's old Royce, getting dirt behind him, making a place for sin-sick souls to stand on. He's making a little place for your feet. That's invaluable. No matter how your head whirls, or your heart flutters, so long as you've got a little sure place for your feet!"

III

Mr. Bartlett's house was as original as his mind. Indeed, it was rather like it. His sociality, generosity, and width of interest were symbolized in the life-masks, death-masks, casts of hands, and photographs of his two chief hobbies, Greek sculpture and Lincoln, that covered the walls, and in the texts and quotations that he wrote in pencil on their unvarnished pine boards. There was comfort, even luxury (in spots), without any special attempt at order. Above all there was perfect freedom for all who came, and any young man seriously interested in any of the arts was welcome. Moody spent several months in 1899, Walter Griffin the painter came off and on, I represented music, somewhat after my time Edwin Arlington Robinson spent, I believe, the entire summer of 1910, and there were others. "I wish you could see us breakfast," I find myself writing my future wife. "We make rich creamy coffee in a big tin pan, and roast bread and crackers in the oven until they are black, and all the kitchen smells of them. Then we have 'sass', as Mr. B. calls it, of apples or blackberries, and eggs that never get cooked the same way, for we always forget what time we put them in. The butter is in a large dish at the center of the table, and the cleanness of knives and spoons is always hypothetical. We drink out of a common water pail with a tin dipper. The dishes, after breakfast, are roughly washed and piled in the strainer, a little fresh water poured over them, and there they remain until they are called into requisition again the next morning. Similarly, our beds are never made; we get into them at night as we left them in the morning."

Our routine at Chocorua was a simple one. We worked mornings, each in his own quarters. For afternoons there was walking or swimming for the more active, carpentry, photography, or billiards for the sedentary. The evenings were sacred to talk and bézique, for which Mr. B. had a boundless zest. If you told him it was immoral for him to make such a big score he would give you his most Bacchic smile and agree: "Immoral? Positively obscene." If you asked him if you might open the window, he would cry, "Take out the side of the house!" But if you tried to write a letter, especially at the ritual hour of go-to-bed-lunch, he would call from the kitchen in his cracked voice: "Come on, my boy. Don't go fol-de-roling there. Tend to business!"

The outside of the house was characteristic too. The useful, in the shape of hogsheads for water and such homely objects, was oddly juxtaposed with the ornamental, of which the chief monument was the long-projected pergola, realized after my time. And then there was the ten-foot fence. Thereby hangs a tale, for the truth of which I will not vouch. Dr. Chadwick was the patron who was supposed to foot most of Mr. B.'s bills. Someone asked him once why he supported "that old reprobate", and his reply was that while some men maintained steam yachts, he got more fun out of maintaining Mr. B. . . . To the house and land, as they were close to his own, he naturally gave only a life interest; and that, says rumor, did not satisfy

Mr. B., who wanted to will them away. It was when this was re-fused that he retorted with the ten-foot fence, to hide from his eyes the estate of the erring Chadwick, also greeting his dog with stones whenever he ventured near. It might well be. One wonders too whether the Chocorua trades-people, not always, according to ru-mor again, promptly paid for the beefsteaks we ate so blithely, con-sidered "old man Bartlett" as generous as we did. Idle questions! What would he have been without his inspired inconsistencies? His climate was naturally gusty. "Mother Kenerson," he writes in 1913 of his housekeeper through long years, "played out a year ago, and turned out as I had long suspected one of the most adroit tricksters I have ever seen. Queen of hypocrites. It's truly great to see excel-lence of any kind in an abandoned farm locality."

Of this almost superhuman power of prejudice the supreme epic is no doubt the newt story. It seems that in his student years in France some friend advised him to have a rose garden, an enterprise on which he embarked with his usual enthusiasm. Meeting him a little later, and hearing that the roses were flourishing, his friend cau-tioned him to beware of newts, those pests that destroy rose-plants. The next time they met, Mr. B. wore a different face, one gathering gloom. "Well, Bartlett, how is the rose garden?" "Ruined," groaned Mr. B., "ruined by those damned newts." "What," said the friend, "got at it, did they?" "Ruined it," shouted Mr. B., "I dug up the whole garden looking for them, and there wasn't a damned newt there!"

To those who did not live through, as impecunious and unknown young artists, the desolate period of the nineties in American civili-zation, it is hard to make clear all that Moody, Robinson, and I—and many others—owed to the generous understanding, the inspiring friendship, of our beloved Mr. B. But perhaps they can divine it if I end my account of him by reprinting a letter he wrote me at a time when, as a contributor to the *Outlook*, I had suffered some rather un-discerning criticism from one of its editors, that agreeable man but rather conventional writer, Hamilton W. Mabie. I will make no at-tempt to tone down its genial scurrility.

"Your state of intense disgust with work is perfectly natural, com-

mon, and you will get over it too; that is, as soon as you get it diag-
nosed and understand its nature you wont bother about it. . . .
Everybody works for ultimate results, and often the best fruit
doesn't ripen till late, say at the age of 300. When the aspiring soul
runs up agin Hamilton M. he strikes the largest amount of rot in the
literary line now living, C. D. Warner having 'passed on.'

"This affair will teach you two good truths. First, that there is always some idiot attached to a popular publication, and second, what
tribulation every decent soul has to go through in trying to do anything sincere and genuine. You are beginning to smell sulphur, and
you want to suck the sweet side of the orange.

"Poor American sculpture doesn't appeal to me, but it is my business to *know* without prejudice just what its rot consists of, and I
do. My sympathies are pleased with good work, while the necessity
of knowing what is bad is a bit of coldblooded castor oil. And the
court takes it. ["The court" was a whimsical phrase by which Mr.
B. referred to himself.]

"You are a trifle over-anxious about accomplishing. In the first
place you have *lived*—in good air—that's something. Again, you
have been occupied in good directions as much as you were able.
That's much. Thirdly, you wish to do well. That's fine. Now, it's
commonplace to say, keep at it as far as your strength will permit,
and don't worry about the result.

"You have worlds of practical life to learn; to find out why all
the concentrated sentences of the best minds are based on blood,
grief, and martyrdom. The literary charm of these sentences is pure
mist in comparison to what *caused* them to be said. It is that aspect
of life that you need and will get, to your great good, and Hamilton
M. is giving the first dose. Dan, my dear, I have lived through forty
years of such stuff, 1,000,000,000,000 times *wuss*—and yet I chirp
like a baby chipmunk.

"Again, the subject of American composers is a serious one, and
worth all respect. You are one yourself. Sail in; H. M. wont hurt
you.

"Emerson is rotten with good things, but he nailed them with
cold hands and an empty stomach. Think of his going lecturing in

the wilderness of Illinois, in 1855, for fifty dollars a night, eating tough pork, sleeping in a cold room, and obliged to be pleasant with idiots. Every sentence of his cost Pain. That's the price he paid for being remembered by you and me. Cheer up and go ahead.

"Ever yours, T. H. B."

CHAPTER VII

"FROM GRIEG TO BRAHMS"

"CHEER up and go ahead": the advice was good, but not entirely easy to put in practice for a young man with rapidly fading financial prospects, interests perplexingly divided between music and writing, and a lame arm that made remunerative work in music next to impossible, and in writing difficult. For the next six years accordingly, as it turned out, from that spring of '96 when I gave up my first venture into New York and into music, until that of 1902, when the articles eventually forming my first book, *From Grieg to Brahms*, began to appear in the *Outlook* magazine, I was going through that long dark tunnel in my life I have already described. Those six years made a baffling, interminable, sometimes almost unendurable period of trial and error—especially error. They were my first conscious facing of the agonizing alternative between the two horns of the dilemma: writing-plus-livelihood *versus* music-minus-livelihood-but-plus-happiness, which my whole life has been a not very successful effort to resolve.

The purely literary side was represented for me by Thoreau, for whom I had as ardent a hero-worship as for Brahms. In 1897 I published in the *Harvard Monthly* an essay on *The Idealistic Basis of Thoreau's Genius* which won me the friendship of the best of the Thoreau biographers, Henry S. Salt, tireless humanitarian and reformer, crusty critic of English life in his *Seventy Years Among Savages* and many other books, still living, as these lines are written, at well over eighty, partly paralyzed but not discouraged. "I am a socialist and a vegetarian," he wrote me early in 1898, "and many other things which are regarded as wickedness or lunacy." He still is!

An amusing contrast to Salt, so fastidious and distinguished, was his friend and fellow-student of Thoreau, Dr. Samuel A. Jones, a man with the energetic enthusiasm of a school-boy, convivial, voluble, chatty, slangy, but withal kind. In the course of his reams of letters to me (now preserved in Professor Raymond Adams's collection of Thoreauana at the University of North Carolina) was a sentence I shall never forget, it so turned the knife in the wound of my indecision. "You cannot serve both God and Mammon," it said, meaning both letters and music. "The beautiful tinkle dies in the ear, and the ear is filled with dust some day. But the written word liveth forever. Take the plain hint of fate: your arm is disabled; music must be not a pursuit but a pastime."

Meanwhile my friend Savage, as ardent a Thoreauvian as I, obtained for me a commission to write a twenty-thousand-word *Life of Thoreau* for the *Beacon Biographies*. I was to receive for the finished manuscript one hundred and fifty dollars, by no means a negligible sum to me in those days. And at the hospitable house of "Mr. B." in Chocorua already described I did actually draft the twenty thousand words. But I did not think much of them; they seemed tame and pallid—a poor substitute for a single strain of melody. And Will Moody was all the while advising me in precisely the opposite sense from Dr. Jones. He was pointing out that it was hardly fair to compare critical prose, which was all I could do in literature, with the imaginative creation of which he thought me capable in music. Once after I had played him one of my sonatas he exclaimed with his usual picturesque hyperbole: "If I could do that I should let Thoreau rot." And his memorable summary of my situation was: "For you to give up music for 'letters' is for an oyster to renounce pearl-making in order to devote its energies to the composition of seaweed pills. I hasten to add that this isn't saying a damn against the pills." [1]

What should I do? . . . To a young fellow with a lame arm and next-to-nothing a year, pearls seemed for the moment out of reach. Yet I could not forget that Thoreau himself had said: "To please our friends and relatives we turn out our silver ore in cartloads, while we neglect to work our mines of gold, far up in the Sierras, where we pulled up a bush in our mountain walk, and saw the glittering treasure. Let us return thither. Let it be the price of our freedom to make that known." Also there was that terrifying poem of Emerson's, *Days*. . . . Thank heaven I eventually summoned enough foresightedness to renounce, not the pearls, but the pills. I have always been glad I found the courage to burn the twenty thousand words and to say goodbye to the hundred and fifty dollars. I am even glad I did not resist the temptation to write and ask Dr. Jones what became of the "tinkle" that died in Beethoven's ear.

II

The next step was gradually to work my way back into music: not yet into composition, of course, that was too much to hope for; but at least into writing *about* music, which was better than nothing. The problem was somehow to turn to practical use certain insights and deep convictions that by the turn of the century had formed themselves clearly in my mind, and that since then have never essentially changed. "It is a satisfaction," says Thoreau, "to find that our oldest convictions are permanent, resting with more than mountain breadth and weight on the world, the source still of fertilizing streams, and affording glorious views from their summits if we can get up to them again." Similarly, reversing one's gaze sometimes to look backward from present to past, it is satisfying to find one's mature convictions voiced, with whatever crudity, in the falsetto of one's youthful words, when their glory first burst upon one, and in the excitement one proclaimed them with almost hysterical fervor.

[1] *Some Letters of William Vaughn Moody,* page 80.

Now one of my deepest convictions has always been a sense of the supreme value in art of balance, restraint, proportion—in a word, of classic beauty. Hence my lifelong adoration of men like Bach, Mozart, Schubert, Beethoven, Brahms, in whom this ideal is supremely realized. Contrariwise I have always felt an instinctive antipathy toward excess, unbalance, romantic exaggeration, sensationalism, typified for me in such composers, great artists though they be, as Wagner, Tschaikowsky, Liszt, Strauss. Therefore it amuses, and yet a little thrills me, deciphering from the unformed boyish handwriting of my early journals those old callow enthusiasms and priggish exclusions, to recognize even in them the same convictions, struggling to birth. On Thanksgiving Eve of my first New York autumn, for instance, I was repelled, exasperated, and bored (as, if I am to be honest, I must confess I have been on all subsequent occasions) by a performance of *Tristan und Isolde*. Recognizing its technical mastery, I yet felt stifled and a little nauseated in its overheated atmosphere—its "sentimentality", to borrow Meredith's immortal phrase, "fiddling harmonics on the harp-strings of sensuality". Accordingly, with the headstrong excess a boy likes to indulge, I celebrated Thanksgiving by writing in my journal: "Thank God Wagner is dead, and thank God Brahms is alive. And here's to the great classical revival of the twentieth century in America!" I even appended a ludicrously primitive sketch (for I have never been able to draw) of a ship marked in large capitals ART, between a Scylla labelled "Mawkish hysteria and constructive license", and a Charybdis labelled "Acid pedantry and practical utilitarianism", adding below "Three cheers for Captain Brahms." And at the time of Brahms's death, April 1897, I gave a whole page, surrounded with a mourning line ruled in black ink, to the inscription: "Brahms died:—the last great conserver of the classic spirit in music."

If I allow myself to exhibit, not without blushes, these early ebullitions of fatuity, it is because precisely what I want to show is this subjectivity of these early feelings that now had somehow to find their way out into the practical world of reality. They were I hope not utterly despicable, since they were sincere; but they had to normalize themselves by contact with actual life. To this health-giving egress they were helped by a casual suggestion made by a Harvard classmate of my brother Harry's, William P. Daniels, a man of rare cultivation. "There is a glorious field," he urged, "absolutely unopened thus far, for the man who will tell educated people what music is, what its place and relations are, in words they can understand. There is a chance for sense on music, couched in good prose."

My mind was ready to fertilize this seed. Though the idea of essays on music was not, to be sure, new to me, and I had even published in the *Harvard Monthly* as an undergraduate a paper on *Robert Schumann's Relation to Romanticism*,[1] I now began to think more practically about the possibilities of such work, both as to its immediate help in solving my economic problems and as to its more gradual effect in helping to mold standards of public taste.

I tried writing a sort of confession of faith called *Two Tendencies in Modern Music*, in which I illustrated the tendency to sensationalism by Tschaikowsky (whose music nevertheless I have always admired) and the tendency to classic balance, or, as I preferred simply to call it, beauty, in which all hope of a fine future seemed to me to lie, by Brahms. This got a step further than the romanticism paper toward ultimate clearness, but was even more uncompromising. No easy matter was it to place in a commercial magazine, and to be paid for, a paper running so counter to fashions then prevailing in musical aesthetics.

---

[1] This little essay, never reprinted, was an attempt to expound romanticism in terms of Browning's answer to his own question, "Greek Art and what more wish you?" His answer is

> To become now self-acquainters,
> And paint man, man, whatever the issue!
> Make new hopes shine through the flesh they fray,
> New fears aggrandize the rags and tatters:
> To bring the invisible full into play!
> Let the visible go to the dogs—what matters?

My paper insists that the future progress of the arts, already adumbrated in the work of Browning and Brahms, must be in the direction of expressing the romantic message in classic forms, and concludes: "Then shall we be travelling the path that leads to an art at once transcendental, beautiful, and perfect." I was young then!

Even so convinced a classicist as Arthur Whiting, who generously offered to read, criticize, and help me place it, was doubtful as to how the public would receive it. "The general reader," he wrote me, "will not appreciate the full beauty of it, and for a magazine article I should try to get the vulgar standpoint a bit more; that is, try to see it as the commoner will see it. With him, your descriptive words will incline him still more to the 'expressive' side, as he has no interest in 'symmetry' or 'device' in art. The word *dry* will frighten him, even if you balance it by applying *putrid* to Tschaikowsky. [Which I did not do; this was one of Arthur's jokes.] To the vulgar one the vices of Tschaikowsky are endearing, while the virtues of Brahms are chilling; so that, if you are writing for him, don't suggest the prodigal and elder brother too vividly.

"I salute you!—the spokesman of our subtle art.

"I advise these few modifications for the benighted and hope you will be able to make them. Then I will write to Abbott of the *Outlook* or Johnson of the *Century* if you wish."

As a pupil I fear I was never docile, often refractory, and sometimes maddening. This must have been one of the times. I agreed that one should clarify one's subject as far as possible, but insisted that if one makes hard things easy one defeats one's purpose and emasculates one's readers. "People have got to learn," I went on, thumping the pulpit a little, "to look at music as an art and not a belch of emotion, and the sooner they begin to handle such conceptions as 'symmetry' and 'form' the better." And I ended by inquiring: "Do you think Abbott would like a short article on Brahms? If so, how long and how treated? (Also how paid?!)"

Arthur's answer, not unnaturally, was brief and to the point. "I enclose your letter, hoping that if you still have mine you will be able to see how completely you misunderstand my suggestion for getting the public to understand your meaning. If you still see a suggestion to 'popularize a subject in the sense of vulgarizing or degrading it' in my note, letter-writing at least is a hopeless medium of communication for us.

"Abbott wants an article on Brahms and will no doubt be willing to give his ideas of what it should be like if you write to him."

Eventually the *Two Tendencies* appeared in the *Atlantic Monthly* for February, 1902, and I was commissioned by Lawrence F. Abbott, one of the best and kindest of men and a true music-lover, to write an article on Brahms for the *Outlook* of January 4, 1902. This was followed through the year by others on Grieg, Dvořák, Saint-Saëns, Franck, and Tschaikowsky, and by two of a more general nature, *The Meaning of Music*, and *The Appreciation of Music*. It is worth recording that at the beginning of the century a general weekly magazine was willing to print so serious a group of studies in a non-utilitarian subject like music; the *Outlook* gave up the practice a few years after this; one wonders where such papers now, if anyone wanted to write them, could find publication. However that may be it was lucky for me that I could find a market for my wares. It fixed and strengthened me in the new path by enabling me through work I felt to be worth doing for itself to earn an income, small to be sure, but having the invaluable quality Stevenson desiderates in incomes—that of "coming in."

Later I revised the entire series of essays and combined them in a book, which appeared in time for Christmas with the unfortunate title, *From Grieg to Brahms*. It was a name no one was to be blamed for not understanding, since it arranged the composers in an order not even chronological. To tell the truth I was still preoccupied with the hierarchy of aesthetic values suggested in the earlier *Two Tendencies*, by which objective imagination and impersonal beauty are of higher nature than romantic fancy and personal whim; and I tried to explain in my preface that when we estimate the composers by their scope and intrinsic importance we are obliged to pass from Grieg the charming lyricist to Brahms the great dramatic and epic master. But so comparative a method undoubtedly gave a certain aid and comfort to that very tendency to regard artists as competitors, instead of the peers, each unique, they really are, which is the bane of most music criticism; and Henry T. Finck of the *New York Evening Post*, who could usually be counted on to be wrong, was right for once when he found my lay-out offensively like "a rank-list". My title was thus misleading; and to people unfamiliar with musical proper names it could be incomprehensible. One New England library catalogued the book under "Geography".

III

In spite of the title the book took hold well, and has made many friends from that day to this. Even before it appeared as a book, but while the articles were running in the *Outlook*, I found in my mail one morning a letter in an interestingly foreign-looking envelope, imprinted *"Le Grand Hotel, Bruxelles"*. Wondering who could be writing me from there, I opened it up and found, at the end of two pages of rather crabbed handwriting, the name, long admired from afar, of Charles Villiers Stanford. No one had done more for English music (or perhaps, in view of his being Irish I ought to say for British music); no one in England had better understood Brahms. It was encouraging to read:

"50 Holland Street
"Kensington. London, W
"Ap 7, 1902

"My dear Sir: Passing through Brussels tonight I picked up a copy of the Outlook Magazine containing an article of yours of the greatest interest on Johannes Brahms. I should like to thank you for it, because in these days of almost hysterical worship of the realistic, it strikes exactly the healthy note which we want. The term "academic" which has been worked to death as a kind of term of reproach for everyone who takes the trouble to know his technique before he foists his work on the world has been too often lately applied to Brahms as the Arch-Academic. Yours is an admirable counterblast to this view. I knew Brahms well enough to know how true your view of him is. There are one or two tiny mistakes in the article: e.g. the remark about Strauss' Blue Danube was written, not in the Album of Strauss' daughter, but on the fan of Strauss' wife. *Liebestreu* Op. 3, which I see you mention in the note, is the identical song which he showed to Joachim at Hanover in the early 50's, and which Joachim sent on to Schumann at Dusseldorf and elicited the famous dictum of S. that 'the one whom he had long awaited had now arrived'. 'Er dass ich so lang erwartet hat ist jetzt da' were the words if I remember rightly. I have often heard the account straight from Joachim himself. He gets too little of the credit which attached to Brahms' 'discovery', if you can apply such a term to the first sight of work which was obviously epoch-making.

"Excuse my writing to you a stranger but perhaps you know my name. I felt grateful for your excellently expressed words, and feel sure that they will do good: and I am lucky to have come across them tonight by accident in the reading room of a hotel where I am only for one night!"

A month later came another welcome letter from England. With Edward Carpenter I had already had some correspondence in the hope of meeting him during a short trip I had made to England the year before; but plans had come to nothing, and I had remained

merely an admirer of his books, which were doing for us young
men something the same liberating service Walt Whitman's had
done a generation earlier. He now wrote me:

> "Millthorpe, Holmesfield, near Sheffield
> "11 May, 1902

"Dear Mr. Mason

"I am very much obliged to you for sending me your articles in
the *Atlantic Monthly* and the *Outlook*. I had seen and read the *Two
Tendencies* before, and thought it good; but the *Meaning* of course
gives the key to the other. Music, as Schopenhauer showed . . .
gives the key to the interpretation of the universe, so much more intimately and directly than the other arts; but so few musicians
hitherto have been philosophers or literary folk. Your suggestion of
how art (by a prudent exclusion) leads us to behold that unity of
things which is Beauty is very good.

"I hope your health, my friend, is better than it was. I am
pleased to think that my books have been so helpful to you. . . ."

Early the following year, after I had sent him a copy of the complete book, and also a copy of my *Elegy* for piano (the same that
Gabrilowitsch later played so widely) he wrote a most friendly letter, praising the "broad handling" of the subjects, the "clear sympathy with different sides and characters", and the style—which he
thought "all the better and rarer for being free of many modern
affectations". But he rather spoiled the effect of all this, from my
point of view (and the reader, remembering the dilemma between
music and writing in which I was still struggling, may perhaps have
a smile of sympathy to spare for me) by adding: "I do not somehow
feel that inspiration in your *Elegy* which I am sensible of in your
writing. Somehow I think your real self comes out more spontaneously in your literature than in your music." Fortunately for my
peace of mind he went on: "However I do not lay very great store
by my own opinion, especially as regards modern music. I confess
I find a good deal of Brahms terribly dry, and sometimes regret that
he gave up the splendidly romantic vein of his early sonatas—so you

see you find yourself in good company!" I certainly did; and as I happened to like those turgid early sonatas less than anything else of Brahms's I knew—except possibly the *C minor Piano Quartet*—I took comfort to go ahead with my own brand of "dryness". . . . The letter ended in the writer's kindest, most friendly vein: "Anyhow you will write what you feel constrained to—and you cannot go wrong there. . . . Well, no more now. It is a great pleasure to me, dear friend, to know that some of my work (*Love's Coming of Age*, for example) has touched you so nearly. . . . Blessings on you and all good wishes."

There was a forthright affectionateness in Carpenter that could warm the heart even of one who had never seen him.

Whiting had continued his good offices by sending some of my articles to his friend—soon to be mine too—W. H. Hadow, later Sir Henry Hadow, that delightfully cultivated Oxford don who wrote *Studies in Modern Music*.

"It seems to be now or never," Arthur wrote me, "to acknowledge your last letter in which you warn me against *The Meaning of Music*. You mistook your man in this as I was highly edified by, and entirely responsive to, it. (This last comes from having literary friends.) I think the piece completely justifies itself, if not its name —this seems to belong to something else, perhaps to your next essay; but we won't quarrel about the label when the liquor is so good.

"This sort of thing, rhapsodical and erudite, is a necessity and will help bury the Hales and Hunekers.

"I sent your articles to Hadow, and enclose his reply. I hope you will have a good summer, and never, never write for a newspaper."

The Hadow enclosure has been lost, but in the summer of 1903 Hadow himself came to America, and fascinated us all. I find in my journal this snapshot.

"Colonial Club, Cambridge, August 19. Hadow lunched with me here. He is very English, with a strong accent, rather ruddy color, fine yellowish moustache, blue, kindly eyes set wide apart, and a sensitive mouth. The most striking feature of his face is the fine domed brow, the brow of a thinker, which is impressive when compared with his mouth, more that of an artist. He is a remarkably handsome man, with an especially noble profile. He reminded me of Stevenson, in spite of the entirely different coloring.

"He talks in a loud voice, with a good deal of the English sing-song. I was talking with another man in the path when he came, and when I asked him if he would wait a moment on the piazza he said "Rather!" with a broad A, highly inflected.

"He finds Strauss extremely interesting, thinks he has enlarged the 'dictionary' of the musical language, and writes wonderful poly-phony, when it 'comes off'. His main criticism is a lack of really fine themes, but he is very hesitant about making any adverse criticism, well saying that adverse criticism of new tendencies is nearly always wrong. He thinks Strauss will tire of pictorial music, and show us what the next step in the symphony is.

"He heard Fauré conduct one of his operas. 'Nice old man, but nobody paid any attention to the music.' Spoke of the utter lack of understanding by the French of writing music for their own language. 'If possible they put a dotted minim at the beginning of a bar on "*le*", "*et*", of the final "*e*" of a feminine word!'

"He has no use for MacDowell. 'Eight times as much music in Whiting'.

"He met Brahms and saw something of him. Brahms treated him very well, possibly because he had a letter from Joachim. Stanford's article he praised as giving a highly just impression of Brahms. I asked him if Brahms's conversation did not reveal humor, and he said not only that but great width of interest."

Hadow told us an amusing story about his first lecture at the Royal Institution in London. He was a young man, highly nervous in the face of the novel experience. He seemed to have made a fair start when everybody's attention was distracted by a most dignified, distinguished-looking old gentleman who slowly made his way down the aisle, found a seat in one of the front rows almost below the nose of the lecturer, and proceeded to draw out of a back pocket a formidable-looking ear-trumpet, in two sections, which he slowly screwed together and pointed at Hadow. And as if this were not enough, just as poor Hadow was getting used to it and accepting the inevitable, with equal slowness he took down the ear-trumpet, deliberately unscrewed it, and replaced it in his back pocket.

At the end of 1902 Hadow wrote me with his customary amenity: "My dear Mason: *Bis dat qui tempestive dat.* [He gives twice who gives opportunely.] I got your book on Christmas Eve just as I was starting off for home, and found it the most delightful of travelling companions. . . . It was very pleasant to renew acquaintance with the old friends in the volume, and to be introduced by them to the rest. Here's a merry Christmas to the company; and many a happy new edition." He went on to an estimate of Strauss worth preserving.

"We're all being exercised over here about Richard Strauss. How does he strike you on your side? I've heard little of him as yet: but I've been working at the score of *Heldenleben* with immense interest. I don't care twopence about his poetic basis—anyone can write programme-music—but his technique is full of problems. At present he strikes me as a sort of Monteverde smashing away at the accepted grammar in order that a looser and more flexible language may result: but the immediate effect is that there are a good many passages in him which don't construe. In short he seems to me essentially a pioneer—a discoverer: and to say that is (on all historical analogy) to deny that he is a great artist. Bach and Beethoven invented nothing: they organised and governed country already won. This man will make possible some immense future development of the art: but I very much doubt whether his own work will endure. However this is a very tentative opinion which, no doubt, I shall have to revise later on."

Of all English musicians the one I admired most cordially at this time (and have never ceased to admire) was Sir Hubert Parry. I could never, to be sure, find very much in his compositions, though I made an attempt to study his much-praised choral work, *Blest Pair of Sirens*, and some of his *Choral Preludes* for organ, which, from a Bachian of his discernment, ought to have been better than to me they seemed. But as a writer, a critic, an uncompromising upholder of fine traditions in a lax time, a character of singular

transparence and nobility, no one could help admiring Hubert
Parry. How full of shrewd wisdom, even more applicable to musical conditions now than when he wrote them, are the chapters on
the influence of audiences on taste in his *Style in Musical Art*! How
inspiring is his analysis, in his great study of Bach, of the place of
tradition and workmanship in the work of a great genius—above all
of the greatest genius! It is a striking instance of the importance of
qualities of character and spirit in artistic work that even those who,
like me, cannot admire Parry's compositions, almost revere him as an
influence in the renascence of English music.

It was in November of 1902, after I had sent him some of my articles, and told him how much his work, especially *The Evolution
of the Art of Music*, had meant to me, that I got from him a cordial
letter, written on Royal College of Music paper.

"I was very much pleased," he said, "to get your kind and friendly
letter. That sort of thing helps one along." (He was at this time, the
reader will remember, one of the most influential and respected
musicians in England; and he was writing, not only to an American,
but to a young student as yet but slightly known.) "The apprecia-
tions of both Grieg and Brahms," he continues with the same cordiality, "are quite admirable, and *The Meaning of Music* is just after
my own heart." And with his fine modesty he actually goes on to
say: "I only wish I could express myself half so well." The sentence
is worth quoting if only to show how free of that "certain conde-
scension in foreigners" even a Briton can be, if only, like Parry, he is
a true intellectual aristocrat. His own style, as all music-lovers know,
if sometimes a little diffuse, is always noble and finely balanced.

He was shrewd as well as modest, too, nor was there ever any
stodginess in his peculiarly British dignity—he had too detached an
intelligence for that. There is an anecdote, hitherto unpublished so
far as I know, of how he was once conducting the student orchestra
of the Royal College of Music, of which he was Director, when the
persistent playing out of tune of one of the violinists so annoyed
him that he was at last compelled to ask the young man to leave the
hall. As the boy passed out of the door, thinking Parry's back was
safely turned, he placed his hands to his nose, tandem, and pointed

towards the conductor. "My boy," said Parry, "don't you know that parallel fifths are not permitted in this building?"

IV

THREE of the most prized letters my book brought me were from my own countrymen. One, addressed not to me but to his old friend my uncle, Dr. William Mason, was signed with the august name of Theodore Thomas, and was worthy of him in its spartan spareness.

"Dear William:

"It may please you to know the impression the studies *From Grieg to Brahms* made on me. I read the book with interest. Of course Daniel Mason is a young man, but shows knowledge and talent. When he has learned to condense his style, he can be of much benefit to the cause of music in his country. He is the first of a kind, and shows the soil he sprang from. It is not necessary to agree with him in everything—the world moves, and we with it—but I hope he may develop and remain sincere."

The second letter is from an equally great artist of entirely different temperament: Abbott H. Thayer the painter. With him I had had several meetings at his house in Dublin, New Hampshire, where his own genius and charm stood out incongruously against the extreme disorder of his surroundings (I recall a pair of rubber boots on the dining table). I do not wonder he mislaid one of my articles; the wonder is that he held the other long enough to read it; but these details melt away in the recollection of his generosity and warmth of spirit, his passionate devotion to the classic universality of true art.

"Monadnock, N. H.
"April 27 [Doubtless 1903]
"My dear Dan Mason

"Imagine my luxury of heart in sitting down to write you, when I explain! Your two *Outlooks* came long ago, when you sent them, and, think of it!—one of our conversations had left a false impression (and by leaving it had robbed me of a detail of the great comfort in you that I felt at our very first talk). It was: that you were proving to balance toward the self-expressionists; and when the *Outlooks* came I kept on postponing reading what I thought would be irritating, till two days ago. Of course I was also eye-tired and very busy too.

"Well, how can I manage to get, out of now telling you what your article *is* to me, all the fierce joy I want to?

"I am fifty-three, with all that means of accumulated passion for the Truth, and longing to have Beauty *seen;* and *you write* FOR ME. . . .

"In what are called the great artists but what it were better simply to call the few live souls, the art faculty—or let me begin back. The art faculty is a Being inhabiting a person, and commonly ill-communicant with the rest of this person, somewhat like a plant growing on his lawn,[1] but in the greatest artists, all the rest of the man, his character and his intelligence, is laid out along roads that symmetrically conduct to the high citadel of his art-garrison, so that a call to arms brings all the citizens swarming to its ramparts.

"I am walking on air today with the wealth of a new *eye*.

"Yours always, Abbott H. Thayer

"I ought to tell you that even now I have only read the second part, the other being mislaid. I have written the *Outlook* for the other part."

The third letter, a little too technical and perhaps too complimentary to print here, was from my composition teacher Dr. Percy Goetschius, to whose enthusiastic four-hand Brahms-playing with me at his house in Jamaica Plain, all through those difficult years, I owed a good deal of what has since proved a life-long devotion. I am happy that as these lines are written, thirty-six years later, he is still, at eighty-four, as good a friend of mine as ever, and as eager a Brahmsian.

[1] Compare C. G. Jung, *Modern Man in Search of a Soul,* pages 194–199. D. G. M.

LINES TO MY DEAR FRIEND PERCY GOETSCHIUS

ON HIS EIGHTY-SECOND BIRTHDAY

AUGUST 30, 1935

In the dim dawn of time, in Boston, Mass.,
Lessons I had, like many a youthful ass
From him who loved to try and test and search us—
Our ever-youthful, well-belovèd Goetschius.
(However stupid we, never the worse he,
Enthusiasm's darling, dear old Percy.)

Diminished or augmented, plain or altered,
For all the chords his passion never faltered;
In choral figuration, fugue, or canon,
He taught us to love God, despising Mammon;
And wisely pitiless to all our moans,
Insisted that we must "command the tones"
Even if thus reduced to skin and bones—
Our wits were razors sharpened on his hones.

One popular heresy, thanks to you, dear Goetschius,
None of us youthful asses have to smirch us—
For UGLINESS you never had to birch us!
One truth you taught us outlived all the rest:
"Music hath Brahms to soothe the savage breast."

CHAPTER VIII

POETS

ON JUNE 4, 1899, after an illness of only four days, Philip Henry Savage, the first of our group to go, died at thirty-one. The whole of his short life, outwardly uneventful, had been devoted to the disentangling of his mind from the stifling conventions it had been born into, and to the patient happy search for poetic beauty. In my introduction to his collected poems [1] I quoted some of the sayings that showed us how vigorously he had learned to think for himself:

"Master of a little beauty which, because it is born and bearer of the divine essence, I will cherish at the expense of most of the concerns of life."

"What is true and beautiful is absolute; and what is stupendous and gorgeous and impressive and wonderful is inferior to it."

And as he lay on his death-bed: "A man may attain completion through concentration."

No more perfect lyric has been written in our country than these eight lines of his:

> Brother, Time is a thing how slight!
> Day lifts and falls, and it is night.
> Rome stands an hour, and the green leaf
> Buds into being bright and brief.

[1] *The Poems of Philip Henry Savage*, Boston, 1901.

115

For us, God has at least in store
One shining moment, less or more.
Seize, then, what mellow sun we may,
To light us in the darker day.

II

It was in the fall of that same year, 1899, not long after Robinson's departure for New York, that Moody arrived in Boston from
Chicago for one of his periodical leaves of absence from the university, and established himself in a tiny room perched high on Beacon
Hill in an apartment-house called The Hermitage. There he completed in January 1900 the first of his poetic dramas, *The Masque
of Judgment*. Early that month Robinson wrote me: "Give my regards—what are regards?—to Moody and tell him he made a great
mistake in not coming to New York for a few preliminary whiffs of
Pan-American CO^2 before adjusting his Pierian lights for six
months of Boston ozone. I am looking in all directions for that book
of his." [The volume *Poems*.]

"Will and I lunched together," I wrote in my journal on the
twenty-fifth, "and repaired to his room. He made coffee . . . to
celebrate the fact that he has today

COMPLETED   HIS   MASQUE

and begun to copy it. While he copied I sat with my shoes off, working at fugue. It was great fun. The rain was pouring outside, and
we glanced up every now and again at the beautiful soft view of the
city, misty with white fog. I am almost as delighted at his having
finished the masque as I should be at completing myself some large
work. I look to it to begin the founding of his reputation."

The publication of the *Masque* at the end of the year was the
occasion for letters in which we can read the opposed temperaments
of the two friends, Robinson so cautious and reserved, Moody so
warm-blooded, and also their regard for each other despite all differences. "I have not yet read Moody's *Masque* for what is really

in it," Robinson wrote me at once, "but I can see that it is a big thing. The mere fact that I can stand it at all is enough to convince me that it is a work of genius." A month later he confirmed this first impression: "That man Moody has really done a prodigious thing in his *Masque*. Contrary to my expectations and wishes I find it the best of all his poems, so far as I know, and most wonderfully put together. I don't like his archaisms, and I am far from discovering what good they can do, or how they can do anything but stop the reader and irritate him; but there are not many of them, and in the light of the poem as a whole they are hardly worth considering. The man's scholarship is still a little in his way, I think, but I am confident that he will shake himself clear of all his shackles in the course of a few years and make the welkin resound."

That he must have written something similar to Moody himself in Chicago we can see from Moody's answer: "What you said gave me the deepest—joy, I was going to say; but remembering your distrust of exuberant language, I will say satisfaction. Still, it was joy, all the same—the feeling was exuberant enough to warrant, this once, my florid vocabulary. I thought in New York that you were bravely trying to be generous (you would have said 'just') towards a thing you rootedly deplored but suspected yourself of being by nature prejudiced against. As you had more than done your duty on this hypothesis, I could not but consider this later testimony as being the voice of the natural man, speaking the faith that was in him; and therefore I rejoiced." (*Some Letters . . .* January 24, 1901).

In 1900, that great poetic year, spring was early in Boston, but, if we may trust a letter of Robinson's dated March 13, not so early in New York, even if his outburst of doggerel suggests some of its intoxication already in the air.

"Dear Mason: Your confidential postal cards are always messengers of joy, and this last one is particularly reassuring. It tells me that your jokes are tuneful and that there are things in Boston to make you think of the vernal equinox. Here it is different, but even though cold retards

The patient shards [1]
In my back-yards,
And postal-cards
(With my 'regards')
Are not for Bards
Who flee towárds

James Everard's on Twenty-third Street for beer after improving
and encouraging conversations with pleasant people who hope most
assuredly—still there is comfort in the knowledge that mercury
must begin to climb to a Christian altitude before very long. How is
Moody and his History of the World? And when am I to see one
or both of you two resplendent gentlemen here in my pale blue
box?"

III

"Bard", with a capital B, was the nickname, alternating sometimes
with "the Little Singer", that Robinson, Moody and I applied to
Josephine Preston Peabody, later Mrs. Lionel S. Marks, author of
poems and verse dramas of which both my friends thought highly.
In those days of 1900 she was a very beautiful girl in her twenties,
dark, with a peach-bloom complexion, wonderfully clear eyes, and
a voice of thrilling low sonority. I can still hear how she intoned
Daily Bread, from her forthcoming volume *Fortune and Men's
Eyes*.

DAILY BREAD

When the long gray day is done,
Spent at weary seams,
Homeward comes my Heart to me,
With the flock of dreams.

"And what tidings, ruddy Heart?
Shall we never share,
Hand in hand, the sun and wind,
Seeking all that's fair?"

[1] of June-bugs.

"Not tomorrow, Dear-to-me!
Ours are parted ways:
Thine the spinning, mine to seek
Fortune of the days."

Oh, and it is cold without
My own Heart to sing;
Oh, and 'tis a lonely way
My Heart goes wandering.

But I fold the web, at dusk,
As a maid beseems;
And my sunburned Heart comes home,
With the flock of dreams.

My copy of her earlier volume, *The Wayfarers*, bears on the title-page in her flowing hand the words "For my true friend, Daniel Gregory Mason", and at the end, a slip of paper on which she has written "Finally, dear spirit: let us always be good and very young." Each writing bears as signature the initials J. P., written as one letter, with decorative dots at either side. This love of the ornamental in Josephine, mixed with her full share of feminine vanity, used to puzzle her masculine friends, especially when she would preen herself like one of the birds that appear so constantly in her poems. It seemed to mate oddly with the fine friendliness shown also in the two inscriptions. Sometimes those birds would become maddening to mere man, as in the verses beginning "Words, words, ye are like birds" in *The Wayfarers*.

On the other hand, whenever Josephine could forget herself enough not to be a bird, or a flower, or a martyr, or anything else except a woman with a passionate, a truly consecrating love of beauty, she rose to heights of loyalty, both as friend and as artist, of which few are capable. I had occasion myself to prove both loyalties when she wrote my wife, after hearing Gabrilowitsch play my *Elegy*:

"Dearest Mary: It was beautiful, beautiful, beautiful. . . . Its strength particularly struck me, this time, and as ever, Dan's richness of resource. Do you remember his passing doubt, once, as to whether the *Dolce e semplice* one—my special pet star—ought to stay in? I thought upon it with smiles yesterday! For that one appeared to me so perfect in beauty—like mourning flutes.

"I hadn't the fun of talking it over afterwards: for the youths rose up and departed after the Chopin things, doubtless to walk over Harvard Bridge and discourse of it. But I remained.

"I contributed my humble significance by looking like a perfect Lady (I'm sure!) and applauding like a base-ball player."

Josephine was almost as devoted to music as to poetry. In music her lack of technical sophistication doubtless helped her to forget her quirks and conceits, and love best what was simplest. It was for Schumann's *Nachtstück* in F, one of his divinest, most child-like melodies, that she wrote her lovely *O far-off rose*. I still have her manuscript copy of it pasted into my Schumann. In *The Wayfarers* it appears on the very next page to that where the words and the birds disport themselves, and illustrates refreshingly the sincere feeling which was the other side of her nature.

> O far-off rose of long ago,
> An hour of sweet, an hour of red,
> To live, to breathe, and then to go
> Into the dark ere June was dead!
>
> Why say they: Roses shall return
> With every year as years go on.
> New spring-time and strange bloom, my rose,
> And alien June; but thou art gone.

IV

It must have been before Moody left Boston that spring for Gloucester that he wrote his great *Ode in Time of Hesitation*, for I remember vividly how overpowered with its grandeur I was when he read or rather intoned it to a group of us, I think at my mother's apartment in Newbury Street. His musical sense made him modulate his song—for it was almost that—from the tender *dolce espressivo* of

> Soon shall the Cape Ann children shout in glee,
> Spying the arbutus, Spring's dear recluse;
> Hill lads at dawn shall hearken the wild goose
> Go honking northward over Tennessee.

to the *maestoso largamente* of

> Then Alabama heard
> And rising, pale, to Maine and Idaho
> Shouted a burning word.

Two decades before, Stevenson had written in his *Across the Plains:* "The names of the States and Territories themselves form a chorus of sweet and most romantic vocables: Delaware, Ohio, Indiana, Florida, Dakota, Iowa, Wyoming, Minnesota, and the Carolinas; there are few poems with a nobler music for the ear: a songful, tuneful land; and if the new Homer shall arise from the Western continent, his verse will be enriched, his pages sing spontaneously with the names of states and cities that would strike the fancy in a business circular." He had even tried putting his theory into practice in a letter of the same period, in the verses with the lovely refrain, "Beside the Susquehanna and along the Delaware". But it was left for Moody, whether or not with knowledge of Stevenson's tentatives I cannot say, to realize the full possibilities of this "noble music for the ear".

The ode appeared in the *Atlantic Monthly* for May. A week or two earlier Robinson wrote me: "I am glad to know that Moody has written another poem, but I am sorry that he calls it an ode. That however, is his business, not mine. I am keeping an eye out for the next *Atlantic*, and am wondering what the deuce the thing is like; for I could no more get together a poem on the Philippines than I could write a description of the human brain. All I know about the human brain is that it seems to be indispensable and that it gets to be damnably tired; and this is more than I know about the right of our incomparable republic to make a game preserve of the Philippines. My knowledge of politics is meagre and my knowledge of Destiny is so small that it doesn't count. I have to content myself with a jew's harp and a bass-drum and let the other fellows blow the trumpets. I have a prophetic feeling that Moody has sounded a clear note—partly on account of your word 'magnificent' and partly on account of a way the man has of making laddered music spring skyward from prophets' pillows and other kinds of music do things in a way on which he seems to have the God-given bulge—so to speak."

In the same letter he gave me news of his own principal poetic undertaking of the year: "I am particularly optimistic just now because I am on the home stretch with the Pauper. It gags me to look at the twelve hundred odd lines that have come back from the machine, but I have a satisfying consciousness of having done something and that's what makes me an optimist. By the time the thing has come back from six or seven publishers, I may be more rational, but for the present it pleases me to give myself a place among the possibilities."

Early in May came Robinson's comment on the ode, coupled with some amusingly characteristic self-depreciation and apology: "Last week, for sheer love of industry, I wrote four pages about Moody's ode and sent them along to him. Now it is not criminal to write four pages about an ode, but surely it is unprofitable—not to say unkind—to do it before the ode has been read; and I am writing this to you that you may carry my confession to Moody and tell him that my letter was written after looking, or glancing, at his poem for something like two minutes and a half—which was time enough to show me that the thing was alive, but not enough to show me just how it was put together. Hence my remarks on his billiard process with American geography—remarks which I see now to be nonsense.—On reading the ode, I find it even bigger than my first glance at it led me to think. Your own adjective is quite safe."

To this may be added part of a letter written later in the same month: "Mr. Stedman is very much wound up by Moody's ode. We talked about the man for nearly an hour the other evening and I was mighty glad to know that the greater part of the poem is to go into the anthology which Mr. Stedman has been solidifying for the past three years—I say three, but it may be six. I believe my uncomfortable abstraction called *Luke Havergal* is also to be soused in antho-

logical pickle—along with two or three others of the forlornly joy-
ous breed.—The Pauper, or rather *Captain Craig*—for that is what
I call him now he is typewritten—is temporarily off my hands.
Two friends of mine have read him and they are still friends of mine.
More than this I cannot say for the present."

For my Easter holiday the last half of April, and for the greater
part of June, I joined Moody at the Harbor View Hotel in East
Gloucester, where he was making the struggle to stick at his desk
and at his *History of English Literature* in the glorious spring
weather, described so drolly in his letters.[1] He found time none the
less for many walks, on one of which we came, one cloudy day, to a
headland whence we gazed over a leaden sea at a tiny row-boat that
seemed as if bewitched in that melancholy scene, unmoving. As he
wrote later, in *A Grey Day:*

> O'er the grey deep the dories crawl,
> Four-legged, with rowers twain:
> Midgets and minims of the earth,
> Across old ocean's vastly girth
> Toiling—heroic, comical!

I have told in my introduction to the letters how much I admired
the power to apply his humor to himself which made him give his
heart-warming shout of laughter when someone at the hotel suggested the "baby blue-eye" for the flower stanza in *Gloucester
Moors*. He improvised on the spot the line:

> Baby-blue is the baby blue-eye.

Moody has been justly praised for taking seriously, thoughtfully,
even passionately, social problems like those treated in *Gloucester
Moors*, in a period before such a modern attitude was common, and
when poetry was still considered, like music, a decoration of life, a
"frill", not a part of its serious business. I agree; but I praise him even
more because, passionate as were his hopes for man's social better-
ment, they were not fanatical or narrow, as they so often seem to be
in contemporary proletarian poets; he never forgot how much more

[1] *Some Letters of William Vaughn Moody*, page 126.

fundamental the culture of the sense of beauty is than all social, economic, and political arrangements. I fancy this was what Robinson felt in writing me: "Moody's Gloucester poem is better than his more splendiferous ode, I think." It was at this very time, when he was most deeply exercised over all these problems, and was writing not only *Gloucester Moors* and the *Ode*, but *The Menagerie* and *The Brute*, that I find in my journal:

"May 25, 1900. Will down from Gloucester. Most inspiring talk apropos of Edward Carpenter and socialism, and the present transition-stage of society. When I said that I often felt I must give up my music, because it was not the thing most needed now, and speak and write and study for better conditions, he answered that he felt that there were a good many men who could work for the reforms we contemplate in the social machine; that, in the second place, it *was* a machine, and that the words of Christ were as true now as when he said them—'The Kingdom of Heaven is within'; and that, in the third place, there were few men who could reveal the soul of the machine, who could give the world 'not a syllogism, but a song.' "

V

In July Will Moody, Josephine Peabody and I visited my brother Edward and my sister-in-law, later my wife, in Falmouth on Cape Cod. Mrs. Mason asked Robinson to join us, but he replied:

"450 Manhattan Avenue
"July 24, 1900

"My dear Mrs. Mason—

"As I have an exceptionally good opportunity to go on with some work that I have been trying to do, and partly doing, for the past five or six weeks, I have concluded to stay in New York until the first of September. In coming to this conclusion I write myself down a past master in self-denial, for I assure you that the sad sea waves and all the other things that go with Falmouth have a mighty attraction for a man in Harlem who sees nothing from his window that is more sparkling than Grant's Tomb. . . . "

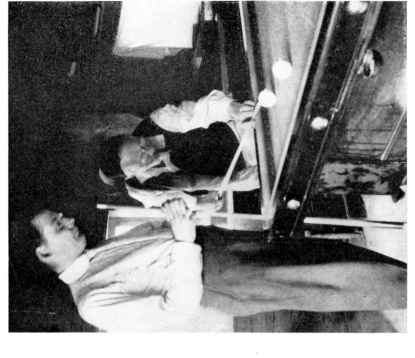

Left: William Vaughn Moody and Truman H. Bartlett at Bartlett's Chocorua house
From a photograph by the Author

Right: Edwin Arlington Robinson and Truman H. Bartlett playing billiards
From a photograph by Hermann Hagedorn

This work that he had been "partly doing" (his poem *Aunt Imo-gen*), Robinson wrote to me about in more detail a week later: "I am wearing poetical petticoats and making a regular analysis of an Old Maid—120 odd lines of blank verse. I did it in the rough two years ago, when I had my eyrie over Brown's dry goods store and smoked *Before the War* cigars. I had a good mill-pond to look out on and somehow conceived the notion of writing down this particular spinster. Maybe I thought she ought to have drowned herself; at any rate, the mill-pond had something to do with it. I have no mill-pond here, but I have five or six bottles of beer in the ice chest and a sweet sense of security. I know they are cooled through by this time. I know, also, a good deal about Heinz's Baked Beans, with Tomato Sauce. I wish I knew as much about the unearned increment—pro-vided I had it."

Meanwhile, he was in the midst of his long struggle to place *Cap-tain Craig*. He wrote me early in July that he had failed with Scrib-ners, and was now trying Small, Maynard and Company. "I suppose this move of mine," he added, "will give you a chance to read the business if you care to; but I warn you now not to feel obliged to like it. Parts of it will jar your nervous system, I think; and I am inclined to fear that the second part, as a whole, will make you thirsty; but there may be other places that you will approve just as a rather con-ventional friend of mine has approved most unexpectedly of the second part just referred to. The chief difficulty in getting the book published lies, I think, in the improbability of any single reader's caring for the whole of it. But anyhow, the thing is what it is and it is something like what I intended it to be—too much a matter of 'at-mosphere' I am afraid, but that will take care of itself if the work is good for anything."

By August Moody and I had moved on to Mr. Bartlett's in the mountains. "All I know about Chocorua," Robinson wrote me from New York, "is that someone of the Burroughs-Bolles-Miller ilk wrote a book about its tenants—which I had naturally supposed hitherto to be chiefly birds and bullfrogs. Your letter, however, tells me that other things abide there, things of the human sort, which are more interesting to an unobserving cuss like me. I am glad to know that you and the man of odes are enjoying yourselves and I hope you may be able to keep the thing going as long as the water remains warm enough to 'scald your tails' in. Your account of Mr. Bartlett makes me think that I should like much to meet him some-time".[1]

"My chief recreation is riding to Bronxville on Sundays and consuming Mr. Stedman's tobacco. His doctor will not allow him to consume it himself, therefore my work in that line is a kind of profitable charity. Sometimes we go to the back lot behind his house, where we sit on ant hills and talk about farming and what is Art. He likes me because I wrote a thing called *The Clerks* and because I represent so many distinct varieties of imperturbable asininity. I am always pretty much the same, and I fancy my influence is rather restful."

As the long summer in the city and the long suspense about his book drag on, we can read between the lines that even his philosophy is wearing thin. "We have had a damnably salubrious summer here in New York," he confesses mildly in mid-September, "but I think the worst of it is over now. I may be with you for a while this fall, but I can't say for certain. The last smash in my western real estate has left me guessing a little, and I am amusing myself by trying to transform a draggle-tailed poet into something practical.

"I sent *Captain Craig* to Maynard on the strength of what you said on the subject in New York. . . . I have not the ghost of a thought that Maynard will publish it, but I can't get over a persistent feeling that the thing is artistic. I don't think you will agree with me, however; nor do I think that you will care much for any of it—except, perhaps, the last two hundred lines; and I prefer to have you wait (for a century or so) until the book is between covers before you read even so much as that. The one thing that the Pauper will not stand is a hasty examination. My only hope is that people will not read him rapidly; and for once in my life I think my hopes will be fulfilled."

---

[1] Robinson himself later owed much to "Mr. B's" generously open house at Chocorua and to his whole-hearted faith in the young poets, even those—perhaps especially those—still unappreciated by the public.

Robinson was now approaching the year that marked for him the lowest, most hopeless, and most monotonous period of his long struggle with poverty and obscurity—1901. As that year was also the worst one of my own life, common misfortune brought us together; I find in my journal the note: "February 9–14. Visit to New York. The beginning of my deeper friendship with Robinson." I saw much of him, both on these visits and more especially after I moved to Princeton in 1902. By that time he was living in a "hall bed-room" at the back of the fourth floor of a rooming house in West Twenty-third Street. You had to grope up ill-lighted flights to reach his eyrie. Arrived there, you took the only chair while he draped his long legs along the bed. We used to pick up inexpensive meals at Childs restaurants, or if we were in funds indulge in a steak or English chop at Cavanagh's.

Admirable, all through this time, were his half serene, half humorous detachment from his surroundings, the long stride and quizzical smile with which he walked through all incongruities. He had a kind of dumb patience, I envied him. He told me once that I wanted to "bottle things up too much—not leave them fluid and indeterminate". "You can't have seeds and fruits in the same package," he said Another time, when we had been discussing the free will problem, and he had mentioned that Seneca or someone had killed himself because he could not find the truth about it, and opined that there was no use trying to find out, though thousands had wasted their lives in the attempt, I burst out in despair: "But how is one to get strength to live without knowing?" He answered: "Isn't the mystery and vitality and energy of the whole thing enough to give interest and confidence?" "The great art of life," he summed up, "is to suffer without worrying." So I was not surprised, on his writing me that *Captain Craig* had been "turned down by five houses", to have him add: "But he is still on the march. His trousers are pretty badly frayed, and his general appearance seems to be more and more disreputable at each return; and perhaps that is all right. He is a sort of disreputable cuss, anyhow, as you know." Once when I asked him if he did not think his sense of humor had lengthened his life, "I think," he replied, "my life has lengthened my sense of humor."

This mellowness that came to him with experience fills two of his longest but also wisest letters. The first, suggested by my edition of Savage's *Poems*, goes on to more universal matters. It was written at the end of 1900, from Yonkers, where he was visiting a friend.

"Your letter came as a welcome visitor on a somewhat bogus Christmas, and I will add that it came just as I was about to write an acknowledgment of your book—which I am glad to own. . . . You have done a good work, and I think now that you did the best thing in not trying to sift the verses out any more than was absolutely necessary. One of the godlike things about me is that I can change my mind as easily as I can change my trousers—perhaps a little more so, for my trousers always stick on my damned heels.

"In regard to the long letter which you wrote but did not send there is nothing for me to say except that if any suggestion of mine, or any safety valve of sympathy, can be of any worth to you, it is always ready. I have supposed that things were somewhat snarled with you, but of course I have not carried my supposition any farther than that. I appreciate your confidence in me, and I want you to know it; and at the same time I ask you to believe that I have always had a good deal of sympathy—more or less vague, but still of what I may call the solid sort, with your ambitions to do what you were born to do and with your difficulties of which you say so little.

"Being such a cheerful abortion as I am in many ways, I suppose I can partly understand a few things that some other people cannot; and I have thought sometimes that my chief usefulness in the world lies in this faculty of mine to encourage a fellow now and then to shin up tall trees while I sit on the ground and tell him what an artist he is. Shinning—I hope the word is not strange to you—is the first of all the arts and I am beginning to fear that I have not done much of it. I can't look back and feel honestly that I could have done more but this feeling is rather a sorry poultice for the present and it isn't altogether an elixir for the future; but as long as I can see that the few real things that I have done are things that nobody knows about except myself I am willing to give the future a chance.

"All this may seem irrelevant, but I am really trying to preach a sermon on the folly of measuring one's success too much in the scale of external evidence. The Ass-Demon of Quantity raises the devil with most of us and makes us forget that the test of a man is his willingness to measure himself by what he has tried to do—which is truly what he has done. It is right here somewhere that those 'other things' begin to be added on, and one wonders where the deuce they come from. Forgive me throwing all this antiquated hay in your crib, but don't forget that I am keeping myself alive with the same crop. Remember, also, that I believe in the most modern of all oats, and that I am quite impervious to the trivial recriminations of little things like mixed metaphors. I began by watching another man go up a tree, and here I find myself a horse—which is well enough for Christmas in Yonkers."

The second letter was written to help me at the time of a personal crisis, which requires no comment here except that my friends, including that incomparably sympathetic and wise one, Josiah Royce, had advised me to go away for a time, and that I did in fact sail for Europe early in April. This beautiful letter, to which that of October 4, 1904 may be regarded as a pendant or foot-note, is offered for its revelation of Robinson's clairvoyant sympathy, and as an evidence that his insight into poetic truth could lead him to much the standpoint occupied by Royce's equally sympathetic and more philosophic mind.

"29 East 22nd Street
"March 26, 1901

"Dear Mason: I don't want you to go anywhere with the idea of giving up anything, but I cannot help telling you that Royce's advice seems to me to be the wisest you could receive just now. If you go to Paris you will have at least the satisfaction of knowing that you have made a definite move in the matter, and the probabilities are that you will not find the separation so hard to bear as you think now that it must be. And then again, the very question of test and probation, or whatever you choose to call it, comes to me now in the light of something like a duty.

"You will say to yourself that I am thinking only of you, perhaps, and I assure you that I do not forget that there is the other, and that it is more on her account than on yours (you will not misunderstand me) that I hesitate at all in advising you to go away at once. The man can always get along somehow, and the woman knows it; and in this case, I doubt if there is any real question in her mind as to her own belief that she can do the same. It is easy, of course, for me to say all of this; but I cannot be quite honest and say anything else. When two people are sure of each other, as you are, perhaps it is not so much a question of what one of you can bear as it is of how the other is going to suffer while he is bearing it, and when it comes to a solution of this difficulty I suppose there is nothing better or less emotional to be said than that she must look on it as the price she has to pay for the right to believe in the possibility of a great happiness.

"As things are going I find it utterly impossible to disagree with Royce; and as I am sure that both of you agree with him I can only hope that you will be able to make the change without losing any of your courage or your faith. There is no reason why you should lose either, on the contrary there is every reason why you should have new surroundings for a time and a better opportunity for new ideas. You know by this time that there is a good deal of the brute in the artist, and, you know, it is chiefly to him that I am appealing when I venture to remind you of the other side of the question at a time when you are not expecting this sort of treatment from a friend.

"What I am most afraid of in your case is that you are in danger of forgetting that even the more hellish of human complexities are not to be considered too bitterly in the beginning. We cannot measure anything until we have seen it through; and I am sure that she will be willing to make this trial if you are, and to do all she can for you and herself. God knows it is a bad business at the best—bad, I mean, as we see things—but I believe that some definite measure like this that you are contemplating will end in making the whole thing clearer. If you will put away all thoughts of hopelessness and start out with thoughts of strength and faith, she will do the same. And this, as I see it, is all that either of you can do just now. As there is no immediate solution possible, you must have courage to do what you believe to be the wisest thing, no matter how hard it may seem at first.

"If you make up your mind to do it, you will soon find a kind of joy in the sheer intensity of the immediate sacrifice, and another in the consciousness that you have not only a moral but also an artistic ideal to live for. You must remember, even when it seems almost like selfishness to do so, that your art is to be the concrete expression of your life. If you are loyal to that, you cannot be disloyal to yourself; for all of your largest ideas have come from this new life, which you think just now to contain nothing but unhappiness. Refuse for once and all to measure anything by the moment and you will realize before long that the picture will take on new colors—and brighter ones. This again is easy enough to say.

"Personally, I shall be sorry to have you go—but of course there is no need of my telling you this.

"I am sorry that I cannot be of more service to you—but you understand all that.

"All this is horribly 'preachy', but I won't try to improve matters by saying the same thing in a different way."

CHAPTER IX

RIDGELY TORRENCE

AFTER I left Boston for Princeton in 1902, and especially after I published *From Grieg to Brahms* at the end of that year, my fortunes, both personal and worldly, began slowly to improve. A second book, *Beethoven and His Forerunners*, appeared in 1904, and a third, *The Romantic Composers*, in 1906. These were published serially as well as in book form, and brought me a good many opportunities to lecture. Through my classmate Winthrop Ames, I got the editorship of a new magazine, *Masters in Music*. This brought me in fifteen hundred dollars a year, making the nucleus of my income for several years. As a result of all this I was able to my great joy to leave Princeton and establish myself (this time permanently) in New York. My former sister-in-law and I were married on October 8, 1904, and with her two younger children, Ellen, aged ten, and "Billy", aged eight, set up housekeeping. The two older boys, Gregory and Lowell, were at boarding school. Robinson wrote me (October 4th):

"Dear Mason: While your letter was in no way a surprise to me it gave me a great pleasure. Now that you have finally wrestled with your worst difficulties, and beaten them, I look for in '*incipit vita nuova*' expression on your countenance next time I see you. If ever two people deserved to be happy in this life, I know who they are.

133

"I am glad to know that you think of me as a good friend through it all, but I am still at a loss to know what in the name of Jehoshaphat and the Delectable Mountains I have ever done, or what I have even been able to suggest. Beyond the honor of your confidence, I have no part in the clearing up of one of the worst tangles that the gods and devils ever delighted themselves with."

II

We began married life in the small city apartments necessitated by our poverty, with all the difficulties unavoidable where children who need freedom are crowded in with a professional man who needs quiet. Fortunately in the summers, which were my only time anyway for work needing concentration, we could rent slightly larger cottages, sometimes with barns that could be turned into improvised studios. Two contemporary snapshots may suffice to picture the life of the next few years, in which, if there could not be much composing there was a good deal of writing and lecturing, and plenty of amusement. The first is from a letter about the wedding itself:

"When I arrived at about 8 A.M. the children were both singing *Merrily clink the wedding cake* (from the Hasty Pudding operetta *Proserpina*) and Billy had changed the line 'Her daughter's engaged to a Prince' to 'My mother's engaged to a Prince', which he delivered in a *basso profundo*. The children were altogether charming—so interested in their wardrobes, and so full of questions about everything. Billy determined on wearing a pair of heavy white woolen gloves, very dirty, and thought he would wash them. Counselled against this, he proposed sprinkling them with flour to whiten them. Finally just as we were leaving we found him in the bathroom with his blouse sleeves rolled up. The first idea had overcome him, and the gloves had to be left behind, in the dirtiest bowl of water ever seen. At the elevator we discovered about six feet of skipping rope in his pocket. This was left behind, and at last we got started."

The second glimpse belongs to the summer of 1906, when we rented the so-called "Coles Farm" at Washington, Connecticut, partly to be near the older boys in their boarding school. It was there that our landlord, Walter Russell the painter, commemorated my barn studio in a sketch of a horse eating hay out of my grand piano. Everything at the Coles Farm was rather impromptu, including a shower-bath we rigged up in the wood-shed, consisting of a garden

" On the Good Old Summer Time "

hose carrying the water to a tin-can perforated with nail-holes, the whole dimly illuminated by a kerosene lamp that always either smelled, smoked, or went out, frequently all three together. The bewildered and petulant artist thwarted by a recalcitrant physical world is revealed only too clearly, I fear, in this outburst in my journal.

"August 1. Billy and his friend were so bent on making a fountain yesterday that they practically demolished the shower-bath Lowell and I made with so much interest. When, tired from my New York trip, I went out at bed-time to take a bath, I found the hose pulled entirely down out of the shed-loft window, lying on the ground, but still connected with the faucet so that there was a miniature lake about the shed. Two carts, the fountain, a rake, a hoe, a screw-driver, oil cans, etc., were left cluttered about in the rain, while upstairs the bottom of the curtain was ripped off, the spout of the shower-bath was mislaid, soap and towels were on the floor. Indescribable havoc. . . . I mended it enough, in spite of the rain and the frequent extinguishment of my lamp, to take a bath, and this morning at breakfast I talked it over with Billy. . . .

"I am going to put the whole thing out of my mind now, and work at Chopin."

At the end of this same summer of 1906, in the early fall days when the Connecticut hills were at their best, Will Moody visited us. He had just had the one great worldly success of his short and so unworldly life, in the production in New York on October 4 of *The Great Divide*. This was the realization of a long cherished dream. "As far back as 1896," writes Robert Morss Lovett in the introduction to his volume of Moody's *Selected Poems*, "he was taking a keen interest in the newspaper accounts of the work of a western faith healer named Schlatter, and speaking of him as a subject for a play." Lovett does not mention, what is however the fact, that Will actually completed a full version of *The Faith Healer* before he began *The Great Divide;* but this interesting fact seems to be proved by an entry in my journal dated July 20, 1900: "Last night Will read Mary his play." My wife distinctly remembers that the play then read was the one about the faith healer. It went through many revisions, however, and was not finished until years later, so that the first play to be produced was the far more successful *The Great Divide*, originally called *A Sabine Woman*.

Will now came to us fresh from this brilliant success. His way of taking it helps us understand his splendidly incorruptible artistic character.

Journal, October 4, 1906. "Will Moody . . . is not the least spoiled by the great success of his play; he laughed and joked about it just as ever. He dropped a good many interesting facts by the way. He has been asked by many well-known managers, including both Frohmans, to write a play for them, and they have offered large terms, but he has in every case refused, as he simply cannot write to order.

"Seats for the present play are selling several days ahead, and hundreds are turned away every night. Miller will take it to England in May, and will open next fall with it at Daly's Theatre. On our walk to Steep Rock Will told me that now when he saw the loveliness of the country he first realized how he was tempted by the offers, of four publishers, of large royalties if he would turn the play

William Vaughn Moody at the Coles Farm, October, 1906
From a photograph by the Author

into a novel. They mentioned such sums as $25,000, and even $50,-
000. He refused all their offers, believing it essentially inartistic to
turn a play into a novel, or *vice versa*.

"On the play he earned about $500 in the one week preceding his
visit, and expects to clear about $5000 from the twelve-weeks' New
York run. He is much beset by reporters, publishers, managers, and
general social invitations, and talks of escaping to California or somewhere.

"We talked of the comic opera I want to write, and he told me
I might use his idea, if I could, of a satire on the acquisition of
Panama by the United States a few years ago. He was most amusing
on this subject, working up incidents and situations. . . .

"He is working on a new drama on the subject of Eve, and says
he is going sometime to develop a scheme he has for making music
and drama interplay in a different way from Wagner's. The gist of
the idea is that they shall not distract the attention one from the
other, as in Wagner, but alternate, the music coming in only when
the action reaches crises, and the action being then suspended while
the music fills the consciousness. Also he spoke of a more imperceptible transition in drama from prose to verse than most writers have
ever tried—said it was exemplified more or less however in Shakespeare's historical plays. . . .

"His delightful largeness of mind and impersonal interest in people and things impressed us more than ever. I never saw a man interested—sincerely—in so many different kinds of people as he is.
He told us about E. A. Robinson, Boardman Robinson, Torrence,
John Corbin, Norman Hapgood, Shipman, Percy Mackaye, and
others, appearing to be cordially interested in every one. This trait
gives him a curious detachment; for it makes it impossible to think
of him as especially one's own friend. Everyone he likes is his friend,
and oneself is only one of these. But to me this broadness and sweetness is restful and delightful.

"In outward appearance he is just the same as ever, with his inseparable companion the briar pipe, his sombrero felt hat and long
dark coat, striped white and black waistcoat, and old coat and
trousers. He still wears the ruby and sapphire ring."

III

That autumn, leaving the younger children as well as the older boys at school in Washington, we took rooms in the Judson, at the extreme southern end of Washington Square. Already living there were Robinson, his friend Ridgely Torrence, and a number of other literary people. One reason for going there was that I hoped Torrence might write me an operetta libretto.

By this time I was ready to try almost any mode of money-earning that would have a closer relation to music than lecturing—as I fondly hoped operetta-writing might. I was heartily tired of lecturing. The few fashionable audiences I got gave only a small fraction of their attention to the music, and the popular audiences, more eager to learn, were often unbelievably crude. Only two days after our wedding I began the endless series of lectures I was to give for years for the Board of Education of New York in various small halls over the city. That first lecture was at St. Peter's Hall in Twentieth Street, between Eighth and Ninth Avenues. In my nervousness I got there half an hour too early, and had to spend the interval walking the streets. After the lecture I always gave the audience a chance to ask questions. My fee for all this was fifteen dollars a lecture, so that it took an almost incalculable number of lectures to earn a hundred dollars.

The director of this early effort towards adult education in New York was Dr. Henry M. Leipziger, an idealist, even a visionary, but wretchedly ill and over-worked and proportionately irritable and domineering. One used to dread the preliminary interviews in his office almost more than the lectures themselves. Even more his slaves than the lecturers, if that was possible, were the local superintendents, officials who for a miserable pittance bullied the audiences as they were themselves bullied by the director. Their manners ranged from the insolence of Jack-in-office to a depressing servility: I remember one of them, at a later period after I had joined the Columbia University staff, introducing me as "the peerless man from Columbia". Another uttered a phrase one evening that hit off so neatly Dr. Leipziger's peculiarities it has stayed in my mind ever since. It was

in March, 1917, just as we were getting ready to join the war against
Germany, and national feeling had to be pumped up. He made a
great show, acting doubtless on orders, of democratically soliciting
opinions from the audience as to whether they would join in singing
America after the lecture. When however they bashfully hung back,
he gave up democracy for a bad job, and announced solemnly:
"Ladies and Gentlemen, it is the consensus of opinion of Dr. Leipziger that we shall sing *America*."

Writing articles, except for a few magazines with intelligent editors like Abbott of the *Outlook*, was not always much more congenial than lecturing. One's independence was too apt to be in inverse proportion to the rate of pay. Once I rejoiced in securing a
commission to write five articles for a popular woman's magazine
for a hundred dollars apiece. I rejoiced less when I was not allowed
to mention that Schubert drank beer. . . .

So I was looking for a closer link between music and livelihood,
and for a while a promising lead seemed light opera. In the end, like
so many other "leads", it proved a no-thoroughfare, but while it
lasted it was amusing. Bert Leston Taylor, who was living near New
York that winter, did for me the greater part of a libretto called *Joan
of Arcadee*, and I composed half a dozen settings. Thomas Ybarra
projected one to be called *The Plutocrat*, and I can still whistle my
refrain for the inspiring lines

Advertise!

Advertise!

That's the only way to make your income rise.

Torrence proposed one to be based on Hawthorne's story of *The
Great Carbuncle*. We gave a party to talk librettos with Wallace
Irwin, Percy Mackaye, Arthur Colton, Will Moody, and Torrence.
(I did write a song for Colton's delicious lyric *When First I Kissed
Susannah*. It saw print thirty years later, transmogrified into the first
of my *Sentimental Sketches* for Trio, and in order not to plagiarize
Stephen Foster rechristened *Rosina*). I made appointments with
managers which they usually postponed. I coached in orchestration
with an operetta conductor who insisted that all violin passages

should be written very high, and that operetta singers were so mediocre that they must always be supported by either violin or clarinet. At last I saw in a comic paper a test offered to discover the
successful operetta: Was it such that a dog, happening to sit in the
front row, would be inspired to bark madly throughout? If so, it
would be a success. It must have been at about the time I realized the
truth of this description that I finally gave up the game.

Robinson and Torrence both had dramatic aspirations too that
winter. Journal, January 13, 1907: "We are certainly a nest of the
arts here. Torrence tells me that Will Moody is going to arrange for
Henry Miller to show Madame Nazimova his [Torrence's] play
which he has just completed. Then W. V. M. asked Robinson if he
had a one-act play, as Miller wanted one for a benefit night which is
approaching. Robinson got an idea for one at 1 A.M. that same evening, and says he can finish it in one day, and is to do it tomorrow.
So that may start him in the dramatic line." And two weeks later:
"January 28. E. A. R. reads me his one-act play, *Terra Firma*. . . .
We hear that Viola Allen has commissioned Mrs. [Olive Tilford]
Dargan to write her a one-acter. . . . Torrence reads his play *The
Madstone* to Henry Miller." A few days later Miller did accept
Torrence's play; but as Nazimova shortly afterward left his manage-
ment he did not give it after all.

At our evening gatherings in the Judson the chief entertainer was
always Ridgely Torrence. Ridgely was tall, thin, and very blonde.
Singularly penetrating eyes gave to the long lean face under his high
forehead an effect of spirituality, almost asceticism. Anyone prepared for that side of him by the mystical beauty of his poems might
well have been puzzled when, in his more social mood, those very
eyes that had just awed you with their seeming penetration into your
inmost secrets would unexpectedly relent in friendliest smiles, or
twinkle at some sudden conceit. Sometimes an almost imperceptible
signal would show you, when the ironic aspect of his subject struck
him, that their seriousness had changed to mock-seriousness. He selected his words with the deliberation of the fastidious writer, and
had a way sometimes of under-emphasizing, almost slurring over,
a peculiarly unexpected and pat one, that made it irresistible. He

talked always slowly, savoring his matter in a way that took for granted and therefore challenged minute attention.

He was an incomparable mimic. He could look drunk entirely by facial expression, with no easy staggering to help out. Then he would become a Fourth of July orator, one hand between buttons of coat, the other with finger-tips on table, head thrown high, stilted voice beginning "Fellow Citizens". . . . Then there was Cap'n Benny, whom he had studied at Cos Cob in the summers. One day the players in a moving picture came to be photographed in the streets of Cos Cob, and Cap'n Benny, his high soprano voice quite silenced by the intensity of his curiosity, followed them fascinated for hours. Once only, when in getting over a fence the leading lady showed a generous amount of leg, Cap'n Benny, startled, piped up in mechanical soprano: "You needn't tell *me* she's a good woman!"

But the greatest impersonation of all was his Missionary. This was originally borrowed from that other great mimic of my day, "Tommy" Safford of Jabberwocky fame, as Ridgely was always most careful to state, protesting that he used Safford's very phrases and invented nothing. But disclaim as he might, not only had he received from heaven a leanness and an ancient mariner fanaticism of eye that made his impersonation unique, but his profundity of imaginative realization wove that missionary into our very lives. Before he said a word, when you simply beheld him swaying back and forth, sucking his lower lip, and giving one of those unexpected but quintessential dips by letting his knees suddenly bend, you would laugh with premonitory mirth until it almost hurt. Then, in a singsong chant, bringing out key words with a sudden rasping of the voice, struggling with a supposedly revolving front tooth that produced strange whistlings and sibilations, and punctuating with dips at the most unlikely moments, he would tell the brethren how he had "landed on the west coast of Africa." "Our first task," he would go on, "was to learn the language [dip] of the tribes there re-s-s-siding" [hissing tooth]. The climax came with the confession: "But after nine years' hard labor, my brethren, we found that what we had learned was not the language of the [dip] west coast of Africa, but that of the [rasped in *fortissimo*] hill tribes of India." It ended, I recall, with the admonition: "One piece of advice I have for you, my young friends. Never lose an opportunity."

Ridgely had in his letters more than any other I have known the Stevensonian faculty of pure, divine nonsense. For years after our Judson winter he was likely at any moment to endue without warning the personality of his missionary, or any other that struck his fancy, and to lapse from prose into poetry, or at least into what looked like prose but sounded like verse—and not "free verse" either. In the summer of 1910, when I had sent to him in his native Xenia a parody, *Chickory's Fountain*, I had made on Robinson's recently published *Vickery's Mountain*, this answer came back.

"Xenia, Ohio, July 19 [1910]

"How are the heavens so full of the sun? That requires no answer, it's only rhythmical utterance. I thought—as the unaccustomed say—that I would write you a letter. I think of you as I think of St. Peter, with your hand upon the keys, with your halo round your neck, in a smock, letting few pass perspirant, with the recording angel not far off, and you on, by, with or in a cloud, hearing heavenly choirs, humming very bold, strike their golden wires never catching cold.

"I cannot go to you but you often come to me and I wish that you would bring your music as clearly as my memory holds your stories and your hearty self. But I am weak, I cannot project you bodily. As the poick so nobly sings

> The feathered tribes on pinions cleave the air.
> Not so the mackerel, and still less the bear.[1]

"I wish that you and I were sitting round some heavenly board, on these hot days, with about half a stigtossel of dogglegammon, (that ghostly porridge) between us. Wouldn't we be a pair of cool ones as ever went up? But here is summer madness, here are summer ants, here the heavy sadness, wearing heavy pance. What's the news of the Muse, does she use any booze? If she does, Professor Mason, you should give it to her strong, you should hand it in a basin till she

[1] See Stevenson's *St. Ives*. Thistle edition, page 404.

lifts a song. But call her Muse, or Maude, or Sadie, never go too far,
Mrs. Mason's more a lady than the Muses are.

"Yours, R. T."

"This is merely to certify that Uncle Dan'l McGregor is a member of the inner council of Poet's Union No. 7, and all members of
Pittsfield Lodge are to yield to him because of his great achievement
in singing of *Chicory's Fountain,* the highest sprouting and the
strongest lyrical ecstasy since the last strike was called. The members
of Xenia Lodge cried with joy over it. It is a perfect thing. More
concerning it later.

"(Signed) With a headache.
"The Talking Delegate"

Three summers later, when my wife and I were spending our vacation in southern France, there came across the Atlantic this edify-
ing advice.

"Now that you have set out in life and are fairly embarked with
a help-mate and an avocation, my advice to a young man of your
age would be: make the most of your opportunities, adapt yourself
to your environment, live within the income which your labours
have won for you and lay up a little each day if it be only a few
pennies, be obedient to those in authority, connect yourself with
some professing body of Christians (I will not urge any particular
denomination upon you but leave that to the behests of your own
judgment) and contribute plentifully towards the work in the
foreign field. Never presume to set up your own opinion against
those of laws and customs established by authority.

"In conclusion I have one injunction which I would always give
to a young man (or maiden) and it is a very precious one. A great
bishop whispered it to me in two words years ago and oh, they sank
into my heart. "Be discreet," he said. Oh golden syllables, they ought
to be engraved over the door of every young man's (and maiden's)
heart. They ought not only to exercise them in the Sunday School
but also abroad, in the daily walks of life, in the counting house and
marts of trade especially. One of the oldest living life members of

the American Bible Society, speaking at our Chautauqua on *The Land of the White Elephant* told us that the same rule applies also in that far-off country."

And again after many years, when in 1928 he was himself spending with his wife (the former Olivia Dunbar) a summer on the Lake of Geneva, his "word" to me was:

"Geneva, May 13, 1928

". . . I hope that you had a pleasant voyage over the Atlantic Ocean, that great body of water, and that your monthly stipend from the American Board arrives regularly. There is a great work to do here among the native tribes. I am at present learning their language so that I can address them in their own native tongue. Thus far I have learned the words *"onze fines—vingt bières—quinze rhums"*—which I find are constantly used among our own countrymen residing here in Geneva, City of Refuge.

"Let me hear from you, Brother, here in the foreign field,

"Ridgely"

IV

I do not fear that any lover of Ridgely's poetry will blame me for thus emphasizing his fun and irresponsibility. It was the other side of the same sensitiveness that shows in the four lovely stanzas of *The Son*, into which he has been able to pack such richness of human nature, and in the incomparably plastic rhythms and spiritual discernments of longer poems like *Eye-Witness*. That most haunting (for me) of all his poems I found in a magazine I picked up in my wife's club on Christmas Eve of 1916.

With what delight I read:

My heart went open like an apple sliced;
I saw my Saviour and I saw my Christ. . . .

He went to the doors but he didn't have the pay,
He went to the windows, then he went away.

Says, "We'll walk together, and we'll both be fed."
Says, "I will give you the 'other' bread."

Oh, the bread he gave and without money!
O drink, O fire, O burning honey!

Early in the new year Ridgely and Olivia dined with us, and I noted in my journal:

"It was fun to tell Ridgely how we loved his poem. He says that some of the tramp ballads use the four-beat line, and that the negroes use the 'Says' (without the 'He'). He got the idea one day when he was working on a *New Republic* article in the Columbia Library, the measure taking possession of him first, and walked all the way down to Waverly Place composing it."

The most beautiful letter he ever wrote me was after Will Moody's death. . . . Since that visit at the Coles Farm in the fall of 1906, only four years before the untimely death by which I lost one of my dearest friends and America one of her greatest poets, Will and I had had no other opportunity for those aimless long walks and talks in which our youth had been so rich. Our later meetings had been brief and at long intervals. At the end of 1907 there had been a Halloween dinner at Mrs. Davidge's, at which Will, Robinson, Torrence, Rodman Gilder and I had twined our brows with grape wreaths and looked like tipsy pagans for the admiration of our women-folk. Will was especially in character, half faun and half Greek god, flushed with punch and genius. A year later, at the end of 1908, he had read us his new play *The Faith Healer*, which had been in rehearsal in Boston.

Then things began to go wrong. Early in 1909 we heard that he had been ordered to Southern California for his health. (He had never been really cured of an attack of typhoid, the after effects of which were long weakness and eventually a brain tumor.) A little later the news was that *The Faith Healer*, which had given him endless trouble and never really satisfied his exacting artistry, had been severely criticised and taken off. The rest of the story, as sad as it is brief, is outlined in a few entries from my journal:

"November 16, 1909. We hear vague and terrifying reports about

Will Moody. He is dangerously ill, in the country in Maryland; his wife's notes are so devoid of detail and filled with Christian Science that we know nothing definite.

"May 14, 1910. We have fine news from Mrs. Will Moody. W. V. M. is progressing, though very slowly, and she says that he will regain his health and his sight.

"Monday, October 17. Will died this morning at Colorado Springs.

"Tuesday, October 18. I cannot think that he is gone, that I shall never see him again, with his pipe and slouch hat and clear, steady eyes, and hear that explosive laugh of his: the dear friend, so generous and loyal, the competent artist, the big-souled poet—the greatest man I have known. Great as my loss is—and I fully know that never can anyone take his place, and were I as young again as when I met him, there is not another who could be to me what he is—still the worst of it is not the selfish pain, but the sense that he—he who was so full of life, such a lover of beauty, is no more in the world, forever. It seems wicked, altogether wrong, that what he was should cease to be, that he should exist now only in our memories, growing dimmer as one after another of us dies in turn. It is a nightmare thought—I can't get away from it today."

Ridgely's letter is too intimate to be given here in full, but parts of it at least may be shared.

"Xenia, October 22, 1910

"Last night at midnight when I returned from Chicago I found a letter from Miss Dunbar in which she said that you had heard nothing about his latter days. . . . Last Saturday—a week ago this afternoon—he was able to take a short walk across a park beside his cottage. He walked perhaps a hundred yards and played with his dog. By 'playing' I mean that he laughed cheerfully at its antics. He was comparatively free from pain.

"Upon returning he felt very weak and was persuaded to lie down. He seemed however to be fairly easy after dinner and retired with no expression of feeling differently. About midnight he was seized with unusual pain, which increased until Sunday afternoon at five o'clock when he became unconscious and so continued until two o'clock on Monday morning when he left us.

"How shall we endure not to hear his glorious voice again? I never heard of a more pitiful example of earthly destiny unfulfilled. . . . Yet his fine gold shall never become dim nor his sacred ashes scattered in vain, for he told us eternally of eternal things."

"He told us eternally of eternal things." That is as true for me now, after twenty-eight years, as it was when Ridgely wrote it. I open his *Masque of Judgment* at Raphael's hymn to man, one of the great documents of humanism, and read:

> O struggler in the mesh
> Of spirit and of flesh
> Some subtle hand hath tied to make thee Man. . . .

> Though now the Master sad
> With vehemence shall break thee,
> Not lightly did He make thee,
> That morning when his heart was music-mad:
> Lovely importings then his looks and gestures had. . . .

> Not in vain, not in vain,
> The spirit hath its sanguine stain,
> And from its senses five doth peer
> As a fawn from the green windows of a wood. . . .

> And the soul utters, as she must,
> Her meanings with a loose and carnal lip;
> But deep in her ambiguous eyes
> Forever shine and slip
> Quenchless expectancies,
> And in a far-off day she seems to put her trust.

CHAPTER X

THE FLONZALEY QUARTET

ONE spring afternoon in 1907 Franz Kneisel, of the famous Kneisel Quartet, was good enough to give me, for publication in the *Century*, some of his ideas on the progress and prospects of chamber music. His quartet still had ten years to run (its last concert took place April 3, 1917); but he was already feeling, as his friend Adolfo Betti of the equally famous Flonzaley Quartet was later to feel, the strain of the continuous travelling, and as he sat that afternoon nursing his usual big cigar he looked a little tired, and sighed, "We grow older." It must have been a bore to have conductors on street cars ask where the dance was at which he and his colleagues were playing —not to speak of having gentlemen who should have known better request the Quartet to give a "Wagner program!"

Yet when I asked him if taste had not improved he answered at once: "Not to compare." "At first they tell me," he went on, " 'We do not care for any Haydn, Mozart, or early Beethoven.' They want the Tschaikowsky, Grieg, they make up programs of a little of this and a little of that—the Boccherini *Minuet*, some Svendsen, the slow movement of the Grieg *Quartet*. . . . But I always say 'If we are to give as many as four concerts, we must have at least one Haydn, one Mozart, and an early Beethoven.' So we insist, and soon they learn to appreciate these, and ask for them each year." The same exacting

148

Franz Kneisel

Inscribed: *"To Daniel G. Mason*
from his friend Franz Kneisel."

taste showed in a comment on Smetana's *Aus meinem Leben Quartet*. "It is a fine thing, certainly," he admitted. "But such a subject is too big for a quartet; it depends too much on painting. It should be kept better in the frame—a certain *noblesse* is lacking. If you have a success with a thing of this kind you don't feel elevated. With Brahms there is more suggestion." I asked if he thought general audiences responded to these subtle qualities as do trained musicians. "Yes, they do. There are a few hundred people in all cities, New York, Boston, Vienna, Berlin, London, Paris, who know just what to look for, and who demand the best. You don't impress them with wrong things. There are many people regularly listening, in private houses, to good music. All this prepares our audiences and we are used to expect the best taste from them, and to know that they go with us in whatever we do."

When I asked him, however, why in that case taste among the people at large was not better than it is, he replied: "There is much musical life in Europe that you don't get at all here. Think of the soldiers, and the way they keep before the people the rhythm of the march. . . . Then there are the Ländler and the Waltz, the *gemüthlich* dances of Austria. When we hear these rhythms in the music of classic composers they are vivid to us. But Americans, when they hear a slow minuet of Haydn, for instance, cannot enter into the spirit of it, for they have never *seen* these things." I felt that in emphasizing this lack of amateur music in a country so over-supplied with professionals (almost all imported) he had put his finger on a crucial matter.

The cellist of the Kneisels at that time was Willem Willeke, Kneisel's son-in-law, replacing the veteran Schroeder. The second violin was Julius Röntgen, and the viola, as always, was the charmingly intelligent and gracious Louis Svecenski. He it was who, being supposed to have less foreign accent than the others, always made any necessary spoken announcements from the stage. Once when Schumann-Heink, who was to have sung with the Quartet, was ill and unable to appear, Svecenski is said to have come forward and announced: "Ladies and Gentlemen: Madame Schumann-Heink cannot sing tonight, she is a little horse [hoarse]." Rather puzzled by the titters that greeted this, he added: "She cannot sing. She has a little colt [cold]." But how graceful, and at the same time how inspiring, was his farewell uttered for the Quartet at that last concert in April, 1917! Those war days were full of the most senseless and depressing prejudices, and the members of the other chief Quartet, the Flonzaley, to whom the Kneisels, despite all their central European associations, were handing on the torch, were two Italians, a Swiss, and a Belgian. But Svecenski ignored all these irrelevancies of nationality like the true artist he was, and simply said: "We are leaving chamber music in the hands of our fellow artists, and it doesn't matter what countries they come from, so long as they are loyal to King Ludwig van Beethoven."

II

Svecenski was right: chamber music was safe in the hands of four such men as Adolfo Betti, Alfred Pochon, Ugo Ara, and Iwan d'Archambeau, not to speak of the sustainer and inspirer of them all, Edward J. de Coppet. In a sense they were all his work of art, a fact gracefully recognized when all five men were sometimes referred to as the "Flonzaley Quintet". Betti and Pochon, who in the early days had been requested by de Coppet to alternate in the post of leading violin, and who had acquitted themselves with equal success, were both distinguished artists and scholars as well as players. Betti was the more poetic and tranquil, Pochon the more high-strung, nervous, and witty; and these differences of temperament were reflected in their physiques. Betti, his softly rounded face with its dreamy eyes framed in luxuriant dark hair, had great charm, a kind of quiet gracefulness and dignity that made him walk slowly onto the stage for a concert, incline scarcely perceptibly but with a sort of noble ease, and take his seat in a way that was already musical. Pochon made a strong contrast in his wiry alertness. He would seat himself squarely and dig his violin firmly into his neck with sidewise shakes of the head to fix it there securely. His observing mind enriched daily life with many amusing anecdotes and keen characterizations. In art it was penetrating enough to see what the vulgar will never know—that a good second violin is just as important as a good first. That is of course the essence of the distinction of chamber music, that it shows up the vulgarity of all personal display, and reveals always the supreme beauty of a just ensemble. Pochon once made a remark that might be taken as a motto by all artists: "If you have only to hold a single note, you can do it for a cent, or for a dollar—and ninety per cent of your audience won't know the difference. You have to do it for the other ten per cent, and for your own satisfaction."

Adolfo Betti on the other hand talked comparatively little, partly perhaps because English never flowed quite so easily on his tongue as Italian or French, but chiefly owing to a greater contemplativeness of temper. His dreamy air made superficial observers sometimes absurdly underrate the keenness of his intelligence; almost child-like as his look might be at times, he had one of the most penetrating minds I have known, discriminating, independent, humorous. Yet he was never sarcastic; a sunny sweetness of nature underlay all his greatest qualities, musical and human.

Of all the original four members of the quartet, the one who left it earliest, after the war-service from which his nervously delicate constitution never entirely recovered, was Ugo Ara. Perhaps that was one reason why I did not get so well acquainted with him as with the others; but he always seemed to me also more reticent in the communication of his thoughts, transparent as was the sweetness of his nature. His spirit was gentle, almost feminine, in expressing its many generous impulses less in speech than in loyal devotion to art and to his friends. The delicate grain of his mind, by no means incapable of humor, as he showed in his speech at the tenth anniversary festival of the Quartet, is revealed in a degree rare with him in a lovely sentence from his tribute to his friend de Coppet:

"Soutenu par les sublimes idées de Beethoven, dont une heure avant de mourir il analysait lucidement les beautés, il s'est éteint presque subitement et sans peine, sous la caresse bienfaisante et le sourire angélique de sa douce campagne; et cette mort, si simple et sereine, semblait être l'inévitable épilogue d'une vie comme la sienne, entièrement dépensée dans la poursuite du Bien et dans l'amour du

Beau." ("Sustained by the sublime ideas of Beethoven, of which only an hour before his death he had been analysing the beauties, he died suddenly and without pain, under the beneficent caress and the angelic smile of his sweet wife; and this death, so simple and so serene, seemed the inevitable epilogue of a life entirely spent, as his had been, in the pursuit of the good and the love of the beautiful.")

And then there was d'Archambeau, the Porthos of these four musical musketeers: d'Archambeau the stocky, the sturdy, he of the ideal cello figure and the ideal cello temperament—dependable as the planets in their courses. Was there ever such a quartet cellist as he? and did he not make most others seem by contrast what Arthur Whiting used to call scornfully "cooking cellists"—by analogy with cooking apples? If there was ever an "eating cellist" it was d'Archambeau; his tone certainly seemed good enough, solid enough, to eat! A quartet needs a foundation; and the strength of a Porthos is good to repose upon, especially when it has the advantage of guidance by more flexible minds. . . . Once the four musketeers were discussing how they might best meet their manager's [1] wish for some novel and striking publicity. Pochon, mischievously: "Why shouldn't we come onto the stage on bicycles, as they do at the circus?" D'Archambeau, round-eyed, and moustache bristling with dissent: "But Adolfo can't *ride* bicycle!" Yet always in a pinch, no matter how round his eyes might get, or how his moustache might bristle, he was *there*.

Betti's policies with the Flonzaley were in every way as severe, independent, and uncompromising as Kneisel's with the older quartet. He exclaims in one of his letters of the autumn following Svecenski's speech: "I have received several letters requesting me to *bar any German work from our programs during next season!* What do you think of that??!!" At a later period, when I was having a controversy with a press reviewer about the sensationalism of a certain New York orchestra, he wrote me:

"——'s attitude seems to me decidedly wrong. The issue—a vital

[1] According to an anecdote of Sandor Harmati's this manager said to Pablo Casals, whose public in America was at first small: "If you could just smile when you come on the stage—audiences like it." Casals' answer was to take another manager. "Now he's playing to sold-out houses," concluded Harmati—"and he's not smiling."

one—should be treated in a quiet dignified way. And he tries to make it as personal as possible, with no reason whatever. Why, it is not your fault if statistics are against the —— and the —— Orchestras. '*Les mathematiques ne sont pas une opinion.*' I think the manager's theory that one must give to the people *what they want* is absolutely wrong. Concessions to the public and sensationalism are not a *sine qua non* of a box-office success. Frederick Stock is certainly not a sensational conductor, his programs are most catholic in taste, and yet the Chicago fares financially better than any other orchestra in the country."

"The Flonzaleys" played on the whole, I think, rather a larger proportion of modern music than "the Kneisels"; but this was done, not from any sensational desire for mere novelty, but from a highly catholic and yet discriminating interest in what was being produced by living composers. It was done too at the cost of untold labor, as anyone who can imagine the task of rehearsing new music from manuscript parts will realize, and in the face of disheartening public indifference. This new music was usually studied in the late summer and autumn, at Le Tronchet in the canton of Vaud in Switzerland, where Alfred Pochon's family lived, not far from de Coppet's estate Le Flonzaley, for which the Quartet was named. It was frequently tried over for a small circle of friends and connoisseurs, either at Le Flonzaley or—after the New York season had begun—at the hospitable de Coppet house in West Eighty-fifth Street. In the spring there were again "reading evenings", when the Quartet's season was over, and, as I have described elsewhere,[1] "De Coppet engaged them for some weeks, to play for his friends, to read new works before a few intimates, and even to rest—for such was his magnanimous idea of what a good patron should expect of a good artist. 'They are tired after the year's work,' he would say. 'If they are to do their best they must have time to relax, to think, to absorb new impressions.' There were again the jovial St. Cecilia Festivals, held from year to year with much good fellowship and good music, ending up after dinner with an octet by Raff, Bargiel, Gade, or

---

[1] See the essay *An Ideal Patron (Edward J. de Coppet)* in *Music as a Humanity,* by Daniel Gregory Mason, H. W. Gray Company, New York, 1921.

Mendelssohn, played by all the available 'talent'. There were other times, too, when some or all of 'the Flonzaleys' listened instead of playing; notably when their friendly rivals 'the Kneisels' supplied the music."

Some idea of the spirit of ideal devotion and of ungrudging hard work in which Adolfo Betti and his associates approached all these activities may be gained from his letters of later years. I find him writing me, for instance, in September, 1921:

"Le Tronchet (Vaud)
"Switzerland

"It is now about six weeks that we are rehearsing daily, and many of the works we are going to play next season begin to be in good shape. . . .

"We have worked a great deal on the Enesco, which we shall play for the first time in Paris, in London, and afterwards in New York. It is a tremendously difficult quartet, but quite a fascinating work:—very original in this way, that it is singularly free from any influence of Debussy or Ravel (a remarkable thing for a man who has been educated in France). It is a very serious deep work, *trés solidement construit*. I think you will like it.

"We shall also play a *Fantasy* by Goossens—a clever piece brilliantly written (*un vrai feu d'artifice*), and also very likely a *Suite* for quartet and string orchestra by Scalero: a sort of modern 'Concerto grosso', a *severe* powerful work, yet quite effective, I believe".

Then a year later came the word, in reply to my advising him of the revision of my own *Quartet on Negro Themes*, which he had played in 1919 and '20:

"Bagni di Lucca, August 4th [1922]

"I was glad to hear about your quartet and am naturally anxious to see the changes you have made. . . . As for us, I am sorry to say we cannot take in consideration reviving the work this winter. We had so many complaints last year about Enesco and Bloch, that we shall be very careful this season about modern pieces and I think we

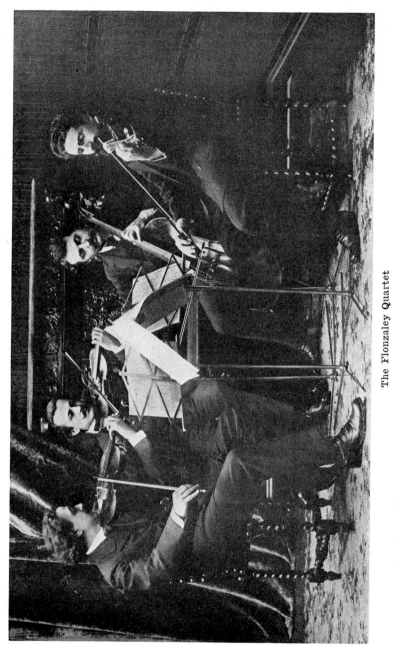

The Flonzaley Quartet

Inscribed: *"To Mr. Daniel Gregory Mason, with friendship and sympathy, The Flonzaley Quartet, New York, May, 1912. Adolfo Betti, Alfred Pochon, Iwan d'Archambeau, Ugo Ara,"*

have already more of them than the conservative stomach of our subscribers can digest."

And a year later still:

> "Le Tronchet
> "September 5th [1923]

"The first two weeks here are always *terrific!* . . . It is hard to get 'the machine' started again (although in this respect the quartet is a little better off than—a Ford!) And then there are so many things to discuss with my colleagues, new compositions to be tried, programs to be arranged, and God knows how many little problems to be solved that necessarily arise after a long period of rest. . . .

"I heard at the Grand Opera a performance of *Le sacre du printemps* with Koussevitzky that made a tremendous impression on me. One may not sympathize with Stravinsky's tendencies in music, but it is impossible to deny that the work is imbued with a sort of elemental power, something really overwhelming ('*Babylonien*', as Berlioz or R. Rolland would say). Koussevitzky did wonders with the Parisian orchestra, I never heard a French orchestra play better (which, of course, does not mean very much).

"We are working on the new Quartet by Vaughan Williams—a real fine work: nothing sensational, nothing ultra-modern, but a fine piece of music and . . . of good quartet writing! I think you will enjoy it."

And as a sort of summary of Adolfo's tireless loyalty to good music of all kinds, of his shrewd understanding of the inertia of the public and the egotism of composers that yet could not disillusion him, and of the simple and ardent love of beauty in nature and in art that always sustained him, let us take this, from the autumn of 1924:

> "Le Tronchet
> "August

"I enjoyed wandering with my mother through some of our little hill towns unknown to me. Orvieto, Perugia, Assisi, Volterra

. . . each of these glorious and musical names brings back to me a
wealth of sensations quite unparalleled even in my pretty long experience as a—professional wanderer. My dear Dan, you and Mrs.
Mason are really lucky, for you still have to 'discover' so many
beautiful things. You think you know Italy, but, believe me, you
don't. In fact, I am far from knowing it myself. . . . The land-
scapes! can anyone describe them? Can anything be more impressive than the view you get from Volterra, looking down through
the Balze into the valley, or the coloring of the Umbrian hills in the
neighborhood of Perugia or Assisi—that delicate blue that only a
Benozzo Gozzoli could reproduce in his frescos? Next time I have
the pleasure of being with you I am going to give you a little lecture
in my own way and to make you a plan which you must follow
when you visit again my country!

"For the present my occupation is . . . much less attractive. I
am here selecting new works for next season. A nice job, as you
know. How often comes back to me Rossini's well-known *boutade*
to the young composer: 'Cher ami, dans votre oeuvre il y a beaucoup
de nouveau et beaucoup de beau, mais ce qui est beau n'est pas
nouveau et ce qui est nouveau n'est pas beau!' ['My dear fellow,
in your work there is much novelty and much beauty; but what is
beautiful isn't new, and what is new is not beautiful!']

"And yet the effort is so vast, there is such a striving after beauty
from so many different sides, that after all one begins to feel encouraged and to hope for some signs of a real dawn in a not very
distant day. *E pur si muove!*" [1]

III

At the very first of the de Coppet musicales, back in October,
1886, long before the later personnel of the Quartet were assembled,
those present, as de Coppet has recorded in his manuscript list of
over a thousand such musical gatherings, were, besides de Coppet

---

[1] "*E pur si muove!*—And yet, it moves!" The exclamation of Galileo, affirming once
more, under his breath, despite his own enforced recantation and in the very presence of his inquisitors, that the earth *does* move, is singularly eloquent in the mouth
of another Italian who believes that beauty, like truth, can never stand still.

himself, Mrs. de Coppet taking the piano, her brother Mr. Charles
Bouis, violin, and Mr. Edwin T. Rice, violoncello. Mr. Rice, a
lawyer by profession but an enthusiastic amateur and patron of
chamber music, had kept up his interest all these years—and indeed
has kept it up until the very moment these words are being written,
now in 1938. He long maintained at his apartment in West Sixty-
seventh Street in the winter, and in the summer at his place, Prospect Hill, in Stockbridge in the Berkshires, semi-professional, semi-
amateur musical evenings that deserve an important place in the
history of American chamber music.

It was an interesting group. Rice himself, a sort of "oldest in-
habitant" in the extent of his knowledge of every concert, it seemed,
that had ever taken place in New York, and a walking encyclopedia
that could name you off-hand the opus number and key of any
chamber work of any standard composer, officiated with his inseparable cigar (as strong as Kneisel's) in the roomy studio of his
duplex apartment, played the cello part in everything from Boccherini to Florent Schmitt with an enthusiasm that made up for
any technical shortcomings, and in a word gave all his guests a
royal good time until the late hour when they adjourned to the
dining-room, Mrs. Rice's marvelous suppers, and the joys of gossip.
Besides all this, he was a trustee of the Philharmonic Orchestra, one
of the leading spirits in founding the Society for the Publication of
American Music, whose try-outs took place in his studio for years
on end, the consulting lawyer of the Flonzaleys, and many other
things. He was an almost fanatical Brahmsian, yet interested himself
in much new music. For several years you could hear his group
working on the splendid but extraordinarily difficult *Quintet* of
Florent Schmitt, long before its composer became generally known
here.

Two professionals who did a good deal to ballast his group, musically speaking, were the brothers Gaston and Edouard Dethier,
admirable musicians both. Gaston had been organist at St. Francis
Xavier, and had as fine a rhythm as any organist I have ever heard
(which is not saying as much as I wish it were). As a pianist he had
not so singing a touch as some, but great brilliance and a heart-

warming accuracy. What is better, as a musician he had courage, independence. Those were the days when the Flonzaleys were bringing forward the first *Quartet* of Schönberg, and many were taking towards it a breathlessly supine attitude that, however convenient, was not exactly heroic. Dethier had more daring, and made at the end of a letter a remark I have never forgotten.

"The Schmitt," he wrote, "made a deep impression; it was to the audience and to us performers, after Schönberg, what was the good Samaritan to the poor, battered fellow of the Scripture. Schönberg left us in a state almost fit for the morgue; he tortured our soul and body like the most fiendish maniac. The apostles of . . . the latest fads find this sublime; they go into ecstasy over the last page, which by the way is the only part which sounds like music. It seems as if Schönberg, who up to that time had been possessed of some tormenting demon, was at last freed and said with a deep sigh: 'Thank . . . the devil, it's all over.'

"The smart ones who frequent Mr. de Coppet's musicales tell me: You must not begrudge an artist for writing as he feels. No, *but a real artist before he expresses his feelings should first ask himself: 'Ought I to feel what I feel?'* "

Dethier may of course have been entirely wrong in his judgment. The point is that it is delightful to find someone who takes art seriously enough to go against the fashionable views, and to do it whole-heartedly. And I for one thoroughly agreed with him.

IV

But after all, the significance of "the Flonzaleys", and of the Kneisels too, lay not in what they played, certainly not in the number of new works they brought forward. New works, unless they have permanent beauty, quickly grow old. In the thirty years from 1886 to 1916 the "new composers" in the Flonzaley programs changed from such men as Bargiel, Goldmark, Onslow, Rubinstein, seldom heard at the end of that musical generation, to Debussy, Ravel, Reger, Schönberg, and Stravinsky, some of whom are beginning to be less frequently heard now. All the while, underneath such surface changes, flowed the steady stream of Beethoven, Haydn, Mozart, Schubert and Schumann. And since it is far harder to give a good performance of so exquisite a thing as a quartet of Mozart than it is to make a sensation with an ugly novelty by Schönberg or Stravinsky, a serviceable test of any performer is: "What can he do with Mozart?" Does he, as do unfortunately the majority of players in every age, merely play by routine, putting into the notes he finds no answering intelligence, no passion, no life?—Is he as a performer, that is to say, a mere *con*former? Or worse still, is he a *de*former?—one who accents here and drags out there until what remains is a parody of the composer's intention? Or finally, is he one of those rare beings a *trans*former—an artist who intuitively catches the composer's vision of beauty, and by his skill, his feeling, his loyal self-subordination, realizes for us not its letter but its spirit, catches for us its inner meaning, gives to us the utterance that is above the notes, in all its magic?

If I were asked to name the supreme transformers, in this sense, of my day, I should cite Ossip Gabrilowitsch, Paderewski, Rachmaninoff and a few others among the pianists; Kreisler, Enesco, and Heifetz foremost among the violinists; the Kneisel and Flonzaley above all later Quartets; and among conductors Muck, Stock, Gabrilowitsch, Bruno Walter, and at his best Toscanini. The conformers are legion. Among the deformers would appear all sentimentalists, most virtuosos, the quartets that habitually hurry and over-accentuate, and the *prima donna* conductors.[1]

What are the exact differences, then, between those performers who conform, those who deform, and those who transform? By what mechanical means do these contrasts, so capital to all musical art, make themselves felt? The differences are in last analysis reducible, it seems to me, to varying adjustments of value, both dynamic (relations of loud and soft) and, more subtly, rhythmic (almost imperceptible lingering on important notes). "To hear Mr. Gabrilowitsch play the first ten notes of the slow movement of the

[1] "Everything exaggerated," says Talleyrand, "is insignificant." Compare my essays *Sensationalism and Indifference* and *Stravinsky as a Symptom* in *The Dilemma of American Music*.

Mozart *D minor Concerto*," I pointed out many years ago,[1] is enough to prove to anyone with ears the supreme importance of subordination. Not that the pianist is necessarily conscious of it; indeed such molding of the phrase is one of the most deeply instinctive of all musical acts. . . . None the less science, in its laborious, intellectual way, might arrive at a formulation of what Mr. Gabrilowitsch does when he plays this meltingly beautiful phrase. Science would measure the dynamic force and deviation from standard time value of each of those ten notes. . . . We may venture the suggestion that the difference between Mr. Gabrilowitsch's exquisite delivery, and on the one hand the perfunctory matter-of-factness of the average performance, and on the other the sentimentality of what we may call an overripe one, will depend quite perceptibly on the length of the sixth note. If it is a grain too short we have matter-of-factness, if an iota too long, sentimentality."

Now it was this quality of beautiful balance in the adjustment of values, the avoidance of flatness on the one hand and of exaggeration on the other, that was the supreme quality of the Flonzaley Quartet. What comes back to mind as one recalls the moments of perfect happiness their greatest performances gave, is not the dramatic shiver of some bold stroke of Beethoven's, not even the rush and excitement of such a thing as his fugue in the C major Opus 59 *Quartet,* but the heavenly simplicity, peacefulness, repose of some quiet melody of Mozart or Schubert, Schumann or Brahms, or that more than earthly theme of the variations in Beethoven's Opus 127. Almost impossible to describe in detail is this perfection of simplicity and repose, partly because it cannot be analysed without the use of technical musical terms, perhaps even more because it depends on no single striking features, no outstanding effects, but rather on the unobtrusive but profoundly right balance of the whole.

An analogy with the sister art of poetry may help us to understand it. Gabrilowitsch picks out just the one important tone in the Mozart phrase, the sixth, and gives it just the right emphasis, neither too little nor too much. To a correspondent who asked me to recall

[1] In the essay, *A Note on Tonal Chiaroscuro,* in *Music as a Humanity.*

my impressions of the Flonzaley Quartet I wrote: "The other day I heard the slow movement of the first Opus 59 of Beethoven (with the deeply spiritual melody in F minor) played by one of our leading quartets. Well played in many ways, it completely lacked the high serenity, nobility, and quietude that it used to have in the hands of the Flonzaleys. It was like taking a beautiful broad line of poetry, such as Shakespeare's

The multitudinous seas incarnadine

where there should be only one main accent, on 'seas', and sing-songing it into

'The MULti TUD inous SEAS in CARN a DINE'."

"Think what it would mean," I have pointed out elsewhere [1] "if I could not read Hamlet's soliloquy for myself, but had to go to a public hall and hear someone recite it. Obviously, if the personal vanity of this reciter, the commercial instincts of his manager, the nose for news of the press, and the imperviousness of the majority of the public to subtly restrained effects were all pressing him toward a sensational way of reading, I should never be able to hear Hamlet speak in the quiet, full, deep way Shakespeare dreamed. Now this is literally the plight in which every lover of symphonic music finds himself today." (And of course, I might have added, every lover of chamber music as well.)

"There is, for illustration, a quietly sustained phrase for cellos that Brahms has put at the opening of the slow movement of his *Second Symphony*, meditative, reticent, profoundly and thoughtfully beautiful. Can I so hear it? Not if it occurs to Mr. X, conductor of one of our most famous orchestras, to italicize, so to speak, each one of its notes by giving it a separate bow-stroke. Thus deformed and overemphasized, the phrase in its bumptious pretentiousness is no more Brahms than Hamlet's soliloquy would be Shakespeare if every other word in it were printed in italics or capitals. "To *be*, or NOT to BE"—how much quiet thoughtfulness remains in that? Alas, our whole musical literature nowadays is so habitually overstressed in this way that many sensitive musicians prefer to stay at home rather than hear concerts that caricature the music they love."

[1] *Music and the Radio, Columbia University Quarterly*, June, 1936.

I would not paint too black a picture. One or two contemporary groups, notably the Roth Quartet, have the same ideal of quiet utterance, of sustained unsensational beauty, as the Flonzaleys, and measurably attain it. The habit of over-accentuation to be noticed in many pupils of Leopold Auer is perhaps passing a little out of vogue; Féri Roth himself tells me that the influence of Enesco and others is leading modern violin playing away from it, and towards a purer style, more like Mozartian *bel canto*. But of course profound influences in modern life produce sensationalism: our hurry, our neurotic restlessness, our inability to relax, the failure so far of our deeper aesthetic and emotional nature to keep pace with mechanical invention, and to assimilate it. Hence we find tranquil beauty less by looking about us than by looking back into a simpler past. And for me at least, supreme beauty in chamber music was realized chiefly in the playing of the Flonzaley Quartet, equalled if at all only by that of the Kneisels. To those two great Quartets of my youth and middle age I shall always look back with gratitude for some of the hours of purest musical happiness of my life.

CHAPTER XI

ADVENTURES IN CHAMBER MUSIC

As to composing any chamber music of my own, I soon found how right was Arthur Whiting in saying that "composing is a luxury." Since chamber music is economically speaking a drug in the market, and yet in order to make it one has to take a great deal of time away from profitable work such as lecturing and teaching, I for one could afford little of it. In the summer of 1907, for instance, after lecturing at Chicago University and teaching in the Harvard Summer School, I had left the tag-end of the vacation, from late August on, in which to write the first movement only of my *Violin Sonata*, a first experiment in chamber music. The other two movements had to wait until the following summer. Similarly a second, more ambitious piece, a *Quartet* for piano and strings, dragged to a tardy conclusion through three summers, 1909, 1910, and 1911. This piece-meal way of working, with long interruptions and many changes of influence even while work was proceeding, carried with it almost inevitably the penalty of changes of style within a single work.

I myself realized well enough that the first movement of the sonata was shamelessly Brahmsian. But I could not help gasping a little when so good a friend as Gaston Dethier, on the heels of telling me that the Flonzaley Quartet thought the sonata a remarkable thing to come from an American, went on to say that Pochon and

163

others criticized the differences of style between the movements, and that he himself found in the first movement Brahms, in the second Massenet (I should have said Tschaikowsky), and in the last —Vieuxtemps! But I tried to remember that one cannot work without models, that as models go Brahms, and even Tschaikowsky, are good ones, and that as Emerson puts it: "Every house is a quotation out of all forests and mines and stone-quarries; and every man is a quotation from all his ancestors." Moreover, I was fortunately no journalist that I should idolize mere novelty of idiom above good workmanship and a healthy grasp of tradition.

Good workmanship—alas, there was the difficulty! I had taken the precaution to use piano in my combinations with strings, although I did not particularly like the way they merge—or fail to merge—because, being a pianist of sorts myself, I had a slightly more adequate knowledge of the piano than of the endless subtleties of strings. But instrumentation is a small part of music, and in all matters of structure and composition I was a tyro, and knew it. . . . This sense of one's own incorrigible inadequacy as an artist, even as a technician, as I am sure all aspiring young composers will agree, is the most formidable of all the obstacles in our path. How shall we conquer it? The best suggestion I can give is what I eventually came to call "spontaneity", in a book, *Artistic Ideals*, written many years later. Spontaneity, the only cure for discouragement, the only road to happiness, is the artist's habit of distinguishing sharply between his personal ambition, his vanity—low motives—and his impersonal joy in art, the finest thing of which he is capable. Spontaneity is his power to work happily at the processes of his art, however far its products may fall short of pleasing others or himself. How those early experiences, many of them bitter, some inspiring, led me slowly to find this out for myself, I may show by one or two journal entries.

"August 18, 1907 [Before starting the *Violin Sonata*]. "We went over to that place under a tree near the golf-links and discussed what I could do.

"I am to work at music, not because my music has any great value (for I can't see that it has) but because it is one of the things that I can to a certain extent do, and want to do. I am going to write notes just as a spider spins web or a butterfly hovers about flowers. A severe utilitarian view would see little use in any of these three activities."

"July 19, 1909 [Before starting the *Piano Quartet*]. M. talked splendidly about how anxious she is that I should go on, not in order to write 'great music', but to have the happiness myself, and to give her the music. . . .

"I feel that I must and will stagger on. However defective my technique, however little originality I may have, there is in me something sacred, that can only find voice in music, and that it is my business to get out, however stammeringly."

"Sunday, December 17, 1911. 5 A.M. [After the eventual success of the *Violin Sonata* at Edwin T. Rice's apartment in New York]. I have been lying awake thinking how fascinating are the subtle interlaced problems of composition, musical or literary. It doesn't matter that perfection, even in a brief bit, depends on so many and delicate discriminations that it is practically unattainable to human faculties. The joy is in the quest for it, and in the even partial success. To use one's mind finely is an incomparable delight."

But no one, I suppose, whatever his experiences, ever learns to maintain spontaneity steadily, without interruptions, backslidings, and forgettings. Certainly I did not. I only generalized my own experience when I said in *Artistic Ideals:* "Even by the most devoted, spontaneity is never definitively attained, nor by the most ambitious ever completely compromised; in all it is fluctuating and precarious. Indeed spontaneity may be said, by a delightful and highly human paradox, to be one of the most laborious of achievements. It is precisely for that reason that conscious recognition of it as an ideal is vital to young artists."

II

Another thing I found almost as hard to achieve as spontaneity was receptivity, hospitality to influences without servility to them. It was hard to cultivate what Arthur Whiting quoted as someone's ideal: "An open mind, but not open at both ends". Perhaps we are all inclined not to be tolerant enough of the slowness with which our artistic individualities have to be formed, of all the testing and tasting, the tentative acceptance, the cautious hesitant rejection, that has to take place before we can discover what influences are truly for us, and what can never be ours. Every young artist must keep himself plastic for years; and if he allows himself to suppose, in maturer age, after he has made his choices and left the alternatives in limbo, that his path was preordained, or that he could have found it any less laboriously than he did, then he is being unimaginative, sadly deceiving himself, and failing to appreciate the venturesomeness of his own youth.

How long it took me to make up my mind what I really thought of the challenging personality of Strauss! His wit and bubbling vivacity, the Till Eulenspiegel side of him, fascinated me from the first, but the ugliness of his realism repelled. "Just at present," I wrote my friend Hill in 1909, "I am wild with enthusiasm over *Till Eulenspiegel*. I think it one of the most irresistible scores in the world. What mazes of color, and what wondrous part-writing! I am particularly struck with Strauss's attitude toward dissonances produced by good voice-leading. He is a true descendant of Bach in this respect." Yet only a few months later, having to review a New York performance of *Elektra* for the *London Times*, I wrote:

"The emotion that to the Greek mind was religious and super-personal . . . becomes in the modern version a blind hate. Accordingly the story is no longer tragic in the sense that it purges the heart by inspiring pity and terror, but is merely monstrous, and plays upon the one nerve of shuddering horror." I summed up my impression: "Here a man of genius has fought a brilliant but losing battle against the requirements of an essentially unmusical because ugly drama. But at moments he has nevertheless emerged above his subject into the pure light of beauty."

The French school puzzled me even more. Looking back, I am surprised to see how long it took me to distinguish between the mastery of Vincent d'Indy, whom, in spite of grave faults, I have come to consider one of the greatest of modern composers, and that puzzling pair, Debussy and Ravel, who now seem to me primarily purveyors of *musique de luxe*. Towards the fall of 1909, when I had finished the first movement of my *Piano Quartet* but was as usual dissatisfied, I wrote Hill:

"I have got to a sort of transition point in taste . . . a little enamored (don't faint) of certain phases of modern style, and of course without the technic to satisfy myself in any new direction. I hasten to reassure you that my 'modernism' would not be so considered by you, it is only a harmless interest in Wagner's chromaticism, in parts of Strauss, and in Debussy's wonderful suggestiveness, tact, and freedom from the obvious in rhythm and harmony—not, I think, in melody."

In early letters to Hill I even coupled the noble if sometimes dry d'Indy with Ravel, whose sentimentality has come gradually to make his music intolerable to me. Debussy's harmonies, especially his sliding, clamped-together ninth chords reproducing a single melody at five levels simultaneously and thus virtually reducing harmony to zero, proved so seductive to the merely sensuous ear, that I used some of them, with really startling inappropriateness, in the first version of my *Quartet on Negro Themes*, and only came to my senses in time to expunge them in a later edition. So slow was I to find my own musical aliment, and to perceive what, though food for others, was poison for me. Only gradually have I come to realize the penetration of a comment Paderewski made to me at about this time: "Debussy is a man of great skill in harmony and orchestration, but he writes music not for its own sake but as a handmaid to something that is not music. Now music is not a handmaid, a slave; it should not be made subordinate to poetry, a mere decoration; it should have its own form, its own meaning, its own *raison d'être*. Not long ago I heard *Pelleas et Melisande* in Paris. It is ingenious, it has many beautiful effects, but from beginning to end it is subdued, soft, monotonous—everything is subordinated to the text, nothing is musically salient—pages and pages without one triad, without rhythmic vigor—never one manly accent."

III

Paderewski himself is another composer about whom I have found it difficult to make up my mind. He is one of those artists who suffer from our labelling system, his label being "Great Pianist". A more intelligent system, it seems to me, might add "Great Composer". We heard his *Polish Symphony* in 1909, and I wrote in my journal: "It is a perfectly wonderful masterpiece: such beauty, tenderness, nobility, majesty." No doubt I was somewhat influenced by the program. Very likely I had Strauss's *Elektra* in the back of my mind when I wrote of it: "What a relief, after all the pettily egotistical, sentimental, and pathological programs that contemporary writers have set themselves, is the simple and exalted patriotism of this work! Its theme is human suffering for an ideal, human loyalty to an ideal. . . . It arouses that sense of 'pity and terror' by which, ever since the Greeks, all nobly tragic art has purged the spirits of men." The program of a piece of music, however, no matter how noble, is of course no more than the menu of a dinner; the question is, what are the viands, and how are they cooked? The symphony, I felt even at the time, was rather over-Wagnerian in style. Deeply as it impressed me—and that is true also of the Piano Sonata—I cannot tell how they would strike me now.

But the *Variations and Fugue on an Original Theme*, opus 23, has always seemed to me one of the finest compositions of my time. In those days—and still more today—it is rare to find the qualities of richly sensuous coloring and splendidly intellectual vitality of form (as in the final combinations of the themes of fugue and variations) united as they are here. It was inspiring to hear a work so firmly founded in its ultimate elements on classic traditions, yet satisfying also the ear used to rich modern color. We first heard Paderewski himself play it at a recital in the Brooklyn Institute, just before Christmas, 1907.

A few days later, by special appointment then made with his secretary, I went on to Boston, to prepare for publication in the *Century Magazine* a conversation with him on his ideas about contemporary music. On arriving at his Boston hotel at 12:30, the hour named for lunch, I made a most stupid, boyish error and asked not for Paderewski himself, but for the secretary through whom I had made the engagement. I was told he was out. So I sat and fumed in the lobby until almost two, while the Paderewskis were fuming in their suite upstairs over my unaccountable absence. When I finally did appear, miserably self-conscious and babbling apologies, Madame Paderewska evidently found it hard to forgive me for having so long delayed the master's luncheon. He himself, the simplicity of his manner belying the formal-looking frock-coat he wore with his usual low collar and white satin tie, was as always cordial and sympathetic.

I told him how much I admired his *Variations*, adding with possibly superfluous candor: "That you may not think I say this in empty flattery, I will tell you frankly that I do not care so much for some of your early pieces."

Mme. P. What pieces? What do you not care for?

D. G. M. Well, for example, I do not care so much for the *A minor Concerto*.

Mme. P. The concerto is one of my favorites among my husband's compositions. I love it more and more.

D. G. M. Oh, I do not mean that it is not a fine composition. But it does not seem to me so strong, so rugged, so original as the *Variations*. They seem to me to combine the most various tendencies of modern music. Besides the modern French impressionism they have a Brahms-like solidity of structure and polyphony.

(Query: After keeping a great man waiting an hour and a half for his lunch, is it tactful for a youngster to discuss his work, no matter how favorably, in terms so—let us say specific?)

I. J. P. I utterly repudiate any debt to French impressionism. . . . I do not believe in the modern French school, because it is not founded in tradition. It is erratic, bizarre, wayward. It strives only for "originality"; it has no true mastery. No, there is nothing French in my impressionism. I used these effects of dissonance, particularly of seconds, long ago, before they had come into common use. In my little *Barcarolle*, published in 1883, you will already find this use of seconds.

D. G. M. Pardon me, M. Paderewski, I do not in the least mean that you imitate the French composers. I mean simply that there is in your *Variations* (for example in that lovely Variation No. XV, which is so deliciously *smeared*, so to speak, with delicate dissonance) a kind of tonal effect which I naturally compare with the effects of Debussy and others.

I. J. P. My dear Mr. Mason, I am not offended with you. . . . When I wrote that fifteenth variation I thought to myself, "Presently someone will label that 'French impressionism'." You say I use dissonances in a certain way. I do this because I am an accomplished musical scholar. The modern French are, many of them, not accomplished musicians; they are in some respects amateurs; they have no polyphony. . . . All of the modern French music of this kind put together is not worth one quartet of Brahms! Originality, originality—is it original to drink like this? [Taking up a glass of water and holding it in the reverse of the usual position, with wrist strained backward.]

I admired immensely this courage to speak his real convictions that I always found in Paderewski, however open they might be to misconstruction.

Before I left that day he wrote out for me, for reproduction in my article, the theme of his variations. Madame Paderewska, who had warned me he had an engagement at three, hovered anxiously over his shoulder. Perhaps she thought my idea of the sanctity of engagements eccentric—at any rate she had the air of somehow blaming me for the slowness of the process of writing music. When at last, reserving as one will the expression marks until all the notes are down, he inserted the direction *forte pesante* for the opening octaves ("loud and heavy") she actually laid her hand on his shoulder—and made him blot it! The *pesante* is hard to read. . . . That was more heavy-handedness than he had bargained for.

Remembering his generous encouragement of my early piano sonata, I ventured to show Paderewski before leaving that day the first movement of the new *Violin Sonata*—the only movement then written. To Hill I reported exuberantly: "He shook hands with me about eight times, and through it kept singing the melody with me and exclaiming 'beautiful!'" This was fortunate indeed for me, destined as I was to go through agonizing fluctuations of feeling about that sonata. When it was all done Ossip Gabrilowitsch told me with his usual straightforwardness that he did not like it; and as late as 1911—the year of its eventual success—I made up my mind, after rehearsing it with an amateur, that I did not like it myself. Yet I had good hours of renewed hope about it, such as all composers will sympathetically understand, especially when I had the luck to play it not with amateurs but with such a great artist as my friend Betti, whose divination could reach through my clumsy technique the soul of my intention. "Betti has dined and spent the evening," I find my journal recording, "and we have had a splendid time. How lovely parts of my *Violin Sonata* sounded—played as I meant them, but have not yet heard them! Detail after detail he took up, patiently and with such heavenly penetration, often playing just the opposite from what I had written. Sometimes it seems as if expression marks were fifty per cent of music. . . . But my themes are often beautiful in their breadth and depth of feeling."

The summer I finished the sonata we were living at East Hampton, where I had my studio in a barn. Above a rough plank ceiling was the hay-loft, and hayseed used to sift down on my head as I worked. One evening as I was improvising there in rather melancholy mood, thinking of the contrast between the careless perfection of nature and our human struggle, suddenly a whippoorwill began to sing. His clear lifting note seemed to symbolize that very ease, that heartless perfection of nature. What was quite as much to the point to the musical side of my mind, he was singing in E flat minor, in perfect tune, and—it is unnecessary to state—with a fairly mechanical meticulousness of rhythm! So I began to improvise with him, amusing myself by seeing how many ways I could think of to harmonize his monotonous cry. In this way I got the germ of the piece called *The Whippoorwill*, the first one written of the set *Country Pictures*. My wife later made these verses for it:

O bird who in the twilight shadows
Thy note of mystery sings,
Who art thou in thy tender mocking,
Thy half revealing of infinite beauty,
Life's secret joy outpouring,
Deaf to our futile pain?

IV

The summer after that, 1909, was the first of the many we spent
in the old "Yellow farmhouse" belonging to our dear friend and
fellow musician Gertrude Watson, of Onota Farm in Pittsfield. Her
own beautiful house, with its communicating music-rooms opening
on the lovely garden, was the scene of many musical afternoons;
her spacious motor-car made all the surrounding Berkshire hills
gradually familiar to us; and her close friend Elizabeth Coolidge was
soon, through her Chamber Music Festivals at South Mountain, to
give Pittsfield a permanent place in the history of music. Meanwhile
our life in the funny farmhouse, almost devoid of plumbing, and as
remote from Pittsfield at four miles as it would be nowadays at
forty, was amusingly primitive. Our aged horse, Dick, the pride of
Billy's heart and the subject of many of his medical ministrations
and experiments, could negotiate the four miles to and from town
once or twice a week, if given his head and allowed his own pace.
The water supply did not usually give out until mid-August, except
in especially dry summers. Then water had to be brought by Miss
Watson's Italians, in milk-cans, until Charlie, her superintendent,
improvised a reservoir for us in the woods, enclosing in very im-
promptu-looking concrete several springs. He piped this to the
kitchen and at last even upstairs. But bathroom there was none. A
poignant family memory is the look of despair Mrs. de Coppet cast
on the small out-building that was the nearest we could come to one,
and her heartfelt comment: "*Mon Dieu!*"

One of our strongest points was my studio, a little one-room frame
building especially erected for that first summer, out of earshot of
the house and the children, in an upland field, with a wood of white

pines behind it, and a big white birch alongside, with even a convenient bend wherein Stillman Kelley, Vaughan Williams, and other
distinguished visitors could sit to be snapshotted. On a sunny day
the air all about it was aromatic with the pine-needles and the wild
thyme. The first musical idea I got there was the opening theme of
what eventually became my *Pastorale* for violin, clarinet, and piano.
That first summer, however, when I conceived it as an orchestral
suite, it obstinately refused to move, and I had to give it up. It was
only when, two summers later, I hit upon the right combination for
it that it took shape fairly quickly. The first theme (violin, D major), voiced the morning mood that filled one in that bright upland
field, vocal with birds, steeped in sunshine and aromatic fragrance.
Then with the change to minor and the entrance of the plaintive
clarinet melody over the murmuring piano accompaniment I tried
to suggest the change of mood that comes as a cloud passes over the
sun. It often seemed to me as if something almost as palpable as a
mist descended quickly and unaccountably on fields and hills.
There would come a sense of pause, of something both melancholy
and ominous that is as characteristic of those Berkshire uplands as
the gayer mood of full sunlight. I used the violin rather than the
cello which more usually accompanies a clarinet in chamber music,
because its brilliance gave just the contrast I wanted with the deeper
liquid tones of the clarinet.

Later that first Pittsfield summer I began the *Piano Quartet* that
I associate specially with Ossip Gabrilowitsch, to whom it is dedicated. When he came to visit us (he had said in one of his letters) he
expected "to have watermelon for dinner and at least two movements of the quartet after dinner". But the watermelon and the
quartet were almost as slow to ripen as his visit, delayed by his
operation and his courtship. When he finally arrived, in mid-September, he had a bandage around his head, and a beard! There were
no watermelons, I fear, and only one movement of quartet, which
he criticized with his usual ardor. "It is a harrowing experience," I
confessed in my journal after his departure, "to have one's music
eviscerated—even with praise—as Ossip eviscerated the quartet.
Perfection is so unattainable, and everything short of it is so un-

satisfying. One's work often seems nothing but a mass of faults, each of which is painfully corrected only to reveal more pitilessly the others."

Yet when my birthday came around, in the midst of his innumerable affairs he remembered it, and wrote me: "May the *Quartet* be completed before you are a year older, and may each succeeding year bring at least one important and beautiful work like the one you so successfully started"? And the following autumn, when I had written two more movements, and he and Clara were starting off to live in Munich and begin his career as a conductor, and when we went to say goodbye and found him, in Clara's illness, receiving all the guests with his usual efficiency and good nature, he seized a moment to tell me "That slow movement is fine".

Glancing ahead at the public performances of the work so slowly completed, I find him as friendly there as in the more important period of its writing. In July of 1914 he wrote me from Dorf Kreuth (he had been settled in Europe for several years then) that he would be very glad to play the *Quartet* with the Kneisels. Then came the outbreak of the war, and for Ossip and Clara a hasty retreat from the home in Munich and all his successful work there as a conductor, and eventually their return to America.

"Zurich, September 20, 1914

"Your letters of August 10th and August 31st both reached me just now. Such is mail service in time of war! Yes, we did have some thrilling experiences, of which I'll tell you more when I see you.

"The principal question to me is whether I shall be able to get the *score* of the quartet from Munich where it is now. We had to leave home in such a rush that we packed almost nothing. And now while we can send for clothes and such things we cannot send for books or music, as all printed matter and (even more so) all manuscripts are likely to be confiscated by the military censure. They might mistake your *Adagio* for the diagram of a fortress, and they might consequently give it a 'blowing up' same as the New York critics probably would.

"However I still hope to be able to smuggle the thing through. If not you will have to rewrite it from the parts. But don't begin that job until you hear from me."

"Atlantic City, November 19

"I went over your quartet this morning two or three times carefully. It is a fine work, but I have the impression now as I had last summer that some revising in the way of cuts, change of form, etc., might greatly improve the last two movements. Under these circumstances the question arises whether it is advisable to play it in its present form in Boston December 1st.

"Please don't misunderstand me. I am only looking out for the best possible way in which your work can first be produced, and Boston seems important, especially as they are only too ready there to find fault with compositions which are not by Debussy or Ravel. I well remember the nasty way in which Philip Hale spoke of your splendid *Elegy*. I think the *Quartet* ought to be presented in Boston in as perfect a shape as possible."

After rehearsing the piece with the Kneisel Quartet, Ossip decided to go on with the performance as scheduled, in spite of his apprehensions about the reception of it by Boston. They proved only too well founded. This time Philip Hale, in the *Herald*, while admitting that the audience had "applauded with a heartiness that approached enthusiasm", headlined his article "Kneisels courteously play *Quartet* by D. G. Mason", and protested that "the Kneisels should not so strain courtesy." And indeed this was a fault from which Hale himself was completely free.

From one point of view, however, Hale's attack did me, if not that particular work, a good turn, by making me more aware of the true supporters of all artistic aspiration—one's fellow musicians and the unsophisticated public. Leland Hall, in more recent years known for his novels and his essays on music, wrote me: "I suppose you saw Philip Hale's review of your quartet. It seemed to me wholly unwarranted. . . . I telephoned the next morning to several people I knew were there and they were unanimous in praise of your quartet. They all mentioned the spontaneous applause which greeted it.

Evidently the public was with you. The more I live the more I am convinced that aside from music which thrills merely by display what gains the approval of the public has the real stuff in it."

As for the musicians, two of those I admired most in Boston wrote me delightful notes, highly characteristic of their contrasting personalities. "I just want to tell you," scrawled on a card Arthur Foote, always so friendly, "that I heartily enjoyed your quartet—and think it a very good work in construction as well as invention. I was ashamed of one Boston criticism—for its spirit—and because it was just the opposite of the truth. I liked it, but whether one liked it or not, it was admirably written—that is undeniable. So I congratulate you on another step onward."

Chadwick was more aggressive. Explaining that illness had prevented his attending the concert but that he had read some of the reviews, he went on: "I was rather struck with the similarity of opinion expressed to those which reviewed some of my early works. While we can't help resenting the insufferable pretence of some of these penny-a-liners, so far as I know a pretty steady stream of discredit and disparagement for the last twenty years from certain quarters has never had the slightest effect, either on my productive powers or on my reputation. So I hope you will be equally philosophical in regard to these creatures."

I fear I am a good deal thinner-skinned, or less well provided with the courage of my convictions, than Chadwick. All through my life the indifference or positive enmity of certain sections of the press has been a heavy drag on my creative energy, a dead weight that had to be lifted with strength needed for all the intrinsic problems of the work itself. The hardest part was the discouragement not only to oneself but to one's interpreters—to the performers or conductors who had devoted their best powers to the ungrateful task of producing new and untried work for an amiable but more or less indifferent public, and who got these licks for their pains from those supposed to be expert judges.

All the more did a helpless composer admire the independence of an intrepid performer like Gabrilowitsch, who in spite of being more at the mercy of the press than the composer himself—since a com-

poser can always afford to wait—set always a high example of superiority to it. When, a few days after the Boston concert, he found me perusing the clippings, he cried, "Are you polluting your mind with those things?" "He began by asking me," I recorded in my journal, "how I felt after my 'triumph', and when I answered that if he and the Kneisels liked it I didn't care what Hale said he answered that he liked it a hundred per cent better than when he first saw it, and that it was a fine work. Nevertheless I know there is some truth in Hale's criticism, and if I can only keep from being too discouraged I may profit by it." As for Gabrilowitsch, he was not in the least disturbed in his liking for the quartet, nor dissuaded from repeating it a year later in New York. I find him writing me in the summer of 1915: "Many thanks for your intention to dedicate the *Quartet* to me. Of course I shall be delighted to have my name associated with this fine work and even to feel myself in a way part owner of it."

Ossip never did things by halves.

V

Perhaps I have now given more than enough illustrations of the self-evident fact that anyone who aspires to navigate the seas of composition had better prepare for squalls, and will be fortunate enough if he escape shipwreck. And after all, when the sun does occasionally come out, how heart-warming it is! The year the sun unmistakably came out for my chamber music was 1911. That summer we twice visited the Rices in Stockbridge, and had the joy of hearing the *Violin Sonata* and other things played and discussed by sympathetic colleagues, professional and amateur. In September the sonata had there its first quasi-public hearing, in the hands of Edouard Dethier and Carolyn Beebe. In December it was repeated, at the Rice's New York apartment, in the presence of the Flonzaley Quartet and other musicians. From that time to the end of the year was one exciting *crescendo*.

"December 22. Wow! Hurray! Betti says he will try the *Quartet* over with the Flonzaley Quartet next March at Mr. de Coppet's!

. . . Then up through the rain to see Winthrop Rogers, and when I asked him about publishing the sonata he said—Wow! Hurray!—that he thought there was little doubt Schirmer would agree."

"December 30. 1 A.M. We had a great time at the Rogers' *Kinder-symphonie* party. Kneisel was awfully funny with the Cuckoo, and Svecenski with the four-note trumpet; and D'Archambeau's eyes nearly popped out when he did on a one-note trumpet the figure, Dum-di-dum. Röntgen was an inimitable leader. Svecenski argued with him a good deal, asking once to go across the street because he had 69 bars' rest. Betti was seriously anxious lest he should not keep time. The whole thing was great fun."

And finally:

"December 31. I hate to have this year 1911 end; it has been the happiest I have ever had. . . . I feel as if it had laid a solid foundation for a satisfactory life as a composer—and though I have been struggling toward that all my life I have never got in sight of it before this year."

CHAPTER XII

PITTSFIELD PEOPLE

OUR musicales in the little studio in the upland field, begun in the summer of 1909 when Miss Watson and Miss Learned, Dr. and Mrs. Coolidge and a cousin were our only guests for the studio house-warming, became almost annual affairs. There was always uncertainty, of course, as to whether the day would be favorable to such *al fresco* gatherings. When it was, the informality of the whole occasion was delightful. The guests would sit about on benches and chairs near the studio, or squat on the grass itself up near the crest of the hill. The music, for the most part ensemble, with scattering soloes, was amateur in spirit even when semi-professional in personnel.

"We had our musicale yesterday afternoon," I recorded in my journal one August day in 1912, "and it was very successful. The weather cleared off beautifully, as if especially for it, and the studio and its surroundings looked awfully pretty. Ellen, Lowell, and Billy worked like Trojans, removing cow-souvenirs (Gregory made a 'Persian proverb': 'He that walketh in the cowpath treadeth in the dung'), carting up the benches, making lemonade, getting wild-flowers, and heaven knows what else." The journal adds a list of the pieces played, among which were two movements of the Brahms *Trio*, opus 8 (Stafford, Miss Zimmern, and D. G. M.), my *Pastorale*

(Stafford, Tuthill, and the composer), a Grovlez *Scherzo* (Sprague
Coolidge and his mother), some Ravel four-hand pieces played
by Mrs. Coolidge and Miss Watson, and the Brahms F-minor
Clarinet Sonata (Tuthill and D. G. M.).

Mrs. Coolidge and Miss Watson, close friends, always made for
us an interesting contrast. Both large, strong women, both passionately devoted to music, both in later years sorely afflicted with deafness, they were different enough in nearly all other ways: Mrs.
Coolidge so ambitious, strong-willed, and efficient, Miss Watson so
large-hearted, so fond of beautiful things from quartets to tea-doilies,
and so loving and kind to her innumerable friends. This was of course
some years before Mrs. Coolidge's more striking benefactions to
music began. Indeed still passing their summers in Pittsfield were
her parents, from whom she eventually inherited the fortune that
did so much for music. The tall, white-haired, courtly Mr. Sprague
made a delightful host, ably seconded by his small but alertly sociable wife, in the modest home they occupied on the same grounds
with their daughter's imposing mansion. Dr. Coolidge, her husband,
was an invalid whose retiring manners hid what only those who
knew his story realized to be a heroic nature. Of brilliant gifts, he
had always been handicapped by ill-health, and in those years when
we knew him, had through his own chivalrous devotion to an infected patient caught a terrible disease, from which he was slowly
dying. I can still see him, sitting with his nurse on an upper piazza
as the rest of us started out for a day's motoring, waving his hand to
us with a cheerfulness that seemed heroic. After his death his wife
donated the Pittsfield house as a hospital for crippled children—a
touchingly appropriate memorial to him.

My own first meeting with Mrs. Coolidge was at the Winthrop
Rogers' in New York in the spring of 1904, when I noted her in my
journal as "Mrs. Coolidge, who composes". She played that evening
a most spirited song of hers, in which the spider sat down beside Miss
Muffet in a chromatic scale that made your flesh creep. When we
came to live in Pittsfield she asked me to give her lessons in composition. Fearing the distraction of any teaching in the only part of
the year I could devote to my own composing, I declined; but it

amuses me to discover in my journal, in the latter part of the summer: "Corrected four chapters of proof, and gave Mrs. Coolidge a lesson." I don't remember now how my change of mind came about. In the long run people usually did what Mrs. Coolidge wanted.

Gertrude Watson was as ample-natured as her friend Elizabeth Coolidge was strong-willed: they were like the sun and the wind that vied with each other, in the fable, to make the traveller take off his coat. And he would have been a surly traveller who would not have done anything for Gertrude. Her retinue of Italian servants at Onota Farm idolized her, even while "talking back" at her as she did at them with an easy familiarity like that of a mother with her children. Rosie, whose round cheeks harmonized with her name, and whose short buxom figure raced about the long corridors on endless services so that the old house shook, acted as her personal maid and mentioned any wish of "Miss Watson" as if it had been the command of a goddess. Silvio, the chauffeur of her big open Packard of an early style, its shiny leather seats as comfortable as her person and as capacious as her heart, argued with her all day long, but defended her against the world. Even Charlie, Rosie's incongruous husband, careless, good-natured, naughty-boyish, took out most of his insubordination in talk, and tried to do what she wanted as well as his makeshift ways permitted. He was supposed to be her overseer, but after bitter experience I preferred to call him her overlooker.

It was part of her easy-going quality (which by no means excluded a firm will of her own) to tolerate any amount of laxness in her dependents in matters of detail without losing her general effect of a delightful feudal establishment, just as she could endure in the old furniture she was always picking up drawers that wouldn't open and doors that wouldn't shut, yet always got the general effect she wanted. There was a newel post in her New York apartment that swayed precariously if you were incautious enough to lean against it; and when we visited her at Onota Farm I usually left a good many of my things in my bag rather than spoil my temper opening and shutting the drawers of her picturesque old bureaus. (Ossip Gabrilowitsch once exclaimed: "I don't see why people like new music and old furniture. I prefer old music and new furniture!") Yet whether things fitted or not seemed a small matter when you caught the charm of her long communicating music rooms, and of the garden on which the last one opened, with its wide green lawn in the centre, luxuriant flower-beds all round, grape-arbors running down both sides, and a row of poplars at the end, with still more distant glimpses of the Taconic Hills and Greylock.

Everything about Gertrude was large—her house, her garden, her car, her person, above all her heart. She seemed to have room in it for everybody. She had two or three other farm-houses scattered about Pittsfield and Richmond besides the one she rented us (later lent us without rent); and everyone of them was apt to harbor a group of "lame ducks" like us. Herself an excellent pianist, a former pupil of Leschetizky, and in our first years at Pittsfield not yet much troubled by her deafness, she used to play endlessly both in solo and in ensemble with various professional friends like May Mukle the English cellist and others. One of the first years we were there she played for the benefit of the Pittsfield Boys' Club. Later she and Miss Mukle and Rebecca Clarke, the English violist and composer, made long concert tours for war relief. First and last she must have helped educate many musicians, to one of whom, Walter Stafford, who took the violin parts in our studio musicale that day, she was especially drawn by their common affliction of deafness. In all the years one knew her one could not keep track of the people she was worrying over, planning for, trying to help: there would always be names cropping up in her conversation one hadn't heard of before. And though a little gullible, I fear, by those who were ingenious and unprincipled enough to impose on her good nature, she was sufficiently high-spirited to resent being imposed on when she recognized it, or seeing others imposed on. A winter day comes back to mind, when she had motored us all, in a closed car this time, to Williamstown for some music or other. As we reëntered the car from the warm house one of the players, whom we may call Merivale, ensconced himself luxuriously in the most comfortable corner of the back seat. Gertrude took one good look at him, one at her women guests shivering on the sidewalk, advanced upon him like some beneficent Amazon, and issued her ultimatum, uttered in her curiously deliberate, syllable-by-syllable way: "Mis-ter Mer-i-vale, come out of that!"

II

As one grows older and sees more of life, one cannot help wondering sometimes at the arbitrary way fame seems to distribute its benefits, such as they are. To some moods those whom the world ignores seem almost more inspiring than its admired favorites, their loyalty is so free of egotistic limitations, their devotion so unrewarded save by its own happiness. Gertrude Watson had no fame at all to speak of; Ulysse Buhler has had far less than he deserves.

A more striking case still was that of poor Cressman. He was a fellow assistant with me to Dr. Percy Goetschius in the music theory work at the old Institute of Musical Art, now merged in the Juilliard School. The name of Forrest J. Cressman is not in any of the biographical dictionaries, his work is unknown, he died early and apparently without realizing any of his possibilities. He was a strange-looking fellow, frail, cadaverous, with slim sunken chest and thin lips that met in a severe straight line. He had a grim humor of his own, and no tolerance for musical mediocrity. Though he wrote at the end of my piece *The Quiet Hour*, when I showed it to him in first draft, "This is something to be proud of," yet he noted on one passage (since deleted): "There are bushels more where this came from." And he said there were too many notes in the Dohnanyi *Cello Sonata*—which I think was also true. He died in April, 1912, I should suppose in his early thirties, though I do not even know what was his age. Dr. Frank Damrosch, Dr. Goetschius, and I tried in vain to arrange for the publication of some of his manuscripts, which for all their beauty were without commercial value. I do not know what became of them.

Yet just after his death I copied a variation of his, from a set he wrote for piano, which still seems to me, after quarter of a century, as hauntingly beautiful as any American music I know. . . . Only last year died an American composer of a reputation we call "national", or, if we are feeling a little heady, "international". (That was the sort of language this particular composer liked.) He had

lived comfortably into his sixties, perpetrated innumerable symphonies, overtures, operas, quartets, and other works, been played all over this country and in Europe. Yet I have never heard a phrase of his not essentially commonplace. Reputation is a queer thing, an irrational thing, a worse confounding of natural human confusion. Let piety at least set down here poor Cressman's variation. Its last few phrases, in their poignant pathos, their passionate aspiration and unwilling abatement, above all in their slow, tentative, but at last deeply peaceful cadence, may symbolize his brief and seemingly unfinished life, yet suggest by their ecstatic beauty different measurements from our mortal ones.

III

Only visiting in Pittsfield that August afternoon of our musicale were Miss Zimmern and Burnet Tuthill. The two Miss Zimmerns, one a violinist, one a cellist, typical English amateur music-lovers, came all the way from London, and were sisters of our friend Alfred Zimmern (now Sir Alfred Zimmern, well known in Geneva and elsewhere as an international publicist). Zimmern was a delightful fellow, an English Jew who combined the Jewish alertness and realism of mind with English tolerance and social magnanimity. Author of *The Greek Commonwealth*, he was a friend of Gilbert Murray and of our friend Hadow. His intellectual brilliance consorted oddly with extreme shyness that made him an uneasy guest. His slight figure, strung as it were on wires, would squirm from one end of the sofa to the other as he talked, so that after half an hour the pillow cushions would lie about the floor. Fascinated by his rich imagination (for his heart was as active as his mind, and his penetration into human nature was singularly free from malice) my wife once gave him tea with lemon and cream, simultaneously. He drank it like a lamb—a very friendly and jumpy lamb. Perhaps he considered it only one more unaccountable peculiarity of American manners.

Burnet Tuthill, a graduate of Columbia College, some time leader of the student orchestra there, and an admirable clarinetist, was musically the product of one of those home groups of amateurs, like the Coolidges, the Rices, and the Rogers, so incalculably important to our musical culture. His father, William B. Tuthill, the architect of Carnegie Hall, was an amateur cellist. Burnet's mother was an able pianist, of discriminating taste. Burnet's own participation in this first performance of my *Pastorale* on its native hill-top confirmed a liking for it he had formed when he and Edouard Dethier and I had tried it over in New York in the spring. He became one of its most devoted friends. He it was who gave it its first public performance in a concert for wind instruments he got up at the Carnegie Lyceum in January, 1913. The following month he played it again in a private hearing at the de Coppets', and in later years many times. Indeed almost the only time he did not play in it, it seems to me, was its first public performance in its "home town", so to speak, at Mrs. Coolidge's second annual Pittsfield Festival in 1919, when Hugo Kortschak took the violin part and Gustave Langenus the clarinet, the composer being as usual at the piano.

Burnet Tuthill was also the "force of detent", as William James used to say, the trigger, so to speak, that fired another composition of mine, the *Clarinet Sonata*, and what is more important, thus released forces that ultimately led to the founding of the Society for the Publication of American Music. That is a story that has never been told. Here it is.

After the try-out of the *Pastorale* at my New York apartment in the spring of 1912 already mentioned, Burnet and I played the Brahms E flat *Clarinet Sonata*. It went so well that I impulsively told him I was going to write him a sonata, and we shook hands upon it. As his August visit approached I tried to redeem my promise, but I was always a slow worker, and this time my mind was a blank— ideas simply refused to come. I had a possible second theme for the first movement, but that was all. Then at last, August 14, less than a week before his arrival, profoundly moved over my friend Moody's letters that I was editing, and a rereading of his *Masque of Judgment*, I improvised the first theme of the sonata. For five days I could not keep away from working at these ideas, and on August 19 recorded in my journal: "I finished the movement this morning, and Tuthill and the Misses Zimmern arrived this afternoon. It sounds well on the whole." On the twenty-second I added: "Tuthill and I went

Arthur Whiting, Ulysse Buhler, and Daniel Gregory Mason at Pittsfield

through the movement again, and it sounded much better. In fact, it sounded fine! He says the theme has been going in his head ever since."

He showed his enthusiasm practically by copying out the movement for his own use, and by urging me to finish the sonata. The other two movements, however, long delayed their appearance, not being finished until three years later, in the summer of 1915. Then the question was, what to do with such a white elephant, commercially speaking, as a clarinet sonata—even worse than a violin sonata. Had I been left to myself, I should doubtless have done nothing. But Burnet was so interested that he proposed, in 1917, to raise funds among his friends, and publish the work privately. This fell through; but towards 1919 he and his father, putting their heads together, did even better. Why, they asked themselves, should they not found a society for the publication, through small fees from individual members, of just such commercially impossible chamber music as this? Their answer to their own question was—the Society for the Publication of American Music. And by a sort of poetic justice, although the founders did not themselves choose the works to be published, but had them impartially selected by a jury, those first to see the light were Alois Reiser's *String Quartet* and my *Clarinet Sonata*.

IV

It was in that happy summer of the cordial reception of my chamber music at the Rices' in Stockbridge—1911—that I first met Ulysse Buhler. He also was living in Stockbridge, but maintained a studio for his piano teaching in Pittsfield—for however perfectly he might exemplify the amateur spirit in his devotion to music for itself, he was by necessity a professional in that he had to earn his living by it. In this respect he was always an instructive contrast to Mrs. Coolidge and Miss Watson, his worldly resources were so much more restricted than theirs, and everything he did had to be done under such handicaps. Yet thanks to a devotion as great as theirs, to the power of the born leader to inspire others with a self-forgetting loyalty emulating his own, and to a singular sweetness and charm of personality, he was able to do a work which Mrs. Coolidge once told me (I like to remember it in her honor as well as his) she considered as important as her own. Her son Sprague, too, speaking at a celebration in Pittsfield of Buhler's sixty-fifth birthday, in August, 1926, turned to him with these words: "Mr. Buhler, where are you to look for the indications of your success? No applause, no press notice, no gate money can measure it. You must look into the hearts of your friends and see by how much you have been able to increase their content of beauty and understanding."

The essence of his work was the bringing of great masterpieces, no matter if sometimes crudely played, to local audiences benumbed by the notion that music can only be made by famous musicians, and to players themselves deaf to what is greatest in music, either through their own technical limitations or more usually through low standards of taste unconsciously formed in theatre, street, or dance-hall. He was, so to speak, a home missionary, such as every town and village in our American hinterland always needs. At that first meeting he told me that he had been incited to his work with the local musicians by an article of Arthur Whiting's in the *Outlook* on using the material one has, even in small places. He had formed, taking the piano part himself, a quartet the other three players of which were chiefly used to only popular music. His viola was a farmer's boy in Lebanon, who would drive sixteen miles over to take his lesson and sixteen miles back again, on cold winter days. Another man he had discovered in one of the Pittsfield theatre orchestras could play either clarinet or double-bass, but had to be taught the standard repertory. At this time the group was already giving ten concerts of good music each winter in Stockbridge, with sixty subscribers at five dollars apiece. It also gave three concerts annually in Pittsfield, but less successfully, since people usually preferred to pay a good deal for one concert by the Kneisels, or the Flonzaleys, or some other famous group, rather than a smaller sum for more concerts by a less known organization.[1]

Of French-Swiss extraction, and always retaining a slight French

[1] See the essay *Domesticating Music* in *Music as a Humanity*. The "Mr. X." there described is Ulysse Buhler.

accent in his precise, clipped speech, Buhler was a widower, but lived happily in Stockbridge—later in Pittsfield, with his sister, his birds and his garden. There was something about his large head, with the iron-gray hair brushed back from the fine forehead, and his rather wide mouth, that reminded me of César Franck, with whose gentleness and sweetness his own character had so much in common. Difficult as it was in the early days to get into Pittsfield with our old horse, and from there to Stockbridge on the electric trolley line, we used to go sometimes, or Buhler would come to us, in order to play Franck, Chausson, Dukas, or d'Indy works in piano duet arrangements. After we replaced Dick [1] with a second-hand Ford it was a little easier—when the Ford did not break down. Those were the days when I was just forming my life-long attachment to d'Indy's music, and when I recall the thrill of first acquaintance with his *Istar, Chanson et Danses, E major Quartet,* and above all the deeply poetic *Summer Day Symphony* I see again Buhler's eyes dancing behind his spectacles, and hear his "Isn't it wonderful?"

Something of his cheerful idealism was echoed in his sister, in whose friendly and comfortable person his equanimity approached placidity. She devoted herself to helping him carry out his ideas, even to the point of taking his protegés into her household. One of the earliest of these was Alphonse Pelletier, a boy Buhler had discovered working in one of the factories, amusing himself in his spare hours playing cornet. Buhler invited him to live with them, bought him a French horn, engaged lessons for him, and himself coached him in such works as the Brahms *Horn Trio* and Dukas' *Villanelle for Horn.* Eventually Pelletier made such progress that he left the factory, became a professional musician, and secured a post as horn-player in one of the middle-Western symphony orchestras.

By 1914 Pelletier must have left the hospitable house of the Buhlers, for another musician, Georges Vigneti the violinist, seems then to have been their housemate. The group was enlarging toward the orchestra it eventually became. From my journal I select two or

---

[1] We sold Dick to a farmer neighbor, for a certain sum of money "plus forty rides". But we had taken only a small number of those forty rides, as I recall it, when poor old Dick fell dead.

three snap-shots. "July 18. We are having a regular musical festival. Last night the ceremonies were at Mrs. Coolidge's, the Vignetis, the Husses, and Burnet Tuthill being the other guests. Today we had our annual studio party, with ideal weather after all the sultriness and rain. There was bright sun and brisk west wind, and the upland field looked lovely. Guests: the Coolidges, Spragues, Buhlers, Vignetis, Husses, Miss Watson, Mr. Pelletier the horn-player, and Burnet Tuthill, who is visiting the Coolidges. We had so much 'talent' that there was much more music to be had than time to have it. To-morrow afternoon we are going to continue the debauch at Miss Watson's."

"July 19. The afternoon at Miss Watson's was delightful. Her garden room and garden are lovely, I never saw them so charming before, the flowers and foliage, the vistas of poplars, and the two arbors, one down each side. She has extraordinary taste. We had tea and cake in the garden, and Mrs. S— read some verses, after which Henry Huss begged her to allow him to express his thanks by improvising, and led the way back to the house, with all of us obediently trailing after, quite as if he had been chief undertaker and all the rest of us mourners. Buhler and his companions played the Reinecke *Trio*, and as we were leaving a little girl started in to play the piano, with much talent."

"September 11. Got up at 7:30 and rode in with the milkman to a rehearsal at Mr. Buhler's of Fibich's *Quintet in D* for Violin (Vigneti), Clarinet (Killian), Horn (Pelletier), Cello (Kingman), and Piano (Buhler), a spontaneous, melodious work, rather trivial."

Our last summer at Pittsfield was 1919, the year I played the piano part of my *Pastorale* at Mrs. Coolidge's festival. So important a public appearance as pianist was rare for me, and in my anxiety to do myself justice I greatly feared the kick our second-hand Ford often gave when one tried to crank it. (In those early days of cars cranking was always such a labor and sometimes so dangerous that I found it in my heart to regret old Dick, who, often as he had had to rest, had at least never kicked.) And strange as it may seem nowadays, Fords had to rest too, at least when their batteries gave out. Late in August, not many weeks before my engagement to play at the Festival, we

At the second Pittsfield Festival, Music Temple, South Mountain,
Pittsfield, Massachusetts, September, 1919

ABOVE: The Music Temple; George J. Dyer and Mary L. Mason in foreground.
BELOW: Louis Svecenski, Leo Sowerby, Mary L. Mason, Elizabeth Sprague Coolidge,
Hans Letz, Richard Aldrich, Eric DeLamarter.

drove Buhler out to the farm for four-hand playing one afternoon.

"Car began going very badly on way out," says the journal, "and finally stopped absolutely just at the entrance to our place. Billy found that it would go again after resting. So at six we started in with Mr. Buhler. We had to stop about eight times to 'rest' it—two or three times on that short West Street hill in the village. In spite of the weakness of the batteries, however, once when Billy left the spark all the way on I got a nasty kick from the crank in the palm of my right hand."

Such was life in the Ford Period. But I played at the festival.

V

In the years that followed our departure from Pittsfield I only saw Buhler at rare intervals, but I followed with keenest interest the growth of his chamber music group into an orchestra. One winter evening late in 1925, when I dined with him in Pittsfield and attended one of his rehearsals, he told me the story of some of his men.[1] Some of his wind players, he told me—two flutes, two oboes, two clarinets, four horns, two bassoons, and bass tuba, had not existed as players of their present instruments a year or two ago, having been encouraged by him to evolve out of what seems to be the pollywog stage, so to speak, of wood-wind players, that of clarinetists. That was the case, for instance, with the oboists and the bassoonists.

The first oboe was a man of perhaps thirty-five or forty who had been not only a player but a teacher of clarinet. With the spirit of devotion to the interests of the group as a whole that such an organization spontaneously generates, he realized that oboes were more needed than clarinets, and forthwith learned to play one, and presently persuaded one of his clarinet pupils to learn to play another —and this second oboist was only eight months old as a second oboe, but already a lusty infant! Years of experience in clarinet playing had stood him in good stead. One of the bassoonists, I learned, produced such queer sounds at first that he made his companions laugh;

[1] Most of what follows is reprinted, with the permission of *Musical America*, from an article of mine which appeared in its issue of January 2, 1926.

but he stuck to it and evolved into a bassoon-player. Being by pursuit a public accountant, he was busy all day, but got up early in the morning in order to practice.

"But how," I asked at this point, "do you get the oboes and bassoons?"

"We buy them," answered Buhler. "A good Lorée oboe costs well over a hundred dollars, a Heckel bassoon nearer two hundred. But you see I am supposed to receive ten dollars from the orchestra for each rehearsal, and I put this back into buying instruments and music. Scores and parts are expensive here, but I have a friend in Paris who has sent me over a number of them."

"And are you sure you never 'put back', as you say, more than you get?" I asked.

"Well,"—the answer came with a deprecatory smile—"Of course I can't tell exactly, as I don't keep my own money separate. But it is so nice to have the music! We have a Brahms symphony that we haven't played yet. I could get it abroad for twenty-seven dollars. We shall play it sometime. And the instruments we must have. We have everything we need but a harp. Oh, if we could only get a harp! It is expensive to hire one, as we have to do for this Debussy suite, and we have nothing left for our money afterwards. But a harp costs almost as much as a grand piano. That is the only important instrument we haven't got now." (I don't know whether Buhler ever got that harp. Maybe he will have to wait for it until he gets to heaven.)

Dinner over, the players began to arrive. Most of the chairs in the house were requisitioned for the drawing-room, as the men were accompanied by their wives, armed with sewing or embroidery. "It is cosier for them so," their host explained. A clarinetist told me the schedule of rehearsals. The director had the four horns rehearse at his house every Wednesday evening, and had even practiced the horn a little himself, in order to coach them more intelligently. He had persuaded these four young men, two of whom had originally played the saxophone and one the cornet, to take up the noblest of brass instruments, and had familiarized them with good music. They had all taken lessons, at their own charges, all last summer, of Pelletier, by this time a skilled horn-player. . . . On Thursday evenings the string players rehearsed, grouped into several string quartets. Friday evenings were devoted to the whole wind group as I was then hearing it. On Sunday afternoons came the full orchestra. And all this, not for a few weeks, but right through the winter!

I began to understand the admission dropped by my indomitable friend at dinner, that after the April concert even he was tired. "After that," he confessed, "I think no more of music. I turn to my garden. And a garden," he added musingly, "is in some ways a good deal like an orchestra. You find a barren place, and you plant something, and for a time it doesn't grow very well, but after a while it grows!" Well, I thought, for some people it grows, for others not. It seems to be a question of patience and faith. And I remembered the summer I planted a small patch of herbs, as much for their names as for their flavors and aromas, and Buhler gave me some tarragon to add to my chevril and chives, fennel and marjoram, sage and sorrel and thyme; and I, as I always did with a garden, forgot about it for weeks and then attacked the weeds with such frenzied energy that the herbs all came up with them! My weeding was as disastrous as those newts that were not in Mr. Bartlett's rose-garden. But Buhler had the genius of gardens.

He had too the genius of fellowship. The humblest member of his orchestra was to him a person. Once when I had spoken of the geniality of his tuba player he wrote me: "I must tell you what that big husky Frenchman and others did for me last summer. I had only casually mentioned the fact that I wanted to build a pool in my garden when Demouge—that is he—and others volunteered to come, after their work for the day was over, and dig up the pool, mix the concrete, pour it in, and make my pool for me. And so they came in the long summer evenings, working as they never would have worked if they had been paid for it, fearing darkness would overtake them before they had completed their task. So they toiled until the work was done and I had my pool. And when it became too dark to work we all sat down and smoked and drank lemonade and had a good time. How can I be discouraged long when I think of all this good fellowship?"

And that very evening of the rehearsal when I spoke of the end-less difficulties he must find in working with so many people, he answered: "Oh yes, there are many difficulties and disappointments. Tonight, for instance, one of my horns has telephoned that he can-not come. He has to play for a dance. He needs the money, poor boy, and I can't blame him. But whatever the difficulties, this work has filled my life, it has made me happy. I don't want anything else, I don't want to go anywhere else or do anything different. I am happy here. My life is full."

This was a philosophy of life, it seemed to me, worthy of Thoreau or Emerson. To understand its sincerity, one had only to witness the rehearsal, devoted to two serenades, one by Mozart and one by Richard Strauss. The leader, I noticed, addressed all the players by Christian name, discussing with them their difficulties and problems, leaving much to their own initiative, but maintaining authority un-obtrusively but effectively. To the second flute he spoke French. This was a courtly-looking gentleman with white hair, one of the few professionals in the orchestra, a retired band-leader who must have enjoyed to the full the musical companionship these evenings brought him. How delightful it was, when the horns encountered a bit of difficult intonation, to watch Buhler patiently explaining to them how to regard it, begging with finger held to lips, as if in con-fidence, for the *pianissimo* that amateurs always find it so hard to give, or visibly beaming at a bit of clear, warm sonority and crying, "Let's begin at F again; it sounds so fine!"

That rehearsal made a picture one does not forget. The rows of players of all ages, temperaments, and types, united in common de-votion to an artistic ideal; the ex-band leader, grown old in music, contentedly playing second flute; the eight-months-old second oboe, proud, possibly a little apprehensive; the three young horn-players, playing horn rather than saxophone and cornet, and Mozart and Strauss rather than jazz, doing their best to make up for the necessary absence of the fourth of their quartet; the immense bell of the bass tuba shining behind the rest like a rising sun of geniality and social warmth; and the leader, guiding, directing, encouraging all, with his pencil baton beating unanimity and every line of his figure radiating enthusiasm and love of beauty.

Witnessing that, one could understand his cry made at dinner with the naïveté of a child—"They all love me!" They would have had to be less than human to resist devotion so tireless, great ability so modestly exercised. If there were only one like him in every large town or small city in our country, what strides America would make in musicality!

In his presence one could palpably feel what we call "musical atmosphere" being created—that subtlest yet most essential of all elements in the musical life of a nation.

CHAPTER XIII

EDWARD J. DE COPPET

ON ONE of our long automobile drives with Edward and Pauline de Coppet, either among the Swiss mountains near their estate of Le Flonzaley or in the environs of New York—I forget which—de Coppet once told us that for many years he had been not particularly successful in business, so that they had finally decided he should retire from it after a certain time, and they should both devote themselves to teaching music. Then came his "happy thought" of some special way of selling stocks and bonds (I did not understand the technicalities of it), its brilliant success, and his acquisition of his fortune. In the years we knew him he was devoting this fortune to the development of the Flonzaley Quartet, to the good in countless other ways of his beloved art of music, and to many more general benefactions about which he was so modestly reticent that the details of them will never be known. His reminiscent story that day helped us a little to understand why we always instinctively thought of him as an artist rather than as a business man. While his supreme work of art was the Flonzaley Quartet, his approach to everything was that of the artist.

Far removed as were his warm affectionateness, his tender consideration of the feelings of others, from the self-centered subjectivism sometimes misnamed by its victims "artistic temperament", the sensitiveness of the real artist he had in full measure. No doubt the delicateness of his physical health intensified a natural nervous irritability in some ways almost morbid. Aside from the affliction of deafness so terrible to one who loved music as passionately as he did he always suffered much from easily jangled nerves. But if this sensitiveness brought him much suffering, it also brought joys keen enough to compensate. What an unforgettable picture he made, in the dimly lighted drawing-room of Le Flonzaley or of his Eighty-fifth Street New York house during a performance by the Quartet, drinking in the music as best he could, though even with his enormous apparatus for hearing he was obliged to sit only a few feet from the players! I have seen him moved to tears by a simple song, and he once told me that such moments "take us above our ordinary life". Late one night at Le Flonzaley, at the end of an exacting evening of social excitement and more or less formal music, after all the guests were gone he sat down at the piano and played that lovely quiet epilogue of Schumann's *Davidsbündlertänze*. Such a response to music as that is possible only to one who deeply understands its spiritual meaning.

He had the patience of the artist. As I have said of him elsewhere: [1] "He never supposed, as do those who aspire to be patrons less for the sake of the art than for that of the patronage, that he could create what he was after (the Flonzaley Quartet) by the simple process of signing checks. His method was that of all genuine art: indefatigable experiment, proceeding by trial and error, requiring endless loving thought, and extending through a long series of years. The books in which are entered in his own hand, and with the painstaking precision he did not spare even when physically ill, the programs, participants and guests of all his musical gatherings, cover thirty years . . . and record one thousand and fifty-four meetings."

He was fond of repeating Pochon's remark, already quoted, that you could hold a single note "for a cent, or for a dollar—and ninety per cent of the audience would not know the difference", but that "you had to do it, for the other ten per cent and your own satisfac-

[1] *An Ideal Patron (Edward J. de Coppet)* in *Music as a Humanity*, H. W. Gray Company.

tion." On the other hand, of course, if anything exhausted his loving-kindness it was slovenliness in art. Here is the first letter I ever had from him. (The little book, *A Neglected Sense in Piano Playing,* on the importance to pianists of the use of the mind and the sense of touch, had been written at his suggestion and on commission from him.)

"Le Flonzaley, Chexbres, Suisse
"June 5, 1912

"We have just reached here after a month's most enjoyable auto trip in Italy. I have found awaiting me some copies of *A Neglected Sense.* . . .

"I hope to persuade you some time or other to write on two other subjects of interest to me. One essay might be entitled *Honesty in Musical Performance,* and might show up the tendency of the day to palm off on the public insufficiently prepared concerts as thoroughly prepared ones. The performers themselves are quite aware that they are not doing at all as well as they are able to do. Really they are selling their second or third grade of goods at the price of the best quality they can manufacture. The really honest artist should be able to say to himself: 'This is the *best* I can do; take it for what it is worth.' But for him to take people's money, when he knows that even one or two rehearsals more would give his listeners much greater value, is not honest. . . .

"Another interesting article might discuss the relative importance of the various elements which constitute the make-up of a great player: his purely musical gifts, his technical ability (which, as you know, I believe has nothing to do with musical ability), and finally the man's personality and character. On this last depends what he really has to say.—Corollary on the importance of general mental and moral education for the musician.

"This is but a hint of what I would like to say to you; but it may set you thinking on the subject, and may lead to our producing something of some value."

When, a year or two later, I did try to act on his first suggestion, he wrote me, with characteristic generosity of enthusiasm: "Your article on *The Quantitative Standard* is magnificent. If I dared I would like to have it read aloud at the supper to be offered us after the next Flonzaley Quartet."

He had too the modesty of the true artist, and the humor so apt to go with it. "What is so stupid," he would exclaim, "as conceit! What a fool a man is, who is satisfied with himself!" And apropos of some especially difficult endowment for ethical research he was undertaking, a cherished plan of his last years, he wrote: "I feel encouraged, for we have surely advanced at least one inch, and we only have ten thousand miles to go." What helped him to endure inevitable delays and disappointments was a realistic outlook on human nature and an unflagging gusto in good works, with a wholesome indifference to whether they were acclaimed or not. "If our little book does nothing else," he says in a second letter about *A Neglected Sense*, "it will start teachers thinking in the right direction. You will presently see piano methods appearing, telling you what particular mental concentration one should have in order to overcome this or that special technical difficulty . . . various new theories will appear, and the feeling between opposing schools of mental work will become bitter and create quite a hubbub. . . . You and I will then be quite forgotten in the general row, as having started the ball rolling. But what fun it will be to remember our first efforts in the right direction."

Above all, de Coppet intuitively understood the impersonality of art so well described by Arthur Whiting when he said that an artist's true friends are those who love his art more than they love him. Always in daily life de Coppet took this attitude instinctively, and on one great occasion—the tenth anniversary of the Quartet—he gave expression to it in unforgettable words. His shyness as well as his deafness prevented his speaking in public, but he wrote out a short address to be read to the two hundred friends gathered that evening of March 9, 1914 to do honor to him, his wife, his quartet, and his beloved art. Whimsically he began by describing his qualms on so public an occasion: "Imagine me rising before a considerable number of people and boldly stating that two and two make four. . . . How much less could I attempt to express any finer sentiment.

And they expect me to talk of chamber music!" But then, he went on to say, "Suddenly there was a change in my mental attitude; something like a ray of sunlight broke through my clouds. It came from the great sun of human kindness and sympathy, and I felt its benevolent heat warming my heart. I said to myself: 'These friends, who are bidding us join them in this festivity, are not going through a pure form. They have something in their hearts which they wish to express.' And then I saw it all. We personally were to be of no importance in the matter. Even our friends 'the Flonzaleys' and their fine ten years' efforts were to count for little. The purpose was to be for us all to assemble as an expression of undying love and devotion for the great art. Ah! That is another thing. Let me in, if you please. And the first thing I knew I was fighting my way to obtain a front seat."

II

De Coppet's rare sweetness of nature was revealed to me just when I was so placed as to appreciate it; he had sympathetic as well as practical help to give, and I was in great need. To a superficial view, it is true, I seemed not unsuccessful. My quartet was highly praised by the players and other musicians when it was read at his house in the spring of 1912, and he himself said to my wife that I was "very gifted", and "ought to have more time to compose". Toward the end of that same year my violin sonata was taken up by David and Clara Mannes, with good success. Nevertheless I was haunted by the impossibility of making any money from sonatas and quartets, or even piano pieces (I could not get my *Country Pictures* published until a foreign house, Breitkopf and Hartel, paid me fifty dollars for the whole six) and by the artistic futility of any music that would "pay". John Jay Chapman, that eccentric genius with the long beard and the fanatic eye suggesting John Brown, told me it was a mistake for me to try the operetta scheme (I had consulted him about a libretto) or to write with an eye on money in any way. "Just write as you feel," he said, "and for yourself, and you will do some things that are worth while. The other way you are very un-

Edward J. de Coppet

likely to hit a paying thing, and you run the risk of spoiling your talent." That was just what I was afraid of. But hack writing, such as articles for the *London Times* and program notes for the New York Symphony Society, and worse still miscellaneous lecturing, seemed almost more futile and hopeless. How was I to boil the pot?

"Le Flonzaley, July 26, 1912

". . . The principal thing I have to say today is to ask whether it would not be possible for me to come to your assistance next winter so as to enable you to do writing in place of lecturing at least for a good part of the season. I have some questions I would like to submit to you for treatment, and you say you have some subjects in mind yourself. Besides there are often things occurring in the musical life of New York which I think ought to be condemned at the time they occur, just as other happenings do not receive their due praise. If you had more free time, and you happened to agree with me in the matters referred to, we might coöperate in doing some beneficial work for the advancement of our art in our country. . . .

"What would it cost me to enable you to do that? Of course any profits from your writings would be yours. I trust you don't mind my asking you frankly an answer to the business side of the matter."

Even this offer of a true friend worried me a little. I did not yet know of what complete devotion to art de Coppet was capable, without any egotistic *arrière-pensée*, how free from "strings" his benefactions could be. I had had one or two other offers of patronage carrying with them a good many obligations, and I must have confessed to him that I was afraid of mortgaging my time, for I find him answering:

". . . You quite misunderstood me if you thought that I would ever ask you to write on any subject that you were not anxious to write about yourself. I merely thought that when you had some idea that you wanted to express, or when I had an idea that really appealed to you, it might be possible for me to give you sufficient help for you to give the necessary time to the matter. We shall talk the question over some time next winter. . . ."

So things went on with me until by the end of the year I reached a really pathological state of discouragement. . . .

Journal, November 24. "Do I not wear myself out needlessly with drudgery for which I am ill-suited? If I had a little more initiative and courage could I not get as much money for really characteristic and unique work as I now get for these fool tasks?

"Sunday, December 1. Working morning and evening, finishing excerpts from the Sibelius Symphony—eleven pages. It has been a job, and, as the music is superficial, rather tedious.

"December 14. Refused to write the preface for the Oratorio Society. I think it wrong to accept work that gives no play to my artistic interests in any way. I'm glad I refused, and hope I shall have courage to refuse all such things.

"December 31. The New Year's horns are tooting their usual hurly-burly. It seems only a few weeks since we heard them last year. The *Outlook* has sent back my Ravel article—a sort of New Year's Eve compliment. Previously it has been refused by *Century*, *Atlantic*, and *Scribner's*. New Year's resolutions are foolish, but I am going to have it in mind to earn as little money as possible, that is, to do as little drudgery as possible. I am going to try and do more what I want, less what the world wants. That is the only way to get anywhere."

III

Then it was, early in the New Year, that my wife solved at a stroke the coiled problems with which I had been so helplessly struggling: "January 16, 1913. Mary has the supernaturally daring idea that we get excused from Columbia work next year, borrow money of Mr. de Coppet on my securities, and go abroad for a year to give me a chance. I don't know. Am I worth saving?" Mary thought I was, and further journal-entries record the stages of the salvation, and illustrate de Coppet's greatness of heart.

"January 22. Mr. de Coppet was awfully nice, and proposed to give me half my expenses if these were twelve hundred dollars, which he thought would keep us nearly a year abroad. He doesn't care whether I compose or not, says to go for 'fun' and a change, and says I must let him have the 'fun' of helping. He is helping half a dozen people, and doing other more organized things. He said he helped ruin a young man once, by adding ten thousand dollars to the same sum the young man had, and he lost all. . . . He is a marvel of sympathy, generosity, and magnanimity.

"January 23. When I told Mr. de Coppet that, while I appreciated his generosity, I did not feel certain enough that I was going to 'show value' as a composer to avail myself of it, he said that my being a composer had nothing to do with it. 'You must realize that this is the way I have my fun. If I can help you have a good time I shall enjoy it.'

"I said I felt as if his family might think I was a queer kind of a man if I accepted help. He answered that his family were used to him by this time. Some of his charities, he admitted, were no doubt a little hard on them. If it were not for what he called his 'nigger babies'—a nursery in Sixty-fifth Street—they could have an oak ceiling in the hall of Le Flonzaley instead of pine. . . . Mr. de C. explained that that had nothing to do with the case. If he wanted oak he would have it, but 'there seemed an element of luxury in it.' Just the same with an automobile, he said. If he wanted one he would have it, but he *didn't want* it!'

"He said he didn't want more houses—they would simply be an added care. It was hard for him to buy the rug in the music room . . . but his family persuaded him it would contribute to the artistic happiness of all who used the room, so he got it.

"He advised me not to plan or worry about composing when I got over there. 'Take a rest, a change, take in new impressions, let yourself be cheered and inspired by the beautiful and new surroundings. If you feel obliged to give music in return, that is a debt—an artistic debt—just as burdensome as a financial debt would be. Eventually your work will be benefited by the change, and that is all you have to consider.'

"One of the people he is helping is the widow of an impresario, and her daughter and granddaughter. The latter has hazy ideas of going on the stage or being a singer, but has been for years in Germany without even learning the language. He told all this without offense—really was amused at it.

"So with young ——, a pianist. He has enabled him and his wife to settle in Paris and teach and play, instead of going back to California to uncongenial relatives. 'They are going to have a couple of happy years,' he said, 'that they will remember all their lives.' "

Of course complications arose. The proposed trip would cost, it soon became evident, much more than we had at first thought, besides shocking the sensibilities of some of our more cautious and conventional relatives. Journal, January 31. "The worldly risk strikes —— and —— forcibly. The real reason is that they have no sympathy with purely artistic success, but only with success worldly, financial, social, or moral. To Mary and me all these are secondary to the artistic. I wish they wouldn't be so confoundedly cautious. . . . One lives but once, and nothing vitalizes and rejuvenates like courage.

"Later: I went over the figures with Mr. de Coppet this afternoon, and when we found that I should need about three thousand dollars for the sixteen months, and could sell my bond for a thousand, and proposed to try to get lectures at Oxford, he said I had better let him give me the two thousand dollars. I tried to tell both him and Mrs. de Coppet that whether we decided to go or not we appreciated their generosity. . . . Lord, these things are hard to talk about, to write about, hardest of all to decide.

"While we were talking it over he said he did not expect anything in return, 'not even a dedication'. I said that he couldn't help how I felt, anyway; and I think this pleased him, for he said that was right, and talked some time about feelings of love for people. . . .

"I feel as if I could never in my life do anything remotely good enough for him. Gratitude like this is so keen an emotion that it restores one's youth."

In March came his check for two thousand dollars, "which," he wrote, "you will dispose of as you see fit, for the purpose of making a stay in Europe." The twenty-fourth of the same month saw the celebration of the one-thousandth of the de Coppet musicales, and the twenty-fifth the gathering of a more intimate group in the

familiar music room, for what Ara, speaking for the Quartet, called
in a happy address to its founder "the thousand-and-first Arabian
Night". It was in the midst of these excitements that de Coppet found
time to write me:

> "March 24, 1913
> "314 West Eighty-fifth Street
>
> "I am so tired, and I ought to go to bed, but I don't wish to let
> another day pass without thanking you for your very kind note. I
> wish I could be as enthusiastic about this matter as you are. To me
> it is a perfectly natural and simple matter, and I remain in my own
> eyes an ordinary mortal, with maybe a little more tender heart than
> some, that is all.
>
> "Now I must ask you most urgently some things that you will
> surely do for me:
>
> "First, don't mention this transaction to outsiders, for it would
> cause me annoyance.
>
> "Second, don't ever, directly or indirectly, try to return the value
> of the gift in any shape whatever. I am selfish enough to want the
> pleasure of giving, all to myself. All that I will see with approval is
> any help you may extend to others more in need than yourself. But
> what will please me most is to see some real joy brought into your
> lives. Now let the incident be closed, and let us forget about it.
>
> "You know we play tomorrow evening for professional musicians.
> If you can, try to join us. I shall be glad. It may be fun. On Thurs-
> day and Sunday next the Quartet will read. All three times at 8:45."

Early in April the de Coppets sailed for Europe. At the end of
May we ourselves sailed, bound on an adventure—to be described
in letters of the time in the next chapter—that was to prove the most
crucial of our lives.

IV

Well before sailing I had written Vincent d'Indy, asking him to
coach me in composition and orchestration, and volunteering to
seek him out at Les Faugs, his chateau near the tiny village of Boffres

in the Cevennes mountains. I had good hopes of his consent, knowing how true was Romain Rolland's description of him: "One can never tell enough the disinterestedness of his life, devoted to the good of art. To what work, to what worker, worthy of interest or appearing to him to be so, has he ever refused his counsels and his aid?" Sure enough, the day after we landed at Liverpool and started on a brief tour of the lake country, I found at Windermere his answer:

"Strasburg, May 28, 1913

"I am so busy that I am only able to reply while I am travelling to the many letters people write me. In Paris I have still on my desk 350 letters it has been impossible for me to answer. . . . I shall have an enormous amount of work to do during my stay in the mountains, but I shall be able nevertheless, if you wish it, to find from time to time a moment to examine whatever you will have to show me.

"Near me there are no towns, but only villages of which the inns are highly primitive and without comforts. [Details given.] . . . All these places are on the line of the little mountain railroad ["*petit chemin de fer de montagne*"] from Saint Peray to Vernoux.

"Hoping to see you this summer in our mountains, I pray you to believe, dear Mr. Mason, in my best remembrances.

VINCENT D'INDY"

So it came about that, spending July and August on our hill-top in the Cevennes, we did not see de Coppet again until toward the end of that ever-to-be-remembered summer he had given us. He sent me, however, frequent letters that revealed him to the life, showing how much "fun" he was getting by sympathy with the fun he was bestowing.

"Nice, May 30, 1913

". . . In the main the news you give me of yourself and yours is quite satisfactory, and it looks as if you would be able to leave for Europe in a reasonably contented frame of mind. . . .

"Encouraged by what you say of Florent Schmitt, I took a few of his compositions in a four-handed arrangement, to try over. We had to consider ourselves thoroughly licked, for we retired with heavy loss. (Of course this means absolutely nothing, I state it as a commentary on our ability and not on the merit of the works.) It is true that the assault was made with the assistance of my daughter. It might have turned out differently had my wife assisted me. I should think that F. S.'s works, in the mere question of intonation, would be a severe ordeal for the Rice Quartet. It is true that the Dethier brothers must have given a solid foundation for the others to build on.

"Now mind that you leave all cares on the other side of the Atlantic, so that you can both fully enjoy your European trip."

"Le Flonzaley, June 24, 1913

"On reading your letter . . . I really envied you. Your description of that evening you spent on Windermere Lake, and of the emotions you experienced at that time, took me back to days now long passed, when several years would elapse between my visits to Europe. The craving for sights different from what I was seeing in the drudgery of my regular business life would become so acute that when I finally managed to get away, and I would land in some country district in Europe with all its special charm, my emotions would be deeply stirred and I would be nearer terrestrial happiness, I think, than at any other time in my life. . . .

"My experience of French *auberges* in general is far from bad. You will often find in such places cooking of a rare degree of excellence. This is most apt to be the case when the proprietor of the *auberge* is himself the cook, a quite common occurrence. Most French villages have a charm of their own, as beautiful in its way as what one sees in England. French villages are rarely as clean as the English; but Oh! just think of the difference in the food.

"I suppose you will not be coming our way for quite a while. Don't postpone it too late however, for the days become short in September. Yet that season is sometimes particularly fine in Switzerland, and it has the advantage that the country is emptied of the mass of tourists who infest it in July and August.

"The Quartet will not begin playing here much before the beginning of August."

"Le Flonzaley, July 21,1913

"Dear friend Mason:

"I felt so proud on reading your inscription on your violin sonata that I have decided to make the most of my chance, and actually be one of your friends. Therefore I shall drop the Mr. in addressing you. When you refer to Mr. de Coppet I shall know that you mean my son André. As to the latter's father, he will always be known as 'de Coppet' with you.

"I think I told you . . . that I envy my friend Mason and his wife who are now visiting Europe with all the relish of what may be called a 'first' trip on the continent. I find that keenness of perception does not completely pass even on one's thirty-first visit, for let it be known that I made my sixty-first trip across the Atlantic in April last. Market scenes are my delight in all countries (except maybe the United States) but particularly in the French provinces. In 1897 we rode on our bicycles from Paris to Nice, and I shall never forget the market scenes we saw in the many little French towns we passed through.

"When you have a moment to write again tell me if you have met d'Indy and what you think of him, and what he thinks of your work. Listen to his advice as much as you like on musical matters, but be careful he does not convert you to Roman Catholicism.

"The Quartet will play here next Sunday for the first time this season. On Saturday we are all to go to the Schellings' for a gathering of professional musicians. I am making great efforts to have my hair grow, so that the fraud of my being present on the occasion will not be detected. On the thirty-first Paderewski gives his annual birthday party. Those parties are sometimes great fun. We are fortunately only asked for the evenings; but the other poor devils are asked for 12 o'clock lunch, and they hang around the place the whole afternoon, and have an enormous dinner at 7 o'clock; then wait for fireworks at 10 P.M. After that those who are humorously inclined are free to show their talents. At 12 o'clock we always leave among the first, so as to try to be home by 3 A.M.

"André leaves us in the beginning of August to return to Princeton. The best part of our summer will be over with his going."

V

When we reached Switzerland early in September we at first took rooms at a *pension* in Chexbres, half an hour's walk from Le Flonzaley, where we spent most of our time for a glorious fortnight, ending up with a visit in the house itself. The musical "jollifications" that always went on at Le Flonzaley in the fall were now at their height. On September 13 came the great gathering for dinner and music (commemorated in the frontispiece) of the Paderewskis, the Weingartners, the Josef Hofmanns, the Rudolph Ganzes, the Ernest Schellings, Sigismund Stojowski, Madame Sembrich, the Flonzaley Quartet, Mr. and Mrs. de Coppet and their daughter Juliet, and ourselves. "The Paderewskis," I wrote my friend Hill a few days later, "kept us waiting, and we did not sit down to dinner until twenty minutes of nine. . . . The stars sat at a big center table, and the rest of us, more intimate friends of the de Coppets, at smaller tables on the edge or penumbra of the luminous tract. Stojowski took out Mary, who also had Schelling, Betti and others at her table. I took out Juliet de Coppet, who talked French most of the time with Ara and d'Archambeau.

"Paderewski was very jovial and merry, and 'jollied' the photographer (named Nietszche, by the way) who took the flashlight picture while we were at coffee in the drawing-room in a way that kept us all 'looking pleasant'. . . . The Hofmanns we found most attractive. Mary took a great fancy to Mrs. Hofmann, and I enjoyed watching Hofmann, he is such an observer and thinker, but found him hard to get at. He was pleasant enough, but looked at you with the detached gaze he might give to one of his mechanical inventions, such as the pneumatic spring for motor cars he is said to be working on now. He has a repertoire of two hundred and fifty pieces by memory, they say, and never practices. We are to walk over there

tomorrow to see the garden and have tea. . . . Paderewski talked
interestingly in the evening. He likened the Ravel *Quartet* to a dancing girl who after years on the music-hall stage settles down and
marries a staid, eminently respectable man, but can't forget her
wiles, and still expects to be pinched by all the men in the corners.
The Flonzaleys played the Dvořák *Quartet*, opus 61.

"The next afternoon, the first of the Sunday musicales this summer, they repeated it, and played with Mrs. de Coppet the d'Indy
Piano Quartet, which I liked in part very much, though he himself
told me he did not think much of the finale.

"On Wednesday the 17th we were the guests of honor at Paderewski's in Morges—an hour from here by train with two changes
—a height of glory I hardly dared hope ever to attain. He took out
Mary and plied her with four kinds of wine until I didn't know
whether she would be capable of locomotion as far as the drawing-
room or not. . . . I took out a baroness of ripe charms, and sat on
the left of Madame Paderewska. I don't think I ever ate a more
sumptuous dinner, considered from a purely gastronomical point
of view. One course was what looked like a whole salmon, and was
in a platter certainly two feet long. There was the tenderest of ducks,
with a marvellous sauce and olives, there was a curiously toothsome
preparation of beef with small roast potatoes in a deep dish—*boeuf
a la cocotte*, I believe—and chicken, wonderful exotic ices, and queer
Polish wines, and two kinds of champagne. . . . It was really painful to one of my Thoreau-like convictions to see an artist, and so
great a one, living so far from simply, and harassing his talent with
the necessity of earning heaps of money to pour out like that! I don't
know what will be the end of it all, for he can't continue these triumphal tours indefinitely. . . ."

The letter may be interrupted a moment at this point for the
addition of a few further contemporary details from my journal:

"The Paderewskis were somewhat upset by our having to return
by the 9:56 train, which mixed up their dinner plans to a certain
degree, but were nevertheless most cordial and agreeable. Paderewski looked over my pieces at once, while we were waiting for
dinner. He said the *Impromptu* (G minor) looked interesting, but

did not examine it in detail. When I pointed out the final cadence
with the unresolved suspensions he said: "Yes, it is just a sigh!" In
one loud place in *Cloud Pageant* he substituted for a passage that
had to be *fingered* another which had, if I may so say it, to be *wristed*
instead, permitting much more force. The most interesting suggestions were in *At Sunset*, to which he took a special fancy, playing
the first eight measures to Stojowski with exclamations of pleasure
good to hear. The middle part he found tame by comparison, and
it was here that he suggested some seconds that add wonderfully
to the effect.[1] The end he played to Weingartner, asking him if it
were not *"schön"*—to which Weingartner agreed almost perforce,
but sufficiently cordially.

"Just as we sat down to dinner, Mary gave me a lovely opening
by telling how the children at Boffres came to look at us strange
Americans, and I said '*Si nous avons des plumes dans les cheveux*'
—an old joke of hers, but greeted with quite a shout of laughter.
Paderewski reverted to it just as we were leaving."

The letter to Hill concludes:

"Last Saturday evening and Sunday afternoon at the de Coppets'
were devoted to the Schönberg *Quartet*, with which the Flonzaleys
have done wonders. The difficulties of intonation alone are almost
unbelievable. Their performance is one of the most remarkable I
have ever heard them give, but of the work itself I hardly know yet
what to think. There are several interesting and novel passages, a
great deal that still seems disagreeable noise, a remarkable constructive power, one or two commonplace melodies that may or may not
be 'giveaways' of the kind of weakness one finds in many moderns
who resort to complexity to hide vacuity, and a peroration of really
great power and nobility. The nervous effect is one of exhaustion,
yet if I can have the strength I want to hear it again—after a while!

"One of the pleasantest of all our adventures happened day before
yesterday. We took the rough, uphill, and muddy walk of about two
hours that leads through forest paths, with vistas across the lake, over

---

[1] These seconds, adopted in the printed edition, are the ones that occur in measures
nine and eleven between the thumbs of the two hands, giving a sort of blur or haze
to the sonority.

to the Tour de Gourze, quite isolated, kept by Madame Pochon, mother of Alfred Pochon of the Quartet. We had lunch in the open air with Betti, Pochon, d'Archambeau—all in working clothes and mood—and the elder Pochons, a lunch *"arrosé"* with some wine of the country and some sweet *Vino di Cipri* the like of which I have never surprised my palate with before. Then we walked with Betti two or three more miles across pretty country to a little place called Savigny, where we got a train for Lausanne. . . .

"I have skipped a great deal, but doubtless said enough to show you how delightful our sojourn in Switzerland has been, in spite of tourists, hotels, *pensions*, and cow-bells. Mary is sitting on the white porcelain stove that is supposed to make us forget the snow over on the mountains across the lake. . . . I enclose a print of me making breakfast at Boffres, which may bring home to your imagination the simple joys of that already mythical existence."

To the letters in which at the time of those simple joys I tried to suggest a few of them we may now turn back.

CHAPTER XIV

SUMMER IN ARDÈCHE

(LETTERS TO EDWARD BURLINGAME HILL)

Villa Mignonne, Boffres, Ardèche, France
July 13, 1913

Dear Neddie:

Behold us *chez nous* at last, after many wanderings, and so pleased with our new surroundings that we can hardly stop to unpack, but keep going out to look at our view, or stopping to laugh again at the absurdly diminutive character of everything. I quite despair of giving you more than the most summary idea of two or three of the hundreds of amusing, interesting, quaint, humiliating, and absurd things that have happened to us. Indeed I have shied off lately from writing you, from a sense of that hopelessness. But now I have decided to cut the Gordian knot by skipping entirely Newcastle, London and Paris, and most of Lyons, and asking you to imagine yourself arriving at Valence with us last Tuesday evening, the eighth.

If you will look at a map of southern France, about seventy or eighty *kilomètres* south of Lyons on the Rhone you will see Valence, and *Baedeker* will tell you that it is wholly uninteresting. But Riboud, the young Frenchman whom we had entertained on his way round the world, had not only given us a royal time in Lyons (which also must be skipped) but had written to innkeepers in Vernoux, Alboussières, and Boffres for us, and had even heard of a little villa to rent, through his friend Mme. Fougeirol, a friend of d'Indy's; and he had decided that the thing for us to do was to go to Valence and prospect the mountains for ourselves. D'Indy had written very cordially of having time to criticise me a little should I come, and we had decided on the move.

The *"petit chemin de fer de montagne"* of which he had told us made only one morning trip to Boffres, leaving St. Peray, across the river from Valence, at seven-twenty. Imagine yourself being awakened at five-thirty then—but this is too cruel. I will recount simply that we were awakened at five-thirty, had *petit dejeuner* in our room, and found ourselves an hour later on a quaint *voiture* with five seats, each holding three or four people, trundling across the river to St. Peray. The line of the mountains to the west is tremendously bold just opposite Valence, and right at the top of the precipitous hill is a ruin—Crussol—marvellously austere. We approached, rounded, and left that, and were set down in St. Peray just as market was assembling—for by greatest good luck we had struck the one market day of the week. Men bartering calves, weighing them on scales that suspended them ludicrously; women with live ducks in baskets; one with a kid in a burlap bag, much afflicted; innumerable dogs and small boys. In the middle of it all the toy railroad train choo-chooing along the road one yard from the house doors and ringing a bell to keep people on the doorsteps from upsetting it with their knees. Engine, one car for *voyageurs,* with an exclusive compartment seating four first-class passengers, apparently never patronized, and the rest of it for the second-classers, and a freight car. This proceeded to clatter and wobble up the side of the mountain, clinging on the edge of precipices and ducking under tunnels like a sure-footed and very sullen goat: and always the view opened up as we rose, Crussol coming into sight again, now remote in the east, and widths of hazy blue, and nearer squares and triangles of yellow and green—farms and vineyards.

Boffres, seven hundred *mètres* above sea-level, is an exceedingly primitive hamlet, clinging about a ruined church on top of a hill, as

In Boffres Valley

ABOVE: Reaping the "*Blé.*" BELOW: The "*Petit chemin de fer montagnard*" from our
chestnut grove

Mary says, like barnacles on a ship. Chief *auberge, Hotel de la Gare,*
Simeon Blaizac, proprietor, to which we at first repaired. His rooms
were impossible, and the plumbing arrangements beyond words.
We persuaded him, not without difficulty, (remember we had been
in France less than a fortnight, and no one in Boffres except d'Indy
and some of his friends we met this afternoon knows English) to
let us investigate the villa of Mme. Ducros which we had heard was
to let for six hundred francs, or *la moitié* for three hundred. As we
eventually took it, or rather the *moitié*, I will describe it.

Fifteen minutes' walk from Blaizac's, cutting through a short cut
where red-tiled sheds cluster and children pop out like rabbits, you
come to this very white and very spruce-looking villa, *toute nouvelle* and unlived in. Not picturesque, compared with some of the
pirates' dens we peeked into, but picturesqueness is better to look at
than to live in, and the newness appealed to us. It stands demure in a
walled enclosure, more gravel than garden, for there are few trees
about and the ground is mediocre, and looks like a very precise little
female fox-terrier telling the gentlemen to stay outside. Two rooms
upstairs and two down we have, the latter *pour travailler* (for
Madame travaille aussi, vous savez), and we can overflow into the
other rooms without any harm done, for we are alone in the house.
The *fermier* of Mme. Ducros lives just across a field, and his wife
brought us this morning a can of milk and four eggs in the pocket
of her apron for breakfast. I wish you could have witnessed our interview. I was sleepy and in my dressing gown. She, with a staccato
and very loud—in fact deafening—utterance peculiar to her, tried
to make me understand, in spurts punctuated by complete silence,
that it would be easier to count the eggs if she delivered them in
tens. . . .

Petit dejeuner we make on two small lamps that burn *"alcool"*,
and it is a difficult problem to make the coffee and the eggs anything
like synchronous. (The coffee opens another chapter: we got it
from an *épicerie* in Valence, buying about twenty-five francs'
worth of things, and having the most heart-breaking struggles with
names and quantities—*litres, grammes*, etc. This was only excelled
by our struggles with a lady clerk to buy some drawers for me. My

dictionary, my inseparable companion, said "*pantalons*", but "*pant-alons*" were wrong. When we finally found "*caleçons*" the material was a stumbling block, and after all obstacles had been cleared the things proved ruinously expensive as well as having a generally wrong air as to cut, and we had to beat a courteous retreat.)

Where was I? Oh yes, after breakfast we unpacked in a desultory way, but I could see that Mary was preoccupied, her heart was not in it. I immediately perceived that her thoughts were still on the plumbing, which indeed, in spite of the assurance of the landlady that it was "*très moderne*" [1] was diffusing a subtle air of cellar and lime through the house—I mean through the band-box. Finally she came out with her ultimatum—the *très moderne* plumbing was not to be used at all! Admire the wisdom of women. She had struck on the one fatally weak point of the house. It is new and clean at present, but woe to us had we attempted to use that plumbing. But our artistic temperament told us in time that it was made, not to be used, but to be looked at, and we are going to sit and look at it all summer.

Late this afternoon we walked over to d'Indy's and found a very austere chateau set high on a hill amid woods, full half a mile of steady climb from the entrance. He received us very cordially out on the tennis court, where twenty or more people were assembled, and I pretty nearly took to English. I did manage to hold my nerve however, and perpetrated some most horrible French which he received with grave friendliness and encouraging grunts and "*Oui, oui's*". He explained that he had written asking us to lunch Tuesday, and wanted me to bring some of my stuff to show him then.

I should like to write a lot more, but it is getting late, and I must leave the rest till another time. We are having, so far, the most wonderful time we have ever had, and though there are of course some difficulties I think it is going to go well on the whole. We take *déjeuner à la fourchette* and *diner chez* Blaizac.

----

[1] In later travels in France we used to be amused by the sign, on houses for rent: "*Confort moderne, prix modérés.*" It always seemed to us it ought to read: "*Confort modéré, prix modernes.*"

P.S. Mary wants me to add, lest you become too envious, that Blaizac's is singularly dirty, having apparently never been *balayé*, and that the common room where we eat is patronized by all kinds of carters, teamsters, tipsters, and so on, who grunt and wheeze very queer French. One old chap stutters—and stuttering in French is quaint! However, we can put up with a little roughing it for the sake of such a chance to be near d'Indy and to see a quite unspoiled and untouristed part of France tucked away in the mountains.

D'Indy said something complimentary about Chalmers Clifton, but I was so intent on what I was going to say that I cannot remember his precise adjective. Talking French makes one singularly self-centered—there isn't time to think of anyone else. All one's faculties are bent on avoiding immediate linguistic shipwreck.

July 25

Why don't you write to me, if only a postal card? I am beginning to get rather worried for fear you or Alison or some of the foot-Hills that surround the twin peaks are ill; Mary and I discuss frequently the chances of a letter from you, but each day as we take our seats at *déjeuner* at Blaizac's and extract our letters from the *liqueur*-advertisement in which they are stowed, the familiar handwriting fails to appear. Do send me a postal on receipt of this, if only to say: "Shut up; all well."

We are having a really desperate encounter with the French language, and confess ourselves considerably discouraged. It is all very well to read a little every day—I have followed with breathless interest a detective story, *Le coffret d'argent*, in the *Temps*, to which we subscribe—but when anybody talks it is a different thing. All the words run together. I have with great pride written several business notes since we came here, to send to Valence and Lyons, and the answers seem to indicate that I have at least made myself intelligible. The last was to order Strauss's notes on Berlioz from Durand, and I am curious to see whether it will come.

That brings me to d'Indy, who is of course here the Rome to which all roads conduct. We lunched with him on the fifteenth, a couple of days after I wrote you, and had a really delightful time.

He was all alone, and most cordial, simple, and pleasant. His chateau, which he built himself about twenty-five years ago, is severe and noble in appearance, spacious but hardly beautiful. But from his room in the tower he gets a wonderful view. It was curious to think as we went up the broad cold stone stairs with him that we were going to the room where he had written the *Jour d'été à la montagne* and many other things. One of the eccentricities of genius is that he has just about the most wretched little upright, as sole musical instrument, that it has ever been my misfortune to play on. Not only was the tone—non-existent, let us say, and the action non-active, but the pedal only barely performed its sustaining office. What with the piano and the effort to express myself in French you can fancy I had some difficulty in doing justice to my pieces. The pastorale did not hit him exactly in a soft spot. The clarinet sonata movement had better luck—indeed he praised it quite warmly, thought it succeeded where the other failed, and urged me to go on with it. But on consideration it seemed foolish to do anything while I am here near d'Indy that I could do equally well alone, and so, with a vivid sense of your probable Homeric laughter when you heard of it, I decided to try something for orchestra. Indeed the first Sunday I saw him he had suggested it. So for the first regular hour of criticism, which was day before yesterday, I had managed to get six pages of score and a good deal more sketch—all new material, "conceived" orchestrally—or at least such was my attempt.

The thing he criticized most frequently, repeatedly, and virulently was doublings, especially between wind and strings. "*Tout a fait inutile*"—"*lourd*"—"*gros*": such were his plaints. He talked a good deal about the "*fond*"—background—of the orchestral tableau and the way one made the characters—melodies—*sortir* from it. Also about changing the "*fond*" when the sentiment changes— that is, *when modulation occurs*. I couldn't quote his words, but I took the impression that he associates modulation quite closely with change of sentiment. In this it seems to me he shows immeasurable superiority to the sloppy modernists like Reger, who modulate in every measure like people who can't sit still, not because they have anything to do, but because a flea is biting them.

As this place is exceedingly quiet and primitive there is practically nothing to do but work at music or study French. We have, for "excitement", lessons in French twice a week from a nice young fellow, M. Bosvenil, *instituteur* in the *école des garçons à Boffres*. While he was here this afternoon a young mite of humanity about three feet high appeared at the front gate of our "villa", and stood there as if petrified with curiosity or terror. While Mary went out to interrogate her—quite vainly—I asked the *instituteur* what he thought she came for. He said that obviously she came to see the two Americans, and on consideration that really is a sufficient reason. If you want to know what fame is, come to Boffres. We walk to our meals down a lane of human courtesy and consideration—"*Bonjour, Monsieur et dame!*" resounding on all sides. Our least wish is known at once to Boffres. If we ask a small boy where to get a loaf of bread, it is quite likely to be the postmaster who comes to us an hour later with the coveted information. I am going to ask the *maire* or the *sous-préfet* or somebody, tomorrow, where I can get my *souliers polis*.

August 7

. . . D'Indy left town for three weeks last Sunday, and I am not to have another criticism until the twenty-seventh. (He has gone, I believe, to conduct *L'Étranger* in Vichy.) We do not feel as completely deprived of social life by his going as we should have expected a few weeks ago. In the first place, Boffres has accepted us in a remarkable way since our friend Riboud of Lyons visited us a week ago Sunday and let it be seen by his treatment of us that we were all right. Even before that we had had pleasant chats with various shopkeepers of the two or three shops of Boffres, especially the very pleasant and intelligent keeper of one of the "*épiceries*" and his talkative, ruddy-faced, one-toothed wife, when we were buying "*alcool*" or "*pétrole*" or leaving our coffee (which we got in Valence) to be ground. That day, however, seeing us with Riboud, they asked us all three into the rear hole of their spiderweb and gave us coffee and cognac. Three hours later Blaizac, our own inn-keeper, had us in to polish off a bottle of champagne with him—champagne

of the country, about two francs a *demi-bouteille*, I suppose, but
still champagne. All the ten days since then have only served to waft
us gently down from these heights.

Then we have French lessons twice a week from the *instituteur*,
who comes on his *bicylette* and talks to us and corrects exercises that
we have written. Finally, there are two little French birds, *Madame*
and *Mademoiselle*, the latter devotedly considered a *"jeune fille"* by
the former for the last twenty or thirty years, *pensionnaires* at
Blaizac's, very correct, very clean, very much afraid of draughts,
and fanatic admirers of d'Indy, of whom *Mademoiselle* took piano
lessons years ago. I fancy they spend the summer here largely to be
near his chateau—himself they rarely see. The daughter knows all
his opus numbers by heart, and both of them talk at length about the
amount of *"coeur"* displayed by his works, and notably absent from
practically all other compositions. They have been to tea with us
twice, and are a severe test on our French, as they usually talk at
once in order to egg each other on, and are apt to come to sudden
stops—when one must be ready to stick in a *Je comprends* or a
Parfaitement, or at least to look sympathetic. The mother makes
attempts to talk to me *tête à tête*, but the moment Mary or *Mademoiselle* pass from smiling looks to timid speech she stops in mid-
sentence to listen, with her mouth open, fascinated. I am naturally
at her mercy. The second day they were here I played for them, at
their request, some pieces of my own, and Mary says they had a
ritual about listening: the moment I began they put their heads on
one side and went into a brown study. It was a serious business. I
was proud to learn that after all d'Indy had not quite a monopoly of
"coeur". My melody however was discovered to have a marked
flavor of Schubert—which was perhaps inevitable considering the
amount of *"coeur"* involved. They were nearly the death of us that
day, staying until 7:05 because of threatening rain. Then they
walked so slowly that in taking a short cut we got to Blaizac's before them and were well on with dinner when they appeared.

It is getting late, and I have told you nothing of work, or of my
third hour with d'Indy on July thirtieth, when things went wonderfully well and he seemed encouragingly pleased with the com-

position of what I had to show him, while even the scoring was fairly well laid out and many of my schemes were allowed to stand. So I have been in good spirits, and have been working from three to five hours a day, trying to finish the piece before he returns.—Have I succeeded in stimulating your curiosity at all? When it is done I shall write some more about it—meanwhile I only want to get you into a mad state of envy at my chance to work with "the master", as his sister-in-law calls him in casual conversation. By the way, his physical energy at sixty-two is extraordinary. He told me that he works from six until twelve, and from two until five every day, and when I go to him at five he is as fresh as possible, and reads score in a way that breaks my heart. He is awfully good-natured about my frightful French, and somehow or other I manage to get what I want with it—last time we neither of us thought once of resorting to English. I am sure I admire his orchestral knowledge and instinct as much as you say Clifton does, and his understanding of the in-dividual is that of the heaven-inspired teacher.

I am in so expansive a mood after my first hour with d'Indy since his three-weeks absence in Vichy and Vienna that I must let off some of it on you. I was *possessed* with the idea of finishing my—but wait, I have not yet told you more than that I was doing or-chestral studies, you do not know that I have bitten off, not a sym-phonic poem, but a symphony *allegro*! There, the cat is out of the bag at last, and I leave you to laugh five minutes at the drollery of the idea. . . . (Laughter) . . .

I was delighted to find that in the twenty-six pages of score he looked at today there were hardly any serious miscalculations. "*Ça va bien*" came with gratifying frequency, and a tuba too heavy in one place and bassoons that deprived the horns of their color in an-other were practically the only corrections. His final comment was that it was entirely a different thing from what I had brought him at first.

Today they are "batting the *blé*", as we call it, at our farmer's, just across a field from us, and we have been over watching the two enormous stocks of *blé* ready for threshing, the busy, eager, animal-like engine in between eating up *blé* with a vicious gr-r-r- and growling for more before each bundle that is fed into it, and the farmhands swarming about the whole like ants. The nice sixteen-year-old hired boy of the farmer cut his hand badly in the engine yesterday, when it was threshing on a farm "*lá-bas*", and has been unable to participate in the great event today.

We had a most absurd fright the other day when a woman appeared during the morning while I was at work, to look at the other half of the villa with a view to renting it. At *déjeuner* we held a council of war and decided that immediate action was necessary, for the place is really so small that work would be impossible with others here. It ended in our walking over to Mme. Ducros's in the heat of the day, and having a long conversation with her, finally paying a *supplément* of fifty francs in order to have the exclusive use of the villa for the rest of the season. We then had a sociable glass of "*sirop de framboise*" (known in the tongue of our childhood as raspberry shrub) and went home in a state of saucy triumph to make ourselves tea and play the piano *fortissimo* with all the doors open. It is amusing now, but it was tragedy then—if you don't realize it get Alison's opinion.

September 3

At present, were I to attempt any detail, I should be inclined to stress the difficult features of Boffres. Impossible to deny that the seamy side has been showing itself rather persistently of late, owing I suppose to the insidious effects of an upset digestion. It has been hot, Blaizac's food has been incorrigibly greasy, and the flies and the fleas seem to gain in energy as one loses it oneself—a vicious inverse ratio. . . .

Among the dogs that haunt the Hotel de la Gare—I like to write the absurdly pompous name for Blaizac's joint—is one pretty but very hungry hound, of the gentler sex, who is always getting in Berthe's way and being ejected to the street, from which, as the door is always open, she soon returns. For some inscrutable reason, she rejoices in the name of "Meess", the one English word we hear with any regularity—and this in spite of the fact that her whole physique cries out that it should be "Meessess" if anything. The father of

"Shorsh" also spoke a little English, but Shorsh, and his father, and his Spanishly-indolent mother who had the prettiness, Mary said, of a chocolate-advertisement lady, and Shorsh's steam cars, have all gone away. Georges, if you prefer the conventional spelling, was about two years old, and was so passionately enamored of the railroad that he really slighted his meals in his haste to go choo-chooing in and out among the chairs and tables. He would look askance at the Americans for some time before venturing on a quick spurt past their dangerous neighborhood, and when they made advances to him he would cover his eyes in shyness. Sometimes in his mimetic enthusiasm he would give an all-too-real series of whistles, and it was then that the singular inefficiency of Shorsh as a name to call anything by was borne in upon us.

There was in Vernoux last Sunday a *Grande Fête d'Inauguration de l'Hotel de Ville, du tramway, et des fontaines, avec le concours d'une musique militaire, bataille de confetti*, etc., etc. Unfortunately the combination of ferociously hot weather with rampant indigestion and fatigue from a former trip made it seem unwise to go, but even in peaceful Boffres, basking on its hill-top in changeless sun, we got intimations of the festivities on foot eight *kilomètres* away. Innumerable bicycles trailed by, our farmer's three sons appeared in *grande toilette*, and above all the *petit chemin de fer de montagne* was fairly distracted. There was a special *horaire* for the day, with extra trains and one of the three regular ones only going as far as Alboussières, three *kilomètres* below us, and then puffing up-hill again to the much-bedecorated little town in its wide plateau. Early in the afternoon an engine, all alone save for a flat freight car loaded with beer cases, went up positively swelling, almost rolling, with self-importance, flying its tricolors from the mast head, so to speak, and making the Sabbath hideous with a whistling fit to bring the dead over the ten-foot wall of the new cemetery—had any of them been buried in it yet. This tramway, you see, was only put in three years ago, and was it not being "inaugurated" now, along with the Hotel de Ville and the *fontaines*? No wonder it felt responsible to contribute all it could to the glory of the day.

September 8

Your Francestown postal-card came today, and was certainly a happy thought. Nothing could more evoke the "home" atmosphere —it was as New England as apple-pie. The uncompromising nature of the sign "Gasoline" and "A. E. Holt" did my eyes good, after a long course of *Épiceries, Boulangeries,* etc. Here is a bit from a circus poster which is as deliciously French as anything I have struck:

Ne manquez pas d'assister a cette extraordinaire et merveilleuse représentation donnée par la famille CATALANI. Le travail artistique qui vous est offert est vraiment incomparable, et vous en garderez un inoubliable souvenir. La Direction ne répond pas des dettes des Employés.

Hotel Victoria
Chexbres, Switzerland
September 12

So much has gone over our heads, or under our heels, since I wrote the above, that I hardly know how to connect with it, or whether indeed to try to, or not rather throw it away and begin afresh. However, as it is the last time I wrote Boffres at the top of a sheet, and probably will be the last time of my life, I must keep it—to say nothing of the family CATALANI.

I began it in a haze of sentiment at leaving Boffres, mixed with excitement at d'Indy's evident interest in the string quartet *allegro* at the fifth and last of our meetings, which took place the afternoon of the eighth. He never says much in praise of anything—"*Ça va*" or "*Pas mal*," but he told me that if I would finish this or the clarinet sonata he would like to have one of them done at a concert of the *Société Nationale.* He also reiterated what he had said before as to the quickness with which I had caught his ideas about not doubling, etc., and I really feel as if the experience with him had given me just the touch I needed, and I could go on by myself now with more confidence.

I wish you could have seen our departure from Boffres. The fifteen minutes' walk up to the top of the hill where Blaizac's is and

Goodbye to Boffres
ABOVE: Mme. Blaizac, Berthe, Simeon Blaizac, a waitress, and the Chef.
BELOW: "Derailed again!"

down on the other side to the *gare* was punctuated by *"Bon jour, Monsieur et dame"*, and by *"Au revoir, Monsieur et dame"* from those who had duly digested the sad tidings that Boffres was to lose on that day its first and last Americans. Our best friend in the village, Mme. Martel the *épicier's* wife, sixty-two, ruddy-faced, jolly, mercurial in temperament, was much dumped, and justly, because Martel had fallen downstairs the night before while searching for the *fromage*, and strained his hip. We could not see him to say goodbye, but had to leave our *grande sympathie*. She was almost too used up to go out in the street and stand talking with Mary while I "snapped" them as a *"témoignage de notre amitié"*. Then at Blaizac's there was another photograph, and this required long preparation: chairs to be brought out, Berthe and the other waitress to be summoned in haste, the *chef* to be found, who lingered so long that I finally raised a laugh at his expense by remarking that *"Monsieur le chef fait grande toilette!"* Blaizac and Madame B. sat in the chairs and let the women stand about them with harem-like effect, disregarding my white-livered American suggestion that the women sit and the men stand. The photograph finally achieved, there were endless hand-shakings and *au revoirs*, and a further snail-like progress down hill to the *gare*. There more friends, and a talk with our farmer's son, who had brought our bags, as to the amount of snow in Boffres in winter and its notable decrease of recent years.

At last the *"petit chemin de fer montagnard"*, as by *metonome* or *synechdoche* or one of those things we call the train as well as the railroad, appeared; but then, after we were in, it still, in its leisurely manner, prolonged the agony about ten minutes more. After many redispositions of baggage and a talk through the window with Mme. and Mlle. Delaire, our Parisian birds, we heard the penny whistle of the guard, and the answering scream-hiccup of the engine, and slowly began to trundle around the hill in the fashion of the far-famed "side-hill winder". Wavings from the window, and a sense of relief and bereavement combined. In five minutes, perhaps less, a complete stop, and a general query: *"Déraillé?"*—not excited or apprehensive, simply interrogatory and just a grain quizzical. It was only too true, the second set of wheels from the back of the engine had jumped the track. There ensued a colloquy between guard, engineer, and one or two self-constituted authorities, and planks and joists began to be extracted from the baggage car, where they had rested probably not twenty-four hours since the last derailment. Progress was slow, and as we sat on a grassy bank—the ten or a dozen passengers—watching the process, we were gradually rejoined by Boffres in a compact and amiably derisive body—children largely in the majority. After a half hour in which everybody was gently laughed at and the recalcitrant wheels were finally coaxed back on to the track we proceeded on our way, and presently saw the uncompromising white spot of the *petite villa* vanish round a curve.

CHAPTER XV

VINCENT D'INDY

It was in May, 1901, twelve years before our Boffres summer, that I had my first glimpse of d'Indy—nothing more than a glimpse—in one of the cold uncomfortable little rooms of the Schola Cantorum that he and Charles Bordes and Alexandre Guilmant had founded less than a decade before. Homesick, ill, bewildered by the noise and confusion of Paris, I was seeking his artistic counsel in the forlorn hope that it might enable me to work. I needed a friend, and in him I found one, even in the strangeness of that environment. I had made my way between the *crèmeries* and *boucheries* of the old winding Rue St. Jacques, which leads from the ugly modern Boulevard Port Royal, where I was lodging, over to the head of the Rue Soufflot and the Pantheon, I had rung the bell in the high wall with the cresset lamp and the overhanging tree, and now from a group of students advanced to meet me, with an ease born of dignity and kindness, the tall, erect, youthfully alert figure of d'Indy. He was already fifty, but the elasticity of his carriage, the black hair brushed back from his finely moulded forehead, the dark moustache and imperial that framed his mouth, above all the striking keenness of his eyes as they looked out from behind heavy brows, gave an impression of vigorous youth. He wore the low collar hiding a little strip of black tie and the rather formal black frock-coat with the

red ribbon of the Legion of Honor that were afterwards to become
so familiar to me. There was in his manner a simple courtesy that
combined self-respect and friendliness, an indescribable, delightful
commixture of cordiality and reserve.

We made an appointment for a more leisurely call at his apartment a few days later. This apartment, which he tells in his memoirs
of 1930 of having occupied for sixty-four years—that is, since 1866
—was at 7 Avenue de Villars, in a quiet and more spacious section
than that of the Schola, dominated by the broad-set gilded dome of
the Invalides. I stayed over an hour this time, and showed him some
manuscripts, so that it was really a "lesson"; yet he would not accept
a centime when I rose to go. I took away from that first talk a vivid
impression of the impersonality of his devotion to beauty. Of course
I had long known of his ardent loyalty to César Franck, and I was
prepared for the pride and affection with which he pointed to a bust
of Franck in his study. But I now learned, from the kindness with
which he wrote on his photograph *"à Monsieur Daniel E. Mason"*
(getting my middle initial wrong) *"en souvenir de bonnes conversations d'art"* (though I had contributed little beyond absorbed
attention), and from the enthusiasm with which he talked of the
masterpieces of Bach, Beethoven, Franck, and Fauré one should
study, and of the unbroken stream of tradition, that whatever degree of friendship he accepted from me, it was not primarily on my
account, or on his, but because both of us were servants of art. And
it was curious that, far from resenting this impersonality, one felt
ennobled by it. "I could not love thee, dear, so much, loved I not
honor more." This is what is meant, I suppose, by the "austerity"
so often and rightly insisted upon, by friendly as well as hostile
critics, in both his personality and his music. But why should everyone have the sweetness of Franck? Is not astringency, is not a severe
nobility, as necessary as sweetness? To me this austerity of d'Indy's,
assuredly one of his most essential qualities, is an inspiring austerity,
like that of Emerson's conception of love or Thoreau's of friendship. And there was a breath as from those greatest of our Americans
in the vibrant conviction of the sentence he uttered that day just
before I left, a sentence that in its solace as well as its challenge has

Vincent d'Indy in 1901

stayed with me all my life: *"Les principes d'art sont éternelles. Ils restent."*—"The principles of art are eternal. They endure."

II

There is another saying of d'Indy's that seems to me deeply characteristic, and that I associate with all my thought of him. In an article on the work of his friend Roger Ducasse he writes: "I am sure that when M. Ducasse is willing to trust himself more to the impulses of his heart rather than to researches in sonorities, he will be able to make very beautiful music." And he draws this more general conclusion: *"Il n'est que le coeur pour engendrer de la beauté."* —[Only the heart can create beauty.] To this creed d'Indy was loyal throughout his long life as a composer, disregarding all the unpopularity it brought him. Most of his active life fell in a period when "researches in sonorities" were infinitely more *à la mode* than beauty through emotion—witness the fame, so far outshining his, of his friend Debussy. It is honorable to both men that, poles apart as were their musical aesthetics, they honored each other. D'Indy was one of the first to defend in the press *Pelléas et Mélisande;* and Debussy as critic wrote of his friend's *L'Ètranger:* "Never has modern music found an expression more profoundly devout, more Christianly loving". . . . But d'Indy's intransigent opposition to "researches in sonority", as well as to other fashionable crazes such as the barbarism of Stravinsky and the ugliness of Schönberg, lasted his lifetime, and cost him dear. A reviewer of his eightieth birthday celebration in 1931 remarked that only one of the Paris orchestras had put a work of his on its program to honor the occasion, though all had given special festivals for the benefit of the Debussy Monument Fund, adding with delicate irony: "Presumably they are waiting until it is time to erect a monument to his memory." But of course they are likely to wait much longer than that.

Whether one like or dislike the role played by the heart in d'Indy's music, however, one could hardly resist the charm it gave his daily life. I saw it even in the hasty call he did my wife and me the honor to pay us during his first trip to America in 1905. We were then

settled in an apartment in uptown New York, where he had the
true kindness, in the midst of endless rehearsals and social engagements, to seek us out, drink a cup of chocolate which I am sure he
did not want, and smoke three cigarettes from his neat little holder.
He had written me too, in his exquisitely precise, legible hand, and
for the first and last time in English, from Philadelphia: "Unfortunately it shall be impossible to me to lunch with Dr. W. Mason, but
I enjoy to pay him a visit, perhaps this same Friday, before one
o'clock, when you think that it is possible." And he did come with
me to my uncle's house in West Sixteenth Street, and discuss with
him their memories of Liszt.

I noticed during this visit a detail that had before escaped me:
his nails were bitten to the quick, making conspicious the rounded
finger-ends often supposed to indicate artistic sensibility. They suggested at least sensitiveness, if not acute nervousness. Assuredly
they were not the nails of the martinet, the pedant, the hard-work-
ing but uninspired academic certain circles absurdly imagined him.
They were minute witnesses to what one believed to be the truth—
that the laboriousness of his life was imposed on a vivid temperament
by an insatiable conscience, and at heavy cost.

Equally absurd was the legend of his penuriousness. He was much
entertained in New York on that visit, and the story went round
that one evening at dinner one of his entertainers asked him for a
cigarette, and he, looking in his case, answered: "I'm sorry, but there
is only one here, and that is for tomorrow morning." It might be
true, for with him everything was planned as carefully as his compositions; but his care was that of the precisian, not that of the nig-
gard. As I have said, he would take no money for our first con-
sultation in Paris. For the five more ample coachings he gave me in
Boffres he would not name a price, saying he never gave private
lessons. I offered twenty-five francs for each (five dollars) but he
would only take twenty, making only a hundred francs (twenty
dollars) for all the trouble I gave him. Precise enough, certainly, he
was. In his note inviting us to lunch and the first criticism, he wrote:
"I count on you both, Tuesday at noon. However, I must tell you
quite frankly that I shall ask you not to stay after two o'clock, since

that is the hour I start work, and I have so little time, above all this year, that I do not want to lose a single day. I am sure you will understand."

It was characteristic of him as a teacher that he always tried to emphasize the positive, constructive side, by praising what was good instead of lingering over what was bad. Thus at that first of our Boffres meetings, when I showed him several already finished compositions, he dwelt on the desirability of letting the imagination flow freely, especially in the second theme of a sonata form, pointing out that Beethoven often incorporates a number of contrasting motives in a second theme, and showed how much more imaginative the second theme of my *Clarinet Sonata* first movement was in this way than that of my *Pastorale*. And I can see him now as we went down the stately cold stone staircase afterwards, turning to me at the bottom to say: "I always divide my pupils (though of course you are not exactly a pupil)into two kinds: those who are too careless and have to be held back and made to take pains, and those who are too timid and need to be encouraged. You are of the second sort. You write well but you are not sufficiently untrammelled, sufficiently willing to go to extremes in the search for your thought, even to be foolish (*"fou"*) if necessary." And he ended by insisting *"Vous êtes trop sage"*, and advising me to dare to be *"fou"*. At our last meeting, when I had learned to some extent to write more freely, and also to avoid the bad "doublings" he had found at first, he dwelt with great good humor on the improvement in this respect, frequently exclaiming *"Bon"* or *"Ça va bien"* with almost as much glee as if my score had been his own, and proclaiming at last that it was now *"tout à fait une autre chose"*—[altogether another matter].

Two memories of that period come back to me. One is of a hot Saturday afternoon at our little villa, when our friend Camille Riboud had come up from Lyons to spend the week-end with us. We could scarcely believe our eyes when the little train puffed and rattled up through the chestnut-bordered field below our villa, and we saw him waving to us from the tiny first class compartment of the rear car, upholstered in magnificent red plush, seating four persons, and never before in our experience patronized by anyone. All Boffres seemed to share our amazement. The effect on our social standing of such a visitor, one who not only arrived first class but mingled with everybody so genially, was immediate and far-reaching. It lasted all summer.

We had asked d'Indy to come down to tea, and he walked all the way from his chateau, despite the heat and the encumbrance of his usual frock-coat. He was greatly amused at our little villa, which for some inscrutable reason had been painted white on two sides and sky blue on the other two. "When he arrived," my wife says in her journal, "I was alone, as Dan had gone to the station to meet Riboud, and he was quite charming in his interest in the villa, looking into Dan's workroom with interest, and very responsive to my amused comments on Riboud's occupying the first class coach in 'le petit chemin de fer montagnard'. He seemed to enjoy his talk with Riboud (most of which we couldn't understand) and the bread and butter, of which he ate a reassuring quantity. He is a delightfully unaffected, kind, great musician."

The other memory is of the following spring in Paris. Despite his crushing preoccupations at the Schola he had given me one further criticism, late in the afternoon of a full day, on the second movement of my symphony; but we had both been so tired that the interview was unsatisfactory. Then came, in April, an invitation from the club, *Autour du monde*, at Boulogne-sur-Seine, for us to be guests of honor at a luncheon, at which "*le mâitre*" had consented to be present. Indeed he took my wife out to lunch, while I sat next M. Kahn, founder of the club and of the scholarships enabling worthy students to travel (it was on one of these that Henri Bergson came to New York). Kahn, a Jew who had made his own fortune, was an enthusiastic humanist of simple and sincere nature, delightful to meet. Fortunately d'Indy was right across the table from me, and my French had now improved enough to enable me to exchange ideas with him more freely. We had brought him a copy of a song of which my wife had written the text and I the music, *The Greeting*, eventually one of the *Love-Songs*, opus 15, and it was good to see the grave courtesy with which he unrolled it, glanced through it in the midst of the distractions of the luncheon, and half murmured, half bowed his interest. Though a member of the club, he had not been to a meeting before for several months. He came out of friendly interest in a young foreigner he might never see again. No one I ever knew acted more simply than he always, more as a matter of course, on Emerson's counsel: "Be an opener of doors for such as come after thee."

III

When we visited Paris in the spring of 1921, he invited us to dine at 7 Avenue de Villars and meet the new Madame d'Indy. He was now seventy; and though he could never be anything but young in spirit, he was evidently experiencing some of the trials of age—going, let us say, through a monotonous stretch of doldrums such as even in the cruise of a genius often separates the brave setting sail of youth and middle age from the coming into port of full appreciation that is too apt to be posthumous. In his new circumstances he was debarred from his chateau of Les Faugs among his beloved Cevennes. He and Mme. d'Indy were spending their summers at Agay, on the French Riviera, where a few years later they greeted us cordially as we passed through on a motor tour. Distressing as this personal exile must have been for one to whom ties of affection and tradition meant so much, his professional exile (as it is scarcely an exaggeration to call it) from the recognition his work deserved must have been even harder to bear. "Modern France," I pointed out in an essay at the time,[1] "is not a good place for a vitalist. It is a wilderness of impressionism, barbarism, and intellectualism. Vincent d'Indy is a voice crying in that wilderness, and his cry is: '*Il n'est que le coeur pour engendrer de la beauté.*' At seventy, despite his imposing reputation, which few trouble to understand, and surrounded by a small group of friends more of whom are sentimental idolators than intelligent supporters, and by many enemies (for he is a well-hated man) Vincent d'Indy is perhaps more alone than ever."

One had to admire his equanimity and perfect patience under

[1] *Vincent d'Indy in America*, in *The Dilemma of American Music.*

these conditions. He invited me to some of his examinations at the Schola, copying out the complete list in his microscopic handwriting. It took nearly the whole side of a sheet, and I could not help wondering whether the Schola included typewriters in the modernisms it distrusted.

Journal. "June 25. Late afternoon. I have been to hear the examinations at the Schola: (1) Violin sonata by a girl, musical but interminably long. D'Indy played what he could of the violin part on the piano, and sang some of it. His criticisms were friendly but firm. (2) Endless truck of a violin sonata by one H—, on terribly common, old-fashioned themes: d'Indy equally patient and considerate. (3) Douglas Moore's overture. (4) Gregorian chant trio, short. (5) Awful improvisation stuff which never began, by that Roumanian M—. D'Indy's sweetness and patience in all deeply impressed me."

After the dinner at his apartment he played for me his new work, *Poème des Rivages*, which he was to conduct on his American tour in the fall (played in New York December 3, it received an ovation). This was a work in four movements, based in part on his impressions of the Mediterranean. He told me that impressions often germinated unconsciously in his mind for long periods, before taking on definite musical forms; and it interested me that both the second and third movements were attributed by him primarily to color impressions, the second to an intensely blue sea seen downward through trees, and the third, a sort of scherzo in which the motion of the train is felt, to the green sea and sky of the Adriatic (high register of bassoon, English horn, oboe, and clarinet, all suggesting intense greenness). Of his method of work I recorded: "He makes a three- or four-line pencil sketch, with few indications of orchestration, mostly melodies. From this he makes a pencil score in full detail, often changing the composition a good deal. Then when that is approved he inks it over on the same sheets. . . . He agreed with me that it was the music possibilities of ideas that determined how they developed, more than any word program. The form could never be determined in advance—it depended on the music."

Of his New York visit that autumn the great event for us was the presentation of the loving-cup. . . . It had occurred to us as a pleasant plan that those of his students then available in New York —unfortunately few—should meet the aging master and his new wife at our apartment, and that we should all express to him our lasting admiration and gratitude. We had heard disquieting stories of the fatigues of his journeyings in a foreign land (a taxi accident, for instance, during a snowstorm in the wilds of Pennsylvania) and we hoped to bring a sense of comradeship to him in his solitary musical position.

So on Thanksgiving afternoon we all assembled: the d'Indys, Seth Bingham and his wife, Edward Shippen Barnes and his, David McK. Williams, Bruce Simonds, my wife and I. After we had all had tea I set up the cup, bearing an inscription put into idomatic French for us by my friend Professor Spiers of Columbia, and read aloud our accompanying letter, afterwards presenting to d'Indy both letter and loving-cup. He said a few words—that he was touched by our kindness, and that he wished to thank those of his American students who were absent as well as those present. Mme. d'Indy wept a little. . . . The afternoon ended with his playing for us all his beautiful canon of *The Quest of God*, from *St. Christophe*.

Here is a translation of our letter:

"Dear Master: Your old students of the United States seize eagerly the occasion of your visit to their country to present to you this cup, a pledge of the friendship they bear you and the admiration inspired in them by a life entirely consecrated to the service of music. In a time when our art has suffered so much from the commercial spirit, when so many have sought personal prestige rather than the pursuit of beauty, you have remained in your acts faithful to the noble ideal your words so powerfully express. In each of us, according to his capacities, you have nourished the cult of art as a principle of life. In acknowledgement of this inestimable gift, please accept this expression of our lasting gratitude and affection."

IV

In my 1921 article on d'Indy in New York I named as one of his most characteristic works his *Jour d'Été à la Montagne*—[*Summer Day on the Mountain*]. Possibly my special love for it may be in part due to my own associations with those austere, almost bleak, but beautiful Cevennes of his. But a deeper reason is that it illustrates, as I tried to show, the inwardness of his art, his dependence on the heart that creates beauty. I contrasted this inwardness with the crass, often vulgarly realistic scene-painting of Strauss in the *Alpine Symphony*. "In the first movement, *Dawn*," I wrote, "there is the empty blankness of the mist before sunrise, the gradually increasing light and animation suggested by changes of key and rhythm, the final gorgeous appearance of the sun in a blaze of B major. In the second movement, *Day: Afternoon under the Pines*, we have almost no tone-painting, but rather the unforgettable evocation of the mood of the scene and place. Then come realistic suggestions of a peasant's song in the valley, and later a sort of marching theme—perhaps a regiment going by. In the last movement, *Evening*, there is first the animation of full day; then gradually an abatement, an almost imperceptible darkening and saddening, and a lovely melody that is like a song as one comes home at evening, a song profoundly characteristic of d'Indy, full of happy serenity and devout thankfulness. . . . Then gradually the shades descend, the passages early in the symphony suggestive of mist and half-light recur, there is a faint clashing of chimes in the distance, and after the song of thankfulness has been sung once more there is a supremely beautiful and characteristic passage made from the theme of full day, in which all is calmed and quieted to the mood of dusk. It is hard to listen to such a passage without tears; for it is not sticks and stones that it gives us, but the very accent of what this beauty of the darkening day means to a responsive spirit."

No doubt the *Jour d'Été*, like all d'Indy's greatest works, is personal through faults as well as virtues. Certain mannerisms of his: a trick of changing the orchestral grouping too frequently and restlessly, so that the ear is bewildered instead of wooed—over-fondness for a texture to which, in something of mine, he once applied the term "a little tortured with counterpoint"—a habit of stopping in the middle of the melodic flow to tease a short motive as a cat teases a mouse—above all a tendency to pile up beauties immoderately, until one kills another and the listener is left gasping instead of entranced—these mannerisms are sometimes maddening in a composer who needs only to be simplified to reveal his unique fascination. It is these things that give the charge against him of academicism, even of pedantry, a half-truth almost more damaging than complete falsity. But is not Emerson right in saying that we understand only what we love? I for one always find that even when d'Indy's useless complexities have most baffled me I suddenly come upon some ineffable moment, like that final twilight meditation in the *Jour d'Été*, or the coda of the first movement of the *E major Quartet*, or the A flat Variation in *Istar*, that carries me into a heaven of beauty where fault-finding is forgotten as an irrelevance.

In December 1929 Nikolai Sokoloff played with the Cleveland Orchestra in New York the *Jour d'Été*, a work still so little understood in our country that Ernest Bloch had dared to say of it that it "might have been written in an office". But at last it was beginning to be heard with the love that creates understanding. "D'Indy, who has spent much time in the wild hill country of the Cevennes," now wrote Lawrence Gilman, "has inclosed the best of himself in this poised and lovely work—a score in which the mountains, for the first time in music, are adequately celebrated." And he ended by declaring: "It is hard to imagine that anyone who knows the moods of the hills, and is not permanently unfriendly toward such music as d'Indy's, could listen to this superb hymn and resist the contagion of its noble and spacious poetry, its free airs, its uplifted and consolatory beauty."

I at once sent the article to d'Indy, who jumped to the conclusion that I had written it—(I only wish I had.) Here is his reply.

"December 15, 1929

"Thank you, my dear Mason, for your kind message and for the charming article on my *Jour d'Été*, which appears to me to be by

yourself? . . . I was happy to see that they have not completely
forgotten me in America, and if you have the opportunity I should
be obliged if you would give my warmest thanks to M. Sokoloff,
who conducted my work. My respects and the best wishes of my
wife to Mme. Mason. And for you, my dear friend, all our very
sincere and unchanging friendship."

I was happy to have been at least the means of bringing to his
attention Gilman's deep understanding of his work.

V

During these years the old master, now nearly eighty, had been
turning more and more towards the most intimate field of his art,
chamber music, writing less for orchestra and for the stage, and
leaving criticism and polemics mostly to younger men. . . . Not
that he ever hesitated, even now, whenever his opinion was asked,
to speak out boldly against what he considered degrading contemporary tendencies. At a festival of his works in Prague in 1925 he
stated frankly that he was glad to note a decline in the revolutionary
tendencies of modern music. He fearlessly expressed the opinions
that Stravinsky had done little that was worth while since *Petrushka*,
that Schönberg's *Pierrot Lunaire* was "small, oh so small", and that
in general the music of the modernists was notable only for its stark
tonal effects, and that "when these were abstracted there remained
only a vulgar residuum."

But in the same interview he insisted that "the anarchy of today"
is temporary, that from early Gregorian church music to Debussy
and Ravel there has been only a development on the same ground
plan, and that when all the present preoccupation with exotic and
jazz elements has been forgotten, "the old original stem of our music
will flower and bear fruit." He mingled more and more with the
Wagnerian and Franckian elements in his own style that vivifying
stream of French folk-song that had flowed beneath it like a fertilizing underground river ever since his *Symphony on a Mountain
Theme* of 1886; and he turned more and more from orchestral music,

with its impersonal massiveness, and from the feverishness of opera, to the intimateness of the quartet.

The longest letter he ever wrote me, following a month later the hurried note about Gilman's article, constitutes, it seems to me, a sort of confession of faith of this final period.

"Paris, January 30, 1930

"I am altogether ashamed not to have given you a sign of life for such a long time, but I am more and more overwhelmed with the most diverse occupations: journeys to direct provincial concerts, my *eight* courses a week at the Schola, examinations, my classes at the Conservatory, and above all, books which editors have asked me for, and which take all my available time. However, I have found some free moments to read your book, *The Dilemma of American Music*, and I want to thank you with all my heart for the way you have treated me—myself and my works.

"I have written in this recent period many new chamber music works; I find that this *genre* is by far the most attractive and the most intimate; it is there that the heart of the artist can best express itself and talk with other hearts and tell them its sufferings and its joys. Nowadays everybody orchestrates well, there is no use making orchestral pieces, as there is a whole nursery of orchestrators both skillful and—amusing, so far as the sonorities employed are concerned, while few are able to make chamber music, a *genre* which requires a particular way of writing, very strict and very intimate. I have therefore abounded in this type in these last years: a *Quintet* with piano, a *Concerto* for flute, cello, piano and string orchestra, a *Suite* for quartet and harp, a *Sextet* for strings, a *Trio* with piano, and finally a *String Quartet* of which the premiere will take place at once. All this has given me much joy.

"Thank you for the details you give me about your young composers, I hope for them that they will not give themselves to the utopias of atonality and polytonality which adroit time-servers, without any knowledge or talent, have made the fashion with us, and I wish them good careers."

de chambre, genre qui exige une écriture particulière, très stricte et très intense. J'ai pu aborder dans ce genre, ces dernières années : 1 Quintette avec piano, 1 Concert, pour flûte, violoncelle, piano et orchestre à cordes, 1 Suite pour 2 flûtes et harpe, 1 Sextuor pour 2 V^ns, 2 altos et 2 V^elles, un trio avec piano, et enfin une Quatuor à cordes dont le 1er méditera une bien incessamment.

Tout cela m'a donné beaucoup de joie.

Mais les détails que vous me donnez sur vos jeunes compositeurs, j'espère pour eux qu'il ne sauront faire avec le mépris de l'actualité et de la polytonalité, qui m'avait anéanti, une œuvre servant mi'talent, ont mis à la mode chez nous, et je ben souhaite bonne carrière.

Mais il faut que je vous quitte, il se me reste que le temps de vous dire, mon cher Mason, toute ma bien sincère amitié.

Vincent d'Indy

Vincent d'Indy in his study
From a photograph by Bonney

The rest of the story is brief. On March 27, 1931 the master cele-brated his eightieth birthday. Three concerts were given in Paris in his honor; the first, a performance under his own baton of his early choral work *La Chant de la Cloche;* the second, a concert of his works, conducted by Pierné, in which the chief item was the *Summer Day Symphony;* the third, a concert of the Société Nationale, bring-ing forward two new works, *Fantasia on an old French Round* for piano, and *French Popular Songs* set for *a capella* chorus. I sent him a brief cablegram and a letter in which I said that it had been given to few individuals to do for music what he had done and was still doing for it. His answer was:

"April 2, 1931
"Thank you with all my heart, my dear Mason, for your kind remembrance. It is precious to me, in these hours of festival, to feel with me, and behind me, a generation which is growing up in admi-ration of the beautiful and in respect for art.
"Your old teacher and friend, Vincent d'Indy"

The old neat handwriting is tremulous in this note, though as full as ever of his character; and in spite of the surprising energy he showed during the festival his strength was somewhat failing, and he lost some days from work through illness in that eighty-first of his years, although he was at work again on nearly the last day. He died in Paris December 3, 1931. Louis Noyer wrote me—in English:

"Paris, December 4, 1931
"I send you a few clippings from this morning's papers on the death of your dear old '*Mâitre*' Vincent d'Indy. You will see how unanimously his genius as well as his great character are acknowl-edged. One may discuss his work or his theories, the younger gen-eration may consider that he was no more '*à la page*' or '*à la mode*', but no one can deny that he was '*une grande figure de l'art fran-çais*'.
"I had the privilege of seeing him a few weeks ago at a concert given by the Calvet Quartet at Salle Pleyel, when his third *String*

Quartet was played. He was sitting in the box next to mine, and struck everybody by his—how could I say—transparent and immaterial appearance. He looked so thin, so aged, so pale, so weak! At the end of the quartet the whole audience turned towards his box and gave him a well deserved ovation, but it seemed as if even a smile was too heavy for him to bear.

"Yet he stood up with some hesitation, and, as I wrote to my sister the next day, he seemed like Lazarus lifting himself out of his grave to receive a last tribute of admiration from a tenderly and respectfully enthusiastic public. It was no doubt his last appearance, and I was not the only one to feel that we might never see him again. It seemed to me as if his soul, which had always roamed so far above matter and man, had hardly any further contact with the world, and that to die would mean for him nothing more than to sever in a whisper a last and hardly perceptible thread."

D'Indy's philosophy of life, in a sense summed up by those sentences of his I have quoted, is one that any artist would find it hard to improve upon. For what is better to remember as solace and guide in times of rapid change like ours, than that "The principles of art are eternal. They endure"? And what wiser counsel is there for the individual artist, bewildered in a world where so much that passes for art is made merely for sensuous charm, or for momentary effect, or to startle the burgesses, than "Only the heart can create beauty"? And if we can find anywhere the answer to the desolating jealousies, the personal animosities, the petty professional politics that tempt us away from our real work, we are most likely to find it in that simple sentence, written at nearly eighty: "All this has given me much joy."

And how about his permanent place in music? In the obituary in the *Echo de Paris* Adolphe Boschot, after pointing out how naturally the ultra-modernists of the period just after the war came to regard d'Indy as a reactionary, because he opposed their formlessness, ugliness, and sterility, insists that the appreciation of more recent audiences has shown them "conscious of what he has brought into the musical patrimony", grateful for the "high example his

artistic conscience has always given with such unfailing courage".
"And thus," he concludes, "by a spontaneous movement towards
justice, the concert public has enabled the artist already touched with
years to see what will be the judgment of the future."

But will it? Who can be sure that the neglect of d'Indy's great
qualities is temporary, that the defects which obscure the real pro-
fundities of his music will ever wholly cease to stand between it and
our love for it? Perhaps it will always suffer that impediment, at
least so far as the mass of the public is concerned. But also, I cannot
but feel, there will always be some to whom, as to me, the aloof and
noble beauty of his best music will make all shortcomings seem
negligible, and will place his work in a niche of its own, so that we
could no more spare him than we could spare Bach, Beethoven,
Brahms, Schumann, or César Franck.

CHAPTER XVI

WINTER IN PARIS

BEFORE settling down in Paris for the winter we made one or two visits. . . . It was now two or three years since, one rainy April afternoon in New York, a stocky young Frenchman whose black eyes positively danced with intelligence had climbed the many stairs to our apartment, presented a letter from Hadow, with whom he had studied at Oxford, and ended by staying two hours for the first of many talks we were destined to enjoy together, ranging from world politics to the intricacies of family life, touching on the way almost all subjects except music. His name was Camille Riboud. He was making a trip round the world with his friend Maurice Schlumberger, as delightful a person as himself though completely different. Schlumberger, as slender and blonde as Riboud was stocky and dark, was of an aristocratic fineness and delicacy of nature that emphasized by contrast Riboud's rougher but rich humanity. Riboud was a man of warm affections and vigorous appetites, a man whose vitality of nature could be egotistic, even ruthless at times, but always righted itself through his generosity of heart and clearness of mind. His background was congruous with this almost earthy quality in him: his father was a banker in Lyons, whose responsible and respected position the son later inherited, and his family, Catholic and well-to-do, had fewer literary and artistic associations than the Schlumbergers. Maurice's family, on the other hand, originally called *de* Schlumberger, and foregoing the *de* after psychological complexities that Maurice detailed to us in a moment of confidence but that rather eluded our matter-of-fact American minds, were Huguenot, or what we in our plain way should call protestant. Both families had ancestral estates of what seemed to Americans a hoary antiquity.

We now visited the Ribouds at La Carelle, their country place in the Department of Rhône, among the Lyonnais Mountains. They drove us out from Lyons on a rather overcast July Sunday, one of those days when the clouds in France have such a peculiar pewter tone, at once sombre and luminous. The lines of poplars were green but severe along the river, villages of stucco houses with pink roofs flew past us, and on the horizon ranged the dark blue hills in the sober light. La Carelle had been in the family at least from the time of our friend's grandfather, the father of M. Riboud senior, who greeted us with a sort of dignified friendliness, picturesque with his little white imperial and kindly eyes; and the quick intelligence we enjoyed in our friend had evidently been in the family at least as long. For the grandfather, having always to give the same answers to his neighbors' criticisms of his house, had conceived the quaint idea of placing both criticisms and answers in panels just below the ceiling of the salon, so that you had only to turn your back on the criticism to find the answer. Here they are:

"*Les domaines de l'hospice sont trop raprochées.*" [The farms are too near.] Answer: "*Il est vrai. C'est le ver dans le fruit.*" [That is true. It's the worm in the fruit.]

"*Le climat est un peu froid.*" [The climate is rather cold.] Answer: "*En revanche le pays est très sain.*" [In revenge, the country is very healthy.]

"*C'est dommage les planchers sont trop bas.*" ["It's a pity the ceilings are too low.] Answer: "*Il a fallu s'y résigner pour gagner du temps.*" [One has to be resigned to that in order to save time.]

"*Les croisées sont trop petites.*" [The windows are too small.] Answer: "*Les appartements sont plus chauds.*" [The rooms are all the warmer.]

Madame Riboud, a Frenchwoman of the old school, efficient,

kindly, intensely religious and patriotic, capable of ferocious prejudices and passionate devotions, and already deaf, ruled her domain
as a benevolent despot. She took us one morning after breakfast for
a stroll over the grounds, unlocking with a massive key the stout iron
gate of the garden, where the fruit trees were pleached in the French
fashion, giving the gardener two peaches of the basketful he had
gathered, giving us one each with elaborate courtesy, and locking
the garden gate again behind her. We noticed two of the women we
had met the night before at dinner worshipping in the private chapel,
and a third making her way towards it. After the dinner the three
men of the party sat in the hall with cognac and coffee; the women
repaired to the drawing room to play bridge or embroider. At the
meals the order of precedence had to be strictly observed by the
butler, though this involved him in a sort of zigzag or stately dance.
For instance, Madame Jourdain, sitting opposite me, came first; I
fourth; my wife, as both a guest and a woman, second; and poor Mlle.
Bourgeot, for all she sat next to me, eighth and last. As each course
came round, I feared nothing of it would reach her. Yet in spite of
what seemed to a mere American so much formality, each person
kept through the entire meal one knife and one fork, and if he forgot
to remove them from his plate for conservation on the little glass
perch, the butler gently did it for him. Also there were served in the
finger bowls tumblers of warmed and scented water, with which
mouths might be pleasantly, but seldom inaudibly, rinsed.

In my journal I find the note: "This morning the six ladies and I
took a walk through the wood of *sapins*, it being my duty to talk to
Madame Riboud more or less—chiefly less—though I could make
her understand little, what with her deafness and my unutterable and
incomprehensible French. At *déjeuner* I gave up all attempt to talk."
My rubicon, however, came one evening when I was luckless enough
to be cast as Madame Riboud's partner at bridge, a game she played
with the passion of a zealot, and I but poorly even in English. At last
at some special enormity of mine she exclaimed, "*Monsieur a volé.*"
Alas, what had I done? I only knew that the literal sense of what
she said was "Monsieur has stolen." When I went up to bed I consulted my trusty friend the dictionary, and found that I had only

revoked. But though La Carelle was rather a strain on one's French, it was an unforgettable revelation of the true France, the France so few Americans are fortunate enough to see.

Val Richer, the Schlumberger's place in Normandy, not far from Lisieux, had been in the family since it was bought, about 1840, by the historian and statesman, Guizot, the great-grandfather of Maurice. All its associations were literary and historic. Memorials of Guizot himself still abounded—books, papers, portraits, busts, medals. His daughter, Madame de Witt, had been an equally prolific writer, whose books seemed to turn up everywhere in the fine library. Maurice's mother, the granddaughter of Guizot, was at that time leader of the woman's suffrage movement in France, a quiet woman whose evident sweetness of nature tempered habitual dignity, a woman of deep convictions and undramatic devotions. Maurice had many brothers, of whom Jean has become a well-known writer, and was at that time already one of the leaders of *La nouvelle revue francaise* and of the just founded *Théâtre du vieux colombier* then producing his play *Les Fils Louverné*, and destined to exercise an important influence on the modern French theatre. It was at his house in Paris that we later met André Siegfried, author of one of the most discerning books ever written about our own country.

As for Maurice himself, he was, and is, one of the finest gentlemen I have known. Gentleman is a title too easily taken for granted; there are few men in any society who have all the fineness of principle, all the intelligence of view, all the sensitive consideration for others, the word should connote. Schlumberger, though by profession a banker, a far richer man than I, and not especially interested in music, always made me feel at ease by the spontaneity and fairness of his views. He was the kind of man who could offer you the garden house on his estate near Paris (as he did one summer—and we accepted) without making you feel that you were imposing on him, or doing anything but indulging with him in an amusing common adventure. The very first time we accompanied him to Val Richer he acted with a delicacy that paints him once for all. We had been a good deal entertained by him in Paris, and he knew I would feel that on the train it was my turn to play the host. But he also knew

that I could not afford the luxuries of French dining cars and wines.
So he arranged it as a great lark that we should pick up lunch baskets
at Nantes and have a picnic supper,—and no harm done to either my
pocketbook or my pride. Small in itself, it was one of those delicacies
that reveal the fine gentleman that is Maurice Schlumberger.

Eventually we met the whole circle of this group of young men,
now some of them, alas, killed in the war, but others, in middle age,
riper and finer than ever. There was Istel, partner of Schlumberger
in the Paris banking-house, keen, nervous, public-spirited, with a
wife both witty and kind. There was Louis Noyer, the other partner, whose mind was of a studious cast and had genuine and deep
culture, the only one of the group specifically musical. Paul Borel,
who was studying to be a doctor but who had the breadth of intellectual interests of all his group, took me once to the Collège de
France to hear Bergson, who had been just elected to the Institute,
so that the crowd was so great we could only stand on chairs and
crane our necks to look through the window. Borel joined the army
and died in action.

II

Another who did not survive the war, one of the gentlest, most
sympathetic spirits of all, was François Roederer. He too was in a
bank; but as Frenchmen have a way of doing, he knew as much
about cathedrals, and old houses, and the writings of Montaigne, and
other beautiful things, as his American fellows do about stocks and
bonds. He wrote me from his post in the air service, after my return
to America, saying little of the war but much of his joy in the mellow
wisdom of Montaigne. His clear-eyed, rather sorrowful realism, even
in those days when we first knew him, before the war had engulfed
his whole world, used to make us doubt a little sometimes our American optimism, so garrulous, assured, and inexperienced, and perhaps
even suspect it of a crudity we were half inclined to be ashamed of.

There comes back to memory especially one day in the rather
formal salon of the apartment we took in the rue Léo Delibes, upholstered in red velvet, when at tea a lively discussion sprang up as

to whether there was such a thing as progress. Chalmers Clifton, a delightful young Mississippian studying music in Paris, defended volubly and with charming enthusiasm the existence and the advantages of progress, with the rest of us Americans rather supporting him as chorus. Roederer, quite quietly, his uncompromising realism illuminated by his transparent good nature, doubted both. After we sailed for home, to enjoy again the comforts of life in America, leaving Europe helpless before its cataclysm, the unspoken drama of that discussion haunted us. Roederer's infrequent but always gravely friendly and self-forgetting letters deepened the impression. "Dear sir and friend," he wrote me early in that fateful August of 1914, "I leave Havre tomorrow morning with my regiment—we do not yet know for what destination. Before leaving I want to tell you again, as well as Madame Mason, all the respectful friendship I have for you, and to address to you, since it is necessary to foresee everything, a second adieu. I hope your views are for us; we certainly do not represent aggressive brutality. I should not wish to judge events entirely after the interpretations of the French newspapers, but in the present crisis German bad faith appears to me indubitable, and makes me indignant."

Three months later, in November, he writes: "These are terrible days, and victory will be dearly paid for. I do not know whether you have yet heard of the death of Paul Borel. He had just been proposed for the Legion of Honor. His brother Jean had been killed some months before. You will share our grief." He tells of an injury to his knee, not grave but making him lame for some weeks, and concludes: "Here are these brief news. Later, if it is given me to see you again, I will recount to you 'my campaigns.'"

In February he tells of how his wound has laid him out in complete inactivity and how he "feels so stupid that he hardly has the courage to write". But he gives the news of Riboud, Schlumberger, and the others, and adds: "Up to now we have not lost any members of my immediate family, but how many have disappeared among our friends! I don't know how to tell you, dear sir, the pleasure I get from your letters and those of Mme. Mason and Clifton. They revive dear memories and express for our cause a sympathy which touches my most sensitive feelings. Thank you then with all my heart."

The time drags on, and one reads between the lines of his next letter, July, 1915, the next to the last, all the tedium and spiritual suffering he is too considerate to voice in detail. "I am always in a situation of waiting. My knee is little better. I have recently passed some time working in a military office, and I am now in hospital. My brothers are now both in the trenches, and I am ashamed to be the only one idle, I the youngest. I have always from time to time good news of Maurice. Have you heard of the sad death of his brother Daniel, who was killed while driving an automobile into Paris?" He tells of his hopes of entering the aviation, since it would be long before he could resume service in the infantry. And after closing his letter he adds: "I dream sometimes of the day when I may see you again and we may set ourselves all four (with Clifton) to discuss progress again. How far-off and problematical seems that day!"

The last letter, written when he had been already long in the air service, is dated November 13, 1916. He thanks me for sending him a sketch I had written of Edward J. de Coppet, and says: "I had great pleasure in making acquaintance, thanks to you, with this personality so noble and so attractive who without being himself creative knew nevertheless how to do something for the great art." Riboud, he tells, has had a little daughter and has left for the front after a brief leave.

"Nothing new," he continues, "for me; always the same trade, not exactly that of the father of a family, but having nevertheless besides its own interest the advantage of considerable freedom and relative comfort. I have time to read a good deal. I have profited by it to make excursions rather far from our epoch, at least when I seek the counsels of a wisdom always timely, and reread certain chapters of Michel de Montaigne."

Not long after writing that letter he disappeared during one of his flights of observation, and was never heard of again.

III

It was fortunate for us that through this splendid group of young men we learned something of the real France that lies under the glittering and distorting surface of Paris. Had we seen only the Paris of the cafés and the Latin Quarter our early months there might have been even more disillusionizing than they were. Some of the letters from home made us a little homesick, not only for New York and Pittsfield, but for Boffres.

"What a grand time you must be having," wrote Ridgely Torrence. "I was charmed with your post-card pictures of Boffres. Do you pronounce it to rhyme with cough or offer? Those peasant accents vary."

> If they offer to cough
> Would you accept at Boff?
> If they offer to sell Boffres
> Would you cough them some offers?

"Such are the French peasants, always willing. From there we took the train to ——. A fine bridge (*12 siècle*) also gorgeous altar pieces.

"And what about M. d'Indy? Does he quiz you much about your native place?

> Said d'Indy to Dan
> Look here, my young man,
> It's been written down
> That Beersheba's your town.
> Said Dan unto d'Indy
> Yes, Beersheba *is* handy
> But my preshent addresh
> Ish right in Ardèche.
> Said d'Indy, 'You're fresh!
> You've been drinking my brandy.'
> Itsh pepp(hic) mint candy
> Said Dan unto d'Indy.

"Well, I've said all I'm going to say, and if you won't stop, then don't. Only it's too bad to see a fine young man in such a state. And now I suppose you're in Paris, where I suppose you're no more moral. Do you rhyme Paris with Harris or Harry? Be careful you don't commit Harry Parree. . . . Having uttered these words he turned his face to the wall and said no more."

We went to a small hotel near the boulevards, and commenced the search for lodgings on the left bank. The Paris autumn can be as exasperating as the spring is entrancing. Each morning we would start out, under oppressive grey skies and fortified only by the meager French breakfast, on our long, discouraging search—prosecuted mostly in busses, partly because taxis were too expensive, partly because it amused me to work out the bus routes. If we took rubbers and rain-coats it would clear off baking hot, leaving us to carry the extra impedimenta all day as best we could. If in desperation we left them behind, it would settle to a steady rain. The busses were difficult too. Studying the map at a street corner, jostled by travellers, was confusing; and I was not surprised that sometimes, though not so often as Mary teasingly insisted, I put her on the right bus—going in the wrong direction. And then there was the hopelessness of being sure we had found a place free of audible pianos. Those were luckily the days before the curse of radio made quiet impossible everywhere, but to achieve it was more a happy fluke than a matter of discretion and pains.

At out first try, in the rue Boissonade, facing an ancient convent that gave delusive hopes of quiet, we found three pianos near neighbors before a week was out. Long diplomatic negotiations secured an hour or two each morning of probable peace, by no means certain. But bureau drawers that would not open, windows that would not fasten, a toaster that would not toast, a tea-kettle that burned one's fingers, thin ceilings through which one could hear one's neighbors drop pins on their floors, a chimney that would not draw, and daily defeat by that diabolic French invention the *boulet*, exhausted our endurance until after a dreary, interminable October and November, we fled. . . . *Boulets* (literally, I suppose, bullets, but bullets we could not have the satisfaction of firing at their inventor) are small egg-shaped balls made of powdered coal held together by some kind of mucilage. You ignite them, if you are lucky, after many applications of those funny little pieces of kindling wood a half inch thick and four inches long, each tipped neatly with resin, that come bound together with a chaste wire. If you succeed in making them burn at all, you have in half an hour a roaring, raging, roasting conflagration, which after another fifteen minutes suddenly expires in a despondent mass of grey cold pebbles. And the only escape from *boulets* is to buy a *salamandre*. . . . But this opens up a chapter too long and too painful to pursue.

With what elation then, early in December, did we leave rue Boissonade, with all its *boulets*, the lady above us still happily playing Mendelssohn's Song without Words appropriately known as *Soul Sorrow*, but now to other ears than ours, and betake ourselves to the other side of the Seine, to the commodious apartment sublet from our friend Stojowski in the rue Léo Delibes, near the Avenue Kléber in the Trocadéro quarter! Besides the luxury of being six floors above the street instead of two, and of having six rooms instead of two, to say nothing of an apparatus for heating a bath that exploded happily the moment you turned the water on, and a maid who cooked us real meals, it was now fully three days before I discovered the two pianos that could be heard from my workshop in the drawing room—one of them playing, of course, that self-same *Soul Sorrow* we thought we had escaped. At least it remained no longer a song without words: I found plenty of words for it! But there were enough exposures in this larger apartment so that by moving my own workshop from the drawing room to my bedroom I was able to work in comparative peace.

IV

All this would have been merely laughable rather than tragic (as it seemed then) had not the utter uncongeniality of the musical fashions then accepted in Paris gradually damped our spirits, reduced my working power dangerously near to zero, and made me feel an outsider and (in down moods) an incompetent. Thus in the two months on the left bank I wrote only the scherzo of my symphony, and later discarded even that. In the happier surroundings of the rue Léo Delibes I managed by spring to finish the symphony.

The maddening thing about the Parisian musical mode at that period was its artificiality, its narrow cliquism, its self-conscious complacency and intolerance, its itch for personal publicity and indifference to any larger beauty. There were of course sincere musicians there—d'Indy, Dukas, Fauré, Florent Schmitt, and within their narrow limits even Debussy and Ravel—but those who made the most noise and succeeded in hypnotising the world of fashion, after all indifferent to beauty, were the *arrivistes*, the *poseurs*, the snobs and the bluffers. "We make the fashion and we follow it"—so d'Indy expresses for them their pose—"Let us be little, let us be original."

It was some comfort to find in the *Guide du Concert* that spring, and copy into my journal, Jean Huré's summing up of their point of view. "They have invented *'l'effet facile'* [the 'easy effect']. Passes a shiver of beauty?—*'effet facile'*. They have invented *'l'art hautain'* ['high art']. Is one bored to death?—*'art hautain.'* Is one inwardly tortured by the worst uglinesses—*'art hautain'*. One might tell them, modifying a little the word of Alceste, that the difficulty has 'nothing to do with the case.'"

If one could only have ignored these *arrivistes* with a good conscience, their effect, omnipresent as they were, might have been less depressing; but of course one could only tell by exposing oneself to them how much of real value might be mixed with their pretentious nonsense. So one went to dreary concerts of the *Société musicale independante*, and endured long quartets by Darius Milhaud written in an idiom exactly as artificial as that of the pseudo-classics like Saint-Saëns whom he despised, rewarded rarely by some really fresh and vigorous work like a trio of the Hungarian Miklos Radnai that made the chief oasis I can remember in that desert. (I brought a copy of it home, and we played it at one of Gertrude Watson's Pittsfield musicales.)

As the year wore on I gradually made up my mind about it all, and wrote my friend Hill: "The net result seems to be increasing distrust of the French itch for 'originality' and for the *chic* and the witty in

music. Debussy and Ravel and all their lesser fellows sometimes interest, often amuse, but never move me. Their modernism, frantic as
it is and taking itself so seriously, strikes me as after all half-baked.
. . . At present the whole world of music is tyrannized over by the
fear that a single natural phrase may escape it. For the creative temperament (creative in however humble a degree) aesthetic battle-
fields are never a wholesome or a congenial environment. To me the
worst thing about Paris is that that same aesthetic battling (or rather
squabbling, for "battle" is a word with too heroic associations) is
merely intellectual and journalistic, and the French have precious
little interest in music one way or the other. They are immeasurably
less musical, I believe, than we are, certainly less so than the Germans. As a result music is an artificial product here, and suffers from
the anaemia of snobbism." [1]

No doubt a good deal of my difficulty was due merely to a personal limitation in temperament; impressionism, the ruling movement
of the hour, of which Debussy and Ravel were the high priests, always left me cold, often painfully bored. I can admire a score like
Debussy's *Fêtes*, with its fascinating rhythms to keep the colors
moving and alive, but such a thing as *Nuages*, in some ways more
characteristic, reduces me to a vacuity positively agonizing. Trying
to listen to it I feel as one does waiting at a remote railroad station
for a train that is very late, and may never arrive. So my efforts to see
what Debussy was "all about" met with but modest success.

Personally Debussy was attractive enough, in spite of possibly a
bit too much suggestion of the familiar *moqueur* type. In my journal
I find in early November the note:

"I have just seen Debussy at his house, 80 Avenue de Bois de Bou-
logne, and had a pleasant talk with him about an article on *Color in
Music for the Piano* which he agrees to write for *The Art of Music*
by the end of May, for one thousand francs ($200). The curious
slant at the back of his head was more noticeable than ever, but his
manner is perfectly simple, quite free from vanity. He said that
while a number of people were interested in orchestral music, more

---

[1] Compare the conclusions of Douglas Moore, Chapter XXIV, page 389.

cared for piano music, and he had written a good deal of that and would like to write about it. As for chamber music, he had only written one quartet, and while he might write another he had none in mind just now.

"He spoke of his dislike for discussing remuneration, saying that he was maladroit about such matters and in perfect good faith made mistakes both ways. He told about the elder Choudens (of the well-known Paris music-publishing house) showing in mimicry how he would weigh a score in his hand to see what it was worth. He mentioned that *S. I. M.* paid him 500 francs for his articles, but that this would require more thought, being for an important work."

We heard him conduct his *Iberia*, but except for the rhythmic precision of his beat were not especially impressed. With Chalmers Clifton, who admired him far more than I did, we heard him play a recital with the violinist Arthur Hartmann. "He plays very delicately and clearly," I recorded, "and with a fine rhythmic equilibrium. But he is by no means free from his own kind of cheapness, even vulgarity." I much preferred Fauré's *Pelléas et Mélisande* suite to Debussy's opera, as having far more real music in it, though it only lasts fifteen minutes.

"I have made myself," I confided one day that winter to my journal, "play through the whole final scene of *Pelléas et Mélisande*, as Chalmers Clifton said it was one of the finest scenes and I therefore thought it would be a fair sample. . . . It violates all my notions of art, presents nothing tangible to my intelligence, and bores me so intensely that any emotion is killed before it starts. . . . I see the justness of the declamation and I see occasional beauties of coloring. But music, to my mind, it is not and never will be. I believe Debussy has contributed something to musical technique—notably the whole-tone scale—which men with something to say may profitably avail themselves of; but he himself, to my mind, has nothing to say."

Debussy admirers may retort that my last sentence is like the answer of the boy to the question about polarized light on the examination paper: "Polarized light, as I understand it, is very little understood." It may well be so. These remarks are offered simply as presenting one point of view which some may find congenial, not as

having any critical value. One can criticise fruitfully only what one
admires.

V

For a much less famous man than Debussy—Florent Schmitt—I
came to have a higher regard. His work, it seemed to me, whether in
such light but delightful things as the *Musiques intimes* for piano or
in the formidable—too formidable—*Quintet*, had real beauty and
strong individuality. His faults were all at the other extreme, an
extreme more tolerable to me than Debussy's. In place of the De-
bussyan sybaritism he has an aggressive masculinity. His music is, it
seems impossible to deny, over-excited, over-voluble, lacking in restraint and in repose; but it is vigorously alive, and fearlessly direct.
And the brusque honesty, not to say the sometimes brutal tactless-
ness, of his character, is at the pole from Debussy's cat-like smooth-
ness.

We only met Schmitt once, at a hasty tea in a little garden near
the railroad at St. Cloud, where he and Madame Schmitt had just
gone to live. Even in that short talk I got an impression of frankness,
of un-self-consciousness, amusingly confirmed at a Châtelet concert
one Sunday afternoon during a learned but uninspired symphony
of his master, André Gedalge. Schmitt, sitting a row or two in front
of us, was made drowsy by the effect of the music combined with
that of the stale air always to be found in French halls. In the middle
of the slow movement, in a quiet passage, he lost himself a moment,
dropping his hard derby hat on the floor with a resounding whack.
Tales of his abruptness were rife. Once after the performance of
Marcel Labey's symphony, meeting the composer he is said to have
greeted him with "Was it you that wrote that *dreadful* thing?" On
another occasion, his admired friend and teacher Fauré shook hands,
more in kindness than from conviction, with a young composer
whose piece seemed to Schmitt intolerable. Meeting Fauré in the
coat-room on leaving, he refused to take the polluted hand. In later
years, when director of the Conservatory of Lyons, he is said to have
sometimes dissuaded parents from having their daughters of little

talent come there to study. No wonder he lost the directorship. But in the midst of the Parisan *politesse*, a surface under which knives were often concealed, one could not but admire Schmitt for carrying his knife at his belt like an honest pirate, and on occasion using it.

A man of equal courage, expressing itself in a quite different personality, was Romain Rolland. As much as Schmitt departed from the usual type of Parisian worldliness in the direction of brusque intransigence, Rolland rose above it in a sort of detached, almost monastic quietude and devout idealism. He was like a priest of art in that hotbed of "artiness". His *Jean Christophe* was to come later, but I already admired him for his essays, especially that on *Le renouveau* in *Musiciens d'aujourd'hui*. In March I made an hour's call on him in his apartment at 3 rue Boissonade. "I found him," I recorded, "a delightfully sympathetic, frank, and thoughtful personality, and he treated me with much kind consideration. He has rather light blue eyes, a high forehead—perhaps a little bald—a thin yellow moustache, a sensitive mouth, and his chin sometimes trembles a little when he talks." I tried to induce him to contribute articles to *The Art of Music*, but he would not depart from his decision transmitted in a letter a few weeks before: "*J'ai abandonné momentanément la musicologie, afin de me consacrer tout entier aux oeuvres d'imagination.*" I am glad I could not persuade him.

That same month of March was illuminated for us by the presence of Ossip and Clara Gabrilowitsch in Paris. They had sent us a wonderful Christmas box with a lobster, smoked salmon, fruit, dates, a bottle of cognac, and two bottles of champagne; and now came a card of Ossip's, accompanying tickets to a recital, with a notation: "Welcome to our city!" A day or two later, when we dined with them, he talked of the fundamental lack of musical enthusiasm of the French, the fact that practically all the music of France is in Paris, and that even there a good hall for music is lacking. He thought the habit of advertising concerts only on the *affiches* a survival, due to French conservatism, of conditions of a half-century earlier when there were but few concerts, and told a story of Rubinstein giving a concert at the Trocadéro to an audience of four thousand, conducting an oratorio of his own, and of Saint-Saëns hailing him on

the street later with "Hello, Rubinstein, what are you doing here?"
In no other city, he said, could this happen. His manager had tried
to get the bill posters at least to put his bills on the same corners, but
they said no, that was impossible. The manager offered to pay extra.
"No, it would make the bookkeeping too complicated." We discussed my piano pieces *Country Pictures*, about which I had just
received one of the great letters of my life from Josef Hofmann,
who was later to play them at his recital of American compositions
in Carnegie Hall. Ossip's favorite, as I should have been able to pre-
dict, was *The Quiet Hour*. Of one passage—that beginning in the
twelfth measure—he said it was "like three nice cats howling."

Towards the end of March came the last real event of our Paris
winter—his playing of my *Elegy* in one of his recitals. "The *Elegy*,"
I noted in my journal, "was cordially received. Ossip played it beautifully. When I went out to the artists' room in the intermission he
was sitting on a red plush sofa, resting. He said that he had felt all
of it keenly, as if he had composed it himself—'though I couldn't
compose anything so good', he added with characteristic modesty."

In May we sailed for home.

CHAPTER XVII

CAPE COD—AND "POINTS WEST"

THERE is an old tale about a man introduced to a southern girl as "from Paris", and interrogated by her "Paris, Kentucky, or Paris, France?". . . . From Paris, France, to the Cape Cod Canal is a far cry, but it is what fate had in store for us. Reaching home early in May, by July we were back in the old yellow farmhouse in Pittsfield, and I was working seven hours a day to finish in five weeks the incidental music for a pageant celebrating the opening of the new canal on Cape Cod. These were the early days of pageants, and I was more than doubtful about how much artistic freedom to do anything worth while I should have. But there was a good fee, and I was frankly curious to see whether composing could possibly be turned from a liability into an asset. I ultimately found that it could not, but I had much valuable experience on the way.

The whole thing had to be timed in the most meticulous manner. One and a half minutes of Indian music, for example—how was one to make sure of that? Never very good at mathematics, I laboriously worked out a method of dividing or multiplying measures, beats, and metronome numbers, and eventually got my exact one and a half minutes, only to find at the first rehearsal that no Indians were to be had. . . . The reports about music in the open air, too, were not encouraging. One friend who had composed a pageant for Philadelphia told me bluntly that "the music had all been blown over to West Philadelphia."

Nevertheless I thought of the check, and persisted. At last the long task was done, and we arrived at the Cape, in unutterably sultry August weather, to be consumed at night by mosquitoes, in the day-time by the most incongruous anxieties. The evening before the final rehearsal, for instance, each of the producers was asked by the director whether all was in readiness in his department. The climax of the whole pageant was to be a gorgeous tableau, *Prosperity*, in which the natural resources of the Cape were to be exhibited symbolically in a formidable pile—fruits, vegetables, the fatness of the earth in all its variety, and of course, above all, cranberries. The property lady was asked whether all was ready. "I've tried everywhere," she answered with reluctant honesty, "but I could only find three good quarts of cranberries."

Next morning, that of the last rehearsal, dawned dark and drizzling. The kettle-drums could not be got over from the railroad station, and one double-bass was missing. In the vast expanse of sand an oasis of boards, painted light blue, made a slight dent in the surface, sunk about three feet, where the orchestra was to sit. Rain water had collected in it, and as the orchestra regarded it ruefully their humorist, the bass trombone, encouraged them with a jovial "Come on, boys; come into the goldfish pond." My own cheerfulness was not helped by the endless errors in the orchestral parts (I did not then know how invariably these accompany all new works), nor by the sprain I gave my ankle as I ran too eagerly to correct some of them down the steep steps of the grandstand.

Over the performance itself I shall draw a veil. I there first met my friend of now long standing, Herbert Dittler, and was drawn to him at once by his ribald and unconcealed mirth, quite undeterred by my authorship of the music. He roared with laughter every time the director, perched high at the back of the grandstand, fiercely waved symbolic signals—squares, circles, and triangles—to which none of the cast paid the least attention. He declared that my *Hymn to Fortune*, one of my proudest efforts, sung by the entire cast in chorus, was a canon, because the procession was so long that the front of it was always about one measure ahead of the rear. At last he completely collapsed at the moving couplet

> We pray thee, God,
> To bless Cape Cod.

But I learned something from that pageant. It was the first orchestral music I had written, and though I long ago burned the score of it I found out a good deal through it, as to both what to do and what not to do. The chief thing not to do was to try to make money by composition. I earned more money by it than by any other piece I have ever written. Yet the time spent on it, save for the experience gained, was completely wasted. I retired from the unequal contest with Cape Cod, a richer but a wiser man.

II

If the *Pageant*, by which I earned nearly a thousand dollars, was thus a failure, my *First Symphony*, on which I sank a good many hundreds, not to speak of more years of work than I like to think about, proved eventually a moderate success, perhaps not so much in itself as in the later work it taught me how to do. We sometimes hear surprise expressed that so few symphonies are written nowadays. When I recall my first one, and what it cost me in years of doubt, despair, and hope, in struggles for infrequent performances, in laborious revisions undertaken again and again as the performances revealed new faults, in damning reviews to digest as best I could, and in rare sweet moments of realisation, themselves almost painful through their intensity, my wonder rather is that there are any. Summing it all up, I would say to the young composer now on the brink where I then shivered before plunging: "If you are looking for an easy life, for worldly recognition, for pudding and praise, let symphonies severely alone. But if what you wish is that, in Thoreau's phrase, life should be 'more elastic, more starry, more immortal'— then go ahead!"

The first problem was to get a performance—any performance. This took just under two years (from April, 1914 to February,

To my good friend
Daniel Gregory Mason
in all sincerity !
Frederick A. Stock
Chicago _ [Ill.] Febr. 10 th.
1928.

Frederick A. Stock in 1928

1916). The first lead came from Mrs. Coolidge. She offered to show my score to her friend Frederick Stock of the Chicago Orchestra, since then a good friend to me and to my symphony, which he ultimately played in two successive seasons (January, 1925 and April, 1926), and even got entirely copied out at the expense and for the benefit of his orchestra. But this is getting ahead of the story. His first reaction, much less favorable, was on the whole, as I now realize, just and far-seeing. I played him the score at Norfolk, Connecticut, in the house of Carl Stoeckel, one of whose choral festivals we were both then attending, in the early summer of 1915. While he was cordial in praise of its musicianship he shook his head over its complexity—to do justice to it, he said, would require twelve rehearsals. It was "more complex than Brahms or Bruckner". It would be "inaccessible to the public, and even to members of the orchestra". He asked me, however, to send him the score for a more careful study.

Here was an opinion, of an admirable musician and a cordial friend, to give me pause. Since then I have learned that the verdicts of the press, through haste and false standards, are often negligible, but that one should always give weight to the response of the public, and especially to that of the musicians themselves. And since then I have also come, slowly and reluctantly, to see that Stock was right, that the symphony in its original form was far too complicated, difficult, and involved. Its best because simplest beauties were often overlaid by elaborations unnecessary and therefore injurious. Some of these I eventually managed to remove (the version Stock played in 1925 and '26 was completely rewritten); others can never be removed.

Over-complexity is in some degree, I think, characteristic of all youthful music; as Haydn put it, all young composers have too many ideas. Besides that, the fads rampant at that time tended to give us all false ideals. Such composers as Schönberg, then spoken of with bated breath, made complexity seem an end in itself, however useless or ugly, and made one almost ashamed to be simple. Musicians saw through such poses a good deal, yet tolerated them through laziness or pusillanimity. I remember Walter Damrosch, at just about the time he played the *Prelude* to my Cape Cod fiasco—my first score

for concert orchestra, since burned like the larger one from which
it was drawn—rehearsing something of Schönberg in my presence,
and saying to the orchestra in his amusing, convivial way: "Now,
boys, let's give Mr. Mason a treat." Yet, however much veiled irony
there might be behind our lip-service to the cacophonists, their influence tended to confuse the ideals of young composers, and had
to be painfully outlived. So I, like the rest, had to find my true path
after a good deal of wandering among the brambles. Transparence,
regard for ultimate dramatic simplicity, belief in one's essential ideas
sufficient to let them stand or fall by themselves, realization that
technical directness is a far higher achievement than complexity,
and that music is made not for one's fellow technicians but for unin-
structed but sympathetic every-day listeners: these are qualities attained only in age and after long study.

The next initiative, destined to succeed, came from Ossip Gabrilowitsch. To realize the loyalty in artistic comradeship of the famous
European virtuoso to a young and almost unknown American composer, we must bear in mind that this initiative came entirely from
him, and that he was then suffering from a chronic eye weakness
that made manuscript scores even more than ordinarily weariful.
Between the lines of his next letters, expressed with his usual matter-
of-fact directness, we shall perhaps smile to discern his characteristic
way of arranging even the minutest details—for he was a born leader.

"St. Albans, Vermont
"15 June, 1915

"Stokowski is spending the summer in St. Albans. Wouldn't you
like me to show him your symphony? You may send it to me or to
him direct."

(Two days later)

". . . As regards the symphony, it will be best if you send it not
to Stokowski but to me. I will show it to him. You needn't say or
write anything to him about it. I think this is the better way."

"20 July

". . . Your symphony has just arrived, but before showing it to
Stokowski I want to get a little more familiar with it myself so that
I can play it for him if necessary."

"31 July

"Last night I played your symphony for Stokowski. I did not do it earlier although I have had the score for more than a week because I wanted to get thoroughly familiar with it so as to be able to play it decently. The effect of your splendid work did not fail. Stokowski was so impressed with it that he declared at once he would play it in Philadelphia. This morning he telegraphed you to that effect, saying that he would put it on his program February 18th and 19th provided you give him the rights of first performance in America.

". . . I am delighted of course that Stokowski was so impressed with your symphony. I want to tell you a lot of things that I personally feel about this finest of your compositions, and will do so in another letter. For the present I just want to say that if he plays it you will hear the very finest performance of your work that can be given in America."

And thanks to Ossip, I did!

III

Before there could be any performance there were weariful months to pass preparing the necessary material . . . I found myself confronted with a dead weight, in short, such as must be lifted to begin with by all ardent spirits who aspire to write for orchestra. This is an aspect of composition that few laymen understand or are able vividly to imagine, and that may therefore be worth dwelling upon a moment, largely mechanical though it be. . . . The score, from which the conductor has to read, was in the case of my symphony a hundred and eighty-one pages long. To have one copy of this made and bound cost me a little over sixty dollars. Next came the so-called "parts" to be used by the individual players. Of these over sixty were required, varying from a few pages for instruments like drums or cymbals to twenty-eight pages for a first violin. In the Philadelphia Orchestra at that time were fifteen first violins, needing (as two could play from each part) eight parts, or two hundred and twenty-four pages of manuscript music for the first violins alone. Similarly one needed seven parts for second violins,

six parts for violas, five for cellos, and four for basses: or, in orchestral men's parlance, the strings in this particular orchestra needed
in parts "8, 7, 6, 5, 4". (In some orchestras less strings are to be found,
in some more.)

The wind, brass, and percussion instruments, one thanked heaven,
could make shift with a part apiece. But doing a little arithmetic, if
one had strength left for it, one found a need for parts costing in all,
with necessary binding, a little over a hundred and fifty dollars.
And as full of errors as Cape Cod ought to be of cranberries—that
went without saying! Just one other point on this distressing subject. If you wanted to change a single chord in your strings you
were in for a pleasant two or three hours with fifteen violin parts,
six violas, five cellos, and four basses, all of which needed opening
up, scratching out, writing upon, blotting, refolding, and stacking.
The concert-goer who hears a symphony for half an hour before it
goes back into the great silence for a few more years, little knows
of the weary months the composer has been giving himself headaches
and backaches over the parts, most of which, after a few performances, get so scrawled over by the players in black, red, and blue
pencil that they are scarcely legible any longer. There is an irony
in the easy good humor and irresponsibility with which players will
scribble anything that occurs to them on a manuscript part (from
the telephone numbers of their friends to none too gentle criticisms
on the music) that can bring a wan smile even to a toiling composer.
Such was the mood of the glockenspiel player who jotted under the
title of a song of mine, *A Drunkard,* which he, poor fellow, was
playing in prohibition days, the scornful notation: "½ of 1 per
cent!"

So that winter before the performance was a laborious and an
anxious one. A composer in the modern world aspiring to write a
symphony should have a larger bank account than I did, with only
my small salary from Columbia University and such extra lectures
as I could pick up. Two excerpts from my journal may suffice to
paint the picture.

"November, 1915. My capital is down to eight hundred dollars
—nothing but that between us and positive want. I may have done

Leopold Stokowski (before 1916)

wrong to write these orchestral things under the circumstances . . . but one cannot live in drudgery alone. . . . The parts are going to cost one hundred and fifty dollars or more, and God knows where the money is coming from."

And a second, a month later, as my nervous resistance wore down under that "consensus of opinion of Dr. Leipziger" constantly encountered in the outside lectures: "A trying telephone conversation with Dr. Leipziger. His usual bullying tone exasperated me so that I let fly at him a bit. I told him that I was tired of being talked to so rudely, and that although I knew he was often tired, I was sometimes tired myself, and overworked in the attempt to educate my son and daughter. It seemed to make little impression on him, and he presently spoke of his 'not living in a dream world like me'. He wants to cut me down from twenty dollars a lecture to fifteen. He ended by saying that his very calling me up showed his interest, and that 'my little outburst was forgotten', the insulting beast! . . . The symphony parts are mounting terribly, and I don't know whether I ought to let de Coppet help me with them or not."

Of course I did let de Coppet help me: that was a foregone conclusion. He came to the rescue by giving me the necessary sum as a New Year's present for 1916, the very day my wife's uncle gave her an even larger sum to help with the children. A month later I was able to chronicle: "Parts off at last. . . . There are sixty-one of them. They make a pile eight inches high, and weigh thirty pounds."

IV

Stokowski had been charming to me. These were early days before the phenomenal success of the Philadelphia Orchestra had tempted him to allow the showman side of his nature to alloy and sometimes corrupt his magnificent musicianship. Indeed the first seasons of the Orchestra in New York were poorly patronized, and he was in no danger yet of becoming a spoiled darling of the public. He was an incredibly youthful-looking boyish young master, with his shock of light yellow unmanageable hair, his large capable hands, and his frank smile and companionable air. We had spent an evening

together in New York over the score. But unfortunately at the
first rehearsal in Philadelphia he was suffering from influenza, felt
very weak, and asked me if I would conduct the first movement and
let him listen. I conduct! I might as well have tried to drive unbroken
horses, or enact Canute with the wild sea-waves. But he persisted,
and in my folly I tried. It was like riding some vast, inhuman roller-
coaster. It would race me away, and I would pull myself together
and resist, and find it suddenly a dreary *adagio*. Then I would try to
move it on, and in a moment be dancing dizzily in its wake. That
was my first and last experiment in conducting. But even then, to
hear my music come back to me from that great orchestra, and
sound so much as I had intended it through all those months of
silence, was thrilling.

After the rehearsal we went to Stokowski's little retiring room, he
armed himself with an enormous red pencil and rumpled up his hair
comfortably, and we went at the score hammer and tongs. "I am
humiliated," records my journal, "that I know so little my own in-
tentions, and am so generally woolly-headed on all practical details.
I can't even seem to hear precisely and fully—I simply get a general
effect. . . . Stokowski was enthusiastic about the main theme of
the slow movement. He said it kept constantly unfolding new feeling, without ever becoming sentimental."

Of the second rehearsal: "We worked over the score again afterwards, and he was awfully nice about listening to my ideas and presenting his. He says all composers want their things played too fast,
they are so afraid there will be monotonous places. He was comforting about the many errors still remaining in the parts, saying it took
years sometimes to get them all out. His wife played the Schumann
Concerto for years with the basses playing G natural instead of G
sharp in quite an important place. 'If this can happen with a well-
known classic work, how much more with rich modern harmonies
like yours.' Apropos of the place in the slow movement where there
is only an A major chord for eight measures of slow time before the
oboe solo comes in (Index number 39) he said it was like the blank
margin of a block of paper he had, on the center of which something
was written in red—it made what was written 'come out'."

Later, in my *Note on Tonal Chiaroscuro*, in *Music as a Humanity*, I worked out in detail this random but pregnant suggestion of Stokowski's, reaching the conclusion that "A common fault of young composers . . . is that of packing a piece too full of interest. It is so natural, but so naïve, to imagine that the more sustained the tension the greater will be the effect. One gradually learns that this is not the case; human attention ebbs and flows, and the interest of a well-composed work will ebb and flow correspondingly. . . . Planes, values, margins: how shall we translate such visual terms into their audible equivalents, and thus learn to find our way better than at present through the mysterious auditory spaces our music inhabits?"

Of the final rehearsal the journal notes that "In spite of the delightful and unexpected presence of Ossip and Clara Gabrilowitsch, it did not go as well as Thursday morning's. My suggestions of changes of tempo had confused Stokowski's reading, and we found on comparing notes afterwards that Ossip's judgment was in every case in agreement with his. I do not think I am dependable on these matters."

This last rehearsal was the morning of the very day, Friday, on which the first performance was to take place in the afternoon. By this time a number of our friends had arrived from New York to hear it: the de Coppets, Mrs. Coolidge and Miss Watson, my cousin Mina, Howard Brockway, who had generously given no end of his time and thought in many seances we had had over the score, and others. Some of them were to lunch with us, including Howard Brockway. At the last moment it was discovered that I had written the trombones, in an important passage, with the wrong clef, which made them play notes agonizingly near the right ones! Howard, devotedly throwing himself into the breach, helped me copy and paste the right notes over the wrong ones. Then Stokowski assembled the brass players in the dressing room just before the concert, and made sure they were not going to split our ears.

Coming on the heels of all these confusions, the performance was for me, naturally enough, almost as painful as it was pleasurable. Gradually I digested my impressions, and thus summed them up in my journal: "The public spontaneously liked the slow movement, but the others elicited only, I think, courteous applause. My own feelings are painfully mixed. Much of the first movement sounded confused and the attention was not securely held.

"Of course it is not fair to blame all the confusion on the scoring, for the orchestra still play it pretty raggedly. . . . The trumpets entirely missed an entrance in the first movement. Stokowski said: 'Just think, all these men have been playing the Beethoven symphonies again and again, some of them for twenty-five years. And then we take up yours last Monday, and play it after four rehearsals. One's impressions have got to form as slowly and unconsciously as glaciers move.'

"But with all allowances made, my score is still to blame for redundancies, confusions, overlayings of register, etc., and I am sure that if I care to take time (and money—for the parts) I can clear it up a good deal.

"Stokowski said that he was 'beginning to like the finale now', which especially pleased me, as I think it the most original movement, and am glad he did not understand it at once. He told his wife it was the most difficult thing, technically, he had ever done. He told me when I said goodbye that in his condition this week it had been a great effort, but added, with a most cordial and frank smile, 'But it was worth it!' "

Thus ended my first lesson. The second was to be postponed five years.

V

In February 1921 Gabrilowitsch, then rapidly turning the Detroit Symphony Orchestra into one of the best in the country, revived the symphony, and we went out to hear it. Indeed, in order to "pay the piper" I made a three weeks' lecture tour in the middle west, and was just fagged enough in consequence to take rather hard the first suggestion of even such a tried artistic comrade as Ossip. The concerts were to be on the Friday and Saturday evenings. On the preceding Sunday afternoon, in the artists' room after one of his concerts, he took me aside and asked me, in his point-blank practical way, what I should think of omitting the scherzo. The idea was rather devastating. I told him that I had already considered it while revising for his performance, and discussed it with Chalmers Clifton, and that we felt the contrast provided by the scherzo to be indispensable. He replied that on the contrary "To go directly from the climax of the first movement to the lyric theme of the slow one was a much finer contrast." I asked him if he had thought it over from all points of view. He said he had. "What," I asked, "about the finale?" "Oh," he answered, "the finale takes care of itself." I finally decided that if he, with all his experience, all his devotion to my music, thought such a surgical operation desirable, it probably was, and might even be essential to the survival of the patient.

The next problem was a practical one. The type plates of the program notes were already locked; no words could be subtracted without adding an equal number. Moreover, when I awoke the next morning there was a heavy snowstorm raging, and the printing office was tucked away somewhere in the wilds of down-town Detroit. However, it was certain that literary verbosity was infinitely preferable to musical; and I managed to find my way to the printer's and to delete the one hundred and sixty words describing the discarded scherzo, adding to the already complete description of the other movements the same number of quite superfluous ones.

This was not too good a beginning, to say nothing of the usual endless errors in the parts. And on the whole the week dragged on badly, with the also usual (thank heaven) gleams of starry happiness caught through the clouds. Journal, Wednesday, February 9. "Pretty awful morning of rehearsal. There is no doubt the first movement is much overscored, things kill other things, too much elaboration of detail, in short, the old story: not conceived in broad and simple enough masses. *Per contra*, it was gratifying to note that all the revised passages seemed better scored and more effectively conceived than the rest, showing that experience and effort do bring their results.

"The finale is cruelly difficult. The five-beat measures are sometimes three plus two and sometimes two plus three, and this ought to have been carefully indicated in score and all parts. Even Ossip seemed almost on the edge of losing his wonderful patience and *sang-froid* at one point. The six-beat measures, he said, were needlessly stuck in, in a way that threw everybody out.

"Thursday. At six Ossip went over the score with me. He made no end of criticisms and only praised two places, but nevertheless I am not wholly downed. Many special points I am keeping for future reference, if I ever have courage to revise again.

"Friday, 6:30 P.M. I have been trying this afternoon to face the truth about the symphony. Despite the fact that Ossip called 'Bravo' after the slow movement, and the orchestra applauded both then and at the end, it has as a whole too many weaknesses, immaturities, and shortcomings to have any permanent intrinsic value. Though it was written when I was forty, I matured slowly, and it is really a 'youthful work', with the turgidity, lapses of expressive justice, and over-complexity that go with youth. The persistent clouds of the last few days cleared away for a moment this afternoon, and we saw shafts of sunlight and later a star and a wisp of new moon in the pale sky. That suggested that the future may bring something better. At any rate it is something to strive and aspire, even if one succeeds only in indicating a direction.

"Saturday evening, 10:30 P.M. Most wonderful, unbelieveable experience. Last night the first movement was so mixed up . . . we were both in the depths (though Mary was a brick to me all through it.) Tonight we went over to the concert as oxen to the slaughter. . . . Then the miraculous happened. It cleared up wonderfully and we were deeply moved. I thanked Ossip for that cymbal roll in the finale, and said I could not hear it last night. He roared with laughter, and said tonight's were new cymbals!"

"Sunday morning. On the train, headed for New York. There is something dramatic, almost melodramatic, in our arranging this three weeks trip, and in not having it become definitely successful until the *very last moment*—even after our Detroit hotel bill was paid. Ossip and I had a good one-minute talk in his office. I said I thought I should set it aside five or ten years and then revise it again. He said, 'I shouldn't wait as long as that.' 'Now,' he said, 'you must begin your second symphony.' "

A few days later he sent me a letter that made me glad for all the work I had spent on the piece, and willing to spend some more.

"Both you and I," he wrote, "were so busy dissecting the weaker points of your symphony and discussing changes in form and orchestration that somehow the days passed by without my having a chance to tell you how much impressed I was on the whole with the beauty of the essential material. The themes, almost without exception, are fine and noble in quality. The harmonic and polyphonic structure is perfectly splendid, and even while the orchestration in some places shows a lack of experience, there are other passages that are exceedingly beautiful and that show you have the makings of a fine orchestrator. . . . The work as it is, is fifty per cent better than it was five years ago in its original form—I hope another year or two will add another fifty per cent to it. . . ."

Thus encouraged, I set to work afresh, and during the summer of 1922 produced a new score, completely rewritten. This had two supreme merits. First, it was, at least for a short period, entirely clean of pencil marks of any color. Second, it reduced the one hundred and eighty-one pages of the original score to one hundred and thirty-eight. With its superfluous flesh thus trained off and its belt tightened, my symphony faced the future.

CHAPTER XVIII

NEW YORK ORCHESTRAS

AT THE end of 1920, only a month or two before his performance of my symphony, Gabrilowitsch had brought his newly formed Detroit Symphony Orchestra to New York, and had thrilled us with the greatness of his conducting. For despite the label "pianist" which many always reserved for him, I thought him almost if not quite as supreme as a conductor. I remembered how, after his first visit to us at Pittsfield, he had got into the train for New York armed with a pocket score of *Tristan und Isolde*, and I saw that from the first he had felt a vocation for conducting, which he was realizing now even at the cost of giving up composing. ("You composers," he once said to me wistfully but with his usual realism, "can wait indefinitely for understanding, while we performers have to be understood at once.") My desire to define exactly the greatness of his conducting led me to discuss in an article [1] three contrasting conceptions of a conductor's function: first, that he is a mere link, a passive medium between composer and audience; second, that what the composer has created, he re-creates for us, by a process no less subtle, no less indispensable; third, that he is in his own right a virtuoso like a star soloist or a *prima donna*, for whom the com-

[1] *A Great Conductor: The Arts*, January, 1921.

position is no more than the tight rope on which he dances. Which of the three conceptions is the true one?

Such a question, I said, becomes highly practical when a conductor like Gabrilowitsch, with an orchestra admittedly still not quite the equal of the two best resident orchestras, succeeds in rousing his hearers to such delight that they listen to Brahms's *First Symphony* in a silence almost breathless—the silence that means even more than the repeated recalls and "Bravos" at the end.

"What was this magic?" I asked, "and why does it so seldom visit our auditoriums? First of all, it is evident that the passive medium theory is quite in error. If all we demanded of a conductor was to play loud when the score says loud, and soft (more or less) when it says soft, some of our conductors, successful enough with composers like Wagner and Tschaikowsky, who depend largely on massive climaxes and rich sonorities, would not fail as they do with that other class, of whom Mozart may be taken as the supreme type, who demand clarity, eloquence, and persuasive beauty in the delivery of each phrase and in the modelling of the piece as a whole. The truth is that the greater the music, the less can the conductor depend on sensationalism or luscious tone color, the more is he required to re-create what the composer has created."

Touching then on some of the criticisms of Ossip's concert made by the devotees of luxurious sonorities—such as that the oboe was here a bit thin, or the heavy brass less mellow there than the horns, I insisted on how insignificant all that was, in comparison with the essential musicality of the interpretation. "What does it all matter?" I urged. "When, starving in the wilderness of this world for the sustenance of thought and feeling, you suddenly hear human, intelligible speech, you do not criticise the voice that utters it. When the other night Mr. Gabrilowitsch made us hold our breath with the mystery of that symphony, made us thrill with its nobility, made us melt with its tenderness—when thus he gave us the soul of this great, manly music of Brahms, we quite forgot about its body; we simply listened spellbound to the beauty of that utterance. It was Brahms himself, the whole of Brahms, and nothing but Brahms."

"Nothing but Brahms," I concluded. "Therewith we discard our third definition of the conductor's function, which makes of his 'interpretation' something personal, peculiar to himself, in last analysis artificial. The self-effacement, the loyalty of an artist like Gabrilowitsch to his composer must reveal by comparison something inferior and essentially inartistic in those conductors who try to color all they do with their own personality, who are always searching out an 'interpretation' instead of letting a work speak for itself.

To this reasoned analysis of Gabrilowitsch's conducting I cannot resist adding a more informal glimpse of Ossip himself, from my journal.

"December 8, 1920. Magnificent concert by Ossip and his Orchestra. Words fail to tell the stimulus and solace of hearing *music* again. Such vitality, flexibility, nobility, tenderness, such seizure and revelation of all there is in the music, and of nothing that is not there. Such cyclopean power in the Brahms *First Symphony;* the brilliance, warmth, and sinister quality in Strauss's *Don Juan;* the exquisite grace and pure beauty of the Mozart *D minor Concerto:* . . . this is the world I would live in always, but most of the time it is a distant dream I can hardly remember. Tonight it has 'come true'.

"The audience was enthralled from the first. After the Brahms there were repeated recalls and 'Bravos', and a big wreath from the directors of the orchestra. Then Howard Brockway and I went out and found Ossip in his shirt-sleeves, wet with perspiration, with three of those Alpine collars of his on the table before him. It must have been surprising to him to see us, but nothing upsets his efficiency, because, Mary says, he is so absolutely sweet-natured that he is never thinking about himself. He at once introduced me to Bodanzsky. William Grafing King [at that time concert-master of the Detroit Orchestra] was on the steps outside, and was fine in his whole-hearted admiration of Ossip.

"What a center of life and vitality is a man like this!"

II

A year or two earlier, before Gabrilowitsch had settled in Detroit, a few of us had tried hard to secure him for New·York. Heaven knows New York needed badly enough the immeasurable stimulus of such a conductor. But our efforts were unsuccessful: the resident time-beaters and the visiting virtuosos were too securely entrenched.

Walter Damrosch, for all his attractive qualities, human and artistic, had more than a little of the time-beater. I have heard him beat four to a measure in Tschaikowsky's *Andante cantabile*, and his rhythm was frequently heavy-handed. Artistically his strongest point was his program-making—it would be hard to exaggerate the indebtedness of us all, in those days, to his curiosity and initiative. He it was who gave us the first performances in New York—often in America—of such modern masterpieces as Elgar's *First Symphony* (January 3, 1909, only one month after its English premiere under Richter at Manchester); *Second Symphony* (December, 1911, its premiere having taken place at a London Music Festival in September); and *Falstaff* (December, 1913, English premiere at the Leeds Festival in October). To him we owed our first hearing of William Wallace's *Villon*, in 1910; Ravel's *Mother Goose*, November 1912; Enesco's *Symphony in E flat*, February, 1911, repeated the following year; Sibelius's *Fourth Symphony*, March, 1913; and Delius's *Brigg Fair*, October, 1910. He gave also early performances of Rachmaninoff's fine *E minor Symphony*. In many cases he repeated these works two seasons in succession, as should always be done with important modern symphonies.

How stale seemed, in comparison with all this, the Wagnerian, Lisztian, and Tschaikowskian pap ladled out to us by Josef Stransky of the Philharmonic Society! Stransky was hard to fight artistically, he had so many agreeable social and personal qualities; he was witty, amusing to meet, an adroit time-server, but a total musical incompetent. Once a party was being got up on the principle of having everybody do something he couldn't do: Harold Bauer was to play double-bass, Georges Barrère was to struggle with a violin, and so on. "But what shall Stransky do?" "Why, let Stransky conduct!"

. . . His inefficiency even in the sonorous show-pieces he did best, his devastating dullness in classic masterpieces, the daily bread of music, had been making us progressively unhappier, especially when we contrasted our state with the sound musical health of Boston, with its permanent orchestra and series of truly great conductors, culminating at the time of Stransky in the greatest of all, the incomparable Karl Muck. As early as 1911 I find in my journal: "March 24. A magnificent concert of the Boston Symphony Orchestra. Fiedler is the man for me. His rhythms are wonderful, his conceptions noble and seen from all round. Conductors differ as much as soloists after all—how easy it is to forget that!" Compare this with the following, from the fall of the same year: "November 5. Philharmonic concert—Stransky a disappointment. Little sense of rhythm, or synthetic power; makes an *accelerando* for every *forte* and a retard for every *piano*! Maddening." And toward the end of the season: "A thoroughly good concert such as the Boston orchestra gives is an experience after one has been hearing so much of Stransky's inorganic twaddle. One ought to hear the Boston Symphony once in a while just to remember what good music is."

On the other hand, when one rarely got away from the time-beaters it was too often only to fall into the hands of the *prima donnas*, more skillful but scarcely more ministrant to true art. "April 28, 1912. Nikisch at the Metropolitan Opera House. In spite of the brilliance and dramatic effectiveness of his conducting there is an element of posing about it all that drives me mad. Insincerity is the one unpardonable sin in art. It not only makes the particular work of art seem nauseous, but trivializes the whole of art for the moment. . . . Certainly the big public must always have the sensational, the exaggerated, the overdrawn."

So we were unhappy. And then Gabrilowitsch, thoroughly trained as a conductor by his years in Munich, but driven by the war back to America again, seemed to open up new possibilities. . . . Two lines of action suggested themselves: first, to arrange concerts where his great qualities could be revealed; second, to induce the Philharmonic Society, formerly conserver of our greatest traditions, to clean house and become so again. In both we met for a long time with what seemed like failure. In both we eventually accomplished, I think, a good deal, though not precisely what we had intended.

III

Oswald Garrison Villard was elected president of the Philharmonic Society in the spring of 1916. On the basis of a slight acquaintance and of our having been at Harvard together, I decided to call on him. "I hoped," records my journal, "a frank description of Stransky's mediocrity from an unprejudiced observer might influence him towards a change. I do not believe it will. He is a hard-shell conservative, admires Stransky, dislikes modern music, and cites Finck as an authority. But he tells me the orchestra is in a hole, and unless he can raise $60,000 this spring may have to disband."

Then, on New Year's Eve of 1917, Gabrilowitsch gave a concert at the old Manhattan Opera House with an orchestra, assembled for the occasion and financed I know not how, of eighty players. "We heard Ossip conduct magnificently," I wrote, "with great power and magnetism, and with the lovely moulding of the musical phrase that makes his playing so incomparable. He had an ovation. Stokowski was in the audience, making notes on points about the conducting. To see those two so full of life and youth and noble artistic feeling was to be encouraged for the future of music. . . . I asked Brockway if he did not suppose the Philharmonic would sometime wake up and engage Ossip, but he thought Stransky was too firmly intrenched with the women directors. I don't know. Perhaps financial losses may make them listen to expert judgment."

At any rate, listening to Ossip reminded some of us of what orchestral music in New York might be, and we began to express ourselves. The first to speak out, so far as my records go, was Richard Aldrich, music critic of the *New York Times*—be it told to his everlasting honor. It is all the more to his credit since he was temperamentally mild and cautious, inclined to take the most kindly possible view of everything, and rather smiled at for his recurrent phrase "There is much to be said on both sides"—especially by those who, knowing him personally, remembered how hard his stammer made it for him to say anything! . . . Yet in this instance he spoke, or wrote, only on one side—the right one. And to his frankness was attributed by some his retirement about a year later from his post on the *Times*.

In his article, after pointing out that the programs of the Philharmonic had become distinctly "lighter" than they were in its great days, and that "some of the noblest works of both the elder and more modern writers now make only a rare appearance", specifying among these Schumann and Brahms, he put his finger unerringly on the disastrous feature of the Stransky regime thus:

"Many of these works, when they do appear, meet with unsympathetic and perfunctory treatment. The public naturally do not respond to them with any enthusiasm, and it is hence assumed that such works have lost their power to give pleasure. The truth is that the public is under a process of education to dislike certain classes of masterpieces. Its attention . . . is directed to those of another kind, in which obvious effects are most easily obtained, 'thrills' most unerringly provided . . . excitement most surely aroused."

What we were witnessing was, in fact, the early stage of the tendency to sacrifice music to sensation which has since grown so formidable, has led the Philharmonic (now merged with the New York Symphony under the name Philharmonic-Symphony) to its long abuse of the star system, culminating in the deification of that great artist Toscanini, has corrupted so sensitive a youthful musician as Stokowski into becoming in middle age scarcely more a musician than a showman, going at last even into moving pictures, and has invaded the oldest and finest of our musical institutions, the Boston Symphony Orchestra, in the *prima donna* attitude of another musician great enough to hold a higher standard. We did not realize all this at the time. All we knew was that the old Philharmonic was being prostituted; and we did what we could to save its influence for genuine music. Paul Rosenfeld followed Aldrich with a fiery article in the *New Republic;* Ernest Abbott had an editorial in the

Outlook. My own contribution took the form of a letter to the *New York Times*, published January 28, 1917.

Beginning by quoting recent assertions of Oswald Garrison Villard, its president, on the occasion of the seventy-fifth anniversary of the Philharmonic, that that society "had kept the faith", had "maintained high artistic standards", and was "the most distinguished musical organization in the American metropolis", I pointed out that these statements were not borne out by the practice of the society in recent years. Its policy had been rather, I said, to sacrifice artistic standards to the box office.

Going on to analyse the tastes of the public, "the great majority," I showed, "prefer the non-musical aspects of music, such as the physical fascination of great or subtly varied volumes of tone, the interest of novelty or oddity, and the satisfaction of curiosity as to the personalities of soloists," and consequently "the box office view tends to cultivate these things at the expense of music itself." The music chosen for performance by the Philharmonic, I pointed out, "is that which appeals by rich modern sonorities (Wagner, Liszt, Strauss) or by dramatic effect verging on sensationalism (Strauss, Tschaikowsky) or by mere prettiness (Delibes) rather than that which nourishes and delights the sense of beauty." And I proceeded to support my statements by the facts: "In the first thirteen concerts of the present season we find sixteen works of Wagner, eight of Tschaikowsky, four of Liszt, three of Strauss, against only four of Beethoven, one of Schubert, two of Schumann, and none of Bach, Haydn, or Mozart, nor of Brahms or Franck. Of these thirteen concerts ten had soloists, one was an all-Wagner program, and one brought forward an important novelty—Strauss's *Alpine Symphony*. Only one had no attraction except that of music."

"It is hardly fair," I concluded, "to blame Mr. Stransky for this state of things. It is true that he evidently does not care for the classics, which he conducts in a characterless way. It is precisely in the qualities most needed for classic music that he is most conspiciously weak. His tendency to metronomic time-beating is at its worst in works which, like the symphonies of Mozart, Beethoven,

Schubert, or Schumann, most need plastic molding of the phrase, because their appeal is more one of line than of color." "But," I finally insisted, "it is the Philharmonic Society that has chosen him to carry out its purposes, and that is finally accountable for the disproportionate performance of sensational works, the admission of third-rate works for their novelty or other specious appeal, the abuse of the star system, and the neglect or perfunctory performance of the classics. Its present tendency is to lower rather than raise standards of musical taste, and to lose the respect it has so deservedly held in the past."

IV

Then began the fun. On the very next day after I had posted my letter the first thing I saw in the paper was the gift to the Philharmonic of a hundred and ten thousand dollars. Three days after the Sunday my letter appeared, the Society announced the reappointment of Stransky for a period of three years. On the following Sunday its president charged me, in a letter to the *Times*, with "bias". (I was later specifically accused by *Musical America* of having attacked the Philharmonic because I was employed, as writer of program notes, by its "rival" the New York Symphony Society!) Villard also published a letter to Stransky from my chief in the Department of Music at Columbia University, Cornelius Rubner (who later, after we entered the war, changed his name to Rybner): "I wish herewith to state to you that although Mr. Mason is Associate Professor in my department I have had nothing whatever to do with his article . . . I am very sorry that the article was written by one of my associates." I confess that this, when I remembered that the President of Columbia was also a trustee of the Philharmonic, made me shiver a little. But it did not, I am glad to say, make me hesitate.

On the other hand there were some crumbs of comfort. For instance, a telegram from Birmingham, Alabama: "Congratulations on your splendid and courageous article. Hearty greetings. Ossip, Clara." And a talk with Harold Bauer, who told me I was too hard on Stransky, he was just the nonentity the Philharmonic wanted, they were altogether well suited to each other. "In accompanying me in the Schumann concerto," he added, "he got out three days in succession in the same place. I finally told the first players to play it right without looking at his beat!" Bauer also told me that Dr. Muck had remarked to him, in German phrase even more amusing than its English equivalent: "Stransky can do nothing; and the nothing that he can do least is accompanying." And there was a note from Arthur Whiting, short and sweet: "Good old Dan, Your letter went to the spot. You are the bravest man in New York and the rest are all skulkers—I will follow it up with another next Sunday and hope to smash everything you have left standing, if such there be."

Arthur did write a vitriolic letter, and after a time even proposed to Aldrich a second one. His enthusiasm was inspiriting. When I suggested trying to dissuade one of the Philharmonic supporters from making a fifty thousand dollar gift, his advice was: "Don't waste time killing benefactors by hand. Let's get the air so full of gas they can't breathe." But Aldrich, wisely I think, did not welcome a second letter. He wrote Arthur: "I am sorry that the circle of articulate critics of the Philharmonic is apparently not likely to be widened. You and Mason have done yeoman's service and have brought odium on yourselves by what you have written. I am doubtful of the advisibility of printing further letters from either of you. I should gladly print strong letters from other sources."

Finally there was for my comfort Ossip himself, dropping in to tea one afternoon in the middle of the fray, after having attended a Philharmonic concert, and remarking: "You can always tell a conductor by the quality of his tone. Stransky's is coarse. Mendelssohn and Tschaikowsky need especially to be played with distinction, they are so easily cheapened. Mozart you can throw down like this (making a hurling gesture), he is always an aristocrat." Apropos of the audience he cited the word of a conductor friend of his: "Audiences listen as cows eat, everything in sight—grass, dry grass, weeds, flowers, roses—all." He made me feel that, whether Stransky stayed or went, I was glad I had spoken out. He had felt the same way, he said, after he had burst out in an early pamphlet that shows his youthful chivalry at its finest,[1] against Krehbiel for an unwarranted attack on Mahler, whom Ossip adored; and he reminded me of the stammerer who replied, when asked if he were not sorry he had called a man a rascal: "T-t-take it b-b-back? I'm g-g-glad I g-g-got it out!" "The cream of the Philharmonic joke," I noted in my journal a fortnight later, "comes in Stransky's announcing, as a result of the pressure, an 'All-classic program'! The whole thing is about as much of a mess as it could be, but one's sense of humor can at least extract that tidbit. If there is anything worse than hearing Stransky play Liszt it must be hearing him play Brahms."

V

As spring came on we turned our attention more and more from the negative to the positive, from Stransky to Gabrilowitsch. He gave a series of three splendid orchestral concerts in the small Aeolian Hall. After they were over he invited me in late May for a row on the lake in Central Park, and chatted somewhat at ease in a vein that let me see why he was so successful as a leader of men. Orchestra players, he said, were like children—you could easily get them interested to a certain point, but their lack of discipline made it hard for them to concentrate. Yet though their union rules called for an extra dollar for any rehearsal time over two and a half hours, they had frequently become interested enough to stay a few minutes overtime without demanding extra pay. Some of them had even stayed still longer of their own accord, to copy down bow marks and so on. As Ossip summed it up, they have good qualities and bad like everybody else, and the thing is to know how to get at the good ones.

Shortly after that, though I had never raised money for anything in my life, and had no talent in that direction, I began active canvassing for funds to guarantee a series of concerts for him, to be held in Carnegie Hall in the following spring. At first it was rather exciting. I began with Otto H. Kahn, who dilated of his own accord

[1] *Gustav Mahler: an Open letter to the music critic of the New York Tribune,* by Ossip Gabrilowitsch. Alfred Schmid, Munich.

on the "shameful orchestral conditions in New York," and the "lot of old women" who ran the Philharmonic, and who ended, though he said he was heavily burdened already, by promising fifteen hundred dollars. The afternoon of the same day I got Mrs. Havemeyer's promise of a thousand. Before the month was out I had been promised another thousand, and Mrs. Coolidge had promised Arthur Whiting two thousand more. That summer I was going west to lecture at the University of California. Before we separated it seemed probable we should be able to finance half a dozen concerts.

When we resumed work in the fall, however, we began to realize the overwhelming prestige and momentum of the established organizations massed against us. Even Otto H. Kahn, one of the cultural as well as financial leaders of New York, was unwilling to act as treasurer of our funds, because of his connection with the Metropolitan Opera and his wish "not to appear," as he said, "to do anything against the present orchestras." He referred me to Felix Warburg, who, my journal states, was "very discouraging". "The scheme for Ossip's concerts," I wrote, "is evidently not going through—at least the best we can possibly do is to give three instead of six. . . . After no end of labor, I have come to the conclusion that New York simply does not want good concerts."

A new and formidable obstacle arose in the rumor that Ossip was "pro-German". I had touched on it myself in my journal as early as April of 1917, the year we entered the war; but whether he was pro-German or not appeared to me a matter of indifference, since I knew what a splendid artist and what an incorruptible man he was. But as the year wore on war hysteria, developing its ugly menace, seemed to jeopardize all higher interests. Its blindness and venom seem almost incredible now. In October the American Museum of Natural History barred lectures on *Parsifal* or any other German subjects, and at the end of the month Dr. Karl Muck, one of the greatest conductors then in America, was condemned by a group of women in Providence for his "deliberate insulting attitude" in refusing to open a Boston Symphony concert with *The Starspangled Banner*, and the Police Commission was asked by the Rhode Island council of defense to refuse permission for further concerts conducted by him. "It half spoils the pleasure of going to concerts," I noted, "that one has constantly to hear that boresome *Star-spangled Banner*. But such things fade into insignificance beside the frightful attempts to suppress free speech, like the recent horse-whipping of Bigelow in Ohio, a brave and public-spirited man."

In November Edwin Warfield, president of a Baltimore bank and ex-Governor of Maryland, said for publication: "Karl Muck shall not lead an orchestra in Baltimore. I told the Police Board members that this man would not be allowed to insult the people of the birthplace of *The Star-spangled Banner*. I told them that mob-violence would prevent it if necessary, and that I would gladly lead the mob to prevent the insult to my country and my flag." He went on to say that *The Star-spangled Banner* was greater than anything ever composed in Germany. . . . Later in the month Youngstown, Ohio barred Kreisler and Frieda Hempel from public appearances, although Hempel protested that she had sung *The Star-spangled Banner*, and that such an attack on a woman alone in this country was "unwarranted and cowardly". Pittsburgh went Youngstown one better, and banned all German music. Early in December a tour of the Boston Symphony Orchestra was actually cancelled.

And all this time it was easy for spineless politicians like Stransky, however mediocre as musicians, to ride high in public favor by coddling the nationalistic passions. When even the head of the department of music of one of our great universities could seriously write in a letter that Bach might be given a rest in favor of—Rameau (!), it is not surprising that time-serving conductors would play anything and everything French. "Some phrases from the *Marseillaise*," wrote Pitts Sanborn in the *New York Globe*, "employed in the finale of Dubois's symphony, make the rest of that work seem so unimportant that you did not wonder Mr. X. swung around to the house each time the *Marseillaise* bobbed up, whipping the air like mad, as if he somehow expected people to jump up on their seats and holler. Some almost did at the relief from lengths of salon prettiness." The same conductor later began a program with a cantata by Bach, who, though German, was too far back to matter, continued with Debussy, and ended with—the *Sylvia* ballet music of Léo Delibes—pretty enough in its place. C. L. Buchanan, an able and outspoken critic, told me early in 1918 that there was no use trying to do anything about New York musical mediocrity. "People *like* it. The subscription to the Philharmonic has never been larger."

In such times the mere whisper that Ossip Gabrilowitsch was "pro-German", untrue as it was, sufficed to obscure the whole issue, and substitute political prejudices for artistic insight. One of the most musical women I knew refused to go to any concert by him, because of that rumor. Later on, after Dr. Muck's arrest in March, 1918, when Ossip was proposed as his successor, Mrs. William Jay publicly opposed him on the same ground—the same Mrs. William Jay who had urged a visiting French orchestra, while it was still in New York Harbor, not yet landed, to omit Beethoven from its programs—and had been answered with true Gallic logic that if a French orchestra could play Beethoven, Americans might listen to him. . . . So raising money was not easy. Journal: "December, 1917: Mrs. O'Day, who is a pacifist, thank Heaven, gives a thousand dollars for Ossip's concerts. This is the more comforting inasmuch as almost everybody else has been refusing lately." Nevertheless we did eventually succeed in raising a little over seven thousand dollars, a modest sum by Philharmonic standards, but enough to pay for three concerts in Carnegie Hall.

Ossip sent us the three programs, and both Arthur Whiting and I regretted that he felt he must appear as a piano soloist in each—in a Mozart *Concerto*, the Schumann, and the Franck *Variations*. His practical sense, I thought, was exemplified in his telegraphed answer: "Please tell Whiting I fully agree with him, and appearing as soloist in these concerts is very distasteful to me. But I feel my duty toward the guarantors to protect them as much as possible against loss, and my appearances as soloist seem the most efficient means of doing it."

In the first concert, April 18, 1918, he began with Beethoven's *First Symphony*, and ended with the *Seventh*. He told me that the droll passage introducing the finale of the *First*, where all the violins feel their way up a scale, one note more each time, in delicate, complicated rhythms, is most difficult to conduct—it is hard to keep the players exactly together. It was mentioned that X. had it played by a single solo violin. "Yes," laughed Ossip, "the ensemble is better that way!"

On the day of that first concert I wrote in my journal: "I am so happy, the concert was so beautiful, so noble, so thrilling. . . .

"I went to his rehearsal yesterday. I was impressed as always with his faculty of forgetting himself completely in his 'job'. Nothing is done to make an impression on others or on himself—but to get the desired result by the shortest and best path. He is tireless in his attention to detail—just where the harp shall be placed, the height of his desk, the choice of baton, not to speak of the infinite more essential musical details. Yet he is perfectly good-natured with it all, does not make problems or allow others to make them—simply solves those that present themselves.

"We had a talk afterwards. I told him of what Sokoloff said of the Philharmonic considering him if it were not for his alleged pro-Germanism. He said he would not make any public statement, it would seem like bribing people to give him a position. It was useless to make any moderate statement. If you did not make an intemperate, fanatical statement you were more suspect than if you said nothing. Justice was not wanted.

"As a matter of fact he was as a Russian outraged by the behavior of the Germans to Russia. As for America, long before the war he had told Europeans—French and British—of our real cultivation, and of the superficiality of their charge of dollar-worship—and they had refused to believe him.

"He told of a lucrative offer he had had from a woman who wanted him to give a recital, but demanded a statement of his political opinions. He told her something of the above, but refused the engagement. His manager could not see the point: 'Now it's all right. Go ahead and play.' But Ossip would not, and I honor and love him for it. 'What have these things,' he said, 'to do with music?'

"He admitted he found it hard now to concentrate on music, but reminded me that Beethoven did much of his finest work during the Napoleonic wars. He was not, to be sure, cursed by the press, from which it is so hard for us to get away. . . . Ossip is one of the greatest men I have ever known—great all through, humanly as well as musically. He is a shining proof of the truth that a man's art rises with his character."

The final concert took place early in May. "The audience," reported the New York *Evening Mail*, "recalled Mr. Gabrilowitsch frequently, and they cheered him. But it remained for the players themselves to crown his effort with a fanfare delivered by the entire orchestra standing." Our work, however, in trying to obtain the immeasurable stimulus of his presence for New York, or even for Boston, had been, like the Stransky exposure, a failure. No wonder we were sometimes bitter—the standards were so irrelevant. "When Ossip is just the man for the Boston orchestra," I wrote after the arrest of Dr. Muck, "and would vitalize our whole life, I had to advise him not to take it, because of the hounding of Mrs. X. and such vermin. . . . So my work there has been fruitless too." No wonder irony seemed sometimes our only comfort. "I told Ossip," the journal goes on, "I should like to write to the paper: 'Sir: I have seen with consternation the charge of pro-Germanism against Mr. Stransky. Could there be any doubts of his pro-Ally feelings in view of the vicious way he treats enemy composers such as Bach, Beethoven, and Brahms?' Oh what detestable rot 'public opinion' is! How admirably the world is adjusted for mediocrity, how disastrously for quality!"

But if the East could only see Ossip through chauvinistic blue spectacles, the Middle West was more intelligent. At the very beginning of 1918 he had received offers from the orchestras of both Cincinnati and Detroit. In March he conducted a concert in Detroit which probably decided his future. He sent me a clipping from a local paper, describing the extraordinary enthusiasm that filled up the Detroit Armory as if for a political rally or a prize fight. "A new method of expressing appreciation," it said, "was hit upon with mob-spirit unanimity. When Gabrilowitsch appeared for the third time in answer to the summons of clapping hands and stamping boots, the audience rose to its feet—a tribute paid customarily to the flag or the national anthem, but seldom indeed to a virtuoso." And Ossip

has pencilled proudly in the margin: "Three thousand people remained standing for several minutes."

And well they might. For of course the press notice was inexact,
and it was not the virtuoso but the musician, the seer of life-giving
beauty, who was for once receiving the glad gratitude we easterners
were too dull to give him. . . . So if we had not helped him into
New York or Boston we had at least helped him into Detroit, which
may have needed him even more than we did, and in which a great
career of selfless devotion to music lay before him.

CHAPTER XIX

JOHN POWELL

Josef Hofmann's letter already mentioned, written by him from Colorado Springs on receipt of the copy of my *Country Pictures* I had sent him, and received early in 1914 while we were still in Paris, had been a great encouragement to me to persist in rather a lonely path. To a musical humanist homeless among the uglinesses and eccentricities of that most cliquish of cities, his blunt statement: "You are a happy combination of modern music and good music" was as heartening as a friendly handshake. Feeling that my *Country Pictures* were in the trend of German romantic music, he always called them *Ländliche Bilder*. And at the end of his letter he added with his usual directness the postscript query: "Are you *really* an American?"

That postscript was characteristic. Hofmann had a brusque way of speaking out his feelings, thoughts, and convictions that was at the pole from the cautious conventionality often found in public performers. There was a bracing quality in his frankness. "I am one of those," he said in an interview of about that time, "who is perhaps known—unfavorably I do not doubt—for not playing much modern music. That is because I do not believe that modern music, taken by and large, is on the same level, mentally, emotionally or artistically, with what has gone before. . . . I think there are but few modern composers who are sincere." This was exactly my own feeling. . . . But after all, even if he thought my pieces sincere, would he play them? In the answer to that question would be the acid test of his own sincerity. That answer came in June, 1918:

> "Hopkinson Cottage,
> "Northeast Harbor, Maine

"I am trying to arrange for an *All-American Piano Recital* and should like to know whether you could help me in finding suitable pieces by *living* American composers for this purpose.

I would of course include your *Ländliche Bilder* and also intend to play McFadyen's *Sonata for the Piano*, which is rather effective. Besides these I found a rather nice piece by Rubin Goldmark, but lack all the rest, especially a suitable piece to begin with, and one to finish up this recital. May I therefore trouble you to lend me your hand and point out the necessary pieces to group around the pieces mentioned beforehand?" . . .

I took up the challenge, little knowing how exacting it was going to prove. But I am glad I did, the correspondence it produced was so characteristic of Hofmann's uncompromising taste and laconic wit. I will give a few specimens.

> "July 9, 1918

"Many thanks for your kind letter and help. The sonata by X. arrived and I sincerely dislike it. I wrote to X. telling him that I was musically old-fashioned and my ears were not quite up to modern music of this sort yet. I returned his manuscript to him with my apology. The fact is I am not looking for another sonata, as I have quite made up my mind to play the McFadyen.

> "July 25

"I am looking forward with interest to receiving the *War Song* by Y. and shall probably dislike it as much as you do, for both you and I are musicians of the good old time. The restlessness and dis-

Josef Hofmann, 1938

content in music of the present day is certainly an unhealthy symptom, but I hope and believe that the cleared atmosphere after the war will have a beneficial effect upon it. [No one realized, at the time Hofmann was writing, how much more disastrous still the effect of after-the-war cynicism was destined to become.]

"I find the Z. compositions somewhat flat, although I will endeavor to use one."

"August 1

"*War Song* is no war song. But worse than that: it is poor music.

"I hope you are having a nice summer's rest and take better care of yourself than I am able to do. I always seem to have more to do than I ought to, and work often as late as 3 and 4 A.M.

"America is no place to rest, I believe!

"So much for tonight. Kindest regards."

"August 12

"A few days ago I looked over your *Elegy* and it seemed to me that this piece would fit better in my program than the *Ländliche Bilder* as it is one continuous one and I need a piece like this—a good sound musical beef-steak! By the way, it is a very beautiful piece indeed. Would you mind if I played it instead of the *Ländliche Bilder*?

"I have received an answer from Breitkopf and Härtel. They will not print a new edition of the *Ländliche Bilder*. The letter was short but not sweet. I am sorry, but I did what I could in this respect."

The letter from the German publishers, "short but not sweet", ran in part as follows:

"We regret that at the present time we shall not be able to print another edition of the *Country Pictures* of Daniel Gregory Mason, as the sales of this composition do not warrant the printing of a new edition, especially at the present time, as the paper output has been curtailed.

"We call your special attention to the new publications we have just issued of Leo Ornstein" . . . etc., etc.

The long-prepared recital finally took place in Carnegie Hall on the afternoon of January 25, 1919. In addition to the McFadyen *Sonata* and my *Country Pictures* it was made up of pieces, mostly short, by Rubin Goldmark, Horatio Parker, Mrs. Beach, Fanny Dillon, and Edward Royce. It opened with the more sustained *Introduction and Fugue* of Clayton Johns. The reception by the public of so many utterly unfamiliar pieces was naturally at best respectful rather than enthusiastic, and the addition at the end of some well known and loved encore pieces by Liszt and Chopin had the equally natural effect of arousing frantic applause. The more cynical and smart-Aleck portion of the press of course made the most of this, even to the point of throwing doubt on the recitalist's good faith in his alleged devotion to American music.

My own feeling was that his effort was sincere but unwise. All-American (or All-Anything-Else) programs, however interesting to producers, are usually deadly to consumers—in this case a hapless audience condemned to a whole afternoon of unfamiliar music, some of it mediocre. MacDowell's courageous letter on a similar occasion came to mind, in which he said: "I write to protest earnestly against this lumping together of American composers. By giving such a concert you tacitly admit that we are too inferior to stand comparison with the composers of Europe. Unless we are worthy of being put on programs with other composers, to stand or fall, leave us alone." [1]

But that is only one side of a complex question. There are other sides equally true and important. Hofmann himself emphasized one in a program note: "There is a decided kinship," he wrote, "between the inventor in the mechanical field and the creator in the realm of music, because . . . the mental activity of both is based upon imagination. . . . The musician does his work psychically, as does the inventor physically. If this nation is especially gifted in a me-

[1] The whole admirable letter is given in an article, *Mr. Hofmann and American Music*, in the *Christian Science Monitor* for January 18, 1919.

Percy Grainger
From an early photograph

chanical way, it also must be granted that among our musicians there are many endowed with fine talents for composition.

"The American public, so far, has treated the native musician with discouraging indifference. Yet if for all commercial infant industries a sympathetic regard is necessary, how much more needful must such an attitude be for the sensitive and eminently personal art of the composer! . . . Once the requisite encouragement and sympathetic attitude on the part of the public are forthcoming, many of our American composers ought to come into their own, and the once halting, unheeded lisp of the infant held helpless in the arms of an older culture will find its voice ring out fresh and bold in the cleared atmosphere of a New World." Brave and friendly words, far beyond the horizon of the smart-Alecks, words that only an artist himself as great as Josef Hofmann could have had the insight to utter.

So one's final conclusions about his experiment were those of the less frivolous New York critics. "Every composition on the list," said the *Sun*—presumably W. J. Henderson though the article is unsigned—"would be better placed in a general program. Edward MacDowell objected to being called an American composer. He wished to be named simply composer. *Verbum sap.*" And Huneker, in the *Times*, ended his review: "We must repeat our old belief: there is no map music, there is only good music. Mr. Hofmann deserves the gratitude of the native composer for his labor of love."

II

Another pianist who, like Hofmann, was himself a composer, and therefore hospitable-minded toward his fellow-composers, was Percy Grainger. This ruddy-haired young Australian, with his cordial attitude, his paradoxical and often wildly fantastic opinions, his quaint way of calling chamber music "room music" and quartets "foursomes", and loading his pages with strange barbarisms like "louden lots" (for *molto crescendo*), his fundamentally genuine musicality shown already in such fascinating things as *Shepherd's Hey*, one instinctively liked. He might be a little mad, but at any

rate he was not in the least a snob (as were so many of the pianists
with anything like his vogue). We met him, I believe for the first
time, at David and Clara Mannes's, in the fall of 1914 just after our
return from France. The following spring I sent him *Country Pictures*, and he returned a hearty note with many underlinings, and
the characteristic sentence: "So far I have had a very enjoyable skim
through, in which the *delicious* page 6 of *The Whippoorwill* very
particularly got home." He was the first, I think, to play any of the
pieces publicly, including *The Whippoorwill* in a New York recital
of November, 1917—on the program of which he is pictured in his
army uniform of a band master, looking incredibly young. He was
at this early period, it must be confessed, a little too devoted to what
one may call muscular pianism—by analogy with muscular Chris-
tianity—to be quite happy with a twilight or moonlight bird such
as a whippoorwill. His playing had a good sunny, broad daylight
effect, especially by its swinging rhythm, but the half-tones were
not always there. One sometimes felt like exclaiming, with Richard
Aldrich's little girl: "Mr. Grainger, you play too loud." But that
was only one side of the early impression of a splendidly sincere
artist. He has matured since then. A year or two later, when he was
teaching summer classes in Chicago, he made a friendly effort to
disseminate my pieces among his students, but was unable to get
copies. At any rate his comradely solicitude was heartening, and I
have never forgotten it.

III

In sending out in 1914, as editor of *The Art of Music*, inquiries to
all our American composers about their work, I included, as a matter
of routine and without any personal knowledge of the man, one to
John Powell. In his reply he struck at once, with a precision now
amusing to look back upon, the keynote of our long comradeship.
"I had the pleasure," he wrote me from London, "of hearing your
Violin Sonata last summer which the Manneses played for me. It
impressed me tremendously and made me feel very thankful that
music of such depth and sanity had been made in these turgid times

—and by an American, too." In this one sentence, I repeat, John struck not one only, but—to make an Irish bull—at least two of the keynotes (though certainly neither of us ever had the least sympathy for polytonality) of our long fellowship: disbelief in the fads and fallacies of what he called "these turgid times", and belief in our native American music.

With a man of John's coruscating many-sidedness, however, even two keynotes are an inadequate allowance; he had at least a dozen. Intellectually he was widely informed, versatile, and alert, but at the same time violently prejudiced, sometimes to the point of riding hobbies into downright fanaticism. It was his strong dramatic sense and love for an "effect", I think, more than any intellectual limitation (for he was brilliantly intelligent) that made him so strongly partisan in all his views: in music, with his detestation, courageously outspoken, for the sophistication then so rife in European music, and with his sincere if sometimes extravagant claims for "Anglo-Saxon" work, whether American or English; in politics, with his tirades and diatribes against this or that, delivered with a rhetoric inherited from generations of his Virginian orator ancestors, and with his keen eyes flashing fire and his muscular hands clenched. (They were singularly small hands for a great pianist: it was only the ingenuity of a brain as large as they were small that enabled them to accomplish miracles.)

But however wild were John's exaggerations you could never hold them against him. Just at the moment he had goaded you to revolt at his caprices the sun of his affectionateness would come out, he would say something touchingly sweet and perceptive, his southern accent, with its funny vowels and missing final G's, would insinuate itself past your defences, and you would find him irresistible. It took some time to get accustomed to these sudden changes of his spiritual weather. One felt as the traveller in the fable would have felt if the wind and the sun had got at him together instead of one by one.

Aldous Huxley, in *Ends and Means*, discussing such contrasts of temperament as always made John's southern impetuosity a bit bewildering to my New England cautiousness, tells how surprised he was at the frequent occurrence in William Blake's poetry of words like "howling", "cloud", "stormy", and "shriek". One day he counted them. "Adding up the score at the end of a morning's reading," he says, "I found that the average worked out at something like two howls and a tempest to every page of verse." That was John's spiritual weather to a T. "John says," records one of the earliest passages in my journal about him, "he was playing *The Whippoorwill* and *The Quiet Hour* at the Wellington one day, when Mrs. Ernest Hutcheson got off the elevator to ask him what they were. He played them again, and when he got through *The Quiet Hour* 'she was sobbing,' (O the sentimentalist he is—not to say the fibber!)." A year later I noted: "John is always telling how music makes him 'cry' and 'sob', and told me that he had to play *The Quiet Hour* seven times for Mrs. Hutcheson, who 'howled'— that was his word . . .

> When music impinged on John Powell
> It got him, body and sowell.
> With emotion in gobs
> He burst into sobs
> And made Mrs. Hutcheson howell."

But of course I was as pleased as Punch all the while.

For praise from a man like John, however extravagantly expressed, was to be cherished. From our earliest acquaintance he has always seemed to me one of the most gifted musical natures I have known. His unerring way of getting at the essentials in any piece of music, of penetrating at once to its fundamental problems, and his willingness to put this instinctive mastery at the service of a friend, make him an inspiring as well as a ruthless critic. . . . In his own music two irreconcilable elements exist side by side. The beautiful melodic simplicity of such things as the variation theme in the *Sonata Noble* or the slow movement tune in the *Rapsodie Nègre* (how few "tunes" there are in contemporary music!) are apt to rub shoulders incongruously with the love of rhetoric, degenerating so easily into pure bombast, into which I thought his oratorical instinct sometimes led him. (His toleration for that bombast in Liszt has

made for years a never-resolved dissension between us.) It seemed
too bad that so base an alloy should ever be associated with the pure
gold of John's themes. Even in the *Rapsodie Nègre*, to my mind his
masterpiece and one of the very few really great pieces in American
music, there are one or two sterile spots where rhetoric elbows out
inspiration.

Fortunately this element has tended to be extruded by time and
experience. There was a good deal of it in the long and I thought
megalomaniac *Sonata Teutonica* he played me at one of our earliest
meetings. There is far less of it in the beautiful *Violin Sonata* in A
flat, played by him with Zimbalist at the third Pittsfield Festival in
1920. There is still less in the *Sonata Noble*, containing the lovely
variations, and prefaced by the verses of Sidney Lanier:

> Vainly might Plato's head revolve it,
> Plainly the heart of a child could solve it.

John added, moreover, to the talent to create beauty the courage
and conviction to pursue it fearlessly in a time enslaved by ugliness.
Lasting influence in a composer depends as much on character as on
talent; and John has both. "He is a real figure in American music,"
I wrote in my journal when in 1919 I first heard him play his violin
sonata with Zimbalist, "a sincere lover of beauty." When the two
friends played the sonata again at the Pittsfield Festival, at which
was also played a brilliant but sophisticated and eccentric prize-
winning quartet, I compared it with another straightforward piece
of contemporary music there, Enesco's *Octet*, and asked: [1]

"Would either, one cannot help wondering, have taken the prize
had it been in the same competition? One doubts it. For both Enesco
and Powell are simple, forthright music-makers, with something to
say and without a thought of being queer, 'effective', or 'ultra-
modern' in their way of saying it. And judges, unhappy men, are
weighed down by their sense of obligation to find not the beautiful
but the novel, not the sincere but the sensational, not what will
sound clear today and fresh in twenty years but what will sound

[1] In an account of the three Berkshire Festivals, 1918–1920, published in *Music as
a Humanity*.

queer today, even if threadbare in a decade." With this may be compared a more intimate entry in the journal:

"Pittsfield, September 26, 1920. Powell, Aldrich, and to some extent Stock, Hutcheson and a few others, appear to be the only professional musicians present who feel as I do (though it was nice to hear Giorni say that the music of Ravel and Debussy seemed a sauce for the viand that wasn't there). . . . The struggle to be 'modern' and 'original' preoccupies almost everyone, and beautiful melodic ideas like the best themes in the Powell sonata are dismissed by people like Salzedo, Gautier, Loeffler, Bloch, Bauer, Leginska, as 'old-fashioned'. . . . One simply must love beauty enough to be unaware of all this. . . . John told me the kind of 'originality' he was after was to present simple thoughts with novelty of cadence, rather than wilfully to multiply oddities."

The sense we thus grew to have of unity of aim in the midst of alien ideals naturally drew us closely together. Our loneliness intensified the solace of our fellowship. When I remarked to him once that few modern pieces were composed, they were mostly mere pictures, he replied: "They are not even pictures, for pictures are works of art. They are illustrations—magazine illustrations." And when I responded to this with an exclamation of despair—"What's the use of it all?" he said : "Well, people like you and me are trying to keep the flame alight, anyway." No idle boast was this phrase of his that has helped me through many a dark hour, but the expression of a conviction he was ready to support with patient work and courageous action. "You mustn't be disappointed," he remarked to me once when he was playing two pieces of mine in a Carnegie Hall recital, "if they don't 'get over'. They have their own individual style. If they *are* appreciated, well and good. If not, we must just keep pegging away at them." "We live in a time," he said on another occasion and in more general terms, "when there is no real musical public, and when current fashions are all against music like yours. [And of course he might have added: "and mine."] You don't care to model yourself on Victor Herbert and Lehar, nor on Schönberg and Stravinsky. You will have to bear the inconveniences of your position. It has its rewards, too." John is always so sure he is right,

John Powell
From an early photograph

and so extreme in his way of saying things, that we who are fortunate enough to be his friends are sometimes painfully conscious of
the exorbitant claims he makes for us. But the essential point is that
he has steadily believed in our finest possibilities, and thus helped us
to actualize them a little—which is surely the very genius of friendship.

IV

Considering how insatiably social John is, it is strange how hard
it is to extract a letter from him. In all our long friendship I have
accumulated only about half a dozen. He will gladly sit up all night
with you, if you will let him, discussing music, or just gossiping—
for he has an unappeasable appetite for personalia, especially when
spiced with a little friendly malice—or declaiming on some of his
pet fanaticisms such as the horrible dangers of intermarriage between Negroes and whites, or the supreme virtues of Anglo-Saxon
folk-songs. But letters, even pressing business ones, he will seldom
answer. Chalmers Clifton, who conducted the *Plymouth Pageant*
to which John contributed part of the music, told us that he would
answer no letters or even telegrams. The only way was to get him
to Plymouth in person, and then sit up nights with him until in two
or three days, or rather nights, he wrote his music between midnight
and three o'clock in the morning. ("Powell," once remarked Arthur
Whiting, "is not for a time but for all day.") Like Mozart, he liked
to be talked to while composing. It excited him and set him in the
vein.

The longest letter I ever had from him was in the summer of
1919, and was coaxed out of him by a subject that happened to in-
trigue his interest. Though it concerns a rather technical matter I
shall present it here, it is so characteristic in its ability, clearness, and
vigor. He had wanted me to write him a piano sonata, but I had
doubted my ability to sustain interest in so long a work without the
help of orchestral color. Early that summer I got some ideas that I
thought would shape into a prelude and fugue for piano and orchestra; and though I knew of no such experiment in combining the

brittle piano with the more sustained tones of the orchestra in that most singing of all forms, the fugue, the problem fascinated me, and I decided to try it. Fortunately for me my letter to John, written in July to announce my intention, did not reach him until September, so that it was not until my piece, for better or worse, was completely sketched, the summer's work was over, and we were about to return to town, that I got his friendly but somewhat skeptical and dissuasive reply.

"Richmond [No date: postmarked
September 12, 1919.]

"Your letter of July 22nd, which was not forwarded to me, just discovered. I am very excited at your news: happy on your account —because you are full of a big work—and disappointed on my own —because I was hoping for a Mason work in the larger form that could be used in recital without having to gain the consent of managers and conductors.

"Besides, I always feel that the combination of piano and orchestra is unfortunate. The dynamic limitations of the former hamper and confine the orchestral possibilities, and the variety of color and sustained sonority of the latter make pallid and dry the timbre of the solo instrument. With the orchestra of Mozart and early Beethoven these difficulties were more easily obviable; hence the pure beauty and perfection of the Mozart concerti and the superiority of the Beethoven C minor to the two later concerti and the *Choral Fantasia*. For as the number and variety of instruments increased in the orchestras, and orchestral effects assumed greater importance, the composer of piano concerti was forced either to suppress his orchestra (note the dry, squawky scoring of the Tschaikowsky and the peculiarly ineffective setting of the Brahms *B flat*) or to assert his solo instrument by means of glittering tinsel or noise-making tricks (note the empty mock-heroics of Rubinstein and the tinkling trivialities of Liszt). I speak only of men who were masters of orchestration, for the Schumann and even the Grieg are much more effective with second piano than with orchestra.

"Indeed the combination of piano and orchestra has hampered the inspiration and creativeness of even the greatest composers. Note the inferiority of the Beethoven concerti to either the sonatas or the symphonies. How much finer are the César Franck *Symphony* and the *Prelude, choral et fugue* than the *Variations symphoniques*! To my mind, and I speak too from practical experience, the piano concerto is a hybrid, and, like the Eurasian and the Eurafrican, possesses few—and these suppressed—of the virtues, and all—and these emphasized—of the weaknesses, of the two parents.

"I suppose however that one ought to take a try at cracking every hard nut, and I am wishing you the best of luck in your adventure and awaiting the result with the keenest interest. For I am sure that in bringing your powers to bear on this hitherto insoluble problem you will, whether successful or not, reach discoveries that will be of vast help to all the rest of us."

V

During the following year I scored the piece, and when I saw Frederick Stock at the next Pittsfield Festival he accepted it for performance by the Chicago Orchestra, with John Powell as soloist. "Of course," he warned me, "you won't expect a barn-storming popular success with it. But it's a noble piece." The next problem was how to manage to be present at this first performance. . . . The only way we could pay our expenses to hear any of my music played at such a distance from New York was to arrange in advance a lecture tour. Fortunately it was now seven years since the Boffres summer and the Paris winter we had spent writing the symphony, and I was entitled to a fresh sabbatical half-year's absence from Columbia, commencing in February, 1921. Gabrilowitsch with his usual considerateness set his revival of the symphony in the middle of February, and Stock with equal considerateness put the premiere of the *Prelude and Fugue* on days convenient for me. I arranged a lecture tour in eight Western cities that would last three weeks, pay the copying charges on the new work, a short one, and on the revisions of the symphony, leave me a net profit of several hundred dollars, and allow us to hear both works!

But this, of course, was too good to be true. In the first days of the new year came word that the Chicago premiere was unavoidably postponed until early March. And by that time we were at sea, starting our sabbatical. . . .

"Steamship 'Providence'
"March 4, 1921

"Quite a celebration tonight in honor of Harding's Inauguration. The smoking room and dining room were decorated with the national colors, and champagne was served to all, in which the Captain asked us to drink Harding's health. Then someone proposed Millerand's health, whereupon the three Frenchmen at the next table led in singing the *Marseillaise*. Later there was rather a weak attempt by the Americans to sing what Arthur Whiting calls 'God bless our 'tis of thee'.

"I suppose the *Prelude and Fugue* has been played this afternoon."

Perhaps in some ways it was just as well: our absence spared us for some months the knowledge that the reception of my work by the press was one of the worst in my long experience. There was some excuse for the pressmen. The piece was in its original form much too long (twelve years later I revised it, amputating two-fifths of the fugue) and it was overscored. But from their point of view its unforgivable sins were that it was called a "prelude and fugue", that it was admittedly "contrapuntal" and that I bore the title of "Professor". No wonder the poor pressmen suffered an unusually severe attack of their usual distemper, breaking out in a heavy rash of such adjectives as "learned", "erudite", and "academic". The piece was "austere in emotional expression", it "contained an unfathomable amount of the lore of composition", it "pretty well managed to divorce itself from human sensibility".

A sneaking sympathy for my critics made their jibes harder for me to bear. John had played also, as he continued to do in many later performances, his own glorious *Rapsodie Nègre*. In comparison with its beautiful folk melodies, its exotic color, its brilliant pianism, of course my piece seemed "austere"—it seemed so to me too: only

I happened to like austerity in its place, as my critics did not. But John felt as I did; and I admired him that in the long course of playing the piece he never wavered.

I recall a characteristic ebullition of his from the time of the performance with the Philadelphia Orchestra. We were talking in the artists' room after the rehearsal with the concert-master, Thaddeus Rich, who as music reporter for one of the local papers was writing a glowing account, as well he might, of the *Rapsodie Nègre*. "He had mentioned me too," says my journal, "referring to me as a professor at Columbia, etc. John, bless him, said: 'Why not try omitting the Professor for once?' and went on: 'You must say how full of life, emotion, passion it is—people have such wrong ideas about fugues.'"

So, that spring of the Chicago premiere, when after some weeks in Italy we settled down in Paris early in June, it did not surprise, much as it delighted me, to get this letter from the doughty and valiant John.

"University of Virginia
"May 17th, 1921

"Please accept my abjectest apologies, and renewed assurance of deep love and admiration for the *Prelude and Fugue*. . . . Stock gave it a splendid performance and the audience received it more cordially than either of us had anticipated. A deep and sombre work can never be grasped at one hearing, especially when it is severely free from all meretricious effects. Nevertheless the applause was hearty and I was recalled four times Friday and three times Saturday.

"For God's sake don't let those barbarians cow you. I am not an utter fool, am I? Isn't my taste and judgment at least as good as that of Mr. —— or Mr. ——? Well, you know what I think of your work, and my experience of the *Prelude and Fugue* has only served to confirm my opinion. If only you could have heard it you would not doubt. But you will hear it next autumn, for I am engaged to play it with the Philharmonic.

"I am almost dead. Have been working night and day to finish my

Virginia Overture [1] and today just as I was completing the score comes the news that it is impossible to secure the necessary players. But I am very pleased with the work and am sure you will like it. I have also been commissioned to compose the finale of the *Plymouth Rock Pageant*. Just got the words (by Frost) from Professor Baker today. It is 4.15 A.M. and it is dawn and I have been working steadily since 10 A.M. yesterday. So Good-night!"

VI

There is a curious irony in the fact that the performance by the Philharmonic to which John refers (especially as it happened to be the first presentation of anything of mine by that Society), should have been conducted by—of all people—Josef Stransky! Had he forgiven my attack on him? Did he consider me a person it was good tactics to conciliate? Or had he simply succumbed, as many did, to John's wayward charm? On such questions my journal throws no light, but merely states:

"November 17, 1920. John Powell came in late to tell me that Stransky wants to have the first New York performance of my *Prelude and Fugue*! I told him I should have to think it over, that I was afraid it would be tantamount to retracting my criticism of his conducting to let him do one of my pieces. John answered that I ought to dissociate my criticism from my composition, and suggested laughingly that I write an article afterwards on the performance. He is anxious that a work of mine should be played by the Philharmonic, because of the prestige, and says there would be plenty of rehearsal. He is also set on winning over Finck to my work! I told him that in such a difficult world he ought to choose something easier."

When a year later the rehearsals began I found, as one often does, that a person criticized from afar may turn out on nearer acquaintance to have many agreeable qualities. Stransky gave my work as many rehearsals, and took as much pains with it, as if it had come from Europe. He was friendly to work with, helpful in suggestion,

[1] *In Old Virginia.*

and witty in comment. For instance, as we left the stage after taking a bow all three together, he turned to me with a quizzical smile, and exclaimed: "It feels like Armistice Day"!

I saw no reason however to change my opinion of him as an artist. His understanding of my piece was superficial, he played it too fast, as he did also, just before it, Rachmaninoff's *Island of the Dead*. Rachmaninoff's five-beat measures, I afterwards learned from the orchestra men, gave him great trouble. This I can readily believe, as when a year later he played my *Symphony* the five-beat measures of the finale, which had irritated even Gabrilowitsch, completely routed him. He unconsciously transformed their five beats into six by holding the last one double time, so that the men in the orchestra were audibly calling out "Six! Six!" But with both pieces I think he tried sincerely.

On this occasion, my first important appearance in New York as a composer, I had a chance to garner some valuable experience on the ticklish matter of writing program notes. One should never give pressmen an opening—a priceless truth I did not then know. So I was naïve enough to write: "While nothing is more deadly than a fugue treated in an academic spirit . . . in itself the fugue is one of the most moving and beautiful of all forms, since it is in its essence melody, all melody, and nothing but melody." This of course gave Deems Taylor an excellent lead for his *riposte:* "True, but first catch your melody." Had I been a little older at the game, too, I might have warned John that not even his insinuating Southern ways could make Finck of the *Evening Post* see much melody or emotion in a piece by one he described as "a pupil of César Franck [!] and a worshipper at the shrine of Brahms, which means that he specializes in the formal side of music," or save him from committing the sapient platitude: "Bach's fugues are often strikingly melodious and emotional!"

I was even more innocent in confessing that I was the first to try a prelude and fugue for piano and orchestra. Rummaging through the notices the other day, I chuckled when I came to this, and looked confidently for the sequel. Sure enough, it was supplied by the *Musical Courier:* "After listening to it, one hopes fervently he will

be the last." Q. E. D. In the course of the years I have learned to look
upon Lawrence Gilman as occupying a different world from that
the average pressman fills with his peculiar blend of smartness and
fatuity. Gilman is a poet and a seer as well as a distinguished man of
letters. But on this occasion even he, though praising in a letter the
"imaginative and flexible counterpoint" of the piece, and telling me
over the telephone that he found it "most moving", added: "I don't
know whether you want it to be, but it is."

Arthur Whiting did not care for Stransky's rendition of the *Island
of the Dead*—said it sounded more like the *Island of the Quick*. For
me his word, delivered with his usual dry impersonality, was: "It
is inspiring to see a man with nerve enough to attempt a fugue for
piano and orchestra—like seeing a man ride at a six-bar gate—inspiring even if he misses it. . . . That is not to be applied too literally."
Yet the next morning came a note that showed a more personal side
of him, a side so seldom shown that one sometimes suspected it of
being resolutely suppressed by his pride and reticence, yet as characteristic as his irony.

"Dear Dan: Just a line to say I was considerable proud of you last
night, and glad to claim you as a friend who is both a scholar and an
artist, with high ideals which are realized. You have indeed made the
most of your talents, and no greater reward than that awaits anyone
at the Judgment Day.

"Stick-to-it-iveness was not your strong suit as a youth, I remember, but by some inward grace (or was it Mary?) you have achieved
it. You and Mary make a strong team, and have pulled out of many
a bad bit of going to the applause of the by-standers, and especially of
                    "Your affectionate friend, Arthur Whiting."

A few days later we dined with Grace and Arthur, finding him
in particularly good form. He told how a friend of ours, a painful
stammerer, had ordered a drink with other men at the club. A: "Martini cocktail." B: "Martini cocktail." Stammerer: Splutter, mumble,
particularly long subterranean passage. Then "The S-s-same!"

I told of my inflicting a great deal of very broken French on
Rachmaninoff before learning that he spoke perfectly good English. A. W. "You wanted your French back!"

Apropos of something, I now forget what, he told a story of an Irish captain haranguing his men on the eve of battle.

Captain, oratorically: "Will ye fight, or will ye run?"

Men, enthusiastically: "We will."

Captain, severely: "I said: Will ye fight, or will ye run?"

Men, after consideration: "We will not."

The tale seemed a fairly good summary of my own ultimate state of mind in the matter of Stransky.

GABRILOWITSCH IN DETROIT

THE summer of 1918, following the brilliant success of Ossip
Gabrilowitsch's guest appearance with the Detroit Orchestra in
March and preceding his first appearance as its permanent director
in November, was a time of intense preparatory work for him.
The orchestra was young, had played together only a few years,
was made up largely of local men, and had to be winnowed out, sup-
plemented by imported players, and increased from a personnel of
sixty-five to eighty-five. . . . One of Ossip's most inspiring traits
was his ability to combine endless, painstaking kindness to individuals with ruthless resistance to mass movements tending to de-
teriorate quality. He would go miles or spend hours to help the
humblest player in his orchestra; but he would also fight the degrading influence of union or other mass attempts to subordinate
artistic to economic values with a fierceness that to those who did
not understand him seemed autocratic.

After the war-time dismissal of Dr. Karl Muck as conductor of
the Boston Symphony, Ossip was asked to succeed him, but declined,
remarking to me that the orchestra would probably have to be
unionized, and that if it was unionized it would never again be what
it had been. Nevertheless only a few weeks later, after his acceptance
of the Detroit offer, he was struggling with the same situation.

"Ossip told us the other night," says my journal, "some of his experiences renovating the orchestra. He heard all the Detroit men first, but had to discharge many of them, they were so bad. But when he tried to bring good players from other cities the Detroit local union would not permit it, and he is still in controversy with them. It may break up the renovation altogether." In order to win his point Ossip was actually obliged to offer his resignation. A letter by him, explaining the whole episode, published in *Musical America*, June 17, 1918, is characteristic in its combination of loving consideration for individuals with uncompromising championship of artistic integrity.

During all his early years in Detroit efforts and worries of this kind were unremitting. In the spring of his first season, I find in my journal: "Poor Ossip is terribly used up. He says he is working from eight in the morning until one at night, largely on endless details of correspondence, telephones, and interviews, never practices, and often does not read a score for days. It seems as if there were something radically wrong in our civilization, to use a razor like an ax."

Toward the end of his fourth season he again offered his resignation, and came near acting upon it. "Of course," he wrote me in February, 1922, "it would be a pity if the Orchestra were to disband, but let me tell you that I would not cry my eyes out if I were to be released from the duties of a conductor in this country. The work is interesting and inspiring, to be sure—at least the musical side of it is, but there is altogether too much of it, and the many sides that are *not* musical do not appeal to me. I find that I spend many more hours on these things than I do studying scores. Nor is this my experience only—I know that Stokowski suffers from the same conditions, although his organization is an older one and very thoroughly equipped and apparently running by itself. I really should like to be able to devote a little more time to my piano than I have been able to do during the last four years. There have been many days—sometimes weeks—when I have not touched the instrument. I have been working almost twenty-four hours a day the last four years, and I do not believe that any one's nervous system can withstand that sort of thing indefinitely."

Ossip's long and fruitful devotion to music in Detroit was carried through quietly, without splurge of any sort. The scene of his labors was not a brilliant metropolis but a middle western industrial city. His orchestra had no prestige, made no impression on the conventional-minded, especially in the early days; he had to fight for every inch of his progress against the indifference, even the contempt, of those who can only see established labels. An amusing instance comes to mind. Once when the Detroit Orchestra gave a concert in New York, the critic of the *New York Times* wrote patronizingly that the brass was rather weak, one could not expect anything better in a young orchestra, etc., etc. Olga Samaroff-Stokowski, then music critic of the *Evening Post*, had to remind the gentleman in her next article that the conductor of this "young orchestra" had had the good sense to take over the complete horn choir of the Boston Symphony! Ossip himself, of course, matched his "young orchestra" with an unassuming directness of manner that, like that of his friend Bruno Walter, made little impression on those who expect from a conductor visible as well as audible results. He never had any of the airs of the *prima donna* conductor—he was thinking not of himself but of music. None of us, alas, not even his intimate friends, quite realized, until his untimely death at fifty-eight, at what terrible cost to him was accomplished the long task which gradually transformed a provincial city into one of the centers of musical progress in America.

II

My own first view of his new work in Detroit came toward the end of his opening season, when, on March 27 and 29, 1919, he performed my *Russians*, with Reinald Werrenrath singing the solo part. Ossip had been taking an interest in these songs ever since I had shown him sketches of some of them in the spring of '17. In the fall of the same year he had gone over three of them with me in detail, advising revision necessary because I had written the voice parts too low. The revision accomplished, I had shown them to Werrenrath, who suggested doing them with Stock in Chicago or Stokowski in

Philadelphia. It was deeply characteristic of Ossip, almost alone among conductors in this respect, that if he liked a work he was totally unselfish as to whether or not the performance to be marked with those magic words "First time" came to him or to one of his rivals, or, as he preferred to regard them, colleagues.

> "Seal Harbor, Maine
> "July 16, 1918

"Werrenrath is going to be one of my soloists in Detroit next season. I believe he was the one you had in view for introducing your *Russians*. Have you made arrangements with him to include them in his program in Detroit?

"Your letter informs me that there is a possibility of *Russians* being sung in Philadelphia. This is, I assure you, no doing of mine, and you have nothing to thank me for. I shall be delighted if the Philadelphia performance goes through, and it does not make the slightest difference to me whether we in Detroit have the first or the second performance.

"The principal question is now whether you have finished orchestrating all the five songs and how soon you could let me have the score."

I sent him the score at once; and then followed a characteristic correspondence between him and Werrenrath. The texts of the songs, by Witter Bynner, were highly unconventional both in substance—utterances in the first person of the feelings of Russian types such as *A Drunkard, A Concertina-player, A Revolutionary*— and in form—a kind of free verse verging on prose. The first one, for example, *A Drunkard*, began

> They ask me what I sing about.
> Who knows?
> Vodka bakes me in my innards
> Drops of it are on my beard.

but ended: "I am comforted and cheered." *A Revolutionary* was the cry of agony of a boy in prison, condemned to death:

I must give up, go out,
I who have cared so much.

The music too, obliged by its subjects to flout most of the conventions of song-writing, was aggressive, violent, and harsh. No
wonder Werrenrath, asked by Ossip to sing such things, had
qualms. He wrote back that while he was much impressed with
their "vigor and originality", he wondered whether, in view of the
Russian situation developed by the war and Bolshevism, it might
not be as well to "consider the temper of our American audiences",
and "perform nothing that would give offense."

"Dear Mr. Werrenrath," answered Ossip, "I quite realize the
importance of what you mention in regard to the Russian situation,
but it seems to me that . . . we need have no apprehension. The
feeling toward Russia in this country is as friendly as it can be. . . .
Of course unexpected political events may happen, but those we
must never count upon or else we should never be able to plan even
for the near future.

My feeling is that if you are sufficiently impressed by the musical
significance of Mr. Mason's songs it would be very desirable to put
them on the program. . . ."

Werrenrath saw the point, and accepted the songs. The first performance fell, however, as it turned out, to Chicago (November 15,
1918). By this time Frederick Stock as well as Dr. Muck had got
into trouble through the war hysteria, and the songs were conducted not by him but by Eric DeLamarter, who telegraphed me
that they "went over big". "Journal, December 16. At ten who
should come in but Ossip, tired from weeks of playing, conducting,
and travelling, but fine as ever. He said that Werrenrath declared
that he had 'made him sing Russians', but thanked him for bringing
them to his attention, said they were 'great' and the audience was
'crazy' about them, and the press down on them—'and what more
could you want?' "

Ossip's own performances, March 27 and 29, 1919, in the old and
barn-like Arcadia Auditorium (for the beautiful Orchestra Hall he
was to persuade Detroit to erect was still a thing of the future)

proved to be one of the great events of my life; and I love to remember that we owed our being there at all to him. Toward the end of February, realizing that the trip to Detroit was entirely beyond our means, I wrote him that we could not come, trying to put a good face on the matter by mentioning work that kept me at home. He answered:

"Your letter seems to indicate that you do not wish to leave New York on account of your own work. . . . On the other hand, if you are giving up your visit to Detroit for *financial* reasons, let me remind you that during that visit you and Mary were to be our guests, and this, of course, includes your trip from New York and back. Therefore there would be no expense to you connected with it. This has been Clara's and my plan from the very beginning, but I am not sure that I made it quite clear to you when we spoke of your coming."

This was followed after a few days by railroad tickets and a Pullman drawing-room to Detroit! I telegraphed: "Tickets joyful surprise. Who could resist you? We are coming." When we reached the suite in the Statler Hotel he had reserved for us, we found a grand piano he had had installed for my use, and a lovely bunch of roses from his wife to mine. That was the way Ossip and Clara did things.

Of the performances themselves perhaps the reader can divine something between the lines of a few fragmentary notes jotted down in my journal in the happiness and fatigue of the first day back in New York.

"Ossip has proved himself the same generous friend and great musician as always. We made the whole trip as his guests. Thursday afternoon, the 27th, was the rehearsal with Werrenrath. At the end the musicians spontaneously applauded, and Ossip and Werrenrath gave me a 'hand up' to the stage, about five feet from the floor, to bow my acknowledgements. The *Free Press* describes the enthusiastic reception Thursday evening. Ossip came to our rooms and gave us supper and we talked until one. He takes a pessimistic view of the 'democratic' levelling-down tendency of society. Saturday afternoon the songs sounded even more thrilling than on Thursday, and some of the musicians, as later I passed among them, called out

'Bravo, Bravissimo!' . . . An ever-memorable experience, the first great overwhelming success of my life, after so many years of failures and half-successes. When it was over and Ossip gave me the tickets back to New York I hugged and kissed him. He too was much moved."

III

One of the high points in Ossip's own life was his great performance of Bach's *St. Matthew Passion*, in Symphony Hall, Detroit, March 30, 1926 (later repeated in Carnegie Hall, New York). For months he had been straining every nerve to make each detail perfect; indeed he had spent a good part of the preceding summer preparing his own edition of the work. Then it was that with the egotism of composers I wrote him I was going to Chicago for a performance of my symphony, and asked what concerts of his I might hear should I stop off at Detroit. He answered: "We have a performance of Bach's *St. Matthew Passion* March 30th, and we also have a Pop Concert April 4th, which I conduct." I fear I must have indicated my preference for April 4th, for in his reply I find this paragraph:

". . . However, your letter says not a word about the Bach performance. If you can arrange it, I should love to have you here on the evening of March 30th, when we give Bach's *St. Matthew Passion*, first time in Detroit. I think it is going to be a good performance. Can you arrange to spend a few hours with us, both coming and going, always as my guest while you are in the city? Sorry we shall not see Mary."

A few days later came a special delivery letter.

"I got the impression that Mary was not going with you to Chicago because you felt you could not afford the trip. Am I right? Clara and I have been talking things over and we should like to make the following suggestion to you. Mary's trip would only cost a hundred dollars. Allow us to put that amount at her disposal. I am sure you will enjoy your trip tenfold if Mary is with you, and incidentally we shall have the pleasure of seeing her when you stop

in Detroit. I have this plan for you: You both leave New York Monday afternoon and arrive in Detroit Tuesday A.M.—hear our Bach
performance Tuesday evening and then proceed to Chicago for the
rehearsals and performances of your symphony. You return to Detroit (on your way East) Sunday April 4th and spend another few
hours with us.

"I need not tell you how much we shall love to have you. As for
you I think you are both constantly 'cooked up' in New York and
will enjoy a little vacation. Be a good boy and get immediately your
drawing-room for Monday afternoon. We will get your other reservations from here. Send me a wire.

"Hastily, Ossip.

"Of course my offer holds good even if you cannot attend the
Bach performance. But I hope you can."

When we called him up on our arrival, and told him he had sized
up our case correctly, he was delighted, and said "I'm quite a long-
distance psychologist." At the rehearsal, begun by his assistant, it
was decided to add a soft stop to the organ at a certain point in the
accompaniment to an aria, where it could not be heard with the
amount of tone decided upon by Ossip the day before. He arrived
and recommenced the aria. After a few measures he stopped and
announced: "Too much organ tone." "You can't hear it without
the extra stop, Mr. Gabrilowitsch," explained his assistant. "I don't
want to hear it," he replied, "it's there only for background." In
another place Richard Crooks, singing the part of the Evangelist,
had difficulty in catching the pitch from the organ. I suggested
adding just a touch of four-foot tone. Ossip called back to me, with
good-natured exaggeration: "That alone is worth coming on from
New York for."

Some of the program notes reflect amusingly his indefatigable
care for detail: "The piano especially constructed for these performances by the Mason and Hamlin Company is an imitation of
the clavicembalo used in Bach's time. . . . There will be no applause. . . . Ladies are respectfully requested not to appear in
bright dresses. . . ." In a few clear and carefully thought-out remarks he explained to the immense audience (hundreds of people

unable to obtain admission, many standing from seven to eleven
o'clock) the devotional sincerity, sublimity, and beauty of the
music, and the spirit in which it should be appreciated. The whole
was more like a religious service than a concert. . . . The broad
final chorus was made so noble and so touching with its long-drawn
closing chord sinking slowly to silence, that after it died away some
auditors sat long without speaking or moving, as if loath to return to
the confusion of ordinary life.

IV

Early in the season of 1927–28 came, out of a clear sky, a note
from Ossip:

"Who is the publisher of your *Symphony* and how much does
he charge for the complete orchestral material? I am seriously thinking of putting that work on our program this winter."

What such an inquiry meant to a weary composer it is hard to
describe to anyone who has not gone through the ceaseless and often
humiliating efforts necessary in order to get conductors even to look
at one's scores. Perhaps as good a hint as any will be implicit in a
tabular view of the adventures of this same symphony in my native
town of Boston:

April, 1916. Score sent to Dr. Karl Muck (to whom Gabrilowitsch
had recommended it.)

February, 1918. Symphony accepted by Dr. Muck.

March. Dr. Muck arrested as an "enemy alien".

Summer of 1922. I rewrite symphony, bringing total expense of
material up to four hundred and fifty dollars.

December, 1922. Pierre Monteux accepts Symphony for performance in season 1923–24.

September, 1923. Announcement made that Monteux will be succeeded after one season by Koussevitzky.

April, 1924. Monteux writes that he is obliged to give up my symphony, very considerately adding: "That I cannot now see my way
clear is not due to the attitude of the press toward your *Prelude and
Fugue*. That could not affect my own high opinion of your work."

March, 1925. Symphony accepted by Serge Koussevitzky, but postponed from time to time for three years.

March, 1928 (twelve years after acceptance by Muck). Symphony played in Boston—a very fine performance—by Koussevitzky.

No doubt this experience in Boston was exceptional, even for a serious work by an American. During that same twelve years the symphony had had in New York two performances—Stransky's mediocre one already mentioned, and a magnificent one by Bruno Walter in 1925. In Chicago Stock had played it in two successive years, 1925 and '26. Nevertheless its path had been mostly up-hill and its appearance on my finance sheets decidedly discouraging. And here at last was a conductor proposing to buy it!

During this same season he and I had occasion several times to fight shoulder to shoulder in the cause of music. Sometimes our opponents were absurd enough to afford us many a good laugh, despite all our qualms for an art so menaced everywhere by commercialism. Sometimes it was the more formidable enemy of sensationalism against which we fought less hopefully—that hydra-headed monster which trampled all beauty underfoot throughout our period, and against which no individual or group could make much headway. . . . Twenty thousand dollars were offered in prizes at this time by a well-known business firm for the "completion" of Schubert's *Unfinished Symphony!* This was a piece for which Ossip had always reserved a special corner of his heart, and the absurd proposal nearly "finished" him and me, slight as was its effect on the symphony of Schubert. I wrote *Musical America* in protest, asking how a sculptor would feel who was offered $20,000 to put arms on the Venus of Milo, or an architect engaged for an equal sum to bring the Parthenon "up-to-date". (A story went the rounds, probably invented by some humorist, that a poll on these questions was taken of the passers on Forty-second Street, and that one man stated as his opinion that the Venus should be duly supplied with the two missing arms, and the symphony with the two missing movements.) Ossip was delighted with my protest, wrote a letter himself to the *New York Times* (October 8, 1927) and sent me his photograph inscribed: "To my dear friend and ally in all battles for musical ideals, Dan Mason. November, 1927."

Early in the New Year a more serious matter came up. As guest conductor with the New York Symphony he gave such a splendid concert that I was excited into trying once more, through a letter to the *Times* (January 29, 1928) to arouse public opinion to the evils of the *prima donna* conductor system and the great good that would follow if one of our orchestras could be put permanently in charge of a true musician.

"The competition in showmanship that has gone on in New York during recent seasons," I wrote, "is bad for music from many points of view. It vulgarizes the taste of audiences by making them value sensations above beauty, exaggeration and feverish seeking for effect above the moderation and balance that alone wear well. It demoralizes orchestras by subjecting them to many and constantly changing influences and traditions, not giving them time to perfect themselves under any. It retards the growth of our composers by denying performances to new works, to permit *prima donna* conductors to prepare sensational interpretations of familiar war horses. It debauches the conductors themselves by withholding appreciation for their more solid, inconspicuous but lasting qualities and constantly inviting them to make stars of themselves.

"The way to correct this condition would seem to be to put a musician of supreme interpretative gifts and of incorruptible artistic character in permanent charge of one of our resident orchestras."

Ossip wrote thanking me for championing him again, and saying that immediately after his Carnegie Hall concert he had been offered the conductorship of the New York Symphony Society, and that he had also had another offer "even more interesting". This, as he later told me, was a half-the-year conductorship of the Philadelphia Orchestra, which however he reduced to two months in the middle of the season. From this time on he appeared often in New York as temporary conductor of both the Philadelphia and the New York Symphony Orchestras. But New York was not so fortunate as to

Ossip Gabrilowitsch

Inscribed: *"To my dear friend and ally in all battles for musical ideals, Dan Mason. November, 1927."*

get a permanent conductor until nearly a decade later, when John Barbirolli was put in charge of the Philharmonic-Symphony.

On the program of Ossip's revival of my *First Symphony* in Detroit, February 23-24, 1928, I find the notation: "The second (Friday night) performance was one of the high points of my life." And below it: "Another was the performance of *Russians* in Detroit, also by Ossip." How pathetically short it makes life seem to realize that the third was that of my *Lincoln Symphony* by Barbirolli in New York in 1937, and that by that time Ossip was no longer living, and my score could only be dedicated to his memory. . . .

Those rehearsals in 1928 started inauspiciously enough. He was still half ill with a recent attack of grippe, and just getting back into the traces. He had found fifty fresh errors in the parts, and as his third horn was also ill he set me to work all the first afternoon cueing third horn parts into other instruments. The next morning things began to go better. Harold Bauer was to be the soloist, playing the Brahms *D minor Concerto*. We all lunched with Clara and Ossip three days in succession, and gave Ossip a plentiful diet of the funny stories for which he had such an insatiable appetite. Bauer told of playing the *Brahms Concerto* with Mr. X., a *prima donna* conductor with whose interpretation he found himself at odds at every point. They spent the entire afternoon discussing the minutest details, but when the evening came X. played everything exactly as at first, and afterwards, embracing Bauer, exclaimed "There, wasn't it just right that way?" Ossip's fatalistic sense of reality, as humorous as it was melancholy, was tickled into paroxysms by my story of the negro who, asked for his philosophy of life, replied, "I avoids de impossible and coöperates wid de inevitable." He himself told us how someone, congratulating him on his energy, added as if by afterthought: "Some people have intelligence, some have talent, and some have energy."

The first of the two concerts was an occasion of great triumph for him, as it had been rumored that he was to leave Detroit, and the manager read the audience a letter from him denying the rumor and assuring them he would return after a year of sabbatical absence. They rose *en masse* and applauded long, while the orchestra gave him a fanfare. "Ossip was in great spirits afterwards," says my journal, "rallying Bauer, and saying to me 'Your symphony made me do one thing I never did before.' When I asked what, he said: 'Wear my spectacles! I really wanted to see what there was in the score.' "

On the last day too, the Friday when I was so delighted with the symphony, he was in the highest spirits. Journal: "Friday, February 24, 5:30 P.M. Ossip said yesterday's rehearsal was the first overtime one of the season, and cost the Society about $100 extra. 'We're going to charge that to you, Dan.' 11:45 P.M. Sitting in the upper berth, eating an apple. On the way upstairs after the concert Ossip said: 'There are some things in the slow movement that are so delicious I could eat them up.' I said: 'Your performance was so poetic,' and he replied: 'It's all in the score.' "

V

This February of 1928 marked, I think, the high point of our artistic fellowship—the point of maximum youthful enthusiasm and zest. Ossip's vitality, I realize now, reached the apex at about the end of the twenties, and then, sapped by long-continued over-work and even more by his deep solicitude for art in an age of confusion and his despair for liberty in a time of growing tyranny, gradually ebbed during the troubled though loyally borne years of the thirties ending with his death in 1936. That was the coda of the symphony, not less poignant or beautiful for being subdued in coloring. And even in those years there were of course happy, comparatively care-free times still. There comes back to mind his performance of my *Chanticleer Overture* at Philadelphia, on the same January night of 1931 that Stock played it in Chicago, when he telegraphed us: "Chanticleer crowed yesterday and made a great many friends in Philadelphia. He will crow again tonight, and wishes his papa and mamma might be present. Ossip."

I remember with gratitude too his honest friendliness in the matter of my *Second Symphony*. When he gave *Chanticleer* in Detroit he took the opportunity to have the new symphony played over in rehearsal by his assistant. This was the first time I had myself heard it, and his almost sole comment—that it "was not so cheerful as *Chan-*

ticleer"—was hardly encouraging. As the days passed with no word
from him, usually so frank, my gloom deepened. At last I could bear
it no longer, and asked him point-blank, after dinner at his house,
how he liked it. He did not flinch in a situation that must have been
for him, as my host, peculiarly trying, but said quite simply and
kindly: "I will tell you frankly that I do not care for the symphony."
When he saw how upset I was he added: "Well, that does not mean
that other conductors may not like it." After my return to New
York he wrote:

"I have now carefully examined the score of your second symphony. It is a dignified and earnest work; the composer speaks a
refined language. At the same time I think it lacks spontaneity and
that certain naïveté which to me makes the principal charm of all
great works by Beethoven, Brahms, Schubert and others. I do not
know what is the matter with me. I find more and more that works
of modern composers reflect a tremendous amount of mental labor;
and the more I see of that, the cooler I get. It may be entirely my own
shortcoming, but such at all events is my reaction."

There sounds here a note of depression painfully frequent in these
last years. His taste had always been conservative and exacting; he
had none of the facility some people have for hiding disagreeable
facts from themselves; his complete freedom from sentimentality,
the relentless realism of his mind, made him see the aesthetic degrada-
tion of "modernism" without any illusions. And of course his courage
as well as his clear view of things made impossible to him the servile
complaisance by which so many shelter themselves behind accepted
fashions from the bitter winds of truth. He had never been afraid to
admire composers whose stock happened to be low: Tschaikowsky,
Mendelssohn, and Haydn, for example. Nor could he accept un-
thinkingly the popular idols. He did not enjoy the sybaritism of
Debussy, Ravel, Loeffler, and the other impressionists. With that
steady gaze of his he saw the ugliness of Schönberg, the worldliness
of Strauss, the barbarism of Stravinsky. Above all he made no pretence of any interest in the smart-Aleck cynicism so unescapable in
the music that followed the war.

No wonder he felt a little lost in the hurly-burly that now surrounds us. "Is it not remarkable," he wrote me in the fall of 1929 (the "boom year" of rampant materialism) "how alone we stand in this world, musically speaking?" And, more sweepingly: "As regards the radio situation—I entirely share your pessimism. Generally speaking, if there is any pessimism to be shared, anywhere or with anybody, you may always count on me. By saying this I am saying at the same time that if it is to me you come for consolation, you have gone to the wrong fellow. No matter how rotten you may think this world is, I think it is still rottener, so there you are! . . ."

The real root of this pessimism was his tender sympathy with all human suffering and his chivalrous scorn for injustice and tyranny, which he thought increasing in the world, and which wore down his spiritual resistance. The mood of despair had been growing in him ever since the unfair settlement of the war. With the gradual development of dictatorships and especially of the brutal anti-Jewish movement his despair became deep-seated and almost voiceless. He suffered in silence and drugged himself with work, work, and more work.

His discouragement became, it seemed to me, almost morbid; and it was a grief to me that some ill-considered words in one of my books added to it. I had attributed some of the sensationalism of New York music to the Jewish influence—rather mistakenly, I now think, as the degrading tendencies were general, and not confined to any race or group. However that may be, one Sunday afternoon late in 1932, in a talk we had in my New York apartment, he made a hot counter-attack upon my argument, the chivalry of which I could not but admire as much as I regretted the partial misunderstanding on which I thought it based. Then, the next spring, came this letter:

"March 29, 1933

"I must make a confession. A week or so ago, under the impression of the distressing news from Germany, I wrote you a letter recalling to your memory the debate on anti-Semitism you and I had last fall. Just as I had completed it Mary's nice and friendly message came. I was so moved by its warmth and sympathetic understanding that I relegated my letter to a remote desk drawer. Some day, if you should be interested in its contents, it is at your disposal. The views I expressed in it remain unchanged. They are, unfortunately, views arrived at through the sad experience of many years."

Of course I asked to see the longer letter, protesting however that I was "with him heart and soul" in his detestation of all narrow nationalisms such as Hitler's, which I felt to be the enemy not only of the Jews but of all liberty. "Your letter," came back his answer, "was a welcome ray of sunshine in these dark days. Thank you from the bottom of my heart." And he enclosed what he had written me originally, of which here is the gist:

"We are witnessing the spectacle of Germany, the Germany of Goethe, Schiller, Schopenhauer—surrendering to the dark forces of Hitlerism. Why should not the America of Emerson, Lincoln, Walt Whitman, some day in the near future surrender to Ku-Klux-Klanism? The seeds have already been planted. And if such events should come to pass you, my dear Dan, I am afraid you would have to feel that in some measure at least you had contributed in paving the way for them. I should like to save you that distressing experience— hence this letter. You may resent it. But I feel that since we have been friends so many years, we can afford to be frank with each other at a serious moment like this."

A year later I sent him a statement I had published in the *New York Times* for December 6, 1934, voicing my admiration of Furt-wängler for resigning his post in Berlin, and expressing my final views in the sentence: "The Nazis are doing things which, if unchecked, will ruin all science and art." His answer reassured me by showing that the melancholy oppressing him all these years was from time to time at least lightened by his old realistic humor.

"Yes indeed, appalling things occur nowadays among the conductors—some tragic and some comical! The Berlin situation is, of course, tragic, and I am delighted that you expressed yourself as you did. The situation at X. appeals so strongly to my sense of humor! Have you any doubt as to Y. remaining in X., or returning there in a year at the latest? If you like I am willing to make a wager with you that his salary will be augmented at the time of his return, in proportion to the present publicity campaign."

VI

The summer of 1931 was the first we spent in New Canaan, and we were happy there. It was always pleasant to share happiness, as well as jokes, with Ossip. "We are delighted," I wrote him, "with our little place here, and are having the best summer for two or three years in spite of the Economic Situation, which in our family has created great havoc. You will see that the place has little cedar trees around it, and Mary proposed that we call it *Little Cedars*. We later found that the trees had a fungous pest, and might die; but I suggested that in that case we might simply amend the name to *Little or No Cedars*."

Promptly came back his answer: "It was a pleasure to get your letter and to know that you and Mary are so happily situated in your new summer home. I think the picturesque name invented by you, *Little or No Cedars*, is delicious. Clara and I had a hearty laugh over it."

Two summers later we actually coaxed him to *Little Cedars*, though only for one night. He arrived with friends by automobile in time for lunch, and as he was already having trouble with his digestion was anxious to have plenty of fruit. Before leaving the village to drive out to our place he cross-questioned my wife as to just what fruit she had on hand, and although she had three kinds decided it was not enough, and bought some more.

Immediately after lunch he told me he wanted me to drive him to the hospital at West Haven (nearly a two hours' trip) to see a friend who was ill there. I was a tyro at driving, and the thought of nearly four hours on the road as a way to spend my one afternoon with my friend did not greatly appeal to me. But there was no resisting Ossip, who always planned everything for everybody. We went, and he cheered the sick man by a great deal of banter and chaff. (The next time I met this man he had entirely recovered, and Ossip, who had been so full of gaiety that afternoon, had died.) Early the next morning, Sunday, we drove him to Katonah to catch a train.

During that hurried visit I had found time to show him a new score of mine, the *Suite after English Folk-songs*. (A composer can

At ''Little Cedars,'' New Canaan, Connecticut
From a photograph by the Author

always find time to show his scores.) By the following summer when
he had the score in hand, he wrote me: "I looked at your *Suite*, and
find it great fun. I am looking forward to performing it in Detroit."
Then, when in the last days of '34 Bruno Walter played it in New
York, Ossip telegraphed me: "Heard your *Suite* at Carnegie Hall
and was delighted with it. Am looking forward to doing it in Detroit. Affectionate greetings."

And I am glad to remember that I did not take all his interest and
affection for granted, as composers are prone to do, but wrote him
for once, as if in unconscious premonition of the approaching end of
our long friendship, a New Year's letter in which I told him:

"January 1, 1935
"I couldn't help thinking the other night, as I sat in Carnegie Hall
and listened to my *Suite*, and caught a glimpse of you in the background of Samaroff's box, that things had changed surprisingly for
me since you first played in the same hall my *Elegy* (February 6,
1909) my first large composition, and that all through those many
years you had been a steadfast and powerful friend to me and my
music."

His own performance of the *Suite* came a month or two later,
early in March, 1935; and great as was my joy in his splendid interpretation, to see him so preoccupied and strained made the occasion
a sad one too. He could never be anything but kind, and a natural
leader; but when in the rehearsal he called up to me "A charming
piece, Mr. Mason," and tapped his baton to encourage the men also
to applaud, I could not but feel something of effort in his gesture.
The only other time I saw him was less than a month later, in New
York—when, desperately ill, he played in one afternoon two con-
certos and two shorter pieces, to close the strenuous series he had
been giving with Leon Barzin's orchestra, and ended the concert
with a little speech of thanks to players and public. When he reached
Detroit he was taken from the train to a hospital. His illness was a
long one, borne with a courage inspiring to all who saw it. The end
came September 14, 1936.

What was in his mind through all those months he lay there, stricken? We cannot know what philosophy he may have been able to summon for himself, but we do know that even then he did not cease to plan for his orchestra and his public. A few days after his death one of his oldest friends, Frances McFarland, associated with him in his piano teaching in earlier years, wrote of him:

"Last spring Ossip planned every detail of his funeral. It was in accordance with his wish that the service was in Orchestra Hall—that the orchestra played the *Unfinished Symphony*. . . . Mr. Paterson [Manager of the Orchestra] said to me: 'This is the end of a golden era of music in Detroit. Ossip Gabrilowitsch built the orchestra through sheer force of genius, personality, and a devotion to music such as I have never seen in any other musician.' "

The funeral itself, with its element of stately ceremony well befitting one who like him so loved order and beauty, has been described by Herman Wise of Detroit:

"Ossip Gabrilowitsch's public funeral, in Orchestra Hall, the scene of some of the greatest triumphs of the master musician, was marked by simplicity and beauty. On the stage was the Detroit Symphony. Fifteen hundred mourners, representative of all Detroit, sat motionless. The orchestra played Schubert's *Unfinished Symphony* and the *Liebestod* from *Tristan und Isolde*.

"There were no eulogies. They were not needed. The man's personality and work were enough. They were near the heart of everyone present. They would be remembered. Throughout the services a great emotional tension could be felt. . . . At the end there was no move to leave. Nearly everyone made his way to the coffin, filing by slowly to pay last respects to one whose contribution to mankind had been of the finest."

As one meditates on this "contribution to mankind" one realizes that, as with all the greatest men, great as was what he did, even greater was what he was. A spirit of love went out from him that cannot be measured. One remembers the incident of the piano-tuner who had long tuned his pianos, and who suddenly died in California. The Mason and Hamlin Company, his employers, sending word from Boston that they wished to pay his funeral expenses, learned that

Ossip had already done so. One thinks of the New York photographer who took some pictures of him, and to whom thereafter he always had tickets sent for his New York recitals. One recalls the episode of his two brothers, Russian professional men, whom he got out of Russia during the Bolshevik horrors, and told to "rest a year" before trying to do anything. One gets a letter from Dr. James Francis Cooke of Philadelphia, editor of the *Etude,* in which he says: "I was ill for about five weeks in the hospital here, and Gabrilowitsch heard of it and made a special trip from New York to Philadelphia to spend some time with me. . . ." One reads in an article by a former pupil of his, Cecile de Horvath [1] how when she was giving a recital, in order not to frighten her by his presence he pretended a conducting engagement elsewhere, but came nevertheless to hear her, crouching behind the seats whenever she looked in his direction —and how on the eve of her return to America he gave her back all the money she had paid him for lessons, to help her get started. In the words of my brother, Henry Lowell Mason, who as president of the Mason and Hamlin Company was for years closely associated with him: "An outstanding quality . . . was his constant thought of others—never spoken of by himself, and, in instances of which I know, never revealed save by those whom he served and aided. Generosity sat at the core of his heart, his spirit was magnanimous, he loved to participate in a worthy cause. It mattered not how lowly one might be, or how far removed from his innermost thoughts, if in trouble physically or socially Ossip's great heart went out to him and such help as he could render was immediately forthcoming. . . . In all my relations with him, never a suspicion of unjust thought or action."

Of all that has been written about him since his death (for none could come in contact with him without loving him) the most clairvoyant, the most deeply understanding picture of him comes, it seems to me, as is only to be expected, from that old and close friend of his, who in so many ways, human and musical, so closely resembles him—Bruno Walter. With his permission a part of his letter may be added here.

[1] In *Music News,* Chicago, December 24, 1936.

"Amsterdam, November 11, 1936

"My dear friend:

"It was an extremely kind impulse that induced you to write to me. . . . Imagine that I had the same feeling: to write to you as to one whose heart is full of sorrow like mine by our friend's death. But I confess that I gave up to write—even to Clara I wrote only about two weeks ago—because I was afraid of using words, of seeking expression for the inexpressible. In fact still now there is a sort of spasm in my soul under the steady weight and influence of that event, and you can understand that your dear words—let me say in German what I cannot translate: *dieser einfache herzliche Erguss eines innigen Gefühls*—had a sort of calming or solving effect on me. It was beneficent for me that you let me have a part in your feelings.

"As you were good enough to compare me with our dear Ossip let me say how far above me I see and always saw him. With all his devotion to our art, full and overfull as his time, his head and his heart were of music and duties, he was every minute free and disposed for every human matter, took part in life, in world affairs, in the interests of friends and, I dare say, of every human being in eyesight, whereas I am so obsessed by music and duty that real life falls far too short (in spite my good will).

"But Ossip was unique. His humanity was as strong in him as talent and spirit—his was the purest, warmest, noblest heart that I found in my life. Most astonishing was—and a summit of love and kindness, that he, pessimist, skeptic, illusionless about man and fate, was at the same time serene, even gay, open-hearted to everybody, generous in thoughts and deeds. His humor, his liking of a good joke, his hearty laughter were the more admirable as by nature and experience he mourned about life and men in general. . . .

"It was marvelous and a comfort—even if one was far from him for a long time—to know he was there, in the distance—to feel his existence. Now he fails, the world becomes darker. The remembrance of this noble, courageous, love-filled soul, this high spirit, this great musician now has to take the place, where our friendship with him enriched, colored, warmed, illuminated our life."

CHAPTER XXI

HOLIDAYS

A GREAT institution is the sabbatical year. For one of every seven years it gives the composer a free time to stretch his mind, to catch up with himself. At Columbia it took the form of either a half year at full pay or a full year at half pay—we always chose the half year, beginning in February. No one can compose who has not some steady means of income. The would-be composer who can command a university position will find the answer to his most persistent problems in its sabbatical years; for they alone—they and the long summer vacations—make it possible for him to *be* a composer. Hence the wise composer of thoughtful tendency will accept the academic life—despite his natural irritation at the persistence with which the press will consequently call all his work "academic"—as the best available to him—and a very good one too. Many of my friends have agreed with me in this: Seth Bingham and Douglas Moore at Columbia, Edward Burlingame Hill at Harvard, David Stanley Smith at Yale, Carl Bricken at Chicago, Albert Elkus and Randall Thompson at California. What a pity César Franck could not have taught in a university instead of running about Paris in omnibuses all day long to girls' schools, with only six weeks in the summer and two hours each morning before breakfast for his own work!

Of our four sabbatical years, three were successful, only one was a failure—and that in many ways a pleasant failure: 1914, in Ardèche and Paris, gave me time to work out my first symphony; 1928, in Florence, provided me with a second; and 1935, though spent at home at *Little Cedars* because of my wife's illness, started the third —so far the last. The 1921 sabbatical was a wearisome time of illness for myself—of utter weariness and emptiness of mind brought on, ironically enough, by the intensive lecture tour in the West undertaken chiefly to finance the holiday. For about the sabbatical year, as about everything else, there is a vicious circle; and in order to accumulate reserves of money to enjoy it one is apt to squander one's even more precious reserves of health, and then be obliged to spend the long-awaited free time reaccumulating them. However, 1921 had its points.

If the American, especially the Yankee like myself, wishes to savor to the full the differences between the Italian temperament and his own, he should land at a port in south Italy, preferably Naples. This is what we did about the middle of March. As I have said in my sketch *Three Restaurants*, written at Amalfi a fortnight later, on Easter Sunday: [1] "The South Italian is notoriously emotional and dramatic. . . . A lira too little, a lira less than can be extracted by enacting battle, murder, and sudden death, is the signal for a brainstorm that breaks into genial sunshine on the appearance of the coveted pennies."

The very first Neapolitan we came in contact with, our *facchino* at the pier, proved to have very little English, a good deal of ambition, and altogether too much temperament. Ambition led him to pick up as one load our three bags, hat-box (in which another bag had been packed) and steamer trunk (with a good many books in it.) After he had fallen flat, as might have been foreseen, cutting his knee and—what from his point of view was far worse—his trousers, lack of English obliged him to call to his aid one of his friends as interpreter. Superfluity of temperament, in which his friend if anything excelled him, expressed itself for all bystanders in tears of agony, cries of rage, and indignant rejection of my offer of first ten, then fifteen, finally twenty-five lire. By this time we were sitting in

[1] In *The Dilemma of American Music*.

stiff embarrassment in a shaky one-seated open carriage, a sort of victoria, surrounded by a crowd fascinated with our altercation. We sat there, first surprised, then angry, then mute. He rejected our twenty-five lire with passionate scorn, his friend shouting at us: "He break pants; he want ten American dollar." When my better half (at least at tipping) fearing I was about to weaken, counselled courage in my ear, he even got enough English himself to explode with surprising clearness: "You shut up!" Almost at the same moment a gendarme, appearing from nowhere, reduced the poor fellow to snatching my twenty-five lire and making off.

I turned my attention to *Baedeker*, while our droschky, or whatever it was, pulled by a skinny horse, wavered off shakily over the cobblestones. At once I discovered that the lamp at my left hand was insecure; I had to grasp it firmly to keep it from rattling. My right hand held the *Baedeker*, and as there remained no hand to shift with from distance to reading glasses I was obliged to keep it stretched at full arm's length in front of me. Thus strangely posed we crawled through the streets until we found a *pension* recommended by *Baedeker*. What recommended it even more was a *major domo* on the front steps who volunteered to "discuss" my fare with the driver. They discussed it in two short but lively minutes of grand opera; the driver, threatened with death and almost weeping with disappointment, accepted five or ten *centesimi* less than I should have given him; and we, reflecting with thankful hearts that we could tip the *major domo* later, mounted to our room to recover. To our further experiences in Naples, Pompeii, and Amalfi, in part related in *Three Restaurants*, I will add here only one episode of an ill-fated trip we made in a heavy rain-storm to Salerno, in the hope of seeing the temples at Paestum. To Paestum we never got, the weather proving too much for us; but in Salerno we had one of those dream-like, mysterious adventures that make so much of the puzzle of travelling while they happen, and so much of the charm of it as one recalls them afterwards.

At that off-season for Salerno, only two restaurants were open—caves they seem in retrospect, quarried from the living rock. Choosing one at random, we were presented with a menu written in an illegible hand, obscured by flourishes, in pale violet ink. Realizing at once how idle would be any attempt at choice on our part, we pointed fatalistically to the heading signifying "Fish", the one legible word in sight, and waited. With gestures of gladness and courtesy, a raw fish was presently brought on a plate and proudly exhibited to us, apparently for our approval. This we gave, in vigorous nods and our prettiest "*Si, si's,*" and again waited. . . . The story has no dénouement. Nothing happened. The fish never appeared again, cooked or uncooked. What we lunched upon I now forget; at least it was not fish. We realized once more, as all travellers have to realize every day, the distance between literature and life.

II

Toward the end of March we went on to Rome, and had much pleasure in meeting the rising young Italian composers, Malipiero and Casella. These two good comrades were strikingly different in type: Casella a "cerebral", long and sallow, witty, rather disrespectful towards everything, with his tongue constantly in his cheek, yet admirably clever, informed about all the latest "movements", and so skilful a caricaturist in his pieces *a la manière de* Wagner, Brahms, Fauré, Debussy, d'Indy, that I could not help wondering whether he ever wrote *a la manière de Casella;* Malipiero stocky, ruddy, of sanguine temperament, his hair dark with one grey lock thrown carelessly back from a strong brow, his eyes restlessly roving or suddenly focussing in a penetrating glance, his utterance rapid and a little impeded with a sort of lisp—a forthright and cordial nature, an impetuous composer and a lively companion.

He took us one day, in another of those funny little open carriages like our Neapolitan droschky, to visit Casella in his apartment in the Via Quirina Visconti, near the Tiber. On his walls were several futuristic portraits, including one of himself in bilious yellows and greens, which Malipiero, a spirited mimic, later reproduced to the life with no more elaborate apparatus than a sudden twist of the jaw and droop of the eye-lids. When Malipiero played us, that first day, his fine setting of the *Canticle of St. Francis,* but could not reach all the notes, I admired the skill with which Casella added whatever was necessary, picking out the needed note with something of the surprising suddenness with which a hen picks up a grain of corn. His mental alertness made him a skillful score-reader, and showed itself in his lively curiosity about all new movements, even to the point of faddism. His latest fad just then was American "ragtime", the equivalent of contemporary jazz. He had included in some pieces for string quartet a *Valse ridicule* and a *Fox-trott* [*sic*]. He told me he felt European music was decadent, but might be resuscitated by— of all things—American ragtime! Malipiero, less brilliant, was better balanced. His view was that fox trot and ragtime represent the worst elements in modern life.

He invited us to go on with him to tea, and as his friend was going to a concert the two took a carriage with us, facing us on the absurd little seat below the driver's back, and keeping up a constant badinage with him over their shoulders, rallying him on his unfamiliarity with Rome. Conspicuously as the central quality of both men was animation, it was curious to see how cerebral was Casella's, how much more social and impulsive Malipiero's. Indeed, whatever reservations I retained about Malipiero's music, the more we saw of him the more I found him as a man delightfully frank and cordial.

Journal: "April 18. Malipiero came to lunch, and was charming. He makes many little jokes, most of which we unfortunately miss, he speaks French so fast and a little indistinctly. When we took coffee, for example, he said: "I cannot take coffee at night, it kills me (*c'est la mort*); but if I take wine at lunch it makes me sleepy, then I must take coffee to wake me up!" At the antiquity shop in the afternoon, in a little lane off the Via Sistina, when my wife was to take our photograph, he suggested we be shooting each other with pistols, and so it was arranged. Under his friendly guidance we bought an *Empire* clock, "*très pure comme style*", for two hundred lire.

"He told us a story of a man who wanted to divide his property between his three sons, one half to one, one third to the second, one ninth to the third. His property consisted of seventeen camels (*chameaux*). How should he do it?

"Answer. A friend lent him a camel. One half of 18 equals 9
One third of 18 equals 6
One ninth of 18 equals 2

Total   17.

—and then the friend took back his camel!"

"April 19. Malipiero came in for fifteen minutes after lunch to give me the letters of introduction. . . . It is really extraordinary what pains he has taken to help us in every way, even adding a postscript to his letter to Prunières to ask him to help us find a clock-maker in Paris to regulate the clock."

With Casella I felt decidedly less at ease, but I admired the incisiveness of his mind. In two *Impressions of Italian Music* which I sent home to the *Freeman*,[1] I drew attention to an analogy that had deeply impressed me, between the situation occupied in the Italy of popular legend by serious composers like himself and Malipiero in Rome, and Pizzetti and Castelnuovo in Florence, and that occupied in the America of popular legend—the America of ragtime and jazz —by the serious composers I knew at home. He had described in a lecture in Paris the "persuasion that reigns in most foreign countries that Italy is the land of 'melody', of *bel canto*, of the romances of composers like Tosti, of Neapolitan tarentellas and Venetian serenades." Just so, I reminded my readers, the thoughtless among us always reserve the label "American" for the feverish and futile inanities of Broadway.

What then would he consider, I wondered, the real Italy. After he had played me some of his own music I remarked as a feeler that it seemed to me to have more in common with Ravel than with Debussy, to which he replied: "We Italians have never been impressionistic. We instinctively demand of our art clearness and force." This helped me to understand the more extended statement in his lecture: "The permanent characteristics of the Italian mind are: grandeur, severity, robustness, conciseness, sobriety, simplicity of lines, plastic plenitude and architectural equilibrium, vivacity, audacity, and the perpetual search for novelty."

[1] Published June 29 and August 10, 1921.

All this was admirable. I realized the width of its sweep only after meeting in Florence the charmingly spontaneous, if rather too facile, Castelnuovo-Tedesco, and his master whom he idolized, possibly the most deeply musical of them all, incongruously tinged as even his chamber music is with operatic elements—Ildebrando Pizzetti. Pizzetti, small and dark, unassuming, so concentrated on his work as to seem almost unaware of personalities, was the very type of the genuine artist. (As for Respighi, destined to make the most resounding name of any of them in America, he seemed and still seems to me merely a man with a prodigious orchestral technique and essentially nothing to say.)

I could not but perceive sadly the irony of Casella's finding in America, however he might look below the frothy surface of his native Italy, nothing but "fox-trots." He seemed, in his sophisticated way, to penetrate little further into the realities of my own country than a sign I saw in Rapallo:

ENGLISH SPOCKEN

JCE CREAM

NIGER (*sic*) JAZZ MUSICK

"Americanism"—I ended my *Freeman* articles by insisting—"Americanism escapes the ragtimer as Italianism eludes the manufacturer of barcarolles. But a temperament alert, nervous, and humorous, such as our Western climate breeds, will write music differing significantly, especially by its rhythmic verve, from that of a more phlegmatic, languid, philosophical, or passionate race, while sharing with it a largeness, a universality of appeal, a wide beauty, forever denied to the chauvinists of all countries."

III

Our next stay abroad was not a sabbatical year but just a summer trip in 1925; and we landed not at Naples but at Plymouth. These contrasts of ports never ceased to amuse us. In Plymouth there were no *facchini*, no temperamental cab drivers or composers, no finocchio, and no vermouth. Yet we adopted the coloration of the place easily enough: so that when the waitress at the hotel on the Hoe asked me the first morning what I would have for breakfast I answered almost without thinking, certainly without reflecting to what later twitting from my wife I was exposing myself: "A bit of fish." (It turned out to be finnan haddie.) The musicians we met were of equally uncompromising English breed: Edward J. Dent, Percy Scholes, Ernest Newman among the critics, Harold Samuel the Bach player, and Ralph Vaughan Williams, whom I regarded as one of the greatest composers of my time, and who was certainly as striking a contrast with Malipiero or Casella as Plymouth with Naples, or finnan haddie with finocchio.

I had first met this shy, friendly, shaggy Englishman, with his loose clothes, his clipped, half-swallowed speech, and his inseparable pipe, at a lunch given us by Arthur Whiting at the Century Club in May, 1922. He had come over from England on commission from Carl Stoekel, then giving annual choral festivals at Norfolk, Connecticut, to produce his new *Pastoral Symphony*. I liked the frank way he told us at once that he and his wife—a delightful woman almost helpless with arthritis—had come over second class, since as an impecunious composer he had had to choose between coming first class alone, or second with her. He asked Arthur about the Philharmonic Orchestra, whence the players for his symphony were to be drawn. Arthur, replying that it was a good orchestra but under a poor conductor—Stransky—added after a pensive moment: "However, they're trying to *float him off* now, by getting in other conductors. That's the only way he can be detached." Vaughan Williams told us about George Butterworth, one of the most genuine of English composers, killed in the war, of whom I was to hear more from Edward J. Dent, who later introduced me to the beautiful settings made by him of poems from Housman's *A Shropshire Lad*. Vaughan Williams, who has himself set Housman with incomparable insight, praised Butterworth's laconic economy of style, his noble reticence (a kind of English under-statement which is of course a supreme distinction of his own *Pastoral Symphony*, one of the most unsensational of the works of a sensational age.) A. W.:

"Yes, the composer's ambition should be to make one note grow where two grew before."

As we were spending that summer of 1922 in Norfolk, where my wife had inherited a small house, I saw quite a bit of Vaughan Williams. He put on no airs, was most companionable. Indeed we were amused at the incongruity between his informal English way of roaming about the roads in the rain with a pipe and a cushion, and the precision of the rather conventional Stoeckel household where he and his wife were visiting. When Gertrude Watson motored over from Pittsfield we all three called, and found both the Stoeckels and their English guests evidently rather exhausted with the effort of mutual adjustment. All parties jumped (though very decorously) at Gertrude's suggestion that the guests become *her* guests for the week end.

We set out to drive to Pittsfield (for we also were invited to the spacious Onota Farm). Vaughan Williams, suffering the inevitable reaction from the success of his symphony, asked for a front seat by the chauffeur, and for about half the way took a covert nap. But after tea he reawakened, joined me in a walk, and gave me those ideas of his on setting English texts to music which I have recorded in *The Dilemma of American Music (A Note on English Rhythms,)* together with some stimulating comments on how one gets ideas.[1] I could not enough admire his freedom from affectations. Journal: "June 9, 1922. He thinks a composer may use anything to start his imagination. The trumpet obligato in the second movement of his *Pastoral Symphony* was suggested by his hearing soldiers practicing bugle in a field, when he was serving in the army. The voice feature in the finale was from a piece in a ballet, which he discarded, salvaging a few ideas—also the heavy rhythm in the scherzo, which accompanied some lumbering movement. . . . That was what Bach did with his co-called realism, which Schweitzer grotesquely exaggerates. V. W. said: "You have to work to get your ideas started, just as one cranks a cold automobile. Once they are started they will generate their own interest."

Vaughan Williams was thus in short that singularly satisfying

[1] See *Workmanship,* in *Artistic Ideals.*

thing to encounter, a man whose sincerity makes him all of a piece with his work. It required the English straightforwardness, direct-ness, freedom from pretence, to write anything so simple as that thrilling solo-voice passage with which his *Pastoral Symphony* ends. And Edward J. Dent told me that when that symphony was played at the Prague Festival of the International Society of Contemporary Composers, of which Dent was president, its composer did not want to go onto the stage, and Dent had to take him by the shoulders "and push him on before the applause stopped"—after which he was re-called ten times.

Besides the stimulus of such a personality he gave me a good deal of light on my own problems and position. "You are now," he told me, "in about the same stage of musical progress in America that we were in England a generation ago. You and your friends are doing the pioneer work that Parry and Stanford did with us. In another thirty years you will have the conscious impulse to emancipate your-selves from foreign influences that we have now." This was corrob-orated by H. C. Colles the following season, when he visited New York as guest music critic of the *Times*. "Your public," he said to me, "does not adequately support your composers. Our men of the Parry-Stanford generation had no less talent than the present one, the one of Vaughan Williams; the difference was that the public was not interested in their work. That is now your condition here. But if your composers keep on what you call 'delivering the goods' it will pass, as it has passed in England."

IV

The real business of the 1925 summer was a motor tour with our friends Susan Rumsey and Gertrude Watson. Mrs. Rumsey pro-vided her splendid long Pierce Arrow (almost too long for safety in some of those mountain roads of the Gorges du Tarne, as we shall see presently) and Gertrude contributed our chauffeur and friend Silvio, of her Italian household at Onota Farm. Silvio, though Italian by birth and Catholic by religion, was a complete American in prac-tical horse sense and a sort of sardonic humor. It was often my privi-

Touring in France: Silvio driving

lege to sit with him on the front seat and decipher our itinerary from typewritten notes supplied us by the firm of Michelin—notes in which the French terms, often to me incomprehensible, were always fascinating.

On the fourth day out from Paris we lunched at Les Eyzies, where are the caverns with the famous wall-paintings made by ancient man. Silvio's orthodox beliefs as to the age of the world were rather strained by the aeons described in the guidebook—it said that the wall-paintings were made a hundred thousand years ago. When our woman guide said twelve thousand, Silvio's scorn came to the surface, and he muttered into his handsome flowing moustache: "Well, she's only cut it down eighty-eight thousand years." To reach the paintings we had to descend what seemed like miles, in a darkness punctuated only by infrequent dim electric bulbs and the sounds of dripping water, now climbing over a jutting rock, now descending into some deeper gully. After about half an hour of this snail-like burrowing, Silvio turned to me with: "Well, we're getting pretty close to the ground." He combined with the dryness of humor which seemed somehow American a native vividness of speech. He told me that a racer once drove him at a hundred and fifteen miles an hour, and remarked: "It makes the telephone poles look like a picket fence."

Where his sturdy manliness laid us under unforgettable obligation was in the Gorges du Tarne a few days later, when, trying to avoid the dizzy hair-pin curves of the Michelin itinerary by taking a short cut recommended by a man in our hotel, we jumped from the frying pan into the fire.

Journal: "Hotel du Midi et de la Poste, Nîmes, July 7. We started over C. G. 19 (Michelin). Soon we got into an even worse place than that of yesterday—far worse. The road was the narrowest, roughest thing, never made for a heavy long car like ours, and going precariously along a gorge, with *tournants* that made your heart come into your mouth. Often there was no wall, and what was worse the road itself seemed none too solid, with places where two or three feet of it had fallen, and the great chasms yawned below.

"We grew deadly silent, and each minute seemed an hour. As

each new turn appeared, often cut out of jagged rock on the inner side, we did not know whether we could round it. Once Silvio had to shift and back a little, suspended as we were between the rocks and the cliff. Twice we scraped the rocks on the inside. Once Sue got out and walked ahead to see if we could go any farther; but in any case it was impossible to turn round, and even Silvio could not have backed down that horrid place.

"We finally reached Cabrillac more dead than alive, and learned from a peasant that the road was '*plus large*' from then on. But it was none too good, and at Col Salides, fifteen hundred meters high, we found ourselves on a sheer mountain edge, with a long descent of similar turns ahead of us—though nothing like the first for terror. It was then 11:10, and those wretches had told us we could reach Nimes for lunch.

"You never saw a happier party than we were when we at last struck Route Nationale 107, a real highway with a real wall. The country grew homely and intimate as we skirted the river Gardon with its green depths and brown shallows, until we stopped at St. Jean-du-Gard for lunch. Nimes at 4, in an intensely hot Midi afternoon."

We later went on through the French and Italian Rivieras, and of course had to spend a few days in Venice, which I heartily disliked.

"July 24. Venice was true to form on our last night there. Serenades on and off all the evening; automobile horn on launch in our canal; siren blasts at 12:30. Much splashing of waves, a waltz by a band, and a harmonica in the offing. And always the futile ravings of gondoliers at the tops of their voices. At 5:50 this morning peals of wedding bells, long continued at double quick. Also snow shovelling, carpet beating, and furniture moving. Whistles for good measure."

Three days later, at Brixen, we lunched, by pure chance, in the same hotel as a motor party of Mrs. Coolidge's, including Frank Bridge and that inveterate *farceur*, mimic, and good fellow, Harold Samuel. He got us aside for a moment to confide his troubles. He had lost a bag, early in the trip, containing all his shirts and his shaving materials. The rest of the trip, according to him, had been one feverish series of telegrams back to the last stop, asking them to forward the ill-fated bag. They always forwarded it, but Mrs. Coolidge, whose methodical efficiency is equalled only by her restlessness, always started before it arrived. If we could trust Samuel, he had bought a shirt at nearly every stop and spent a fortune on shaves.

Samuel was as inimitable an anecdotist as he was a Bach player—his rich humanity filled both activities to the brim. He told us, for example, of a hurried trip he once made from London to Edinburgh to discuss an important problem in their Bach edition with his friend Donald F. Tovey, that fascinating scholar and endlessly discursive talker. The first two hours of his three-hour stay, he declared, were filled with conversation, interesting enough in itself, about—not Bach himself, but some of his minor predecessors, known only to Tovey and the musicologists. As the clock inexorably moved on towards train-time, Samuel at last managed to interpolate: "But now, what about our Bach problem?" To which the response of the imperturbable Tovey was to hold up his hand and murmur: "Don't digress, Harold, don't digress."

We finished our motor trip late in August, but we have often enjoyed it over again in retrospect, and not least the quaintness of the French terminology that makes the commonest objects seem more distinguished, more noble, above all more logical in France than they do at home. Real estate agents are more or less the same the world over, I suppose, and certainly we had heard enough nonsense from them in our own country and tongue. But somehow the climax seemed capped when in a desolate field half weeds and half puddles we read the poetic sign: *"Ici se crée Azurville."* On the train from Dijon to Paris I found this

AVIS

of which I could not sufficiently admire the dignity and the logic:

"Il arrive très fréquemment que des agents travaillant sur la ligne sont blessés par des objets solides, des bouteilles vides en particulier, lancés par les portières et dont le choc est d'autant plus violent que la vitesse du train est plus grande.

"Messieurs les Voyageurs sont instamment priés de s'abstenir de cette pratique."

The thought of these "agents"—not mere hands, oh, far from it —working on the line, often in blissful unconsciousness, we may suppose, of danger, being wounded by "solid objects" ("empty bottles in particular") not merely thrown or tossed but "launched" from the train, moved me for one to the heart. I found not only my heart but my mind stirred by the thought so elegantly added that "the shock is the more violent as the speed of the train is greater." Even my dignity as, not a mere traveller but one of *"Messieurs les Voyageurs"*, did not disincline me to listen to this prayer, and henceforward "abstain from the practice" of throwing empty bottles.

TRIOLET

DON'T THROW BOTTLES

You might do manslaughter
If on a *Rapide*.
—A bottle of wine, or even of water—
You might do manslaughter
You just hadn't oughter.
Even freights get up speed.
You might do manslaughter
If on a *Rapide*.

Thus was it gradually borne in upon me that nothing is the same in France as in America: not only empty bottles but the very sun and moon. By the end of our summer in England, France, Italy, and German-speaking Switzerland, I came to the conclusion that the Latin nations have a matchless natural flair for nobility in names, while we "Nordics" are slovenly in language, and will tie an epithet to an object as carelessly as if it were a baggage tag.[1]

Already in Paris, before starting, while waiting one day for a bus at the Palais-Royal, I had found the time-table (pasted with French meticulousness inside a sort of bird-cage on a lamp post) stating that

---

[1] A portion of what here follows is reprinted, by permission, from the sketch entitled *A Noble Language*, originally contributed to *Harper's Monthly Magazine* for July, 1928.

the busses ran every so often—every ten minutes I believe—during
certain parts of the day, but oftener, perhaps every five, during the
"*heures d' affluence*". I rubbed my eyes. Why, of course, it must
mean "rush hours". But what an august, what a Roman, what an imperial way of saying it! On Broadway, the scrambling street of a
mushroom civilization, there may be rush hours; by the Palais-Royal
there are hours of affluence. I made a mental note of "*affluence*",
resolved to bag other specimens of it in my further travels.

I had to wait until Interlaken. There I found in my tri-lingual
Kur-Karte this note on the *Heimwehfluh-Funiculaire*: "*Départs
toutes les 5 a 10 minutes selon l'affluence.*" This struck me as neat
if not noble, and the German version as somewhat clumsy in comparison: "*Abfahrten alle 5–10 Minuten je nach Frequenz.*" "*Je nach
Frequenz*" was adequate enough, but had a barbarous sound after
"*selon l'affluence.*" With some misgivings I turned to see what my
native tongue would make of it. "Trains leave every 5–10 minutes
if required." About that "if required", tacked on as if by an afterthought, there was a crudely utilitarian air, an effect of makeshift
and dull prose, that filled me with envy for those who by natural
right travel in French. It seemed a fortune almost superhuman.
Mortals may have things "if required"; angels alone must be always
served "*selon l'affluence*".

It is even more absorbing then, to travel in French than to travel
in France; the one is indeed the natural complement and consum-
mation of the other; and the happy motorist may do both with the
kind aid of Monsieur Michelin. Thus we had got no further than
Fontainebleau before my imagination was so obsessed with the
problem of what PN could possibly mean (PN, just like that, capitals without even periods after them) that I had to ask the hotel
proprietor before I could eat my lunch. PN, it seems, is *Passage à
niveau*. Now not only is *niveau* a word beautiful in itself, and interesting both in its likeness and its unlikeness to its Italian equivalent, which I was later to encounter in "*Passagio a livello*", but there
is something distinguished about the very conception "*Passage on
the level*", not lost even in English, which "Grade crossing" hopelessly lacks. A grade crossing is a chore, performed grudgingly, with

the sole aim of getting to the other side alive. A *Passage à niveau* is a privilege, an episode, an adventure. And then, if you are travelling *à la Michelin*, when you get tired of one level you can get variety by going underneath in the PI, or *Passage inférieur*, or overhead in the PS, or *Passage supérieur*, while all you can do in English is to scramble across somehow.

But wait—was it perhaps just the other way? Was I superior to the railroad, or was the railroad superior to me? I must candidly confess I never felt quite sure which; and in general I think it may be reluctantly admitted, even by those who admire French rationality as I do, that language can easily become rational in a degree baffling to mere human intelligence. A good deal of the nobility of French terminology is due to the abstract philosophic account it gives, highly flattering to our *amour propre*, of acts we really perform in a more or less hit-or-miss way. In real life we are liable, if we patronize public conveyances, to sit in a draught and get a stiff neck. It is reassuring to know that in Paris this cannot happen, since in the Paris busses draughts do not exist, but at worst "currents of air". And even these we need hardly fear where the windows, we read, are "always immobilized on one complete side of the conveyance"—not merely closed, be it noted, but *immobilisées*, which is a thing vastly more satisfactory, and indescribably more French. In real life we either take the trolley car where we know it always stops, or else run after it and wave, in the hope that it will pick us up. It therefore solaces our sense of dignity to read on a neat red sign: "*Arrêt obligatoire*", or on a green one: "*Arrêt facultatif*". In real life we try to drive the wrong way through a one-way street, and get reprimanded by the traffic policeman. A sign such as "*Sens unique*" seems with its universality of expression to lift us into a better world.

It is odd what chameleons words are, how they take on the colors of their associates, and how the commonest object, throw but an unwonted light of association upon it, will gleam with novel splendor, like an oily mud-puddle reflecting sunset. In the later stages of our trip that summer, reëntering France from German-speaking Switzerland, we had this borne in upon us in a *crescendo*. At Fribourg, where two thirds of the people speak French, I noticed in my hotel room an *"Avis concernant les pourboires"*, the opening sentence of which suggested with a delicacy of innuendo not lost even in English: "Remunerations to the servants are not included in the bill". (*"Les rémunérations au personnel du service ne sont pas comprises"*—note the gender of *"comprises"*—*"dans le montant de la note"*. I was struck by the tactfulness of *rémunérations*. There is a genial conviviality about even a *pourboire*, but no doubt one might have a slight sense of inferiority in accepting one. But *rémunération!* Why, the word positively coddles one's self-esteem. Even without that *"comprises"* I should have known it must be feminine by the gentleness of its dealing. Then I glanced at the English heading: "Notice with regard to tips". Tips, indeed: the word was a blow in the face! Justly, no doubt, are the French considered the politest of peoples.

At Auxerre I observed the sign:

BOUCHERIE CHEVALLINE

with a modest rider, *"Saucissons d'ânes et mulets"*.

Avallon was still more elegant. Avallon might accept the diet of Auxerre but was not so easily to be satisfied in the more important matter of vocabulary; Auxerre might eat its horses in French if it pleased; Avallon preferred something more classic, and proudly wrote:

BOUCHERIE HYPOPHAGIQUE

Thus did the French teach me that anything worth saying at all can be said nobly, not to speak of some things that might perhaps better remain unsaid. No man, I suppose, likes to receive a summons to the dentist's. To make such a summons attractive might justly be considered a supreme test of literary skill. In our country we do not make much of a hand of it, with our curt "Mr. Jones has an appointment with Dr. Smith for Friday at 5:30." But while I was in Paris I had occasion to ask an appointment from a dentist; and his reply has ever since been treasured among my most precious possessions. It is engraved and on large paper, like a *lettre de décès* or *de mariage*, and looking at a distance hardly less voluminous.

With a slight change of names it is conceived in terms which may be thus translated:

"Dr. Durand addresses his salutations to Mr. Jones, and has the honor to inform him that he will hold himself at his disposition on Friday, July 1st, at 5:30 o'clock."

Who would not willingly exchange a tooth or two for the privilege of receiving so elegant a missive?

CHAPTER XXII

A VILLA IN FLORENCE

WHERE should we spend our 1928 sabbatical year? The answer to a question for us so serious came in a curiously roundabout and casual way. During the summer of 1926 I had completed a choral cycle, *Songs of the Countryside*, on texts from A. E. Housman's *Last Poems*, and had composed also, in lighter vein for women's voices, *Mothers and Children*, to a text by the American poet Orrick Johns. At about the same time I had set another poem of his, *The Tree Toad*. These texts had appealed to me by their blend of sentiment and humor.

> A tiny bell the tree-toad has:
> I wonder if he knows
> The charm it is to hear him
> Ringing as he goes.

Thus commenced one of them; and the other, which some of the more staid women's clubs found too outspoken for them and declined to sing—much to my surprise—ended with the couplet:

> A man may be ninety with a very long beard
> And not be any better than his mother feared.

On this occasion, when I asked John Powell impulsively if he did

349

not like the song, he agreed with the women's clubs—also to my
surprise, and for once cordially disapproved of my music. "I do
not," he answered. "In the first place the poem makes me sick. . . .
And then I don't like those repeated notes a la Puccini." On the
other hand Randall Thompson, one of the most musical of the
younger men, was enthusiastic over what he called the subtlety of
my setting of a text in which he found a combination of Gogol and
Gilbert! Whoever was right, the main point is that Orrick Johns,
then living in Florence, pleased at my having picked his poem out
of an anthology without ever having met or heard of its author,
urged us to spend our sabbatical year in Italy, even taking the
trouble to find us a "*villino*" in Fiesole. So to Italy we went, although, as will appear presently, we missed the *villino*.

II

The incomparable *Last Poems* of Housman had appeared in 1922,
and I had begun to set some of them in the Spring of '23. I began
with *Fancy's Knell,* with its delightful suggestion of a recurring
refrain for flute:

> When lads were home from labor
> At Abdon under Clee,
> A man would call his neighbor
> And both would send for me.
> And where the light in lances
> Across the mead was laid
> There to the dances
> I fetched my flute and played.

In those years the natural fascination of English folk-music to
an American of Anglo-saxon inheritance like mine was rising ever
more and more out of my instinctive feeling into my conscious
mind, and I was therefore happy in this chance to invent not only
the flute refrain but the whole music somewhat in the vein of
English folk-song. Increasingly conscious as I was also becoming
of the psychology of composing, and of how necessary and yet

how hard it was to secure unity either in a complete cycle such as I was now planning or even in a single song, I was stimulated by that problem to work with enthusiasm. I had long realized in a general way that the supreme need in any composition was the summing up and completion in its ending of all that went before, that the ending was thus the crucial point, and that consequently it was in practice often wise to determine the end before the beginning and middle, and to work backwards. Such a procedure was almost necessitated by this text with its magnificent tragic peroration:

> The lofty shade advances,
> I fetch my flute and play:
> Come, lads, and learn the dances
> And praise the tune today.
> Tomorrow, more's the pity,
> Away we both must hie,
> To air the ditty,
> And to earth I.

Evidently the right effect would be secured only if this could be set to a broad, deliberate, sombre melody, which nevertheless should be recognizably only a variant of the tune already heard in the evening dance on the mead "at Abdon under Clee." The two melodies would then express, as they should, different yet related moods of the same person: the first gay, with an undertone of melancholy, the second noble in its full consciousness of tragic fate. "Started precising," says my journal for April 8, 1923, *Fancy's Knell*, and found that it will work out. I had already determined the general shape of the melody, and the flute refrain. I began working at the last stanza. Then I went back to the first, and decided on its general form."

In setting the Orrick Johns text later I adopted the same procedure. Journal: "July 25, 1926. The developmental broadening at the end of *Mothers and Children* has begun to come clear this morning, and I am glad I left the first stanza sufficiently vague so that I can shape this one and then go back. That is always the way in composition. First one gets the germ. Second, one works out the *end* (or, in a large composition, one works out all possibilities). Third, one goes back and works out the earlier parts. The beginning must be treated largely as preparation for the end, the most important part; and therefore one can treat it intelligently only when one knows exactly what is to be prepared for."

When I had got far enough with *Fancy's Knell* to see that it would work out, and had also sketched what eventually proved to be the last song in the cycle, *In Valleys Green and Still* (though the crab-like forwards-and-backwards nature of the composing process is exemplified in the fact that I did not then know it would be the last!), I wrote to Housman for permission to use his texts. His answer, which did not reach me until the middle of May, fired a bomb-shell into my carefully organized unity:

> "Trinity College, Cambridge, England
>   "3 May, 1923
>
> "Dear Sir:
> "You have my permission to publish your settings of poems from my last volume, provided that they are settings of entire poems and not of portions.
> "I do not exact a share of your royalties nor any other fee.
> "I am Yours very truly,
>
>   "A. E. HOUSMAN."

"Provided that they are settings of entire poems": and I in the six weeks I had had to meditate on *Fancy's Knell* had decided to omit a stanza that seemed to me to contain too many British names of slight interest to American audiences:

> Wenlock Edge was umbered,
> And bright was Abdon Burf,
> And warm between them slumbered
> The smooth green miles of turf.

But obviously the condition set by Housman was an entirely proper one; and what did a few more days' work, required for still one more revision, matter in the long run?

I was reminded of another time I had sunk a good deal of inconspicuous work in a song—work that no one but I knew was there. When Werrenrath was first planning to do *Russians* he was troubled by the necessity of singing a certain high E very soft, just before the end of the fourth song, *A Boy*. "Perhaps I can do it and perhaps I can't," he said. "It's an uncomfortable feeling. Be a good feller, and put the song down half a tone for me." At that time the music was only in sketch, not in full score, and I could with only a day or two of work transform my nice B major Boy into a sort of B flat major foundling that never seemed to my jealous parental ear the real thing. But Werrenrath felt sure of his E flat. . . . One day at the end of the season, after the songs had made their triumphal progress from Detroit through a number of other cities, we were chatting desultorily about them. "My only regret," said I, "is that my Boy is no longer a B major Boy, as he was born. In B flat he is dull. But you had to have your E flat, didn't you?" "Why, not at all," answered Werrenrath. "Now that I know my way about I can manage that high note. Put the song back if you like." "Put the song back"! Rewrite the entire score, necessarily changing its conception where certain instruments are not so happy in one key as in the other! How maddeningly casual is the race of singers! But I could not resist—though perhaps I was foolish to do it—spending the weeks and the dollars needed to reinstate my Boy in his native B major.

The problem of unity in the Housman cycle as a whole, as well as in the separate songs, gave me a good deal to think about. What at last I worked out was a correspondence between the second and the last song that I believe links the whole work together. The subject of the cycle is the struggle between love and war, the pitting of the destructive forces of war, in the end vainly, against the creative power of love. The second song, *The Deserter*, is a duet in which the man, awakening in the arms of his sweetheart, hears his regiment passing in the distance, and at last forsakes her to rejoin it.

Hark, I heard the bugle crying,
And where am I?
My friends are up and dressed and dying,
And I will dress and die.

The march to which that cry is set must recur in the last song, but
in an entirely new context. Here all is peace:

In valleys green and still
Where lovers wander maying
They hear from over hill
A music playing.

Distant, unreal, ghostly must now be the march tune that in the
tragic dialogue was so pitiless, so charged with fate. The regiment
then so insistent is now become only a memory, a rumor:

Behind the drum and fife
Past hawthorn-wood and hollow,
Through earth and out of life
The soldiers follow.

I have dwelt at some length on these problems we have to solve
in order to secure unity, because to my mind it is this effect of
unity that is the culmination and final appeal of all deeply moving
music. No doubt there have always been certain sophisticates who
have taken, I cannot but feel largely as a pose, the opposite view
that music should have no form, no development, no themes even:
that it should be nothing but fleeting impressions and momentary
effects. I for my part cannot see how without definite themes, clearly
developed, presented throughout a work in a significant variety
finally summed up in a salient unity, the listener can possibly join
the composer in that supreme experience which is a genuine work
of art.

III

Our cablegram in response to Orrick Johns's letter unfortunately
reached him too late to secure for us the promised *villino;* and when

we ourselves arrived in Florence we had to spend our days hunting villas or apartments and our nights serenaded by mosquitoes and barking dogs. To escape these pests we took temporary quarters at the Villa Bencista, a *pension* half way up the hills toward Fiesole, delightfully fresh and quiet, but nearly an hour from Florence by a squeaky tram with ungreased wheels, much joggling, and many long waits. A compensation for riding in so much discomfort was a familiar view of an as yet unregimented Italian populace, hardly less melodramatic in temperament under their more staid exterior than our Neapolitan friends. The passengers, most of whom seemed to live largely on garlic, paid no slightest attention to the sign not to talk to the motorman; and he in return we have seen at a stop in the route regale them with struttings, orations, and even on one occasion a recitative, worthy of grand opera.

As the securing and occupying of a villa was evidently going to prove a long business, I took a room to write in, and drafted a paper, *Creative Leisure* (later published in the volume *The Dilemma of American Music*), summing up some of the results of my reading and thinking about the psychology of composing, to which I shall return presently.

We liked the Villa Bencista. "I've never known," I wrote in my journal, "a lovelier place for quiet than this: no dogs, no pianos, no victrolas, no motor horns. It is delicious! There was a full moon again last evening, and at dawn there is a little cock near by who crows funnily.

"Our chambermaid is amusing. Though she is old and her face seamed and wrinkled you can see that she must have been pretty once, and she is still full of mischief and high spirits. She teaches us phrases of Italian, such as '*Permesso*' and '*Avanti*'. Then she tries to say words in English, only to break off, exclaiming: "*Difficile parlare Inglese*'. She breaks into peals of laughter over our difficulties of communication. Then we all become sober again, and end up with a '*Bona notte*' spoken with a certain formality and sense of coda."

Eventually, on the opposite side of Florence, south of the Arno, well up on the heights near San Miniato, and commanding a fine

view of the Duomo and other Florentine landmarks, we found a
promising double villa, of which we could rent one half, in a steep
little street lined by high walls called the Via dell' Erta Canina—
"street too steep," I suppose one might translate, "for any but dogs."
Would the other half-villa be noisy? If so, we could not snap it up
ourselves as we had done at Boffres, as it was already occupied. In
our anxiety to make no mistake we took the long trip over from the
Fiesole side to visit it three successive days, on only one of them
indulging ourselves in a taxi. On the third we took the plunge, and
I recorded in my journal: "Villa Bencista. We left here at 1:45 and
at last got to the Via dell' Erta Canina at 3:35, having been *en route*
for nearly two hours. The family of the care-taker are really awfully nice. The little boy came first and I managed to ask him for
'*il signorina qui parla Inglese*', and he got the pleasant, intelligent girl
we saw yesterday. Then the man who would work for us appeared,
Constantino; his wife, Assunta, would be our cook. They ask three
hundred lire a month for both with wine, or three hundred and
sixty if they have to supply the wine. A younger man picked Mary
a bunch of roses, and insisted on our sitting down in the garden—
though none of them would sit.

"Afterwards we walked down the precipitous Via dell' Erta
Canina—well named—giving lovely views of Florence, and dis-
playing a shrine on one wall:

> *O figlio, O sposo, O santa genitrice,*
> *Al passagier la via date felice.*

"It seemed a good augury."

Our troubles, however, were not at an end: Constantino and
Assunta failed us. Our nice English-speaking Norina suggested a
certain Lavinia, who would cook for us for two hundred and forty
lire a month, getting her own wine. "Lavinia," states my journal
with the brevity of despair in an entry made on our first day of
tenancy, "left after lunch. Mary did not much believe in her from
the first. . . . Cold and rainy. I made a fire. . . . The woman that
came from Pistoia to try for the job had gone back by the time
we got to the agent's." Later I added further details. "We took

In the Via dell' Erta Canina, Florence.
The Duomo in the distance.

From a snap-shot by the Author

dinner in Florence and returned in a heavy downpour. The keys to our street gate and inner door are enormous, but I had some difficulty finding the keyholes in the dark. I had taken the precaution to notice where the electric switch was, so once inside we were all right. The fire was still going. The wind whistles in the chimney." The next day came a telegram from the woman in Pistoia, who eventually became our cook (and Alfredo, her husband, waiter and major domo): "*Mercoledì mattina prenderemo servizio.*"

For the next few days the journal naturally enough contains frequent references to Alfredo and Marietta, of which I will give but two. "Wednesday. Alfredo and Marietta arrived before we were up. They are to have four hundred and fifty lire a month (about $22.50). They both look very nice, and treat us like grandees. It is odd to have Alfredo open the door and come out to the gate with us when we start on an innocent walk. Saturday. The 'Countess' next door but one began playing the piano at noon, but I don't believe she will play often. It seems that Alfredo and Marietta brought a little white dog with them! There's irony for you. However, he doesn't seem to bark at all."

These two were really admirable servants, despite Alfredo's superfluity of respect and Marietta's superfluity of inventiveness. (Her trick of serving a whole fish, with its head and tail most life-like and its mouth even grasping an apple, completely took poor Mary's appetite away). As in Boffres fourteen years before, our chief complaint with the food was that it was too rich. One night after we had had for lunch some calves' brains that disheartened Mary and for dinner some chocolate pudding that I ate only out of consideration for Alfredo's feelings we lighted up at three in the morning, and sought solace in literature. We made two parallel columns on a large sheet, headed the left-hand one *Posseamo mangiare*, and made it as encouragingly voluminous as the dictionary would allow, and the right-hand one *Non posseamo mangiare*, making it as laconic and as forcible as we could. For instance, the top line ran, in the left column, *Tutti erbaggi fresci*, with the emphatic addendum on the right: *escludere cipolli*. An item toward the end was *mele arrosta*, with the appended warning *non cioccolata*. The whole list closed with a pathetic appeal: *e cosi semplice*. This not only enlarged our vocabulary, but positively seemed to ease our indigestion and to enable us to sleep quietly the rest of the night. On Marietta and Alfredo we could not see that it had the slightest effect. Nevertheless when rather before the end of June, driven from Florence by unbearable heat, we took leave of them, we gave them fifty lire for *bona servizio*, and were really sorry to say goodbye.

IV

During this spring of 1928 in Florence, first theoretically in the paper on *Creative Leisure* written at the Villa Bencista, later practically in my *Second Symphony* planned and about one third composed in the Via dell' Erta Canina, I worked out for the first time in my life a fairly full consciousness of just how the process of composition takes place. I still feel that the conclusions I reached were sound; and in view of their possible suggestiveness to young composers just starting in I should like to sketch them briefly here.

They were founded largely on three books I found invaluable: Graham Wallas's *The Art of Thought*, Henri Poincaré's *Science and Method*, and T. Sharper Knowlson's *Originality*. My paper set forth Wallas's conclusion that the whole creative process naturally divides itself into four stages, called by him "Preparation, Incubation, Inspiration, and Verification." Of these the first and last are conscious, the other two are unconscious, and hence only indirectly subject to the will of the scientist or artist. It is the nerve-racking effect of this indirect control of the most essential stages in creation—incubation and inspiration—together with the patience-trying slowness of the initial preparation, that make it so sore a strain on our poor human nature. All the writers agree on the *fruitlessness* which is an essential character of the stage of preparation. Wallas describes it as a time of "hard, conscious, systematic and fruitless analysis of the problem", and Poincaré writes:

"Unconscious work is not fruitful unless it is preceded . . . by a period of conscious work. Sudden inspirations are never produced . . . except after some days of voluntary efforts which appeared absolutely fruitless, in which one thought one had accomplished nothing, and seemed to be on a totally wrong track." Or, as John Powell once phrased it, "You have to let your subconscious know what you want." And the second stage, that of incubation, is almost harder to bear, as I pointed out in my paper, because "one is now working in the dark. A process of trial and error goes on below the threshold of consciousness . . . and when a successful combination happens it irrupts into consciousness as an 'inspiration'."

Looking back, I realize that I had been coming slowly, through years of bitter experience of the baffling character of the early stages of composition, to realize that this feeling of futility was an essential part of it all. "From any striking motives that come into my mind," I noted in my journal in July, 1916, "I evolve a number of possibilities, and as some of these are bound to be trite I am always much discouraged at first. But if I only persist I can select the good ones, which come more as I 'get up steam'." The utter banality of my initial ideas (my disgust at which made even the contempt of a Philip Hale seem almost flattering) and the slowness with which I overcame their resistance, had made composing, ever since I had first tried it, almost as much an agony as a joy. Wallas and Poincaré a little reconciled me to it, even if they could not make me entirely philosophic about it. The sweetness and patience of César Franck were almost as hopelessly beyond me as his genius. "One evening," recounts Pierre de Breville, "I saw my teacher Franck at his piano, a blank sheet of music paper before him. 'I have worked all day,' he said to me, 'and I have written nothing. But I am satisfied, my effort will not be lost, and I shall find tomorrow what I have sought in vain today.'"

I also came now to realize more vividly than ever the need of mingling subtly the laboriousness of preparation with the day-dreaming, the idle reverie, yes, the complete shameless loafing, that favors incubation. I found by the best test of all—that of trying it myself—that Knowlson was right when he said in his *Originality*: "One of the conditions of inspiration is that a period of close inquiry and reflection should be followed by . . . a period of inactivity. Idleness gives the subconscious mind its opportunity. Close work, with its constant absorption of eye and brain, monopolizes the mental life, allowing few opportunities for transitions from the subconscious to the conscious. Descartes slept a great deal, and particularly recommends idleness as necessary to the production of good work."

My journal shows clearly how this worked out in my case. "May 22. Morning. I have no ideas, and can't see much chance of getting any. What ought I to do?

"Later. Mary read aloud to me almost all the morning.

"Dinner-time. After tea I began improvising, and got onto a sort of clangorous theme that may work into something orchestral. At any rate it was great fun to improvise over an hour, and feel some musical 'juice.' "

This "clangorous theme" proved eventually to be the nucleus of my *Second Symphony*. Yet as it came to me that first day, oddly enough, it had only in its harmonies the sinister, menacing quality which makes its individuality; in rhythm it was a weakly graceful triple-beat movement, almost a waltz, instead of the peremptory march it had to be when it found itself. As for the second main theme of the movement, a melody for solo horn, it stayed in the banal stage nearly a month, almost driving me mad, until a suggestion of my wife's showed me what was wrong with it. . . . This banality of first thoughts seems to be a general affliction. That even Beethoven was subject to it his sketch-books show clearly.

"June 2. There are two opposing theories of the way one gets ideas. Can both be right? Theory 1. Wallas's scheme. Laborious conscious preparation by trial and error, and at last the inspiration. Vaughan Williams on cranking a cold automobile, or scratching with a fountain pen that won't work. The trouble is I have been trying this, and for me it seems to mean getting my mind pounding relentlessly on a lot of trashy rhythms and bastard still-born themes that go on pulsating in my brain night and day. Can such intense worry and fatigue possibly be the way to anything creative? Theory 2. W. James's, that the way to be productive is to "unclamp", to relax, to cease to be responsible. Then, when "the belts are not so tight", the mind will work, he says, twice as well. . . . Whether this is the best method or not, I must try it for a few days, I am so completely knocked out from the last bout with those awful false themes I thought I had.

"June 4. Stayed in all day until after tea, when I felt more energy and we took a pretty walk round by Arcetri . . . to Santa Margherita a Montici.

"June 5. Began before breakfast to have some new ideas of what to do with that material. . . . I can't believe it, but it really seems to be going to work out."

"June 18. In spite of my not getting new ideas of any apparent value, water is still cool, sun warm, books like Young's *Medici* interesting, Franck's *Quintet* and Beethoven's *Benedictus* beautiful. As Orrick Johns says:

> Oh better let the little things I loved when little
> Return when the heart finds the great things brittle.

"June 19. Used up all day. Stayed at home from Mrs. T's party this evening.

"June 20. How would it be to omit development section, and let those solemn harmonies in strings gradually abate and modulate downwards into a new key. . . . Then a short but serious slow movement, complete and coming to an end in that key. Then a scherzo (with possibly some reference to the main theme of the first movement) and this lead to a restatement of that first movement material, ending in A major?"

Here, complete in all essentials, was the rather unconventional scheme eventually adopted for the form of the symphony. It had come to me in the end rather easily, almost as a "happy thought", but prepared of course by all the early agonies, and incubated in the idleness of walking, reading aloud, and staying at home from parties. And the central feature of it, we may be interested to note, was the return at the end to the material of the beginning, ripened by the emotional and musical experiences gone through in the interim: in other words, I was here, for the first time, letting my plan of justifying the beginning in the end work out over the wide expanse, and with all the subordinate detail, of a whole symphony. With how much success it was hard to tell, and I am not even yet very sure; my old master, Vincent d'Indy, wrote me that while he found the pattern interesting, he thought its equilibrium would be difficult to establish; and the amount of revision I have had to give it seems to justify his doubts. Of course all such experiments are shots in the dark—trials that may turn out errors: that is part of their charm, and in any case unavoidable.

About the expressive individuality of the work I was somewhat less anxious. I completed it, or at least its first version (for it has since had many revisions) at South Salem, New York, late in the summer of 1929. There I showed it to Chalmers Clifton, just returned from a summer in Europe, and always closely associated in my mind with my symphonic adventures, since he had been almost like a youthful godfather to my first symphony back in those Paris days of 1914 when I was finishing it. As I now played him the new one, he exclaimed: "This is better than the other!" I inquired "More original?" and he answered "Oh, I don't know as originality matters much—more expressive." The same evening he sent me a very sweet and characteristic letter:

"I cannot forbear writing you a line of congratulation on the symphony. It is above all expressive, and a sort of ground swell of rich, slow-moving harmonies provides a splendid foundation for its free and natural contrapuntal texture. I felt quite happy about it, and realizing its beauty and sincerity the pleasure of seeing old friends after so long was even greater."

The premiere of the new work took place under Fritz Reiner at Cincinnati in November, 1930. A year or two later Bruno Walter, who had given a memorable performance of my first symphony in New York in 1925, gave the second one there also, writing me of it, to my great joy, that my "musical language had developed the capacity of personal expression without sacrificing musical purity."

V

For all that, it was impossible to publish the symphony. . . . How does so unmarketable a thing as that ever take on permanent

Silver Wedding, October, 1929, at Onota Farm, Pittsfield.
Adolfo Betti, George J. Dyer, Gertrude Watson, D. G. M., M. L. M.

material form? While I shall not tell any more here of its spiritual adventures I cannot leave it without a few words about the material ones, no less checkered.

In the Fall of 1929, just after I had completed the score, Gertrude Watson, always our generous friend, got up a party for us at her hospitable Onota Farm to celebrate our silver wedding anniversary, October 8. My *Chanticleer Overture*, recently completed, was dedicated to her; and through her generosity and that of my brother Harry had been published my first symphony. But after the meager returns it had brought I simply could not bring myself to let her help me with the new one. So I waited and hoped. Gradually, as time went on, with new performances every few years, ever new red, blue and black pencil marks in the single big score and the ten-or-twelve-inch bundle of manuscript parts, ever new revisions by the never-satisfied composer, confusion grew worse confounded. The score was not only getting more and more illegible, more and more dog-eared, dilapidated, and shabby; worse still, the Italian paper on which it was written, of poor quality to begin with, gradually began to flake off, rot away, and visibly disintegrate. The more work I put into it, the more problematical became its mere existence. What if before I got it into any permanent form it should disappear entirely? Eventually it was only in the year of this writing, 1938, ten years after its composition, that a copy was undertaken, in India ink on all-rag paper, by that good friend of American music Edwin A. Fleisher of the Free Library of Philadelphia, that will at least enable posterity, should it any longer take any interest in the matter, to judge whether there was any beauty at all in a certain ancient piece of music.

But all that was in the future that sunny October day when we gathered at Onota Farm for the silver wedding. Gertrude Watson had done the thing in her usual open-handed way, and invited several fellow guests to help us celebrate. There was our old friend Adolfo Betti, who the spring before had completed his splendid twenty-five years of the Flonzaley Quartet. There was a more recent but highly prized friend, George J. Dyer of Norfolk, shrewd and discriminating patron of music, painting, and the other arts, one of the most genuinely cultivated and completely unaffected men I have known. And for good measure there was a new but loyal friend, Michael Florinsky, not long escaped from Bolshevik Russia but already becoming an American citizen with a fully developed American sense of humor. He took a picture of us all after lunch, to commemorate the great occasion, grouped around Gertrude on one of her Italian stone benches. In the autumnal warmth of old haunts, old friendship, and old marriage, I felt as if the coiled difficulties of press critiques, rehearsals, scores and parts, and worst of all the agony of the composing process itself, were not beyond my courage to face again, in a good cause.

CHAPTER XXIII

TOWARDS AN AMERICAN MUSIC

IF COMPOSING, as a series of trials and errors in which the errors bear so staggering a proportion to the trials, is thus always a more or less agonizing process, how much the more agonizing is it when one is working in the dark towards a goal one cannot define—in short when one is trying to write music somehow distinctive—one doesn't quite know how—of one's own time and place!

In this blind search, partly conscious but far more unconscious, which preoccupied some of us through all those years, we needed fellowship, the sense of friends sustaining us. In the finding of such artistic comrades I was fortunate: my chief fellows in the (still incomplete) discovery of America were, among my seniors, Chadwick and Whiting; among nearer contemporaries, John Powell and —not so intimately, less as a personal friend than as an encouraging spectacle of steadfastness under difficulties—Henry F. Gilbert; among the younger men, Douglas Moore and Randall Thompson. We all shared, I think, the intuitive conviction that American music must be more active, restless, humorous and sentimental than European; that to this end it must, or at least might, draw upon naïve elements of folk-song capable of answering and guiding its own naïveté; and that somehow the native style into which its elements were built must be simpler than European styles, more childlike in feeling, yet contented in its childlikeness—in short more naked and unashamed.

How far was our leaning on folk-songs an unconscious means of escape from our shame in our own nakedness in confrontation with the rich raiment of European music? . . . For my own part, I confess that my joy in the use of beautiful simple tunes like *Deep River* in my first experiment in this direction, the *Quartet on Negro Themes*, was partly due to their giving me a chance to indulge my own naïveté without a sense of inferiority. The childlike quality of the tunes answered something childlike in me; they would not have given the same release to a more complex or intellectual temperament. Yet gradually I came to see that there was wisdom as well as wit in Arthur Whiting's question to my brother already recorded, after the first performance of the Quartet: "Is there any Negro blood in your family?" It pointed to a lack of complete correspondence between the temperament of the composer and the material of the composition. The material was scarcely complex enough for me, or I was scarcely simple enough for it—put it either way you choose. One result was that I coupled these highly primitive tunes with more complex elements of style assimilated from elsewhere, with which they discorded.

This discordance in style, which it took me some years to recognize and admit to myself, my friend Hill was keen enough to detect at once. "Despite many attractions and even beautiful episodes," he wrote me, "I feel that there is little stylistic adjustment to the themes. Instead of having the treatment grow naturally out of the latter it seems as if . . . you forced them into harmonic and contrapuntal combinations which . . . do violence to their original character." How true this was I realized very slowly. Ten years later, completely revising the quartet, I came with almost a physical jolt upon *Deep River*, most essentially simple of tunes, harmonized with the luxurious sliding "ninth chords" of the sybaritic Debussy, and realized that I had committed a musical miscegenation that would have horrified John Powell. Debussy among the negroes!—only the sardonic wit of a Whiting could do justice to such a solecism. It was even worse than Debussy among the Anglo-Saxons, for which I had

already myself blamed my friend Howard Brockway in his beautiful
settings of the Kentucky Mountain songs to which our American
music owes so much. . . . I struck out the passage. But there were
others I could not strike out without striking out the Quartet. Thus
I had tried—and erred: and ended by learning something.

II

John Powell's playing of his *Rapsodie Nègre* and my *Prelude and
Fugue* in concerts in many cities, to which I travelled whenever I
could, threw us together a good deal from 1921 on. His mixture of
impish disrespect for conventional standards with sound common
and uncommon sense my wife and I found invigorating. In Detroit
at the end of the year for a splendid performance by Gabrilowitsch,
"We lunched," says the journal, "with John, who was amusing and
sympathetic. He thinks the Freud business exaggerated, and when
Mary said that though Freud exaggerated sex there was nothing much
more fundamental, he patted his stomach and said: "This is; and it's
a simplex, not a complex." He suggested a sketch of the evolution of
the world in an opera, to begin with the chaos of the Schönbergian
style and gradually evolve to the cosmos of—Mozart!" Ossip, after
showing at rehearsal how elastic my piece could sound, was prevented by illness from conducting the first of the two concerts. But
of the second the journal records:

"Ossip led, and did everything magnificently. John outdid himself under such stimulating circumstances, but forgot to come in
once in the fugue, and said when I went out: 'It was wonderful, Dan.
I was so excited I forgot to play!' He was splendid to me all through
this visit. He showed the themes of the *Prelude and Fugue* to X. of
the *Times*—never loses a chance to help my music. What a fine
friend!"

His forgetting to play reminded me of a harrowing experience at
the New York performance under Stransky, a month or two earlier.
(I have blamed Stransky a good deal, but this time the fault, if fault
there was, was all John's, whose shoulders are broad enough to bear
it.) In the *Prelude* are two passages, beginning exactly alike but pro-

gressing differently—always a hard kind of thing to memorize—the first staying entirely in the key, the second gradually modulating further and further away from it. Imagine my sensations, as I sat there in the audience helpless, when John's memory played him the trick of taking the second entrance first! As slowly and relentlessly as in a nightmare he diverged further and further from the orchestra, producing ever more and more horrible discords. What would happen? I sat on the edge of my chair, envisaging breakdown. . . . But John at a crucial moment jumped, like a circus rider jumping through a hoop onto the back of a galloping horse, precisely and neatly onto the back of the chord just reached by the orchestra; and most of the audience never knew anything had happened.

At the end of 1922 came the performances in Boston by Pierre Monteux, and the following spring those under Stokowski in Philadelphia. I could not but be struck by the contrast between the attitudes of the two conductors, both of foreign birth, but one always so friendly to American music and musicians, the other with his equally great gifts already beginning to have his head turned by the adulation of a virtuoso-adoring public.

Monteux was throughout the good comrade. John's arrival at the hall for only the last half hour of the first rehearsal, caused by a train four hours late, did not perturb him, and he generously gave us that afternoon over two hours of his time to go over our scores. One detail in itself trivial remains in mind, it was so characteristic of both men. Monteux made some point about the phrasing of the oboe in the *Rapsodie Nègre,* to which its composer agreed. We were sitting on the platform of Symphony Hall, surrounded by the players' stands on which still lay the instrumental parts. John, to whose brilliant mind the detailed clerical side of composing is always something of a bore, agreed—but continued to sit, think, and talk. Finally Monteux himself rose, got the oboe part, found the place, and made the correction. . . . To those who have known *prima donna* conductors, of whom he might so easily have been one, the little deed speaks volumes.

The next morning, the Saturday following the first performance, of which the reviews had been true to Boston form, was precisely the time, as luck would have it, that he had chosen for me to play him my symphony. With delicate tact he reasserted his belief in me as a composer, listened sympathetically to the symphony, criticised it frankly and helpfully, and accepted it for performance the following season. As matters turned out, he could not play it after all; but his letter explaining why was so kind and so clear as to remind me once again how much the fair dealing of conductors may mean to the morale of composers. "It is with much regret," he wrote, "that I find myself unable to keep my promise to play your symphony this season. That I cannot now see my way clear is not in any degree due to the attitude of the press toward your *Prelude and Fugue*. That could not affect my own high opinion of your work. . . . The fact is that there has been so insistent a demand for a repetition of Stravinsky's *Le sacre du printemps* that I must give another performance in Boston, and on the programme where your work should have appeared. And I think you will agree with me that it would be unwise to include two modern scores on this programme, coming as it does so near the close of the long musical season."

That same Saturday morning Monteux told John and me a curious story illustrating a method of dealing with American composers quite different from his own—and unfortunately more common. He had been obliged some years ago, he said, as one of the conductors in a well-known opera-house, to pass upon a certain one-act American opera, atrociously written. He had refused it, and in an interview requested by the composer had advised him to study harmony and counterpoint, which by his own admission he had never done. A month later the man was back again with the revised score, saying that *now* he *had* studied. Once more Monteux refused it, telling him he should study ten years instead of one month. . . . A little later it was accepted, over the veto of all the conductors, by the manager. Asked to explain so strange an acceptance this gentleman replied, in his broken English: "If I produce a good American work, they ask me all the time to produce American works. If I produce a poor one they get tired of it—they don't bother me any more."

This beguiling incident was equalled by one that happened to John Powell himself a couple of years later. A certain foreign conductor, notoriously unaware of any loyalty to the music of the country that paid his large salary, accepted a concerto of John's for violin and orchestra for performance in an important city, at the suggestion, probably, of the American violinist who was to play the solo part. After spending several rehearsals without even reading it through, he made at last, only a day or two before the concert, to John's justifiable urgency that he rehearse it, this brazen reply: "On the program with your concerto is the Dvořák *New World Symphony*. Everybody knows that, and I must play it just right. But nobody knows your concerto, and so"—John's instinct for dramatic effect may have sharpened the phrasing a little here, but the internal evidence is that he gave the sense of it—"and so it doesn't matter how I play it."

Any such bald confession of the "*prima donna* complex" as that was unthinkable, of course, from a man of the cleverness and subtlety of Leopold Stokowski, who did our two pieces in the early spring of 1923. Yet I could not but feel that in his own way, and for all his skill and brilliance, he showed the ravages of the adulation he lived in, especially when I recalled by contrast the friendliness with which he had worked with me on my symphony seven years before. At the first rehearsal, standing beside him in the orchestra, I asked him for a certain kind of accentuation, which he got so instantly and completely that in my delight I cried: "How did you do it?" His tart reply was: "That's my affair." To turn off an embarrassing moment I laughed and said, "That's your secret, is it?" "Oh, there's no secret about it," he answered. "Anyone can see how I do it." After the Friday afternoon concert I noted in my journal: "He is spoiled, I think; and though his performance had a fine ground swell in it, he overrode John a good deal in both pieces. As Mary says, he has the air of throwing you a bone."

Yet when the whim took him he could suddenly shift, like a selfwilled child, into a winning charm all his own; and he could be as amusing as he was masterful. At the second rehearsal, when he called out "Mason" to announce to his men that he would take up my piece, he suddenly paused, relaxed into a whimsical smile, and asked them: "Isn't there something about Mason and Dixie [sic]?" "Well"

—pointing first to me and then to John—"here's Mason, and there's Dixie."

"Stokowski," sums up the journal, "ended the Saturday evening concert with a performance of *Till Eulenspiegel* that was a marvel of virtuosity, brilliance, and fire, but theatrical in the extreme—far too much so, to my feeling. Some idiots burst into applause at the sudden break in the sentencing scene. Stokowski completely dropped his hands, waited long, and then brought the shrill answer of Till. He spoke to me afterwards, sneeringly, of its appositeness.

"I told him I wanted him to put his name in my score with the others, but perhaps he'd rather wait till New York. He said, 'No, come upstairs,' and led me to his room where a steaming bath and his *masseur* were awaiting him. He paused, pen in hand, and said: "I'm going to sign 'Till Eulenspiegel.'" I laughed, and he added: "No one will know the difference anyway," and wrote the name in a strange, crazy, illegible hand. I said: "I want your own name too. Till was a good fellow, but . . ." He added it.

"On the way upstairs he told me that he had been urging the management for years to put the visiting composers not in the box, where they couldn't hear, but back in the house where they could. 'They don't want to be seen', he said, 'they want to hear.'

"Altogether a personality of great power and charm, you feel, but unbalanced, spoiled, with an acid contempt and derision that corrodes. . . . He has had everything."

III

It would be hard to think of a more stark contrast to Stokowski, who had had everything, than that uncouth, thwarted, pathetic yet somehow stirring figure, Henry F. Gilbert, who had had almost nothing—neither appreciation, influence, nor even much of the private satisfaction of technical skill. Yet Gilbert remains one of our pioneers. "He said, indeed he snorted and swore," wrote Olin Downes of him in 1938 on the tenth anniversary of his death, "that American music was not to be found in our concert halls, completely dominated by German and French conceptions of music-making." There was something inspiring in this sturdy if blundering intransigence of his, with which he "snorted and swore" his way through many of the pretty modes of our day. It went well with his "shagginess", as Downes calls it, with his heavy features like an Indian's and complexion suffused with deep red by some heart ailment, with his physical awkwardness and arrogant manner of a shy man fired with his mission yet painfully inarticulate. . . . In his actual work, I must confess, even in the *Comedy Overture on Negro Themes* so lauded by Downes, I always found the originality of the intent largely defeated by the crudity of the workmanship. But his aims one could not help admiring.

His exact niche in our music has never been better pointed out than by Downes, who in an article in the *Musical Quarterly* for 1918 describes the following three periods in the development of a national culture: "First", he says, there is "the period of imitation of well developed foreign models. Second, the revolt against imitation, and the cultivation of folk-melody in order to formulate an authentic idiom and get back into touch with the spirit of the composer's people. Third, the time when the spiritual consciousness of the people and the musical idioms transmuted from the original folk-songs. . . are responsible for the highly specialized expression of a leading composer, who remains a true prophet of the people." And the analysis concludes with the discerning judgment: "Gilbert appears to me as a pioneer of the revolt that prefaces the second stage in our musical development."

Gilbert and I never saw very much of each other: I suppose our circumstances and superficial tastes made us a little mutually suspicious; as I found him "crude" he may have thought me "snobbish". Yet under the surface we were really working for the same things. We were like the twin brothers in the story, one of whom became "a perfect Harvard gentleman" and the other "a complete Yale mucker"—"and you couldn't tell them apart." But whatever his inhibitions he broke through them generously on seeing two papers of mine destined for my book *Artistic Ideals*, and wrote me:

"Cambridge, Mass. August 21, 1926.

"My dear Daniel Gregory Mason:

"I am writing to thank you heartily and sincerely for writing those articles on *Independence* and *Spontaneity*. The second one is even better than the first. I have read it several times, and am fond of reading it over. You have so happily picked out and quoted just those things which appeal to my inmost heart—and put them in such strong and telling form. To me these articles seem the most serious words yet addressed to the creative artists of America. That you should know and love this truth—which you here set forth—is a pleasant discovery for me. I always had quite a different idea of you. All my life I have been looking for my relatives, and I guess you are one of them.

"I cannot forbear quoting my own quasi-humorous way of putting it; 'He who aims at *success* in art is apt to miss success in *art*.' "

Not long after the book itself appeared I had an amusing encounter with Gilbert. Sitting in the balcony at Carnegie Hall one evening when a piece of his was being played by the Boston Symphony, I spied him in the parquet and decided to go down during the intermission and congratulate him. He rose on my approach, and standing there in full sight and hearing of many neighbors began to tell me, in no measured terms, how inadequately his piece had been rehearsed. I tried to put on a little soft pedal, to make extenuations or qualifications, but in vain. It was an American piece, and he was telling the world it hadn't been rehearsed enough. As at length I turned to leave him he made a sudden transition and congratulated me on *Artistic Ideals*. Bearing in mind that although I myself liked it best of all my books it was yet largely made up of quotations, I tried to be modest. I might have spared myself the trouble. His parting shot, fired with his customary brusqueness, was: "No, it's a fine book—though of course you didn't write it!" When I recounted this example of what I called Gilbert's cloven hoof to Arthur Whiting, he amended "cloven hoof" to "club foot".

Yet of this same Gilbert, John Powell told me one of the finest stories I have ever heard of any composer. When John played his

Rapsodie Nègre at a Norfolk Festival, Gilbert, profoundly moved, told him he was realizing a mission that he himself had been unable to realize. Then Louise and Sidney Homer introduced the manager of the Worcester Festival, who asked to have the *Rapsodie* there. There was no room on the program. Madame Homer offered to give up one of her groups of songs to make room for it. "There is no need of that," answered the manager, "Mr. Gilbert is offering to withdraw a composition of his." . . . And thus it was actually arranged.

IV

Toward the end of each of the three summers 1922, '23, and '24, John Powell visited our Norfolk neighbor Peachey Flagg, one of his innumerable cousins (Peachey was an old southern name) who afterwards married another neighbor, our dear friend Dr. Edward Quintard, true lover of music, poetry, and all other good things. These visits were chances for us all, including our friend George Dyer, to get together in my big barn-studio for evenings of music, and for John and me to have long daytime tête-à-têtes settling the affairs of the universe, criticising each other's work, and playing folk-songs. Vaughan Williams was there too the first year, joining John in powerfully confirming that growing interest of mine in the folk-music of England that had found its first expression in my *Songs of the Countryside*. As I was finishing the draft of these, in the early fall of '23, John showed me for the first time Cecil Sharp's *One Hundred English Folksongs*. I followed his advice and bought a copy, but did not study it closely until, in the following September, I had the stimulus of his company again.

That summer I had been sketching some variations for string quartet on the folk-like theme of the piano variations in his *Sonata Noble*, but had found myself in a depressed mood. As the Pittsfield Festival approached and it was announced that the prize I had been fatuous enough to try for with *Songs of the Countryside* had gone to Schönberg for his highly modernistic quartet with soprano, my gloom deepened, especially when two of my friends, who happened to be on the jury, assured me in the frank manner of friends that all the works submitted were crude stuff. Perhaps my conscience troubled me too, as I had competed against my convictions, disapproving in general of prizes, or at the least, as my wife suggested, disapproving of not winning them!

Anyway there was more than the usual amount of ugly and noisy music to be listened to at the Festival that year. In addition to the prize quartet there were a good many scarcely less strenuous novelties, and between concerts this highly seasoned fare was continued at Gertrude Watson's. She had called for us at Norfolk in the comfortable big Packard, accompanied by her friend the English cellist May Mukle with her two fascinating dogs Wigg and Molly, as restless as the prize quartet and keeping us busy night and day even when there was no music worse than their barking to listen to.

Journal: "Onota Farm, September 16, 10 P.M. . . . After Sharon both dogs became drowsy for a few moments, but only to gather fresh energy. When we arrived at eight they at once took possession of the entire house, and like the creator of the universe on the seventh day, 'saw that it was good'. Nor had they been an hour on the premises before Rosina's hound appeared with paws on the piazza door as we sat at dinner, and galvanized Wigg into such excitement that I told Gertrude she'd better put all her nice china on high shelves. Even after this hound, who had never taken any interest in the house before, had been shooed away, Wigg would fill his lungs from the fascinating smell under the door, and then suddenly empty them with a whish like a bellows. (Molly, though more shy as befits her sex, has her share of curiosity too, and walked over every inch of the car many times during the day, also sitting down anywhere and everywhere unexpectedly.) The dogs are now abed but not asleep. Indeed they have begun the barking for the night. One now sees why they fortified themselves by that nap after Sharon.

"September 17. Arthur Whiting came before dinner. Afterwards Miss Mukle and Mrs. Cole played John Ireland's *Cello Sonata*, a horribly noisy, chaotic thing. The two dogs were very curious, somewhat alarmed, and walked about a good deal. A. W., after the first movement: 'Quite an exciting movement—with the dogs and all.' To Miss Mukle: 'This is the first music the dogs have heard?'— *sotto voce:* 'Their introduction to the gentle art.' "

Arthur may have felt that the dogs made as appropriate an obbligato to the sonata, perhaps as welcome a one as a certain Madame X's
three-year-old daughter to a recital she had recently given in Maine
and we had all been discussing at dinner. The question was why the
small child had been brought to the concert at all (and put in a con-
spicuous position in a box.) Some thought it a method of advertising.
But Arthur said: "Have you ever heard Madame X play? A diver-
sion would be welcome. 'Recital by Madame X and Young' ". His
irony was a comfort during that Festival—it seemed to relax one's
tensions. Meeting Howard Brockway at the deafening reception
in the Hotel Maplewood where everybody was screaming at top
voice, he put his hands to his mouth in the form of a megaphone and
shouted: "Ship ahoy! What ship is that?" Howard replied in like
manner: "This ship is sunk! S. O. S."

The "All-American program" Arthur explained as "a publicity
stunt—like a Liggett's drugstore window all full of salted almonds".
To account for the fragmentary effect of one of the most pretentious pieces on it he suggested that every time the composer got an
idea he may have been called to the telephone. He even had comfort
for the victims of the prize work. Most of us had suffered in one way
or another from the ineptitude and self-complacency of a certain
official, E. N., who had been systematically mismanaging an important musical foundation. "The only comfort in the Schönberg," said
Arthur, "was that E. N. had to hear it."

But most of these troubles were still unimagined, fortunately,
when John Powell and I got together early that September; at any
rate we were busy enjoying the simple loveliness we found in Sharp's
collection of folk-songs. We revelled in the quaintness of *Fanny
Blair*, with its queer scale in which the third and seventh steps were
always turning out minor when you expected major and bobbing up
major when you thought they'd be minor. We discussed how John
could treat in solemn *a capella* chorus the magnificently varied
rhythms and cadences of *Lord Bateman*. We played, whistled, and
sang the lilting phrases of *Henry Martin*, and hotly argued whether
it must be harmonized all in the Dorian mode or not, John quite sure
it must, as always where modes were in question, and getting more

and more dogmatic as I grew skeptical or unwilling to cut off other possibilities. We made friends again over the poignant pathos of *The Death of Queen Jane*, which just had to be plain major, but which I thought "sat down" too soon and needed developing. And for me at least, the most haunting tune in the book was *A Brisk Young Sailor*. How heart-breaking was that dip of a fifth from the highest note, followed by the reluctant descent to the cadence! The words, too, were for once as touching as the tune—as humanly simple, natural and frail:

> Hard grief for me, and I'll tell you why,
> Because that she has more gold than I.
> Her gold will waste, her beauty pass,
> And she'll come like me, a poor girl at last.

Curious is the rich web of associations that gradually accumulates over the years around any music—especially any simple music—that we love. Beautiful as those songs were to me that first summer, they are even more beautiful now, not least by the thought of all I owe them, even for their letter as well as for their enfranchising spirit.

I turn to *Fanny Blair*, for instance. As it stands here in Sharp, I feel all its original quaint charm, but realize now that its phrases are too short and too much all of a length, and that the third one is commonplace; that like *Queen Jane* and so many other folk-songs it sits down too soon, its cadence (literally *fall*) coming almost before it has begun to rise; and that I don't like Sharp's harmonization, so fussy and motion-impeding. And a picture comes to me of a small workroom I had in the delightful *Pension Nuss* in Vevey, on the Lake of Geneva, in August 1927, and an upright piano whereon I pounded out what seemed a better form of the tune, and most of the rest of my *Fanny Blair*, Folk-song Fantasy for String Quartet. I must have made a good deal of noise, for a fellow lodger, an American colonel, complained of me. "I like music well enough," he told Mademoiselle Nuss. "I even give a sou-piece to a hurdy-gurdy player once in a while. But the trouble with this man is, he plays a perfectly good chord, and then he doesn't like it, and plays another. Then he doesn't like that either. Nothing seems to suit him." Finally, after a meditative pause: "The trouble with *him* is, he's an enthusiast!"

The scene shifts, and I see a big basement room in Detroit, filled with people. It is towards midnight of a March evening in 1930, we have all come from a concert of the Detroit Orchestra—though unfortunately its director cannot be with us—and the members of the Detroit String Quartet, Messrs Schkolnik, King, Coffey, and Miquelle, to whom *Fanny Blair* has been dedicated, play it twice, with rarest beauty of tone and understanding of style. (It was they who gave the premiere of it about a year earlier.) They preface with a Haydn, and the evening ends with supper and pleasant talk.

Again I thumb over the leaves of Sharp. Here is that saucy *Henry Martin*, far saucier than the *Saucy Sailor*, who in reality is rather on the plaintive side. I am grateful to John now for making me change my original setting of this fascinating tune, made for the middle movement of my *Serenade* for string quartet, in such a way that it should remain at first strictly modal. He was right that the freer treatment, when it came later, would seem all the better. And here is *The Death of Queen Jane;* it was a happy thought of mine to set that over against *Henry Martin*, the one being as wistful as the other is saucy.

The great difficulty I had with *Queen Jane*, with which that second movement of the *Serenade* opens, was to get away from its short-breathed effect; its flight was like that of an aeroplane that instead of rising sticks its nose into the turf after one jump; and my first care was to make it soar a little. Always that was one of the fascinating problems: how to give these songs, so primitive in structure, a little scope, a little development, a little natural expansiveness, how to cure their short wind without getting an effect of artificial respiration. Another closely related problem, of which my solution here was the first one that ever satisfied me, was how to make one flow into another without break, getting the full value of the contrast in expression but avoiding disjointedness. I found it depended on some sort of community of pulse between the two tunes. Continual restless changes of pulse, such as some composers think necessary to variety, in reality only break up the texture and make the whole

With the Roth Quartet, Mondsee, Austria, August, 1932

Janos Scholz, Féri Roth, D. G. M., Jeno Antal, Ferenc Molnar.

piece restless and fragmentary. What we need is rather a fundamentally regular pulse, like the physical pulse or the even respiration of our bodies, on the basis of which the music may group its
uneven patterns with fantasy, with never-ending variety and charm.
Only as superimposed on unity can we get any real variety. In
these particular tunes a whole measure of the quick *Henry Martin*
equals a single beat of the stately *Queen Jane;* and I still remember
the delight with which I discovered one morning near lunch time
(and could hardly stop to eat my lunch) how this simple mathemat-
ical fact would enable me in my coda to make, without any break,
the liveliness of the one sober down into the melancholy pensive-
ness of the other.

The first hearing of the *Serenade*, given by Jacques Gordon and
his associates at his Music Mountain summer series, July 17, 1932,
was followed less than a month later (August 12) by another from
the Roth Quartet in the completely contrasted scene of the castle at
Mondsee in Austria. And thanks to a commission to study the chamber music of Brahms that summer we sailed between the two performances, and were able to hear both. Consequently another of the
pictures these tunes evoke is that of our arrival one hot morning
among the rolling hills by the Lake of Mondsee. "One of the stupe-
fying changes of travel!" exclaims my journal. "After such an awful
day in that noisy Hotel Stein in Salzburg yesterday, and little sleep,
we got here in the funny little mountain railway to find the entire
Roth Quartet awaiting us at the station. . . . Someone took a moving picture on our arrival, and with all the waving and handshaking
it was really heart-warming. We all set out for rehearsal in a villa
formerly occupied by Strindberg. More pictures on the way—snap-
shots. The *Serenade* sounded really beautiful—fine deliberate tempi
and big tone.

"Dinner was in the Schloss, afterwards speeches and flashlights.
Thursday morning we went to the Strindberg villa at eleven. They
were rehearsing the slow movement of the *Serenade,* and we stood
outside listening for five minutes. It sounded so beautiful and warm,
hearing it in so detached a way, with no social complications. . . ."

Finally, many memories arise as I look at these three tunes I found how to combine, by means of common pulses, in the first movement of my *Suite after English Folk-songs: O no, John, A Brisk Young Sailor*, and *The Two Magicians*. The most haunting of the three, *A Brisk Young Sailor*, (when I began the *Suite* in the summer of 1933 it had already been haunting me for ten years) proved the most difficult of all to treat, perhaps because it was so profoundly moving that no development seemed good enough for it. There is one expansion of it, where bass answers treble, just before its appearance in minor for violin solo, that cost me several morning's work, requiring seven rewritings. The chief theme, on the other hand, *O no, John*, gave no trouble; and its name seemed almost providential as a neat blanket answer to my friend Powell's mono-mania for modes.

His sweetest side came out this time, and modes or no modes he worked hard to arrange the first performance, which took place at the Virginia Festival of April, 1934, with Hans Kindler and the National Symphony Orchestra, and which I was unable to hear. Poor John, according to his account, was hardly able to hear it himself, as he was commandeered at the eleventh hour to play the celesta part, and vowed he was "so scared" he didn't hear a note. Performances I did hear and shall never forget were the beautifully sensitive ones with the New York Philharmonic by Bruno Walter at the end of the same year. At one of these he said to Ossip Gabrilo-witsch, who had joined us in the artists' room during the intermis-sion: "It is high praise, but the composer's part goes perfectly with the rest"—and Ossip agreed. Could it be true? Had I a little learned my lesson since the solecisms of style Hill had found in the *Negro Quartet*?

My mind went back to the morning after Walter's first perform-ance, when the fatigues of rehearsal and the dread of the usual press notices had thrown me into one of those moods of discouragement I never seemed to provide for in advance, although my wife had often told me I must always expect them. "You mustn't expect every-thing to go your way," she had said only a few days before. "You must expect your ups and downs—your Gilmans and Downes." (Lawrence Gilman was the music editor of the *Herald Tribune*,

Olin Downes of the *Times*). Well, that morning I took up the *Herald Tribune* and started to read aloud to her Gilman's notice. "By some rare and doubtless unconscious imaginative process," he wrote, about two thirds through his article, "the music that integrates the songs has been made to sound like an extension of the same material. [The composer] must have been penetrated through and through by the essential quality of these ensnaring tunes—by their gaiety, their beauty, their tenderness, their invincible and resistless charm".

When I came to that sentence my voice, already a little shaky, completely failed me and broke; and I had to pass the article to her to finish.

V

All this, however, was in the future that summer of 1924 when I first grew to know and love these songs. All I knew then was that their sincerity and simplicity, striking an answering chord in my own heart, had helped me to free myself from servility toward alien types of European music. What if the main attraction of the Pittsfield Festival that year was to be the Schönberg *Quartet*? Sharp had died in June; and I sent Mrs. Coolidge a brief address that I hoped might be read at one of the sessions, trying to express the sense some of us had of what he had done for our own music.

"Since we met here last summer," it said, "the art of music has suffered an irreparable loss. The death this summer of Cecil Sharp removes the man who has done more than any other to make widely understood and loved those folk-songs and dances in which England and our own country have an incomparable artistic inheritance. Cecil Sharp has put this inheritance in our hands, ready to use; and as time goes on we shall increasingly realize our debt to him. He devoted his life to making known the beautiful songs and dances which nourish our Anglo-saxon branch of music as Russian folk-songs nourished Tschaikowsky and Borodine, German folk-songs Brahms and Beethoven, French folk-songs d'Indy and Debussy. Without our Anglo-saxon contribution music would always lack something of completeness: that is what Cecil Sharp taught contemporary England, and what he will help teach us."

But when, ten years later, John Powell came to report to me in New York the Virginia premiere of my *Suite*, he summed up even better, in a single sentence, how we felt. "It was played," he said, his face lighting up in his enthusiasm,—"It was played among the people for whom it was made—and who made it!"

CHAPTER XXIV

THE YOUNGER MEN

To THE literal use of folk-tunes, whether Negro or Anglo-saxon, we were by no means committed, John Powell and I; there is no discoverable relation with them in such things as his *Violin Sonata* or my *Second Symphony;* and even such tunes as the one he varied in his *Sonata Noble* and I afterwards borrowed for my string quartet *Variations*, were folk not in letter but in spirit. Even more was this the case with some of our younger contemporaries who, using few folk-melodies, yet produced a music unmistakably American— men like Douglas Moore and Randall Thompson. It seems to me we were guided by a sound instinct in thus stressing the spirit rather than the letter. What we needed to free us from enslavement to Europe was just this sense of our own people behind us and with us —our "folk", their temperament as well as their idiom—or, in the more American and home-like phrase, our "folks". Even more important to us than the "formulation of an authentic idiom", to recur to Downes's terms, was the "getting back into touch with our people". Once sure of that we were no longer intimidated by the contempt of the snobs; having found a path of our own, however obscure, we could follow it with joy.

My *Variations*, for example, begun that 1924 summer of first acquaintance with our folk-songs, but laid aside in discouragement,

were finished with the help of a fresh social impetus. Every spring
we gave at Columbia University a concert of the compositions of our
students in the Department of Music. We announced for April 29,
1925, "An Evening of Columbia Music by Faculty and Students",
explaining that "Mr. John Powell, Guest of Honor, will play the
movement from his *Sonata Noble* containing his own variations on
the theme treated by students and faculty." As the reader will already have guessed, the evening ended in a blaze of glory—or at
any rate of variations: ten by five students, and ten more by four of
us teachers—Seth Bingham, Bassett W. Hough, Berrian Shutes, and
myself. After that I could not leave my own set unfinished. Adolfo
Betti generously helped me get them into shape, copying out in his
own hand the theme and editing it with his usual infinite care for
perfection of detail. The first public performance and many admirable subsequent ones were by the Quartet of my friend Jacques
Gordon, then of Chicago.

Another experiment of about the same period, in which I was
helped to "get back into touch with my own people" less by any
flesh-and-blood group than by a long-loved book, was the *Chanticleer Overture*. Ever since the days of my boyish enthusiasm for
Thoreau I had longed to get into music some of his freshness, some
of his "immortal joy". Even in Pittsfield summers, going up to the
morning's work through that hill-top field sweet with thyme, I had
projected an orchestral piece to be called *Pine Trees and Sunshine*.
To a slightly later period belongs a memorandum in the journal:
"May 9, 1922, 7:30 A.M. *Cock-crow*, Symphonic Fantasy on three
texts of Thoreau." The G-major salute of the rooster follows, with
the three texts appended, of which the first is the one eventually used
to head the score. The third, a good motto for those of us who, contemporaries of Schönberg and Stravinsky, found ourselves dreaming
of something more human, was also from *Walden:* "If a man does
not keep pace with his companions, perhaps it is because he hears a
different drummer. Let him step to the music which he hears, however measured or far away."

To the actual writing of *Chanticleer* I did not get around until
four years later, when, in July 1926, I noted my purpose "to do

something exuberant, high-spirited, cheerful—to be strong, clear and energetic without commonplaceness—to get distinction by interest of rhythm and polyphonic ingenuity." By the end of the year the piece was sketched; but then for a second time I succumbed to the temptation of prizes, forever confusing as they do the scent of us composers by drawing across our trail their commercialistic red herrings.

Musical America (then under different management from now) was offering, with vast decorations of publicity, a three thousand dollar prize for an American work. There were to be five judges, advertised of course as "nationally"—or I dare say "internationally"—known: Damrosch, Herz, Koussevitzky, Stock, and Stokowski. As the scores poured in, a photograph showed them, oceans of them, with portrait vignettes of the judges in the border. I know not whether it was before or after the photograph, or possibly during and because of it, that my particular drop in that ocean was lost. All I learned, by the spring of 1928, after my score had been held out of circulation a year, was that it had been seen by only one of the judges, Walter Damrosch, and had then disappeared. From *Musical America*, after months of correspondence, there was no satisfaction to be got, not even any financial help toward the making of a new score. My only comfort was that this new score, made as a side job during the composition of the *Second Symphony* in our Florentine villa, was far better than the original one.

Chanticleer, thus inauspiciously hatched—incubated, so to speak, twice—proved eventually to be the liveliest bird of all my brood. It went quickly the round of the conductors. The first to see it was Ossip Gabrilowitsch, to whom I played it on a too brilliant piano in the very small workroom of my New York apartment. I asked him if I was playing too loud—if it was painful to his ears. "Oh no," he laughed. "Your score is painful only to my eyes, agreeable to my ears: different from most modern scores, which are painful to the ears and agreeable only to the eyes." That was in late September of '28, and he at once accepted it for performance. The very next day Fritz Reiner called up to know if I had any new scores, came shortly to see it, and gave its premiere in Cincinnati in November. A fortnight later Mengelberg accepted it, and the day after that Stock, always a good friend to my music, wrote from Chicago for the score! This was rather a more exciting career than that of the *First Symphony*.

Even the economic side, always so difficult, reflected the general success. Reiner, a loyal fellow-artist that composers could depend upon, after giving its Cincinnati premiere played it early in the new year, as guest conductor with the New York Philharmonic, no less than six times, seeing that I got a performance fee each time. Two hundred dollars came in from these six performances and the two in Cincinnati—a small fortune! Eventually *Chanticleer* not only earned back all its copying charges, but actually made money for me,[1] as it had over fifty performances before I stopped counting, and was played by nearly every symphony orchestra in the country except the Boston. I made a special trip to Boston by appointment to show it to Koussevitzky on the last day of April, 1929; the first would have been more appropriate, as he accepted it but never played it, a practical joke he also played me with my second symphony, the more disappointing because his performance of the first had been so fine. Two days later, May 2, the Juilliard Musical Foundation accepted *Chanticleer* for publication, issuing it, under the intelligent and friendly direction of John Erskine, in most sumptuous, generous style, giving me the lion's share of the profits. After the *Musical America* contest such help was balm indeed.

In still a third work, written a good many years after the *Variations* and *Chanticleer*, and indeed after the *Suite* in which my experiments with folk-songs had culminated, I tried to feel my way towards Downes's third stage, that in which the composer's "specialized expression" is based on his people's "spiritual consciousness" (for which we might perhaps substitute the less pretentious, more colloquial term, "temperament") voiced in idioms not literally imitated

---

[1] In May 1934 I made an accounting on *Chanticleer*, and also on my *Second Symphony*, a much better work, so enlightening on the absolute disparity between financial and artistic values as to be worth summarizing here: *Chanticleer*. Cost of material, $188.65. Performance fees $200. Royalties $449.31. Net profit, $460.66. *Second Symphony*. Cost of material, $395.13. Rentals. Chicago (Stock), $50. Cincinnati (Reiner), $75. New York (Bruno Walter), $50. Net loss, $220.13.

but rather "transmuted", as Downes says, from their songs. In my third symphony, (*A Lincoln Symphony*) composed in the summers of 1935 and '36, the only traditional theme is the *Quaboag Quickstep*, an actual popular tune of the 1860 period, used to suggest the thoughtless, restlessly trivial people Lincoln had to inspire. The theme of the slow movement, *Massa Linkum*, it is true, is also conceived in the vein of the Negro spirituals, but is not based on any actual tune. Also my own are the themes of the serious Lincoln, of the humorous, gawky, yet tender Lincoln of the scherzo *Old Abe's Yarns*, and of the funeral march made from the *Quaboag Quickstep* in the finale, *1865*. I felt, and Douglas Moore, Chalmers Clifton, and other friends agreed, that this was a step in the right direction, away from the letter and toward the spirit. But it is too soon to say any more here about this line of experiment. Besides, I hope later to pursue it further.

II

My companion and fellow-sufferer on that ill-fated Boston trip was Douglas Moore, who had joined our Department of Music at Columbia in 1926 and who has since done so much to build it up. He and I could afford to suffer a few minor set-backs together, we were in such rare sympathy on all important musical issues. When, on their wedding tour in the early fall of 1920, he and his bride had stopped at our Norfolk cottage to make our acquaintance, he had told me he was organist and curator of music in the Cleveland Museum, but had studied with d'Indy, admired him as I did, and hoped some day to go back to him. The first music of Douglas's I was to see, a year later, the *Museum Pieces* written for organ, which I advised him to transcribe for orchestra, were American less in subject than in their unashamed naïveté. Their titles bore evidence to a side of him as characteristic as his melodic spontaneity—his literary sense and humor: *Fifteenth Century Armor—A Madonna of Botticini—The Chinese Lion and the Unhappy Flutist—A Statue by Rodin*. Of the later orchestral version, conducted by him with the Cleveland Orchestra, he wrote me with agreeable young-mannish enthusiasm and a modesty rare in composers young or old:

"It was really a most exciting occasion. . . . The first piece suffered most by my conducting. It was not nearly as delicate and Mozartian as it should be. The flute player liked the second piece and inasmuch as he had the melody it went very well. The lion, much revamped and with queer orchestral effects, got a laugh but it was really the last piece that got by with the audience and critics. That seemed 'symphonic' to them and made a racket . . . I am awfully grateful to you for urging me to set the *Museum Pieces*."

The next year he wrote his delightful *Pageant of P. T. Barnum*. This is American in subject as well as in style, and remains, youthful as it is, one of the most untrammelled, high-spirited, and genuinely native works we have. The little march, *General and Mrs. Tom Thumb*, scored for flutes and oboes in shrill miniature, was a real "find"; the Negro spiritual *Nobody Knows De Trouble I've Seen* was slily quoted in *Joice Heth, 161-year-old Negress; Circus Parade* ended up with a Babel worthy of Barnum; and best of all, in *Jenny Lind* the composer was not ashamed to write a real tune, even a sentimental one. Here again his inspiration was literary as well as musical. "It seems," he wrote from Paris in April, 1926, "Sokoloff stopped and made the audience read the program notes before he began. The result was a great success, so much so that the *General and Mrs. Tom Thumb* was repeated. . . . Wasn't that nice?"

At about this same period I was amused to receive, stamped with the incongruous postmark of Salzburg, where so many of our expatriates spend their vacant summers, the following highly American "yawp": "I have finished my pioneer ballad to Steve's [Stephen Vincent Benet's] *William Sycamore*. It is for voice, piano, flute and trombone and is in effect very backwoodsy. Before I left Paris G— and I played *Barnum* at the *Revue Musicale* at one of their teas. Prunières seemed to think I must have studied with Satie. This I didn't know whether to take as a compliment or not. . . . I am doing a musical comedy, book and all, and I think it has its moments. The scene is Tennessee and the chief protagonists are Holy Rollers and Rotarians."

Would even such independence as this be able to weather the Parisian sophistication to which we had seen so many apparently sound young Americans succumb? It was hard to tell. We judges for the Pulitzer Travelling Scholarships felt heavily our responsibility when in 1925 we awarded two of them to two of the most talented young men we knew—Leopold Mannes and Douglas Moore. Leopold, in spite of the strong influence toward music of his father and mother, David and Clara Mannes, did actually drop out of it for a while, lured by the fascination of color photography (and possibly by the idea of earning enough by it to be able to compose in peace); but we always hope he will come back.

As for Douglas, "I am doing strict counterpoint," he wrote from Paris early in 1926, "with Nadia Boulanger—stricter than I ever knew anything could be. The result has been quite sterilizing upon my work and I am reconciled to this as a necessary evil. Nadia is marvelous—quick as lightning and keeps up your spirits when discouraged. . . . There is an immense mass of propaganda about Fauré which has succeeded in making me dislike him utterly. . . . Debussy's Frenchness I like because it is universal but that of Fauré seems just aggravating."

Then in May: "I am afraid I cannot grasp the Fauré-Ravel idiom, in fact I dislike these young men who write in that style and prefer what traces of d'Indyism are left me. . . . I really don't know where to turn or what to believe. I am going to write another orchestral piece before I return and try to combine a reasonable modernity with attention to melody."

And in June, after I had sent him the article that eventually formed the first chapter of *Artistic Ideals:* "You are right in saying that independence is necessary to the artist everywhere but I for one know how difficult it is to achieve. . . . Every age is dominated by someone and it takes a super-genius to lead the revolt. It was Debussy who broke Wagnerism and it is Stravinsky who has broken Debussyism. . . . I rebel from his style although in it I believe there are excellent things. . . . I can't write in the modern idiom because I don't like it and yet I haven't got one of my own to substitute. . . . I think all this will pass in time . . . but this winter has had a sterilizing influence on me."

The summer, however, spent in Gerardmer, enabled him to get

far enough from the Parisian cliques to make up his mind about them; and a letter of August is worthy to stand as a sort of *vade mecum* for young Americans far from home, materially or spiritually. "I read with . . . much stimulus your article on *Spontaneity*. . . . I agree with you perfectly about the proper attitude towards art. If it is not for pleasure what in thunder is it for? We start out in art to the greater glory of God and it is pathetic the way we wind up. As I have seen this winter particularly, the sickening nest-feathering that goes on, the egomania that betrays even the most talented make one want to go out and sell bonds or be a motorman.

"Idealism and art hit us mightily in the early twenties. Then we start acquiring the technique to put our idealism into practice. At about thirty we get our chance in the world and come riding up with the gayest of banners apparently invincible. Then we run into a mushy person like —— or a cynic with good moments like —— with the result that idealism becomes discredited and we seize upon anything that is hard and solid and honest. . . . I believe this is the condition of most of the world today and if we could only get beyond and recover our idealism but retain our armor against mush and the awful uplift around us we might really be quite useful people here and there.

"I saw Ravel in a festival of his works this spring. He played accompaniments to some of his songs perfectly quelconquely. . . . My, but what a thin evening that was! It was like a whole meal of cucumbers, some of them a little rancid.

"We recently took the Rhine trip and of course came back violently pro-German. How the Germans sing! Rhine steamers that passed seemed always doing something in thirds and sixths, whether people or jolly little bands. And the music itself is so truly music, something lovely to hear, not an ingenious arrangement of notes."

Thus Douglas, with his gaiety, his power to express what was going on in his mind and heart, his willingness to "try everything once" without throwing overboard everything he had tried and found good, and the boundless intellectual curiosity that made him investigate even what he disliked (for he is by no means free of prejudices) made him in those formative years a particularly vivid example of the species Young American Composer. By no means did he cut himself off as I, less tolerant, was inclined to do, from the young modernists whose sophistication and egotism repelled us. He was amused, sometimes a little bored, and on the whole instructed by them. There was X, for instance, of whom he wrote:

"Cutchogue, Long Island, July 8, 1928. When we finally did see the X—s and had them to our house to a meal, we discussed exhaustively the problems of X—'s music, we analysed it and laid wreaths upon it . . . and he did not have the imagination even to ask me if I had written anything since we last met abroad. You can't tell me that these great people who spend so much mental energy in building up the concept of their own greatness get the most out of life. There must be some place left in the world for Christian humility.

"Having delivered myself of this homily, I will now proceed to the genial topic of my own music. . . ."

Such a sense of humor as that is the best protection against the dry rot of egotism. Douglas's later music, such for instance as the droll scherzo of his *String Quartet,* continues the vigor of *Barnum,* with more of technical maturity.

III

In surprising contrast with Douglas's boyish impetuosity, a little careless of detail but always outgoing and warm, was Randall Thompson's precocious, almost elderly caution, precision, and exquisite workmanship. He was singularly mature, even when I first knew him in his late thirties; he seemed to have looked deliberately over the whole musical field and decided what it was worth his while to cultivate. His reticence made it difficult to know just what was going on in his mind, and things like his *Jazz Poem* and his later *Americana*—which in its exploitation of the smart-Aleck type has always seemed to me a libel on true Americanism—made one suspect him sometimes of worldly compromises. But all one's defenses crumbled before the exquisite simplicity, sincerity, and musical distinction of such a little song as *The Echo Child,* contributed to a collection called

New Songs for New Voices as early as 1927. Here the tune was as naïve as the text of the nine-year-old poet: it simply went up the scale and came part way down again; but the way it did this three times, the third with much more subtle harmony, showed a sense of construction rare in modern music. And the poetry of the whole was as fine as its technique. Other songs in the same volume showed in the stamping of the simplest materials with distinction the rarest kind of originality—for instance the witty *Someone Came Knocking*, with its inexhaustibly ingenious "knocking" repeated notes. Here, evidently, was a real composer.

In 1930, in Europe on a Guggenheim Fellowship, he wrote me he was working on a symphony I was eventually to consider one of the finest of American works, and added a snap-shot of Gertrude Watson among the modernists:

> "Chalet Tip-top, Gstaad, Switzerland
> "5 VIII, '30

". . . Since the end of June I have sketched three out of four movements for a second symphony. You remember my alarm at finding that you and Mr. Hill were each a symphony ahead of me. I am doing my best to catch up.

"In Paris we had the pleasure of seeing Miss Watson on several occasions. She was in high spirits, ready for anything, and we had some delightful times together. . . . One hilarious and interminable session at the Sorbonne where excerpts from Gluck's and Lully's *Armides* were performed in a very desultory manner. The whole thing was preceded by a late-beginning dissertation by a weak-voiced and ineffectual professor of musical history, and Armide herself had not reached the hall even when he had finished. So there was another stall. The seats were far away, narrow, and so hard that we were numb with pain almost before we sat down. But through it all Miss Watson was resilient and undaunted, and in the duller moments produced several reprints of the most subversive and ultra-modern paintings, showing them to us successively with a sidewise glance out of the corner of her eye, implying at once connoisseurship and the most despairing contempt . . . I don't know anyone who honestly

Bruno Walter

Inscribed: "*To Daniel Gregory Mason, the artist and the man, in high appreciation of his work and tendency. New York, January, 1935. Bruno Walter.*"

enjoys modern art more acutely. And withal such reserve, such astute judgment! She exhibits her treasures like a guide in the Louvre who closes his eyes and points with his thumb at the Mona Lisa, as much as to say: 'Need I say more?' "

When he played me the new symphony, in Paris a month later, even my delight at its rare technical mastery—every note rightly placed and not a note too many—disappeared in the fascination I felt in its folk-like quality, its simple straightforward lyricism, especially in the Stephen-Foster-like theme of the slow movement and the splendidly sustained melody of the finale. But the full daring required of a man of Randall's generation to write in that romantic vein I realized only when I first heard the symphony actually played, at the second annual festival of American Music directed by Howard Hanson at Rochester, May 5, 1932. Randall and I were both there, I for a hearing of my conservative and romantic *Prelude and Fugue*, Randall for his conservative and romantic *Symphony*. Between us sat one of Randall's most belligerently radical contemporaries, his guest at the Festival, (who distinguished himself by saying not a word to either of us about our pieces!) and the program opened with a *Divertimento* by that genial but incorrigible modernist, Bernard Wagenaar.

So I was as much delighted with Randall's courage as with his symphony, and happy to be able to send his score to Stock, to Gabrilowitsch, and to Bruno Walter. November 3, 1933, when Walter played it with the Philharmonic-Symphony in New York, seemed to Douglas Moore and me a red-letter day in American music. "When I came out to the artists' room," boasts my journal, "Bruno Walter said: 'Here is the guilty man,' meaning that it was I that got him to play the symphony. I am so glad he has had such a success with it." And I wrote the composer himself that his work had renewed its Rochester fascination for me, adding: "I was proud to have the New York public hear such a fine American work and respond to it with such evident satisfaction. Our music has got to be a social experience if it is really to live, and yesterday was a move in that direction, and away from snobbish disillusion."

IV

In this period toward the end of the '20's I was having a chance to try Emerson's good doctrine: "Be an opener of doors for such as come after thee, and do not try to make the universe a blind alley." I was learning to say with Robert Frost:

> Now I am old my teachers are the young.
> What can't be moulded must be cracked and sprung.
> I strain at lessons fit to start a suture.
> I go to school to youth to learn the future.

Our Pulitzer Travelling Scholars of those years formed by themselves a goodly company of such youthful teachers. 1925, as we have seen, brought two of the most highly endowed of them all, Douglas Moore and Leopold Mannes. (1920 had discovered Bernard Rogers, now one of our most serious composers, and 1922 the gifted but over-ambitious Sandor Harmati, who burned himself out to a sadly early death.) 1927 and '28 brought two flute players and conductors, Quinto Maganini and Lamar Stringfield, one as practical and good-humored as the other was romantic. Carl Bricken, Pulitzer Scholar in 1929, was a close friend of Leopold Mannes and Randall Thompson, and fellow-pupil with them (and with Samuel Barber) of that splendid teacher of theory who has possibly done more for our music than any other single scholar, Rosario Scalero. Like all Scalero students Bricken was solidly founded in a living tradition. Another pupil of Scalero, William Dinsmore, though he did not happen to take the Pulitzer Prize, wrote delightfully fresh chamber music. Mark Wessel offered in 1930 a romantically conceived piece for horn and orchestra as full of promise as Bricken's string quartet. Both men, occluded by university teaching, are in momentary eclipse as composers, presently, one hopes, to emerge once more. Ernst Bacon, who wrote us a vigorous Whitmanesque symphony in 1932, gave me one of the most inspiring books I have ever found: Robert Henri's *The Art Spirit*. Samuel Barber, now so well known (and so deservedly, since like Randall Thompson he is a splendid craftsman) was Pulitzer Scholar for both 1935 and '36.

Memories throng about all these names. . . . In the old rooms of the Beethoven Association, in its first home in West Forty-fourth Street, less magnificent and more intimate than the present marble halls, a fluctuating group of us used to meet from time to time, for dinner and a leisurely evening to hear and discuss one another's music. Why these evenings ever stopped I do not recall; perhaps what more needs explaining is how they ever started, in the hurly-burly of New York, and with no economic benefit for any of us. . . . While they lasted they brought us together, I think, really together, far more than do meetings with economic aims likely to foster egotism more than comradeship. Here is one for a sample:

Journal: "January 2, 1929. Composers' party at Beethoven Association. Seven of us sat down to dinner.

"After dinner we had, first, Dinsmore's *Violin Sonata*, then his *Trio*, sketched by him alone at the piano. Both have lots of spontaneous lyric feeling.

"Then Leopold showed us his *Piano Concerto*—really music of prime order— such imagination and charm, good solid musicianship, planning, awareness of effect!

"Randall Thompson's *Jazz Piece*, brilliant *tour de force*, which appeals to me much less than his songs.

"Finally *Chanticleer*."

"January 4. The picture stays in my mind of the other evening. Quinto Maganini and I sat on the sofa and looked across at the Steinway piano in the corner. 'Billy' Dinsmore sat playing his sonata, a pipe in his mouth, his hair curly and rough, his face serious and pleasant. Carl Bricken was in the extreme corner, hidden by the music. To the left of Dinsmore was the dark head and keen alert smile of Leopold Mannes, enjoying all the 'points'; and left of him again the blond head of Randall Thompson. In the middle foreground was Wolfe Wolfinsohn in his shirt sleeves playing his Strad, of wonderful rich tone. . . . It is a good picture to have in one's head."

What we were trying to do in these meetings was to develop a sense of fellowship in art as a protection against the chaos by which we were surrounded. . . . As I look back I realize that we could hardly hope for much success—we were in too desperate a minority. Already Van Wyck Brooks was painting in his magnificently courageous and original *Reviewer's Notebook* in the *Freeman*[1] a picture of American letters in which we could recognize an equally exact likeness of our music. "In America," he there wrote, in the essay on *Literary Generations*, "a complete anarchy prevails; the individual writer is thrown entirely on his own feeble resources, he follows the lead of this European writer or that, he doubles and turns and hesitates, he loses touch with a contemporary life that criticism has not interpreted for him, and the total result is a literature that is incoherent, without characteristic principles, and incapable of development."

Excited by the exactitude of this description, for music as well as for letters, I wrote to tell him how, in the group I knew, the same lack of fellowship made it impossible to sustain professional standards. He answered:

"Westport, Conn. January 2, 1933
"My knowledge of music is *not much*, but after all, the arts are all closely connected, and I am growing not to care very much for any criticism that is not based on a fairly generous understanding of art in general, though I still suspect the kind of criticism that professes to *deal* with more than one of the arts. I wonder if you know the *Prétexte* of André Gide in which he shows that the ages of greatest energy have preferred the strictest forms? It seemed to me when I first read it the final comment on the 'free verse' movement then in vogue."

The lack of that sense of the calling Van Wyck was pleading for gives the retrospect over our group of young composers a certain sadness. Sandor Harmati was not, in the deeper sense, the only one that fell by the way. Many of us wandered or strayed into other than creative paths, temporarily or permanently, and not one realized his possibilities as he might have done in a society of artists more

---

[1] Since collected in *Sketches in Criticism*, to me an even finer book than his richly beautiful *Flowering of New England*, so seminal it is, so concerned not only with the past but especially with present and future.

consciously bound together by a group loyalty. Yet it was towards such a group that we were working, however haltingly—towards what Van Wyck himself describes in another of the *Sketches in Criticism*, the one called *A School*.

"If Europe is more fortunate than America," he there explains, "it is because, even if the great spirits are lacking, the 'neutral terrain' is always, in some degree, maintained. There is preserved a sense of the dignity of letters in the abstract, and the rank and file continues to subordinate itself just as rigorously and just as impersonally."

And he ends with the inspiring assurance, all we have as yet any right to: "If we still lack our neutral terrain we have evolved something that approaches it: a *cordon sanitaire* . . . against the crowd-spirit and the habits of commercialism. A race has grown up . . . who have never thought of 'making good', to whom 'success' and the 'high standard of living' are as idle sounds as the rumbling of the street. . . . There honest work is respected, and honest work is done. There is the germ, at least, of our neutral terrain, the germ of sincerity and expectation. And out of this class will surely come in the end the rare, directing spirits who will give it the Forward, march."

V

A more generalized movement, of a slightly later period, that helped give us fresh hope was the advent of the "emergency orchestras" fostered by federal relief work, with their potent democratizing influence on conductors, composers, public, and even the press. In New York this work was at first, before the appointment of Nikolai Sokoloff as national director, under the wide-visioned guidance of two men, Chalmers Clifton and George Crandall, to whom I have always thought it owed much of its far-reaching influence for good. In last analysis however probably no individuals created it, not Clifton and Crandall, not even the gifted conductors like Modeste Alloo, Franco Autori, Eugene Plotnikoff, André Polah, Alexander Thiede, and others who so helped to sustain its artistic level, but rather the general instinct of music-lovers, beginning to feel at last that we must own rather than beg, borrow, or steal our music. The movement in short was a social one—therein lay its steady impetus.

How refreshing, how invigorating it was to find conductors who regarded us composers as comrades and friends! That of course had always been the attitude of men like Frederick Stock, Ossip Gabrilo-witsch, Bruno Walter, Fritz Reiner, Goossens, Kindler, Stokowski in his earlier period, and a handful of others—without their help there could have been no American music. But for the *prima donnas* we did not exist. Even so great a musician as Toscanini, dominating a decade, and playing innumerable Italian mediocrities, never gave our own music a chance. (Here I speak from personal experience, as in the spring of 1928 he promised to play my *First Symphony* the following season, a year later postponed it to the next, and in November 1929 indicated that he would not play it at all.)

"The W.P.A. concerts," I wrote to Lawrence Gilman in 1936,[1] "have given our composers a chance to be heard, to hear and criticize and amend themselves, such as they have never before known. . . . My first symphony had been last heard in New York, under Bruno Walter, in March 1925—eleven years ago. 'This symphony,' you yourself said in the *Herald Tribune* at that time, 'is not one of those that have had to languish in silence; and this is fortunate; for the symphony is an admirable work, and a credit to American music.' Nevertheless the symphony did have to 'languish in silence' from that day for more than a decade. I doubt if under the star conductor system it could ever again have been heard in New York. But Chalmers Clifton, under a more human system, played it with the New York Civic Orchestra five times in one week. . . . I had not only the chance afforded by his friendly and adequate rehearsals for the revision which a conscientious workman always likes to make, but the sense of communication with a sympathetic public which is the very breath of an artist's inspiration."

The sense of friendly social give-and-take with the audience here emphasized was quite as important as that with conductors; indeed

---

[1] Mr. Gilman published my letter, with some rather disingenuous comment that unfortunately obscured rather than clarified the issue, in the *Herald Tribune* of April 12, 1936.

the latter was but the means to the former. Here again the emergency orchestras were revolutionizing conditions. By allowing audiences to hear works frequently, which is of course the only way to grow to love them, they were insensibly changing the composer-audience relation from the sterility of exhibitionism stimulating curiosity to the fruitfulness of shoulder-to-shoulder music-making. Let me give, once more from personal experience, an example of that.

Early in 1936 were performed for the first time, in their orchestral version, the *Love Songs*, opus 15, that I had written more than twenty years before to texts by my wife. Probably they would never have been scored for orchestra at all had it not been for the friendly interest of Franco Autori, who as conductor urged me to score them and helped me with invaluable suggestions, of his wife Paolo Autori, who gave her musicianship to singing these quite unsensational songs, and of George Crandall, who lifted a heavy economic burden from my shoulders by having the parts copied. At last they were scored, rehearsed, revised, and performed, again like the symphony in five centers.

The text of one of them began:

> Though I am dead
> Count me as still beside you,
> My heart with yours.
> In words long said
> My voice, though hushed forever,
> Still endures.

In the intermission a gentleman asked me whether I could give him a copy of the poem. In further conversation he confided to me that his wife had died thirteen years ago, and that for that reason this song, which he had now heard three times, especially spoke to him. Seldom have I had a moment of deeper happiness in music than that. Art, essentially social, comes to life only when communication of the emotion of beauty leaps the gulf between mind and mind. That life was what these concerts were bringing to us composers. Is it any wonder we saw in them a new hope for American music?

In the light of such a hope a little technical roughness appeared a small matter. The snobs and the sophisticates, of course, would never let us forget that among these players, who were "on relief", were naturally, among the many highly competent ones, a few incompetents. I remember my discomfort at a performance of my *Lincoln Symphony* when two oboes, two bassoons, and an English horn with singular unanimity agreed not to come in at all with the main theme of the *Funeral March*, and all that was to be heard was the accompanying chords of the strings, with silences between. But we could retort that in the wondrously perfect string tone of the Boston Symphony or the fact that in a whole Philharmonic concert there has not been a single false horn-note it is possible to take a pride more mechanical than aesthetic. We could remind ourselves what fearsome scraping and blowing Beethoven, for example, and indeed all composers in more creative and therefore more groping and experimental periods than ours, had had to put up with. The concert at which the *Fifth* and *Pastoral Symphonies* were first performed lasted four hours, in an unheated hall, in midwinter. There were a good many false entries among the inadequately rehearsed players, and one complete breakdown and fresh start. It must have sounded more like an emergency orchestra than the Philadelphia or the Boston.

And after all an orchestral concert should be not a show, but an utterance; whatever tends, as hyper-polish does, to arouse awe and admiration for a show, and to encourage in performers, press, and public the attitude of showmanship, is really injurious to art, while healthful is whatever invites us to hear in it a communication of beauty from heart to heart. For it is our hearts that we should open to music—not our mouths!—our hearts, together with our ears and our minds.

Randall Thompson, I feel sure, would agree. In November, 1935, he wrote me:

"Thank you very much for suggesting my *Symphony* to Mr. Autori and for all the trouble you took to bring about a performance of it. I take a childlike pleasure still in finding one composer who will speak kindly of another's work. I am much indebted to you for giving me that pleasure." A year or two later, hearing an unusually spirited performance of this symphony by another of the W.P.A. conductors, Alexander Thiede of Boston, I wrote Randall: "I must tell you once more how *beautiful* I find your symphony, and how happy I am about it. After all the times I have dragged myself to concerts in the hope of liking the music of my fellow-countrymen, sat through a long evening, and gone home with a headache, it is such a joy just to savor something, without an afterthought or analysis. Whatever chauvinism I ever had has pretty well evaporated, but it is satisfying to hear something that could not have been written anywhere but in 'these States'."

His answer was: "Your note makes me very happy. I wrote that music not to obliterate my fellow composers but shoulder-to-shoulder with them as it were. What you say makes me feel that something of the spirit that prompted the music came out of it and has come back to me through you.

"*My* deep thanks to *you*—for renewing my faith in something even more abiding than music, old or new, can very well hope to be."

So it seemed to us that the new orchestras were bringing to our music an atmosphere of coöperation favorable to the experimental, often hesitating growth of art rather than to its finished or even decadent perfection. Their chief gift seemed rather an attitude than any tangible result: an attitude expectant, interested, friendly, tolerant of imperfections in its zest for discovery. We remembered Thoreau's question: "Is not the attitude of expectation somewhat divine?—a sort of home-made divineness?" Growing art is always full of faults, stumbling, uncertain, not merely childlike but childish. It is always ignored by the conventional who can see only what already exists, despised by the snobs, ridiculed by the smart-Alecks. In such an atmosphere of indifference or contempt its crudities can hardly survive long enough to seek their own maturity—it can breathe only the more generous air of democratic humility.

Therefore we felt that in addition to the great orchestras, exhibition places for the high achievements of the past, inspiring us with a sense of what man has done, we needed also the emergency orchestras, the music schools, the amateur groups, all the crude and weak embodiments of our aspirations, to feed our dreams of what we too might accomplish, even now. What did it matter that such groups must always be, to the sophisticated eye, a little ridiculous? What is more ridiculous than a baby, so weak, so helpless, so shapeless? Yet within that ridiculous lump of red flesh lie the germs of the future.

INDEX